Gender and Discrimination

Recognizing the importance of macroeconomic policy in women's welfare and empowerment, this volume engages with the key challenges faced by our policymakers in achieving gender equity. With contributions by experts from diverse fields, the volume provides fresh perspectives on gender bias, wage inequality, and discrimination.

The essays span a wide range of issues from differential wages in agriculture, work participation, and sex ratio imbalances to cultural constraints underlying discrimination, HIV transmission, and role of maternal literacy. Rich in data and analysis, the volume presents studies from India and other South Asian countries and provides alternative methods for a better understanding of gender differentials.

Manoranjan Pal is Professor, Economic Research Unit, Indian Statistical Institute, Kolkata.

Premananda Bharati is Professor, Biological Anthropology Unit, Indian Statistical Institute, Kolkata.

Bholanath Ghosh is Assistant Professor, Sociological Research Unit, Indian Statistical Institute, Kolkata.

T.S. Vasulu is Associate Professor, Biological Anthropology Unit, Indian Statistical Institute, Kolkata.

W0234599

Gender and Discrimination
Health, Nutritional Status, and Role of Women in India

edited by

Manoranjan Pal
Premananda Bharati
Bholanath Ghosh
T. S. Vasulu

OXFORD
UNIVERSITY PRESS

OXFORD
UNIVERSITY PRESS

Oxford University Press is a department of the University of Oxford.
It furthers the University's objective of excellence in research, scholarship,
and education by publishing worldwide. Oxford is a registered trademark of
Oxford University Press in the UK and in certain other countries

Published in India by
Oxford University Press
22 Workspace, 2nd Floor, 1/22 Asaf Ali Road, New Delhi 110002, India

First Edition published in 2009
Oxford India Paperbacks 2011
15th impression 2023

ISBN-13: 978-0-19-807664-3
ISBN-10: 0-19-807664-9

Typeset in Adobe Jenson Pro 11/13
by Sai Graphic Design, New Delhi 110 055
Printed in India by Manipal Technologies Limited, Manipal

Contents

Tables, Figures, and Maps

TABLES

Figures

Maps

Foreword

It is hardly necessary to deliberate on the importance in any exposition of gender bias that exists in the developing world and in certain forms in the developed world as well. This book deals largely with the situation in India and with current Indian concerns in taking inclusive growth to a new level of understanding, the perennial timeline of this book is unquestionable. The edited volume brings together a collection of essays that deal with various aspects of gender discrimination that manifest mainly in areas of health, nutrition, and work.

The recent strides in public policy towards a more rights-based approach, have brought on board many schemes for the relatively disadvantaged such as the National Rural Employment Guarantee Act (NREGA), the *Panchayati Raj* Institution etc. The intention would definitely have also been to improve the situation of women as of other disadvantaged segments of society. However, unfortunately, even in these schemes there was no focus that would make them more accessible to women. A contemporary study on the access to such flagship programmes by the disadvantaged carried out at the National Council for Applied Economic Research (NCAER) and funded by the UNDP (2008a)[1] showed that women do not even get proper information regarding employment opportunities under government schemes. In case of *Gram Sabhas*, women's groups have complained that they do not get information about meetings being held and more sadly they are not even aware of reservation of seats for women in the *Panchayats*. Bina Fernandez, at the start of the book, rightly points out

[1] See NCAER (2008a), Report on "Perception of disadvantaged in Seven States of India", sponsored by United Nations Development Programmeme, prepared by Anushree Sinha et al. (mimeo), NCAER, New Delhi.

that schemes targeting the poor in general need to be gender sensitive if they are to make any impact on women's welfare.

The pages that follow provide evidence on the constraints that women face in accessing decent work. Reasons of failure to do so include women's unequal access to land and other resources, exploitative labour markets, macroeconomic policies of structural adjustment, and the social relations of caste and class. Madhura Swaminathan deals with differential wages for women in agriculture and how low these are, in absolute terms, in relation to not only male wages but also shockingly, in relation to minimum wages for urban industrial workers. Amal Mandal further argues that access to employment by women workers is restricted due to their lack of education and training. Moreover, there is also a gender bias revealed by employers as they generally prefer men to women. The low participation rate of women workers has always been a matter of concern. Labour force participation of Indian women was recorded to be as low 22 per cent according to the Census of India of 1991[2] and has not moved beyond 26 per cent even in a decade since then (as per other evidence).[3]

However, it is now accepted that there are certain areas in which rural poor women have been somewhat empowered which allows them some freedom only in voicing their concerns. An NCAER (2008b)[4] study on the role of self help groups (SHGs) has shown that to a large extent women have been empowered through the SHG initiative. Nevertheless, the role of religion and socioeconomic environment perpetuates the century-old biases that generally maintain women in subordinate positions compared to men in the Indian society and have a strong negative influence on their freedom to voice their concerns. Discrimination against girls and women should address underlying basic cultural constraints and there should be a systematic process to promote freedom of thought in women in our society.

[2] See Amitabh Kundu (1999), 'Trends and Pattern of Female Employment: A Case of Organised Informalisation', in Alakh Narayan Sharma and Trilok Singh Papola (eds) *Gender and Employment in India*, Indian Society of Labour Economics, Institute of Economic Growth, Delhi.

[3] Anushree Sinha et al. (2003), 'Impact of Globalisation on Indian Women Workers: A Study with CGE Analysis', (mimeo), NCAER, New Delhi.

[4] See NCAER (2008b), Report on 'Impact and Sustainability of the SHG Bank Linkage Programme', sponsored by German Development Corporation, prepared by Anushree Sinha et al., NCAER Publication.

A large part of this volume very appropriately deals with gender differences that exist in access to health and education. Vani K. Borooah deals with the role of maternal literacy in reducing the risk of child malnutrition in India. Borooah argues that households that were headed by women or those in which the women had access to information would have better-nourished children than households in which women were not so informed. Sadly, the study reported that, when it came to the nutritional well-being of the children, literacy of the father was but a poor substitute for the literacy of the mother. In order to reduce the risk of children in India being stunted or underweight it was far more important that the mothers actually be literate. Following this, Koumari Mitra articulates on the very vital issue of poverty and HIV transmission in India. Mitra writes that access to health services by women is critically important in addressing women's welfare.

This book has a significant role in providing us with alternative methods that could help in better understanding gender differentials by using indices and measures of gender discrimination. The last part of the volume dealing with methodological aspects of gender indices propose some new measures on gender discrimination. Further, through a survey of gender indices Manoranjan Pal and Premananda Bharati very compellingly argue that there is some scope for refining these measures. The major limitation of all the indices of gender inequality, gender segregation, and gender discrimination, is that they do not provide information on wider social pattern—how women are oppressed if at all. Such a proposal is relevant to other developing countries as well. The indices should also be complemented by gender analysis. The cause and also the effect of low and high values of the indices from the agreed norm should be thoroughly investigated so that some policy prescription towards gender equality could be provided with more certainty. Complementing this argument on a better measure, Diganta Mukherjee provides a new measure of gender bias. He looks at the parents' decision problem at the procreation stage rather than at household budget allocation decisions where the daughters are discriminated against in terms of expenditure on health and education.

Worldwide, an estimated 60–100 million girls are 'missing' and South Asian countries contribute to this imbalance to a large extent. It is now widely acknowledged that regional variations are very large and in some parts of the Indian subcontinent the sex ratio has fallen

to as low as 770 women per 1000 men. Gender discrimination at
each stage of the female life cycle contributes to this imbalance. Poor
access to health care for girls and women, selective abortions, neglect
of the girl child have all been cited as reasons for this difference.[5] A
global perspective is provided in this volume by Stephen Klasen and
Claudia Wink.

Using the third round of India's National Family Health Survey
(NFHS), conducted in 2005–2006, and data from the National
Sample Survey (NSS) 2004–05 for India,[6] it was found that the
relative increase in boys' height must come from something that
happens after early childhood, perhaps during the adolescent growth
spurt, even though much of the literature argues that adult height is
largely determined by the age of three. This aspect is also examined
in the volume by Moradi and Guntupalli. However, the authors
do not claim to know the contribution of individual programmes
such as health, transport, labour welfare, and nutrition in reducing
gender dimorphism. Stature, an outcome of nutrition and health,
definitely serves as a complementary indicator for measuring gender
discrimination compared to conventional ones. So, it is aptly stated
that 'gender dimorphism in stature' is important for measuring gender
discrimination in future research.

This book confronts a central challenge faced by our policymakers
in achieving gender equity. It also complements the growing recognition of the importance of macroeconomic policy in influencing women's
welfare and their prospects for economic empowerment. For example,
research that started in the mid-1990s[7] shows that economic reform
with decreased incentives can reduce women's output or restrict their

[5] See Fikree, F. Fariyal and Omrana Pasha (2004), 'Role of Gender in health
disparity: The South Asian Context,' British Medical Journal, Vol. 328, No. 7443, pp.
823–6.

[6] See Deaton, Angus (2008), 'Height, Health, and Inequality: the Distribution of
Adult Heights in India' Research Programme in Development Studies, Center for
Health and Wellbeing, Princeton University, January.

[7] See: Cagatay, Nilufer, Diane Elson, and Caren Grown (1995), 'Introduction,'
World Development (Special Issue on Gender, Adjustment and Macroeconomics), Vol.
23, No. 11, pp. 1827–36; World Bank (1995), 'World Development Report', 80–81; and
Palmer, Ingrid (1995), 'Public finance from a Gender Perspective,' World Development,
Vol. 23, No. 11.

access to education and hinder their ability to develop their human resources.

Economy-wide analysis is essential when the indirect impacts of policy changes are wide and other groups and other markets are affected as well as the welfare of women as a result of a trade or financial policy. It is, therefore, important that for policy analysis economy-wide models should distinguish between men and women[8] in distinguishing between socioeconomic variables and institutional behavioural relationships. In such a gender aware multi-sector model, the economy[9] by factors of production could be distinguished by gender and further households and industry sectors could be distinguished by regions such as rural, urban, formal, and informal. Further such a model could be augmented even by identifying home-based workers as a separate category if such data could be culled out from nationwide data sets.[10] Another type of model allows for capturing the interactions between productive and 'reproduction' or 'care' sector of the economy. Female wage rates rise when the leisure and 'reproduction' sectors are omitted.[11] Further, a more nuanced version of economy-wide model analysis could examine the impact of policy shocks on informal workers and hence on women workers as informality includes a high share of women. Empirical evidence has shown that informal workers face a dampening in their wages during a period of reforms[12] and hence flanking policies may be necessary to mitigate the exclusion of women from the benefits that are attributed to reforms.

[8] See Faye Duchin and Anushree Sinha (1999), 'Structural Economics and the Quality of Life', *Feminist Economics*, Vol. 5, No. 2, July.

[9] See Sinha, Anushree and N. Sangeeta (2003), 'Gender in Macroeconomic Framework', in S. Mukhopadhaya and M. Sudarshan (eds), *Tracking Gender Equity under Economic Reforms: Continuity and Change in South Asia*, Kali for Women and IDRC, Ottawa.

[10] Ibid.

[11] See Fontana, Marzia and Adrian Wood (2000), 'Modelling the Effects of Trade on Women, at Work and at Home', *World Development*, Vol. 28, No. 7, pp. 1173–90.

[12] See Sinha, Anushree and Christopher Adam (2006), 'Reforms and Informalization: What Lies Behind Jobless Growth in India', in Basudeb Guha-Khasnobis and Ravi Kanbur (eds) *Informal Labour Markets and Development*, Palgrave Macmillan, Basingstoke; and Sinha, Anushree (2009), 'Impact of Global Slowdown on Employment and Income in India: A CGE Model Analysis', Paper prepared for The World Bank, New Delhi.

It is obvious that an analysis of gender with macroeconomic and micro perspective is critical in any policy making. Policymaking can be made more interested through a macro analysis of gender if that makes it possible to examine the impact of various policy measures such as changes in taxes and subsidies on the welfare of the more vulnerable sections of our society and on that of women.

June 2009   ANUSHREE SINHA
                                                   NCAER, New Delhi

Preface

This book does not aim at introducing readers to gender perspectives. Dealing with gender perspectives is much more difficult than looking at gender bias. Gender perspectives have many dimensions and gender bias may be viewed as one of those dimensions.

GENDER BIAS VERSUS GENDER INEQUALITY

The term gender bias carries different misconceptions to applied researchers. Gender bias is taken as synonymous with gender inequality. There is nothing wrong with it. The problem arises when gender inequality is just taken as a special case of inequality. When gender inequality is taken as a special case of inequality, the members have identities only in terms of the groups that they belong to, that is, male or female groups. To make it more clear let us first understand what we mean by inequality.

Inequality arises because of deprivation. Two persons will be said to be unequal if one is deprived of a given facility with respect to the other. Economic literature is replete with discussions of income inequality. Consider the comparison of incomes between two persons. It is natural to assume that the two persons are or should be equal in every other respect and therefore should also get equal share of income. If not, then we say that the person getting the lesser income is deprived compared to the person who is getting the greater income. The degree of deprivation may be measured in an ad hoc manner or through utility functions. A measure of inequality is a summary of all such deprivations.

When the comparison is between two groups, one should first make sure that the two groups should get equal share with respect to the given facility. Males and females should get equal amount of income if they have equal skills as manifested by their performances, which are initially judged by their qualifications and experiences before being absorbed into the job. One should be cautious in making similar judgments in other aspects especially when the two groups are none other than males and females. Here we give two examples to illustrate this concept.

Life expectations of males and females are not same. This is because given the same environment age specific survival rates are higher for females than for males. It would be wrong to compare life expectancies of male and female populations; thus putting them on an equal footing.

The growth patterns at different age groups are not same for males and females. Direct comparisons of heights, weights etc. between males and females at different age groups are not meaningful.

It is clear that the concept of gender inequality is different from the concept of gender bias. A measure of gender inequality is arrived at by assuming that every individual, regardless of whether the individual is male or female, should get an equal share with respect to the given variable concerned, whereas in case of gender bias one looks at whether males and females get their due share. A value of 1.05 as sex ratio (female—male ratio) in a given region may be regarded as the existence of gender inequality, because it implies the female—male population sizes to be unequal. However, it definitely does not imply gender bias, because in the ideal case of equal treatment given to males and females, the chance of survival of females is more than that of males and in that case the value of sex ratio should be approximately 1.05 as is seen in the Scandinavian countries.

Here we would like to bring the attention of the readers to one more dimension of gender bias which is different from gender inequality. We prefer to call it gender discrimination. A measure of gender inequality does not reflect gender discrimination fully. Suppose a female gets half the salary of that of a male for the same occupation and for the same service rendered by them. Suppose all males get the same salary in the given occupation. It naturally implies that each female also gets the same salary in that occupation, but the amount is less. A measure of gender inequality takes a different value if the proportions of males and females change in the same occupation. The discrimination between males and females remains same but the measure of inequality differs. So it calls for a new measure, which is termed as a measure of gender discrimination. A measure of discrimination between males and females should be independent of the number of males and females in the given population. This measure need not be confined to only male and female populations; it may very well be applicable to any two groups of individuals in a given population. It can even be extended to more than two groups. We should only assume that the size of each group is same while arriving at the measure.

Gender Bias versus Development and Growth: Development implies improvement in all directions. Development and growth are different concepts in economics. For development, variables such as per capita income, life expectancy, literacy rate etc. which may be termed as positive variables, should increase and other variables such as infant mortality rate, maternal mortality rate, crime rate etc., which may be termed as negative variables, should decrease. A uniform increase of all positive variables and decrease of negative variables implies development. The variables are usually seen to be highly correlated. Thus it suffices if we take only a few of these variables to get an overall picture. Sometimes we are not satisfied even with this. We need a single overall measure. The Human Development Index (HDI) is one such measure. It was observed that the HDI is unable to capture some special features of development, for example, it does not capture the uniformity of development among the male and female populations. Again, HDI tries to capture the aspects of inequality by taking minimum and maximum possible values, but it fails to take account of the degree of poverty. New measures are thus called for. So we fix one aspect of development and get a single measure of development on that aspect. Thus, the Gender Related Development Index (GDI) and Gender Empowerment Measure (GEM) considering the gender aspect, and Human Poverty Index (HPI) considering the poverty aspect were introduced. It is also not advisable to look at too many aspects as it becomes difficult to make a comparison across regions. One country may be better on some aspects and worse on some other aspects compared to some other country.

However, we may not be interested in an overall measure. We may be interested in only a single aspect of gender bias and seeing how much we have achieved in respect of equality of men and women. One of the aspects is women's right to property. Women should be brought into the mainstream by including them in all activities. The Ninth Five-year Plan (1997–2002) identified the empowerment of women as a key strategy for development (see 'Engendering Poverty Policy in India' by Bina Fernandez). Women's work participation, that is, participation in work involving the production of goods and services for the market is one of the prerequisites for the empowerment of women. But it is low in countries like India.

Since it is mainly women who are adversely affected, gender bias is usually looked at in terms of whether women are getting the benefit of development and whether/how they are involved in developmental projects. Besides finding the extent of gender bias, one also sees causal factors like religion, superstitions, women's decision-making power as well as effects like status of health of women and their children, status of education of other members in the family etc. But it may not always be true that it is only the women who suffer. One should keep an open mind to all the possibilities and proceed.

Moderate to high economic growth has been witnessed in India in the last few years. Even during the global recession India has registered more than 6 per cent growth rate last year. Growth in income is correlated with the reduction of the anti-female bias in childhood mortality (Ueyama 2007). But the gender gap in wages in India is increasing over time (Chandrasekhar and Ghosh 2007). The gender gap is also increasing in many other aspects: it has increased in unemployment; juvenile sex ratio and child labour have deteriorated for women. However, the gender gap in life expectancy has narrowed down to some extent (Vepa 2007). Again, the fertility of women is declining in India (Basu 1999, 2000) but fertility decline has not generally led to an intensification of gender bias in mortality (Klasen 2008).

Intra-Household Allocation of Resources

One important aspect of gender bias which is not touched upon in this volume is the intra-household allocation of resources among the members in the household. The literature on this topic is very scarce. This is mainly because of dearth of data on intra-household allocation. There is also an inherent difficulty in ascertaining the same. For example, it may not be possible to know how much a female member consumes a particular item vis-à-vis a male member even if the respondent cooperates fully with the investigator. Special types of surveys may be necessary for this purpose in which the daily consumptions are recorded by actual measuring devices (Basu et al.

1986). As an alternative to this, one can build up economic or statistical models with measurable variables, which give the male—female differences of household allocation as a solution to the optimization principle.

Within household distribution of resources, especially to see the gender bias has been addressed by authors like Deaton (1989), Pitt, Rosenzweig, and Hassan (1990), Ahmad and Morduch (1993), Haddad and Reardon (1993), Haddad et al. (1996), Udry (1997), Bhalotra and Attfield (1998), and Duflo (2005). Deaton (1989, 1997) argues that for a given level of income, families with children will spend less on adult goods in order to purchase children's goods. If household purchasing favours boys over girls, smaller expenditures on adult goods would be made by families with boys as compared with those with girls. This procedure for detecting gender bias was applied by Deaton to data from Côte d'Ivoire and Thailand. The data show no evidence of inequality between boys and girls in Côte d'Ivoire, and a small and statistically insignificant bias in favour of boys in Thailand. Deaton (1997) also observed the changes in household expenditure on a particular good due to changes in the gender composition of the household. In particular, change can be seen due to the addition of a boy or a girl member in the household of a given composition. The difference in the average changes will give the gender bias. Lancaster, Maitra, and Ray used and extended the collective household model (Bourguignon et al. 1993; Browning and Chiappori 1998) to find the gender bias within households. It was derived from an economic model in which utilities of male and female members were maximized under certain constraints.

Very recently, Song (2008) proposed a statistical model to find intra-household gender bias. In a regression model taking an augmented Working-Lesser expenditure function where the dependent variable is the total household expenditure on goods of a particular type and the explanatory variables are per capita total household income (predicted), household size, ratio of wife's years of education to that of both husband and wife, number of household members in demographic groups, other control variables, and a dummy signifying whether the head of the household is male or female, Song found that less is spent on girls' education[1] and the presence of young girls in the household

---

[1] Some inferences are possible based on the effect of household demographic

is associated with much smaller increases in the share of spending on health care than the presence of young boys.

The inferences that can be drawn from such models are very limited. Ray and Lancaster (2004) derived a set of age-gender breakdown of daily normative calorie requirements corresponding to the overall per capita calorie norm of 2400 kcal/day for the average rural Indian. Their proposed procedure incorporates the changes in household size, composition, and other characteristics in the calculation of the household-specific poverty lines and borrows the idea of Coondoo, Majumder, and Ray (2003) in which the unit values of the major nutrients, namely, carbohydrate, protein, and fat are estimated using a cross-sectional household budget data set on food expenditure, total consumer expenditure, quantities of nutrient consumed, and related variables.

Chesher (1997), Bidani and Ravallion (1997), and Deaton and Paxson (2000) and others have proposed schemes for breaking up an aggregate expenditure into its household members. Mason, Montenegro, and Khandker (1999) offered a straightforward way of disaggregating household expenditure into age—sex composition of the household by taking linear regression with no constant. However, there is a danger of not taking the intercept term. The intercept term absorbs expenditures not reported or not taken into account because of various reasons. Pal (2008) and Pal and Bharati (2008) decomposed total calorie consumption into the calorie consumptions of individual member groups in the households using the identity that the sum of individual consumptions is the total consumption and found that there is no indication of inequality against female members in the households at all levels of income except for the age group 4—6 years at high income levels. On the contrary, results indicate that gender inequality may be present against male members especially grown up members in the households. For further exposure on this issue, readers are encouraged to go through papers by Gibson and Rozelle (2004), Gong et al. (2005), Kingdon (2005), Lancaster et al. (2007), and Subramanian and Deaton (1991).

---

composition on the pattern of household expenditures. For example, if a higher proportion of boys in a household is associated with more educational spending than an equivalent higher proportion of girls, then this suggests that less is spent on girls' education.

REFERENCES

Ahmad, A. and J. Morduch (1993), 'Identifying Sex Bias in the Allocation of Household Resources: Evidence from Linked Household Surveys from Bangladesh', (mimeo), Harvard University.

Basu, A. (1999), 'Fertility Decline and Increasing Gender Imbalance in India, Including a Possible South Indian Turnaround', *Development and Change*, Vol. 30, pp. 237–63.

———(2000), 'Fertility Decline and Worsening Gender Bias in India: A response to S. Irudaya Rajan et al', *Development and Change*, Vol. 21, pp. 1093–5.

Basu, A., Subrata K. Roy, B. Mukhopadhyay, P. Bharati, R. Gupta, and P.P. Majumder (1986), 'Sex Bias in Intrahousehold Food Distribution: Roles of Ethnicity and Socioeconomic Characteristics', *Current Anthropology*, Vol. 27, pp. 536–9.

Bhalotra, S. and C. Attfield (1998), 'Intrahousehold Resource Allocation in Rural Pakistan: A Semiparametric Analysis', *Journal of Applied Econometrics*, Vol. 13, pp. 463–80.

Bidani, Benu and Martin Ravallion (1997), 'Decomposing Social Indicators using Distributional Data', *Journal of Econometrics*, Vol. 77, pp. 125–39.

Bourguignon, F., M. Browning, P.A. Chiappori, and V. Lechene (1993), 'Intrahousehold Allocation of Consumption: Some Evidence on French Data', *Annales d'Economie et de Statistique*, Vol. 29, pp. 137–56.

Browning, M. and P.A. Chiappori (1998), 'Efficient Intra Household Allocations: A General Characterisation and Empirical Tests', *Econometrica*, Vol. 66, No. 6, pp. 1241–78.

Chandrasekhar, C.P. and Jayati Ghosh (2007), 'Recent Employment Trends in India and China: An Unfortunate Convergence?', Paper presented at ICSSR–IHD–CASS Seminar on Labour Markets in India and China: Experiences and Emerging Perspectives, 28–30 March 2007, New Delhi.

Chesher, Andrew (1997), 'Diet Revealed?: Semiparametric Estimation of Nutrient Intake—Age Relationships', *Journal of the Royal Statistical Society: Series A*, Vol. 160, No. 3, pp. 389–428.

Coondoo, D., A. Majumder, and R. Ray (2003), 'Estimation of a Set of Multi Lateral Consumer Price Indices for Nutrients', Working Paper No. ERU/2003-12, Indian Statistical Institute, Kolkata, India.

Deaton, A. (1989), 'Looking for Boy–Girl Discrimination in Household Expenditure Data', *World Bank Economic Review*, Vol. 3, No. 1, pp. 1–15.

———(1997), *The Analysis of Household Surveys: A Microeconometric Approach to Development Policy*, The World Bank, Washington, DC.

Deaton, Angus and Christina Paxson (2000), 'Growth and Saving among Individuals and Households', *Review of Economics and Statistics*, Vol. 82, No. 2, pp. 212–25.

Duflo, E. (2005), 'Gender Equality in Development', (mimeo), MIT, US.

Gibson, J. and S. Rozelle (2004), 'Is It Better to Be a Boy? A Disaggregated Outlay Equivalent Analysis of Gender Bias in Papua New Guinea', *Journal of Development Studies*, Vol. 40, No. 4, pp. 115–36.

Gong, X., A. Van Soest, and P. Zhang (2005), 'Sexual Bias and Household Consumption, a Semiparametric Analysis of Engel Curves in Rural China', *Journal of Applied Econometrics*, Vol. 20, pp. 509–27.

Haddad, L. and T. Reardon (1993), 'Gender Bias in the Allocation of Resource within Households in Burkina Faso: A Disaggregated Outlay Equivalent Analysis', *Journal of Development Studies*, Vol. 29, No. 2, pp. 260–76.

Haddad, L., C. Peña, C. Nishida, A. Quisumbing, and S. Alison (1996), 'Food Security and Nutrition Implications of Intrahousehold Bias: A Review of Literature', FCND Discussion Paper No. 19, Food Consumption and Nutrition Division, International Food Policy Research Institute, Washington, DC.

Kingdon, G.G. (2005), Where Has All the Bias Gone? Detecting Gender Bias in the Intrahousehold Allocation of Educational Expenditure', *Economic Development and Cultural Change*, Vol. 53, No. 2, pp. 409–52.

Klasen, Stephan (2008), 'Missing Women: Some Recent Controversies on Levels and Trends in Gender Bias in Mortality', Discussion Paper No. 168, Ibero-Amerika Institut für Wirtschaftsforschung Instituto Ibero-Americano de Investigaciones Económicas Ibero-America Institute for Economic Research, January.

Lancaster, G., P. Maitra, and R. Ray (2007), 'Household Expenditure Patterns and Gender Bias: Evidence from Selected Indian States', Paper presented at the Indian Statistical Institute Platinum Jubilee Conference on 'Gender Issues and Empowerment of Women', Kolkata 1–2 February.

Mason, Andrew D., Claudia E. Montenegro, and Shahidur R. Khandker (1999), 'Can We Say Anything More about Gender and Poverty using Household Consumption Data', Poverty Reduction and Economic Management Network, The World Bank.

Pal, M. (2008), 'Estimation of Gender Inequality in the Average Consumption of Calories in the Households from NSSO Data', Paper presented at the ISI/ISS (Academia Sinica)/ISM Joint Conference, 19–20 June, Taipei.

Pal, M. and P. Bharati (2008), 'Some New Methodologies towards Measuring Head-Count Ratio: Illustrations with NSS Data', Paper presented at the Seminar on 'Issues in Measurement of Level of Living Based on NSS Surveys', 17 March, Ministry of Statistics and Programme Implementation, Mahalanobis Bhavan, Kolkata.

Pitt, M., M.R. Rosenzweig, and M.N. Hassan (1990), 'Productivity, Health and Inequality in the Intrahousehold Distribution of Food in Low-income Countries', *American Economic Review*, Vol. 80, pp. 1139–56.

Ray, R. and G. Lancaster (2004), 'On Setting the Poverty Line Based on Estimated Nutrient Prices with Application to the Socially Disadvantaged Groups in India during the Reforms Period', Discussion Paper 2004–09, School of Economics, University of Tasmania, Tasmania.

Song, Lina (2008), 'In Search of Gender Bias in Household Resource Allocation in Rural China', University of Nottingham and IZA, Discussion Paper No. 3464, April, available at *http://mpra.ub.uni-muenchen.de/8348/*

Subramanian, S. and A. Deaton (1991), 'Gender Effects in Indian Consumption Patterns', *Sarvekshana*, Vol. 14, pp. 1–12.

Udry, C. (1997), 'Recent Advances in Empirical Microeconomic Research in Poor Countries: An Annotated Bibliography', *Journal of Economic Education*, Vol. 28, No. 1, pp. 58–75.

Ueyama, Mika (2007), 'Income Growth and Gender Bias in Childhood Mortality in Developing Countries', IFPRI Discussion Paper 00739, December.

Vepa, Swarna S. (2007), 'Gender Equity & Human Development', *Indian J Med Res*, Vol. 126, October, pp. 328–40.

Manoranjan Pal
Premananda Bharati
Bholanath Ghosh
and
T. S. Vasulu

Abbreviations

AFMR	Adult Female-Male Ratio
ART	Anti-Retroviral Therapy
ARV	Anti-Retroviral
AS	Anganwadi Sevika
AWI	Agricultural Wages in India
BDO	Block Development Officer
BFOs	Bank Field Officers
BIA	Benefit Incidence Analysis
BMs	Bank Managers
BPL	Below Poverty Line
CAD	Coronary Artery Disease
CDC	Centres for Disease Control and Prevention
CDP	Community Development Programme
CFMR	Child Female-Male Ratio
CHD	Coronary Heart Disease
CSIR	Council for Scientific and Industrial Research
CVD	Cardiovascular Disease
DSB	Differential Stopping Behaviour
DWCRA	Development of Women and Children in Rural Areas
EAI	Educational Attainment Index
EOs	Extension Officers
FMR	Female-Male Ratio
FPP	Family Planning Programme
FYP	Five Year Plan
GAD	Gender and Development
GDI	Gender Related Development Index
GEM	Gender Empowerment Measure
GIT	Gastro-Intestinal Tract

GoI   Government of India
GPG   Gender Poverty Gap
GSs   Gram Sevaks
HDI   Human Development Index
HDR   Human Development Report
IAP   Indian Academy of Pediatrics
ICDSP   Integrated Child Development Services Programme
ICMR   Indian Council of Medical Research
ICPD   International Conference on Population Development
IDA   Iron Deficiency Anaemia
IDD   Iodine Deficiency Disorder
IHD   Ischaemic Heart Disease
INSA   Indian National Science Academy
IRDP   Integrated Rural Development Programme
IUD   Intra-Uterine Contraceptive Device
LAC   Latin America and the Caribbean
LEI   Life Expectancy Index
LIG   Low Income Group
NACO   National AIDS Control Organization
NACP   National AIDS Control Programme
NCAER   National Council for Applied Economic Research
NFHS   National Family Health Survey
NICED   National Institute of Cholera and Enteric Diseases
NSS   National Sample Survey
NSSO   National Sample Survey Organization
OLS   Ordinary Least Squares
PEM   Protein-Energy Malnutrition
RLE   Rural Labour Enquiry
SDP   State Domestic Product
SGSY   Swarnajayanti Gram Swarozgar Yojana
SHG   Self-Help Group
SLI   Standard of Living Index
UNAIDS   United Nations Programme on HIV/AIDS
WHO   World Health Organization
WID   Women in Development

Introduction

'We must spare no effort to free our fellow men and women from the abject and dehumanizing poverty.'
—Former Secretary-General Kofi Annan in his Millennium Report.

The United Nations (UN) former Secretary-General identified seven goals and set a specific timetable for their implementation (United Nations 2000). One of the goals was to provide 'primary education to all girls and boys on an equal basis' by 2015. Undoubtedly, reduction of poverty and imparting primary education are among the seven basic goals. Observe that in both the cases the Secretary-General mentioned development of men and women (boys and girls in the case of education) together. Development in human society is a many-sided process involving women as well as men. Both have an equal right to share the benefits of developments. The United Nations Development Programme (UNDP) has recognized that investing in women's capabilities and empowering them to exercise their choices is the surest way of contributing to economic growth and overall development. The UNDP introduced Gender Related Development Index (GDI) and Gender Empowerment Measure (GEM) in 1995 as measures of development in addition to the Human Development Index (HDI). Despite efforts from UNDP, United Nations Children's Fund (UNICEF), World Bank, and other organizations, gender disparity is still one of the leading problems in today's world.

Available data on gender statistics suggest that there exist pronounced differences between men and women. Women are less paid than men for the same type of work. There exists severe inequality of ownership of properties. Women's right to land is conditioned by local customs and laws. In many countries, females get fewer opportunities than the males, for example, opportunity of schooling, opportunity of participating in social functions etc. Females also miss special opportunities such as those for higher education, professional training, etc. Job prospects for women in many countries are far less bright than those for men. The number of women employed gradually decreases as one goes to more senior positions. The number is virtually absent at the highest level of occupations. This phenomenon is usually known as 'Glass Ceiling'. Several disturbing facts such as the limited access of women in science-related careers as well as the glass ceiling in their profession were reported by the Indian National Science Academy (INSA) in 2005. In the Indian Institutes of Technology (IIT), the number of female students is less than 10 per cent of the total students. Out of the 42 laboratories of the Council for Scientific and Industrial Research (CSIR) spread over different states of the country, not even one is headed by a woman. So far no woman has held the post of Director-General of CSIR or President of INSA (*The Telegraph* 25 April 2005).

There are gaps between men and women in terms of literacy rate, intra-household distribution of food and other resources, health facilities received, and so on. It is even taken for granted in many countries that women are responsible for household work regardless whether they are engaged in outside work or not. These issues are also interlinked. Gender discrimination in the labour market may imply women having more limited access to employment and hence having lower earning capacity than men. Intra-household discrimination of resource allocation between male and female members may lead to differences in health status. Poor health among girls and women leads to low birth weight babies and continued health problems for both men and women, including the increased incidence of cardiovascular disease (CVD) later in life. Further, gender inequalities slow the pace of development by stalling economic growth and poverty reduction (Sen 2001; World Bank 2001). Reducing gender discrimination is not only a legitimate development outcome for equity reasons, it would benefit the overall social and economic development in many ways. In this volume we have not only tried to capture different aspects of gender bias, but have also presented some analysis on the causal relations.

In an inauguration lecture for the new Radcliffe Institute at Harvard University, on 24 April 2001, Amartya Sen illustrated with examples the different kinds of inequality between men and women that exist in most parts of the world (Sen 2001).[1] These are: (i) mortality inequality; (ii) natality inequality; (iii) basic facility inequality; (iv) special opportunity inequality; (v) professional inequality; (vi) ownership inequality; and (vii) household inequality. At first it may seem that mortality and natality inequalities between men and women, if they exist, are pre-ordained and outside the control of human intervention. However, with the advancement of science, many new techniques have been developed by which one can determine the gender of foetus. Gender discrimination is prevalent in South Asian countries, which is manifested by natality and mortality inequality. The extreme preference for a son in this region leads to sex selective abortion. In fact, it has become a common practice in many countries. Mortality inequality may also be ascribed to differential treatment to females, starting from childhood, by society. The end results of gender discrimination among both adults and children in South Asia are high rate of excess female mortality, unnaturally low life expectancies for females relative to males, and population sex ratios which is skewed disproportionately in favour of males. The skewed distribution of population sex ratio is reflected at an aggregate level by the evidence of millions of 'missing women' in the region's population. Amartya Sen defined the *number of missing women* as the difference between the actual number of women and the number one could expect to see if there were no 'bias against women in terms of health care and other attentions relevant for survival' (Sen 2001, Klasen 2005).

Beck (1999) stressed the need for developing a national level database of *gender sensitive indicators* which can support national level planning towards gender equality (also see Commonwealth Secretariat, 1999). He pointed out ten key areas for gender-sensitive indicators. In each area he gave a list of indicators which are important at the national level. These are: (i) population composition and change; (ii) human settlement and geographical distribution; (iii) households and families, marital status, and fertility; (iv) education, (v) health, health services, and nutrition; (vi) economic activity and labour force participation; (vii) access to land, equipment, and credit; (viii) political and public

---

[1] A shortened version of this chapter was published in *The New Republic* on 17 September 2001.

life; (ix) indicators of gender-related violence; and (x) macroeconomic policy and gender.

Amartya Sen's Capability Approach can also be used in the discussion of gender bias. In this approach, one usually focuses on people's capabilities when making normative evaluations. Robeyns (2003, 2005) proposes the following list of capabilities.

1. *Life and physical health*: being able to be physically healthy and enjoy a life of normal length.
2. *Mental well-being*: being able to be mentally healthy.
3. *Bodily integrity and safety*: being able to be protected from violence of any sort.
4. *Social relations*: being able to be part of social networks to give and receive social support.
5. *Political empowerment*: being able to participate in and have a fair share of influence on political decision making.
6. *Education and knowledge*: being able to be educated, and to use and produce knowledge.
7. *Domestic work and non-market care*: being able to raise children and take care of others.
8. *Paid work and other projects*: being able to work in the labour market or to do projects, including artistic ones.
9. *Shelter and environment*: being able to be sheltered and to live in a safe and pleasant environment.
10. *Mobility*: being able to be mobile.
11. *Leisure activities*: being able to engage in leisure activities.
12. *Time-autonomy*: being able to exercise autonomy in allocating one's time.
13. *Respect*: being able to be respected and treated with dignity.
14. *Religion*: being able to choose to live or not to live according to a religion.

Nussbaum (1995, 2000) has also produced a very careful and elaborate list. Since capabilities are nothing but functioning, Robeyns describes how to measure *functionings* based on individual-level data. Three major types of techniques have been used—descriptive statistics, factor analysis, and fuzzy set theory—to measure functionings. Robeyns, however, resorted to descriptive statistics and scaling techniques to address gender issues.

There has been an extensive research on what should be relevant data to be collected in order to see gender inequality. The World Bank publishes sex-disaggregated indicators on population, labour, education, enrolment ratios, life expectancy, and maternal mortality on an annual basis. For baseline data on the gender issues, one can also see CIDA[2] (1996a, b, and c) and UN (1995).

Sex ratio is perhaps the oldest measure of gender inequality proposed in the literature. It is defined as the ratio of male population to female population known as male–female ratio (MFR) or the ratio of female population to male population known as female–male ratio (FMR). It may be expressed either in terms of percentages or in terms of numbers out of thousand (that is, number of females per thousand males or vice versa). This ratio is certainly linked with the mortality rates of males and females. The ideal sex ratio would have been '1', if—given similar health care and nutrition—the male and female mortality rates were equal. But, surprisingly, it is not so. Women have lower age specific mortality rates than men. The FMR in North America and Europe is around 1.05. However, the FMR in the world is around 0.97, which is not only less than 1.05 but also less than 1. It is believed that in North America and Europe, women get more or less equal treatment as compared to men. It automatically implies that in many of the other countries women receive less attention and health care than men. It is argued that more enlightened regions have higher FMR values than those in less developed regions. Thus FMR value is regarded as an indicator of development.

'The UNDP Division of Women in Development was established in 1987 with a policy guideline for each UNDP country resident representative to identify the nature of women's participation in each project and area of interest. However, in 1989, out of 106 resident representatives to give gender perspectives in UNDP programmes, only seven were women' (Ramji 1997). Since the UN itself is male dominated, it is expected that the Human Development Reports (HDRs) will have fewer gender perspectives than expected. Fortunately, UNDP, UNICEF, and WHO have started recognizing egalitarianism and are at present concerned with equality of people, at least for income, besides poverty. One aspect of equity is gender equity, and UNDP introduced the GDI and GEM in 1995 to augment the

[2] Canadian International Development Agency.

HDI. The need for sex-disaggregated data was stressed by UNDP and Commonwealth in international conventions and declarations.[3]

The two composite indices of gender equity measures, GDI and GEM, can be better understood if the HDI is discussed first. The HDI was introduced in the very first issue of the Human Development Report (HDR) in 1990. It is a composite index comprising life expectancy, adult literacy, and real GDP per capita. The index was further refined in later years (See section I in Appendix).

The composite index HDI uses only the simple arithmetic means of the concerned variables and ignores the distributional features to the extent that any transfer of the value of the variables among the individuals in the population leaves the value of the index unchanged. In other words, this index is not concerned about the differences between people/groups of people which may be defined through social classes, regions, or races. Thus male–female differences are not captured by this index. Potentially, women have a higher life expectancy due to lower age-specific mortality rates than men. So far as literacy is concerned, it is not known whether women have biological advantages or disadvantages over men. But even in this case there may be situations where the overall literacy rate may be the same in two countries, but if we compare the rates separately for males and females there may be vast differences. Should we say that two countries with same overall means have the same development index even if one country has large differences between men and women than the other country? Of course not. Development of all groups in a uniform manner should be the aim of every nation. The GDI is one way of looking at uniform development so far as male and female populations are concerned.

The GDI uses same variables as the HDI, but gives due consideration to male and female population (See section II in Appendix). The GEM measures the relative empowerment of women and men in political and economic spheres of activity. It is a composite index having three components. The first component represents political participation and decision-making power, the second component

---

[3] For example, Platform for Action of the Fourth UN World Conference on Women in Beijing in 1995 and Commonwealth Plan of Action on Gender and Development in 1995.

represents economic participation and decision-making power and the last component reflects power over economic resources (see Section III in Appendix).

Choice of the different components of GDI and GEM is somewhat arbitrary and is not rigorously based on objective criteria. For example, instead of women's and men's percentage share of parliamentary seats, if one takes women's and men's percentage share in other spheres say, in legislative assemblies, then the ranking would be quite different. Moreover, the weightage system considering the relative importance might be different. The aversion to inequality factor is also some kind of weightage between different values of the same variables. This factor can also be different for different components. There is no reason why this aversion factor should be the same for longevity and education while calculating GDI. In fact, Bardhan and Klasen (1999) are of the opinion that this should be equal to 6 for longevity, 3 for education, and 1.5 for earned income.

Besides GDI and GEM, other measures of gender equality/ inequality have also been proposed in the literature. The sex ratio (FMR or MFR), the Index of Relative Equity proposed by Anand and Sen (1997), gender poverty Gap (GPG) etc. are worth mentioning. The measures of gender segregation, strictly speaking, cannot be viewed as measures of gender inequality, but some modifications of these segregation measures may well be regarded as measures of gender inequality.

THE GENDER POVERTY GAP

A concomitant, disturbing aspect of rising poverty throughout the world is that poverty has increasingly become feminized—women are much more likely than men to be poor. This phenomenon was first noticed in the US (Pearce 1978, 1989; Pressman 1988), but more recently the problem of feminization of poverty has become an international concern as well (Pressman 1998, Casper, McLanahan, and Garfinkel 1994). (Pressman 2000).

One way to look at the feminization of poverty is through the GPG. The GPG is defined as:

$$GPG = PovR_f - PovR_o,$$

where $PovR_f$ and $PovR_o$ are poverty rates of female-headed households and other households, respectively.[4] The calculation of poverty rates is based on the methods developed by Orshansky (1965, 1969). The poverty rate is calculated as the percentage of families whose income falls below the poverty line (for their family size and type) in a given year.

The GPG is also defined as the ratio of $PovR_f$ to $PovR_o$ (Christopher et al. 1999). Since the poverty rates give the probability that a household headed by a female is poor, the difference can be interpreted as excess of probabilty of household headed by a female to be poor over that of the others. Thus the GPG through the difference of poverty rates is preferred to the ratio. Moreover, when both the poverty rates are low, say four per cent and one per cent, the ratio gives unusually high figures—that is one is four times the other. There may also be large variation in this figure due to a small error in the reporting and even rounding off.

The possible reasons for GPG are as follows:

1. The education level of women who head households is usually lower than that of the heads of other households; and income has been seen to be positively related with the education level.
2. Women usually receive lower salaries than men even when they do the same work.
3. Gender segregation exists which puts women into jobs with lower pay.

Gender Segregation Measures

One way of looking at the gender discrepancy is through segregation measures which refer to the tendency of men and women to be employed in different occupations/work places though it is not exactly what we mean by gender inequality. Concentration of sexes in different organizations does not necessarily imply that any of the groups are in a disadvantageous position. It is just a measure of a kind of polarization. We first define two distinct set of occupations: male occupations and female occupations. These are defined through the proportion of male/ female employment being less than the overall proportion considering all occupations. The segregation measures consider the deviation of

---

[4] The comparison is made with other households and not with male-headed households just to make it exhaustive. Effectively, it is the comparison between male- and female-headed households.

male/female employment from that of overall proportion. A perfect segregation occurs when there is only female employment or only male employment in each occupation/work place.

A large number of gender segregation measures have been proposed in the literature (see Harrison 2002). Among these the Duncan and Duncan index is perhaps the oldest index proposed so far and is also the most widely utilized of all the indices (See section IV in Appendix).

Gender Bias in Children

The discussion on gender issues will not be complete if children are not paid special attention. It is not only because the children constitute the future generation, but also because the treatment of gender bias for children is different from that for the rest of the society and because the problem is more severe than initially thought.[5] Aspects of health and nutrition come to the forefront for children especially for under-five children. Non-availability of gender disaggregated data sometimes puts a constraint on the analysis of gender bias among children. Studies have indicated that the girls often receive less attention than boys. Intra-household differences on food consumption were seen to be prominent in some regions (Basu et al. 1986). Girls are not taken to the doctor as often as the boys for the same type of illness. The parents are sometimes not serious about sending the girl children to school. Parental investment in the marketable skills of their children may not give a good measure of gender preference by parents, because in a society where the females are not allowed to work, parents may pay less attention to the education of daughters. Instead, mortality of children may give a better insight.

Kurz and Johnson-Welch (1997) described six categories where the health and nutrition information for children can be sought. These are (i) mortality; (ii) morbidity; (iii) health care practices; (iv) nutritional status; and (v) feeding practices and psychological development.[6]

---

[5] '53 million children have died since the Millennium Development Goals were adopted, 32 million of these deaths could have been prevented' (as on August 2005 from *http://www.basics.org/index.html*).

[6] Mortality includes infant mortality (<1 year), child mortality (1 to <5 years), and under-five mortality (<5 years). Morbidity may refer to incidence of diarrhoeal disease, respiratory infection, measles, malaria, etc. Health care practices relate to immunization rates, oral rehydration therapy, etc. Nutritional status involves weight for age, height for age, weight for height, anaemia, Vitamin A deficiency etc. Feeding

Except for neonatal death (that is, deaths within one month of birth) female children suffer from higher death rates for all ages up to age 10. Among children aged 1–4 years, the difference in mortality (child mortality) is most prominent with female child mortality exceeding male mortality by more than 50 per cent (D'Souza and Chen 1980).

Children in general, and especially young girls represent a particularly vulnerable section of the population. Nutritional deficiencies combined with inadequate sanitation, overcrowding, and contaminated water sources predispose this already weaker section of the population to a number of serious infections such as diarrhoeal diseases, parasitic infections, measles, tuberculosis, etc. Prevalence of these diseases is not only widespread, causing nearly three-fourth of all death sunder-5, but frequently reaches epidemic proportions (Mahmud 1987).

In many poor societies, the biases in attitude and behaviour within the family, favouring sons over daughters, could be a major issue in explaining nutritional and mortality differentials among particular age-sex groups of the population such as children (Sen 1981: Chen et al. 1981).

The assessment of nutritional status weight for age (WAZ), height for age (HAZ), and weight for height (WHZ) is done through z-scores. Z-score is defined as the deviation of the value observed for a child from the median of the reference population divided by the standard deviation of the reference population. If this value is less than '−2' then the child is termed malnourished. WAZ, HAZ, and WHZ signify three aspects of malnutrition. WHZ index is an indicator of thinness or wasting. Wasting is a short-term malnutrition due to acute starvation or severe disease, famine, etc., but may result also from a chronic dietary deficiency or disease. HAZ is an indicator of stunting which means chronic malnutrition of health; however, the genetic factor is also related to it. The third index, WAZ is primarily a composite index of HAZ and WHZ that is, the indicator of both acute and chronic malnutrition. A study by Bharati et al. (2005) reveals the nutritional status of children in 26 states in India aged 0–35 months (see also Arokiasamy and Pradhan 2005). Percentages of underweight, stunted, and wasted children of 0–35 months were seen

---

practices are supplementation, breast feeding, etc. Psychological developments deal with interaction with parents, participation in child development programmes, etc.

to be 43.8, 43.9, and 16.5 for boys and 45.0, 42.9, and 15.1 for girls, respectively. Female children were found to be more underweight, less stunted, and less wasted, but the gender differences were not very much prominent. Nutritional status can also be seen through mid-upper arm circumference (MUAC). Choudhury et al. (2000) attempted to study the gender inequality in nutritional status among children in a remote rural area of Bangladesh. Thirty-three per cent of children were found to be seriously malnourished. Of the severely malnourished children, 54 per cent were female and 45.8 per cent were male.

In order to reduce child malnutrition and gender differences among children it is necessary to: (i) provide health infrastructure facilities to children as well as to mothers; (ii) make mothers aware of the necessity of health care and sanitation facilities for children; and (iii) make the parents capable so that they can afford these facilities. All these can be achieved only if the status of women in society is enhanced through literacy and empowerment of mothers.

ABOUT THE VOLUME

We now turn our attention to the chapters included in this book and see how the gender bias is addressed. This volume first introduces general issues of gender discrimination and critically examines the position of women in different spheres of life. It discusses the nature of women's participation in the workforce and other spheres. The effect of religion in deciding the age at marriage of men and women is also discussed in this part. The first four chapters deal with these aspects.

Concern for development planning for women in India was felt before India's Independence. In 1938, a Sub-Committee on Women's Role in the Planned Economy was constituted. The Sub-Committee demanded recognition of women's rights to property and recognition of women's role as workers. The Government of India Committee on the Status of Women in 1974 documented the deteriorating condition of women in all spheres. The report compelled initiatives for the integration of Women in Development (the WID approach) policy and academic research. Parallel to the WID initiatives for women's economic self-reliance through self-help groups (SHGs), the late 1980s and 1990s also witnessed major feminist incursions into state programmes designed explicitly with a 'Gender and Development' (GAD) agenda for consciousness-raising and empowerment of women. A parliamentary Committee on the Empowerment of

Women was established in 1997. The committee reviewed impact of gender mainstreaming in ministries and various departments under the ministries (see Bina Fernandez's chapter in this book for details).

The book begins with the chapter entitled '(En)gendering Poverty Policy in India' by Bina Fernandez. It investigates the poverty policy in India named the Swarnajayanti Gram Swarozgar Yojana (SGSY). Translated from Hindi, SGSY reads as the Golden Jubilee Village Self-employment Programme. SGSY is one among several central and state government programmes which, taken together would comprise the welfare component of poverty alleviation policy. Although SGSY has designated 40 per cent of resources for women, women officers are few and generally at the upper levels of the bureaucracy and bank hierarchies. SGSY ignores the gender division of labour in social reproduction. The policy ignores the reality of women's double labour burden, and the fact that self-employment would further increase this burden. The author correctly points out the possible reasons for the failure of fulfilment of most of the programmes in India. These reasons are: (i) the high levels of leakage of resources due to corruption; (ii) targeting errors, (excessive target orientation); (iii) low participation of the poor, particularly women; and (iv) political interference, etc.

Madhura Swaminathan concentrates on women as 'workers', engaged in different types of agricultural activity in India. In rural India today, the majority of women continue to be engaged in agriculture and related activities. In fact, as men move away from agriculture and diversify their occupations, women are being further concentrated in agriculture. There is thus an urgent need to focus on the concerns of women in agriculture. For women agricultural labourers, who are growing in both absolute and relative terms, the major issues of concern are the abysmally low levels of wages for tasks that women perform, the insecurity of employment, and the lack of adequate days of employment. One of the marked features of wages in India is the disparity between men and women. Occupations in which women are concentrated tend to be paid poorly. The chapter is mainly concerned with the problems such as the lack of diversification in agriculture among women workers, the feminization of the agricultural labour force, and the casualization of the rural workforce.

In the chapter 'Gender, Religion, and the Age at Marriage in India' by Sriya Iyer, the effect of gender and religion on the age at marriage in India is explored by examining gender differentials in the context of the textual theology of Hinduism and Islam on marriage. Women and men are treated differently with respect to marriage, polygyny, and divorce. Iyer's findings show that the effect of socio-economic factors on marriage age is especially pronounced for Hindu and Muslim women compared to men. Marriage is dictated by prevailing local norms that encourage early marriage. Remarriage and divorce, although sanctioned by the religion, are not regarded as feasible options for women. What is striking is that the women in the sample did not blindly accept religious prescriptions on marriage. However, they still appear to hesitate in translating their personally-held views fully into actual practice. Women's ability to enforce their views is determined by their access to socio-economic characteristics, which does vary considerably among religious groups. In the light of the recent debate in India about gender, religion, and the legal age at first marriage, these qualitative and quantitative findings have significant implications for gender inequalities, for differences between religious groups, and for development policy.

According to Amal Mandal, the women work participation rate continues to lag far behind that of men. Women workers have consistently been confined to low paid, unskilled manual, seasonal, casual, flexible, and above all leftover occupations. Over 95 per cent of total women workers are engaged in agriculture, animal husbandry, beedi rolling, labelling, and packing; building and construction; collection of raw hides and skins; handlooms weaving; brick kilns; stone quarries; saw mills; oil mills, etc. The labour market is highly sex segregated and biased. Women perform different work and their labour is perceived and valued differently. The massive concentration of women in agricultural activities is not for their deliberate preference, but simply because they do not have any other option. Those income earning activities of women fall in the broader category of the unorganized sector of the economy. Modernization and technological advances in the production process are either pushing women out from their traditional occupations or pushing them down the job hierarchy. Over the years women's work participation rate has been increasing, but the rate is nowhere near that of men. Three-fourths of total women are still recorded as non-workers. Women's work participation rate is substantially higher than the official estimates. Work without payment for example, cooking, cleaning, child care are either unreported or not taken into account.

It is also important to investigate how the gender differences transmit to the children and how women's decision-making power, maternal literacy, etc. affect children's well-being. Apart from this, there is a complex nature of interrelationships between gender, poverty, and HIV transmission. Chapters 5 to 11 discuss demographic, health, and nutritional differences among male and female populations in different geographical regions and at different stages of life.

Women's decision-making power within households is known to be lower than that of their husbands. Women are the main caretakers of children in most of the developing countries. If the decision-making power is increased for women, then it is expected that women will use it to direct household resources towards improving the health and nutritional status of their children.

The chapter by Lisa C. Smith and Elizabeth M. Byron tries to find if there is any relation between gender empowerment, especially mother's empowerment, and the well-being of, and gender bias among, children. The answer must be yes. This phenomenon is verified in the chapter in the context of South Asia. Increasing women's power is an effective force for reducing discrimination against girls. Will women use increased power to direct household resources towards equalizing the well-being of girls and boys? The measure used for examining gender discrimination among children is girl–boy comparisons of the nutritional status of 0–3 years old children. Nutritional status is the outcome of a child's nutrient intakes and health status, both of which are strongly influenced by the quality of care for children. Applying multivariate regression analysis with statistical tests for significant differences in effects for girl and boy children to demographic and health survey data from Bangladesh, India, Nepal, and Pakistan, the authors are able to prove that increasing women's power not only improves the well-being of children as a group, but also serves as a force to reduce long-standing discrimination that undermines female capabilities in many important areas of life as well as human and economic development in general.

The study by Vani K. Borooah uses unit-record data on over 50,000 rural children, from the 16 major states of India, to analyse the determinants of the risks of severe stunting and of being severely underweight. The study focuses on the role of maternal literacy in reducing the risk of child malnutrition. It concludes that when the mother is literate, real benefits flow to children in terms of reduced risk;

the same benefits, however, do not flow when the father, but not the mother, is literate. Literate mothers make more effective use of health care institutions such as *anganwadis* and hospitals. Consequently, the benefits to children from expanding the supply of such institutions are greater when these institutions interact with mothers who are literate. This chapter employs a bivariate probit model to estimate equations for risk of rural children in India being stunted and being underweight. The results of the bivariate probit model indicate that the likelihood of being stunted and underweight was lower for girls than for boys. Children living in female-headed households were less likely to be stunted/underweight than those living in male-headed households. Children from households with one, or more, 'empowered' females, as defined earlier, were less likely to be stunted and to be underweight than children from other households.

Koumari Mitra's essay provides an anthropological analysis of risks and vulnerabilities, pertaining to HIV/AIDS transmission experienced by women and men living in the urban slums of India. In the developing world, most women with Human Immuno Virus (HIV) infection regardless of their marital status, are living in poverty, thereby symbolizing the social forces of gender inequality and poverty responsible for HIV transmission. Barriers to diagnosis and treatment of sexually transmitted diseases including HIV/Acquired Immune Deficiency Syndrome (AIDS) are often specific to women, varying in different cultures but with common themes: lack of information; differential access to health care; violation of norms of personal modesty; including ignorance or denigration of women's needs. However, these barriers can be lowered with education, economic opportunities, better and more easily available health services, including preventive methods that women can control themselves.

Aparna Pandey's study on 'Gender Differences in Early Childhood Feeding Practices: Rural West Bengal', was undertaken among a cohort of 530 (273 boys and 257 girls) pre-school children residing in four demarcated villages of West Bengal by following them over a period of one year from June 1998 to May 1999. The study has highlighted the prevailing gender differences in feeding and nutrition of young children at the crucial juncture of rapid growth and development. Initiation of breastfeeding was delayed for girls. Boys are breastfed for a longer period. Weaning started early for boys. Boys also received protein-rich items and expensive commercial foods more frequently.

Discrepancies in feeding practices have resulted in poorer nutritional status of girls. It was observed that 92.9 per cent boys as against 73.9 per cent girls received protein-rich food such as meat/fish/eggs during the weaning period. During illness they were also offered expensive ready-made foods more often (72.8%) than girls (48.2%). Difference existed in prevalence of underweight (45.8% for boys and 57.6% for girls) and stunting (49.5% and 56.4% respectively for boys and girls). The reason for the observed differences seems to lie in the mothers' behaviour rather than lack of resources. This needs to be addressed by a well-planned and directed intervention acceptable at the level of community.

Tara Gopaldas in her chapter 'Health and Nutritional Status of School Age Children: Some Gender and Age Differentials' observes that severe malnutrition existed among the boys and girls in the age group 10 to 15 years. The author highlights dominant nutritional disorders and contributing factors in the schooler of the developing world. These are: (i) hunger, (ii) endemic protein-energy malnutrition, (iii) unsafe water, (iv) iron deficiency anaemia, (v) endemic iodine deficiency disorders, and, (vi) vitamin A deficiency. The team has worked with school age boys and girls (5–15 years) in about 40 of the free municipal schools (out of the existing 200) in Baroda, for over a decade and has executed comprehensive intestinal parasitic and nutritional status surveys on large cohorts. In this Chapter, Baroda has been used as a case study to depict the sad and deplorable parasitic/ nutritional status of these children. It is to be noted that only about half the children (5–15 years) had a normal weight for height index. Older children (10–15 years) had an even poorer growth rate. Among girls (10–15 years), only 31 per cent had a normal growth. Stunting was noted in 40 per cent of all older children, being seen more in the older boy vs the older girl. As many as 73 per cent of the boys and 67 per cent of the girls were mildly to moderately anaemic. Gopaldas suggests using a database wherein the heights and weights and other relevant information of children entering primary school and leaving it can be ascertained. This will help in monitoring school health at the most basic level. It will also throw light on the deterioration of health and nutritional status in the older boy and girl (11–15 years).

Apart from growth and malnutrition, studies have also been made on 'Gender Bias in Family Planning Progamme in India' by Amitabh

Tewari and Suruchi Tewari and 'Heart Disease among South Asians: Role of Gender' by Sumita Das Sarkar and Ahana Sarkar.

In the Chapter by Tewari and Tewari, an attempt has been made to analyse the gender bias that is inherent in the Family Planning Programme (FPP) in India. The analysis in this study is based on secondary data published by the Government of India as well as in various independent researches. The presence of gender bias was felt in the beginning of FPP in India. Despite this realization, no perceptible change has occurred in the FPP in India. The gender bias in the FPP is also manifested in the basket of fertility control methods, which are presently available. The Fourth Report of the Committee on 'Empowerment of Women' pointed to the health disabilities and morbidity that are gender specific. Gender power relations existing between men and women place women in a situation where they are often without power and authority in negotiating sexual relations with men. The International Conference on Population Development (ICPD) held at Cairo in 1994 as well as the World Conference on Women at Beijing in 1995 highlighted the hitherto neglected area of need of male involvement and the unnecessary and uneven burdening of women with the task of regulating reproduction to meet macro goals (Jayalakshmi et al. 2002). Still, around 51 per cent of currently married women in 1998–9 were not using any FP method because of opposition from husbands. Thus, the woman who bears the pain and responsibility of giving birth to a child has very little say in deciding when to have a child, the number of children to have, and whether to use a contraceptive or not.

A review of the prevalence pattern, etiology, and psycho-social aspects of cardiovascular disease shows that South Asians (natives and migrants to other countries), compared to other ethnic groups of the world, are at highest risk of suffering from the disease. Gender differences within the South Asian population have been noted, with women being at a higher risk than their male counterparts; yet, the scope of research has not targeted this gendered phenomenon. Genetic predisposition, urbanization, westernization, and the unique social and cultural milieu of the South Asian population may be responsible for the high prevalence amongst the population. Decline of cardiovascular disease in developed countries show that this disease is preventable, predictable, and treatable. Thus, the South Asian population should be targeted through research, education, and awareness to reduce the high prevalence of the disease amongst them.

The last few papers in the volume deal with methodological aspects of gender issues. Some new measures on gender discrimination have been proposed. Attempts have been made to find gender discrimination through the adult height difference between the genders. One chapter also proposes a simple measure of gender bias through quantifying differential stopping behaviour (DSB) by parents. Efforts have been made to find the number of females who died as a result of discriminatory treatment in access to health and nutrition in parts of the developing world.

This part of the book starts with a chapter by Manoranjan Pal and Premananda Bharati. The chapter proposes some measures of gender discrimination that can be derived from the existing measures of inequality by decomposing into 'within' and 'between' population groups—the groups being male and female populations and then modifying these measures by giving equal weights to male and female communities (that is, assuming equal number of male and female members in the population).

There are mainly three kinds of measures of gender bias proposed in the literature so far. These are: gender inequality, gender segregation and GPG. Gender inequality is concerned with the difference between male and female members of the concerned variable (say, income) in the population. Segregation measures refer to the tendency of men and women to be employed in different occupations/work places though it is not exactly what we mean by gender inequality. GPG is the difference between the mean income of female-headed households and other households. Pal and Bharati propose a new kind of measures of gender bias known as gender discrimination measures, which are different from gender inequality measures. Gender discrimination measures the difference of income between a typical male member and a typical female member. It is not concerned with the number of male and female members in the population.

The chapter by Guntupalli and Moradi explores a new measure of gender discrimination: the adult height difference between the genders in excess of normal dimorphism. Mean adult stature (or net nutritional status) of one gender contains information on nutritional and health conditions which the individuals of that gender have faced during their physical growth period. In taking the relative difference in stature of the sexes (height dimorphism), the authors argue that one can get an insight on differential treatment during youth and hence also on the discrimination between girls and boys. In a regression analysis, they statistically test possible explanations for the observed differences in height dimorphism over space and time. They focus especially on economic variables which are significant in the context of rural areas. Besides agricultural output, poverty, rural real wages, and development expenditures, they also consider amount of monsoon rainfall as an important determinant of living conditions in rural India. Here they find, that monsoon rain does decrease height differences between the genders, which means, that girls benefit to a larger degree. They argue that rural households were typically better-off because there was a higher amount of rainfall leading to high rural output. If rising output is associated with an increase in female labour input, the boy child benefits disproportionately.

The chapter by Diganta Mukherjee proposes a simple measure of gender bias through quantifying DSB, a particular method of obtaining a higher proportion of sons by parents. It also interprets the measure theoretically and illustrates it using household level data from the state of Tamil Nadu in India. This measure uses data on only the actual distribution of children and not stated ideal numbers, which is suspect in any context. In particular, it uses the actual (age, sex) composition of children in a family. The author formulates the procreation decision by parents as a dynamic utility maximization problem and hence shows that changes in the sex ratio are more important in gauging the extent of bias of the parents than the actual proportions. That is, a couple's decision to procreate further is affected more by a favourable or adverse change in the sex ratio than the actual value of the ratio.

Based on demographic information, Amartya Sen (in 1989) and Coale (in 1991) estimated that some 100 million women are 'missing' as a result of excess female mortality in parts of the developing world, most notably South Asia, China, West Asia, and parts of North Africa. More rigorous estimate gave rise to a number much lesser than 100 million. By examining the latest census returns and updating the number of 'missing women', Stephan Klasen and Claudia Wink in 'A Turning Point in Gender Bias in Mortality?' "An Update on Missing

Women"' showed that the number of missing women in absolute terms is in the range 65–107 million and that it is still rising. In relative terms (as a share of women alive), it has, however, improved in most countries. India had the highest absolute number of missing women in the early 1990s. Among the countries considered in earlier studies, the largest relative problem, indicated by the share of females that are missing, appears to be in Pakistan, followed closely by Bangladesh, and India, while more moderate problems exist in West Asia, Nepal, China, and Egypt. Improved female education and employment opportunities have generally reduced excess female mortality. The comparative neglect of female children, which is generally worse in rural areas, appears to be particularly severe for later-born girls and among them even worse for girls with elder sisters. In addition, sex-selective abortions seem to have played an increasing role in some countries experiencing missing women, most notably China, South Korea, and possibly India. The most important evidence of this is the rising observed sex ratios at birth, which appear to be indeed due largely to sex-selective abortions rather than the under-registration of female infants.

REFERENCES

Anand, Sudhir and Amartya Sen (1997), 'Gender Inequality in Human Development: Theories and Measurement', Human Development Report Office Occasional Paper No. 19, New York, United Nations Development Programme (UNDP), http://hdr.undp.org/docs/ publications/ ocational_papers/oc19a.htm.

Arokiasamy, P. and J. Pradhan (2005), 'Gender Bias Against Female Children in India: Regional Differences and Their Implications for MDGs', manuscript, Indian Institute of Population Sciences, India.

Atkinson, Anthony B. (1970), 'On the Measurement of Inequality', Journal of Economic Theory, Vol. 2, pp. 200–63.

Bardhan, Kalpana and Stephan Klasen (1999), 'UNDP's Gender Related Indices: A Critical Review', World Development, Vol. 27, pp. 985–1010.

Basu, A., Subrata K. Roy, B. Mukhopadhyay, P. Bharati, R. Gupta, and P.P. Majumder (1986), 'Sex Bias in Intrahousehold Food Distribution: Roles of Ethnicity and Socioeconomic Characteristics', Current Anthropology, Vol. 27, pp. 536–9.

Beck, Tony (1999), 'A Quick Guide to Using Gender Sensitive Indicators, Commonwealth Secretariat', Marlborough House, London, UK.

Bharati, S., M. Pal, and P. Bharati (2005), 'Growth and Nutritional Status of Pre-school Children in India', manuscript, Indian Statistical Institute, Paper presented at Second German Conference of Auxology, Glucksburg, Germany, 17-20 November 2005.

Casper, L., S. McLanahan, and I. Garfinkel (1994), 'The Gender Poverty Gap: What Can We Learn From Other Countries?', American Sociological Review, Vol. 59, pp. 594–605.

Chen, L.C., E. Huq, and S. D'Souza (1981), 'Sex Bias in the Family Allocation of Food and Health Care in Rural Bangladesh', *Population and Development Review*, Vol. 7, pp. 55–70.

Choudhury, Kaneta K., Manzoor A. Hanifi, Sabrina Rasheed, and Abbas Bhuiya (2000), 'Gender Inequality and Severe Malnutrition Among Children in a Remote Rural Area of Bangladesh', *Journal of Health, Population, and Nutrition*, Vol. 18, pp. 123–30.

Christopher, K., P. England, K. Ross, T. Smeeding, and S. McLanahan (1999), 'The Sex Gap in Modern Nations: Single Motherhood, the Market and the State', LIS Working Paper.

CIDA (1996a), *Developing Baseline Gender Indicators and Analysis for Country Programme Planning: A Resource Guide*, CIDA, Hull, Asia Branch (Author: Tony Beck).

——— (1996b), *Guide to Gender-Sensitive Indicators*, CIDA, Hull, Asia Branch (Authors: T. Beck, and M. Stelcner).

——— (1996c), *The Why and How of Gender-Sensitive Indicators: A Project Level Handbook*, CIDA, Hull, Asia Branch (Authors: T. Beck, and M. Stelcner).

Coale, A. (1991), 'Excess Female Mortality and the Balance of the Sexes', *Population and Development Review*, Vol. 17, pp. 517–23.

Commonwealth Secretariat (1999), *Using Gender Sensitive Indicators: A Reference Manual for Governments and other Stakeholders*, Gender Management System Series, London (Author: T. Beck).

D'Souza, S. and L.C. Chen (1980), 'Sex Differentials in Mortality in Rural Bangladesh', *Population and Development Review*, Vol. 6, pp. 257–70.

Duncan, O.D. and B. Duncan (1955), 'A Methodological Analysis of Segregation Measures', *American Sociological Review*, Vol. 20, pp. 210–7.

Harrison, Jane (2002), 'Gender Segregation in Employment in Australia: A Workplace Perspective', Working Paper No. 186, *Economics*, Murdoch University.

Jayalakshmi, M.S., K. Ambani, P.K. Prabhakar, and P. Swain (2002), 'A Study of Male Involvement in Family Planning, Health and Population', *Perspectives and Issues*, Vol. 25, pp. 113–22.

Klasen, Stephan (2005), 'A Turning Point in Gender Bias in Mortality? An Update on the Number of "Missing Women"', in Bharati, Pal, Ghosh and Vasulu (eds), *Gender Disparity: Its Manifestations and Implications*, Oxford University Press, India.

Kurz, M. Kathleen and Charlotte Johnson-Welch (1997), 'Gender Differences Among Children 0-5 Years: An Opportunity for Child Survival Interventions', A Review Paper Prepared for the BASICS Project. Published for the US Agency for International Development by the Basic Support for Institutionalizing Child Survival (BASICS) Project, Arlington, VA.

Mahmud, S. (1987), 'Gender Aspects of Nutrition and Mortality Among Children in Rural Bangladesh', BIDS Research Report No. 63, Bangladesh Institute of Development Studies, Dhaka.

Nussbaum, Martha (1995), 'Human Capabilities, Female Human Beings', in, Martha Nussbaum and Jonathan Glover (eds), *Women, Culture and Development*, pp. 61–104.

Nussbaum, Martha (2000), *Women and Human Development: The Capabilities Approach*, Cambridge University Press, Cambridge.

Orshansky, M. (1965), 'Consumption, Work and Poverty', in B.B. Seligman (ed.) *Poverty as a Public Issue*, Free Press, New York.

———(1969), 'How Poverty is Measured', *Monthly Labour Review*, Vol. 92, pp. 37–41.

Pearce, D. (1978), 'The Feminization of Poverty: Women, Work and Welfare', *Urban and Social Change Review*, Vol. 11, pp. 28–36.

——— (1989), *The Feminization of Poverty: A Second Look*, Institute for Women's Policy Research, Washington, DC.

Pressman, Stephen (1988), 'The Feminization of Poverty: Causes and Remedies', *Challenge*, Vol. 31, pp. 57–61.

———(1998), 'The Gender Poverty Gap in Developed Countries: Causes and Cures', *Social Science Journal*, Vol. 35, pp. 275–86.

———(2000), 'Explaining the Gender Poverty Gap in Developed and Transitional Economics', Working Paper No. 243, Luxemberg Income Study, CEPS.

Ramji, Shiraj (1997), 'The Peak', *Simon Fraser University's Student Newspaper*, Vol. 96, Issue 11, July 14.

Robeyns, Ingrid (2003), 'Sen's Capability Approach and Gender Inequality: Selecting Relevant Capabilities', *Feminist Economics*, Vol. 9, pp. 62–92.

——— (2005), 'Measuring Gender Inequality in Functionings and Capabilities: Findings from the British Household Panel Survey', in Bharati and Pal (eds), *Gender Disparity: Its Manifestations and Implications*, Anmol Publishers, India.

Sen, Amartya (1981), 'Family and Food: Sex Bias in Poverty', in P. Bardhan and T.N. Srinivasan (eds), *Rural Poverty in South Asia*, Oxford University Press.

———(1989), 'Women's Survival as a Development Problem', *Bulletin of the American Academy of Arts and Sciences*, Vol. 43, pp. 14–29.

———(2001), 'Many Faces of Gender Inequality', *The Frontline*, 9 November.

Siddhanta, S., D. Nandy, and S.B. Agnihotri (2003), 'Sex Ratios and 'Prosperity Effect": What Do NSSO Data Reveal?', *Economic and Political Weekly*, 11 October, pp. 4381–404.

The Telegraph, 25 April 2005, Kolkata, India.

UN (1995), *The World's Women, 1970–1990: Trends and Statistics*, United Nations, New York, Social Statistics and Indicators, Series K, No. 12.

———(2000): *http://www.un.org/Pubs/CyberSchoolBus/briefing/poverty /index.htm.*

World Bank (2001), *Engendering Development*, The World Bank, Washington DC.

Appendix

Equally Distributed Equivalent Achievement (EDEA) Approach

This approach was first developed by Atkinson (1970) while deriving a measure of income inequality of income through social welfare function (SWF). For simplicity, let us assume the SWF of incomes $y_1, y_2, ..., y_n$ of n individuals in a society is the sum of individual utility functions which are assumed to be the same for each individual,

$$W(y_1, y_2, ..., y_n) = \Sigma\, U(y_i),$$

where, W is the welfare function and $U(y_i)$ is the utility of y_i for the ith individual. The equally distributed equivalent income is defined as:

$$y_{ede} = U^{-1}((\Sigma\, U(y_i)/n)).$$

In other words, it is that income which, if given to each individual, gives the same value of the SWF as that of the existing one,

$$W(y_{ede}, y_{ede}, ..., y_{ede}) = W(y_1, y_2, ..., y_n).$$

Since the utility function is assumed to be increasing and concave, it can be proved that $y_{ede} <$ m, where m is the arithmetic mean of y values. The difference m - y_{ede} goes on increasing as the utility function becomes more and more concave. Thus maximum welfare is attained when y_{ede} = m, that is, when the total income is distributed equally to each person—the case of perfect equality.

Dalton has proposed the following measure of inequality:

$$I_D = 1 - \Sigma\, U(y_i)/(nm).$$

This is nothing but $1 - U(y_{ede})/U(m)$. As a refinement to the Dalton's measure, Atkinson has proposed the following measure:

$$I_A = 1 - y_{ede}/m.\text{[1]}$$

This measure is invariant under any positive linear transformation of the utility function. Calculation of both the Dalton's and Atkinson's measures needs knowledge of the utility function. The class of utility

---

[1] $1 - I_A = y_{ede}/m$ is known as the index of relative equity (Anand and Sen 1997).

functions can further be narrowed down if we assume that the inequality measure is invariant under the change of unit of measurement. In this case the utility function boils down to:

$$U(x) = A + B x^{1-\varepsilon}, \qquad \text{for } \varepsilon > 0 \text{ and } \varepsilon \neq 1, \text{ and}$$
$$= C + D \ln(x), \qquad \text{for } \varepsilon = 1.$$

The constants A, B, C, and D are unimportant in our analysis since, under the above specifications, I_A becomes

$$I_A = 1 - ((1/n) \sum (y_i/m)^{1-\varepsilon})^{1/(1-\varepsilon)}, \text{ for } \varepsilon > 0 \text{ and } \varepsilon \neq 1, \text{ and}$$
$$= 1 - GM/m \qquad \text{for } \varepsilon = 1.$$

The equally distributed equivalent income y_{ede} now becomes:

$$y_{ede} = ((1/n) \sum y_i^{1-\varepsilon})^{1/(1-\varepsilon)}.$$

The justification for defining EDEA can be found in the above definition of y_{ede}.

$$y_{ede}^{1-\varepsilon} = (1/n) \sum y_i^{1-\varepsilon}$$
$$= (1/n) \{m(1/m) \sum_{i=1}^{m} y_i^{1-\varepsilon} + f(1/f) \sum_{i=m+1}^{m+f} y_i^{1-\varepsilon} \},$$

(where the first m individuals were assumed to be all males and m+f = n),

$$= p_m \cdot (1/m) \sum_{i=1}^{m} y_i^{1-\varepsilon} + p_f \cdot (1/f) \sum_{i=m+1}^{m+f} y_i^{1-\varepsilon} \},$$

where $p_m = m/n$ and $p_f = f/n$ are the proportion of male and female population in the community and are regarded as weights.

If incomes are replaced by corresponding life expectancy index (LEI) and since we take the expected values, the LEI will be same for each man and also it will be same for each woman. Thus assuming that there are almost equal number of male and female population we get,

$$LEI_{ede}^{1-\varepsilon} = (LEI_m^{1-\varepsilon} + LEI_f^{1-\varepsilon})/2.$$

Otherwise we can take $LEI_{ede}^{1-\varepsilon} = p_m \cdot LEI_m^{1-\varepsilon} + p_f \cdot LEI_f^{1-\varepsilon}$.

Anand and Sen call it $(1-\varepsilon)$-averaging.

I) Measurement of HDI

The HDI is now based on three indicators:

1. Life expectancy at birth.
2. Educational attainment, as measured by a combination of the

adult literacy rate (two-thirds weight) and the combined gross primary, secondary, and tertiary enrolment ratio (one-third weight).

3. Standard of living, as measured by GDP per capita (PPP US$).

For each component there are fixed minimum and maximum values of the respective variables to compute the index. The formula is:

$$\text{Index} = \frac{(\text{observed value} - \text{minimum value})}{(\text{maximum value} - \text{mimimum value})}$$

The maximum and the Minimum values are fixed as follows.

	Minimum value	Maximum value
Life expectancy at birth (years)	25 years	85 years
Adult literacy rate (age 15 and above) (per cent)	0	100
Combined gross enrolment ratio (per cent)	0	100
GDP per capita (PPP US$).	$100	$40,000

To find the index for the standard of living component one has to take logarithms of the observed value, and also the minimum and the maximum values. This is just to bring the concept of diminishing marginal utility of money. In other words, one does not need an unlimited amount of money to achieve a decent standard of living.

The HDI can be symbolically defined as:

$$\text{HDI} = (\text{LEI} + \text{EAI} + \text{SLI})/3,$$

where, LEI = life expectancy index = (life expectancy at birth – 25)/(85–25),

EAI = educational attainment index = (ALI×2/3 + CGEI×1/3),

SLI = standard of living index = (ln(GDP)–ln(100))/ (ln(40,000)–ln(100)),

where, ALI = adult literacy index = (adult literacy rate – 0)/ (100 – 0),

and CGEI = combined gross enrolment index = (combined gross enrolment rate – 0)/(100 – 0).

Observe that the adult literacy rate and CGER were measured in percentages so that the ALR and CGEI are effectively same as ALR and CGER. Also note that while combining the gross enrolment ratios, it matters whether the enrolments are combined first and then ratio is taken or whether the ratios are taken first and then arithmetic mean of the ratios are taken. It is the former one which is done.

II) Measurement of GDI

The GDI uses same variables as the HDI (that is, LEI, EAI, and SLI), but gives due consideration to male and female population. It first finds the LEI, EAI, and SLI values separately for male and female population and then suitably combines them to get LEI_{ede}, EAI_{ede}, and SLI_{ede}. Finally, the GDI is found from the following simple average:

$$GDI = (LEI_{ede} + EAI_{ede} + SLI_{ede})/3.$$

The Calculation of the First Component (LEI_{ede}) of GDI

To find LEI separately for male and female population, the maximum and minimum life expectancy for men and women are taken to be different as follows.

Table AI.1: Minimum and maximum life expectancy for males and females

	Minimum Life Expectancy	Maximum Life Expectancy
Male population	22.5*	82.5
Female population	27.5*	87.5

Note: *Anand and Sen (1997) used 32.5 and 37.5 instead of 22.5 and 27.5.

The LEI for males and females (LEI_m and LEI_f) are calculated as

LEI_m = (life expectancy for male − 22.5)/(82.5 − 22.5)
LEI_f = (life expectancy for female − 27.5)/(87.5 − 27.5)

The combined life expectancy is calculated through the EDEA approach.

$$LEI_{ede}^{1-\varepsilon} = p_m \cdot LEI_m^{1-\varepsilon} + p_f \cdot LEI_f^{1-\varepsilon},$$

where p_m and p_f are the proportion of male and female population in the community and are regarded as weights. Since p_m and p_f are almost equal we can well approximate it by

$$LEI_{ede}^{1-\varepsilon} = (LEI_m^{1-\varepsilon} + LEI_f^{1-\varepsilon})/2.$$

The Calculation of the Second Component (EAI$_{ede}$) of GDI

Equally distributed equivalent educational attainment index is found in a similar manner.

$$EAI_{ede}^{1-\varepsilon} = p_m \cdot EAI_m^{1-\varepsilon} + p_f \cdot EAI_f^{1-\varepsilon},$$

where EAI$_m$ and EAI$_f$ are calculated from

$$EAI_m = (ALI_m \times 2/3 + CGEI_m \times 1/3), \text{ and}$$

$$EAI_f = (ALI_f \times 2/3 + CGEI_f \times 1/3).$$

The subscripts $_m$ and $_f$ correspond to the indices for male and female populations respectively.

The Calculation of the Third Component (SLI$_{ede}$) of GDI

Computation of SLI from male and female SLI is also similar.

$$SLI_{ede}^{1-\varepsilon} = p_m \cdot SLI_m^{1-\varepsilon} + p_f \, SLI_f^{1-\varepsilon}.$$

Note that SLIs were calculated from per capita GDP indices using maximum and minimum values with natural logarithmic transformation. Calculation of GDP for male and female population is not that simple due to lack of proper data. We consider percentage share of the economically active male and female population (say, p_{ma} and p_{fa}). Suppose, the ratio of female non-agricultural wage to male non-agricultural wage $= w_f/w_m = r_{f/m}$. Then the female and male shares of non-agricultural wage are:

$$S_f = (w_f \times p_{fa})/(w_f \times p_{fa} + w_m \times p_{ma}) = (r_{f/m} \times p_{fa})/(r_{f/m} \times p_{fa} + p_{ma}), \text{ and}$$

$$S_m = (w_m \times p_{ma})/(w_f \times p_{fa} + w_m \times p_{ma}) = (p_{ma})/(r_{f/m} \times p_{fa} + p_{ma}).$$

Per capita GDP for male (PCGDP$_m$) and female (PCGDP$_f$) can now be found by the following formula:

$$PCGDP_m = PCGDP \times S_m/p_m \text{ and } PCGDP_f = PCGDP \times S_f/p_f$$

Finally, the SLI$_m$ and SLI$_f$ are found from

$$SLI_m = (\ln PCGDP_m - \ln 100)/(\ln 40{,}000 - \ln 100), \text{ and}$$
$$SLI_f = (\ln PCGDP_f - \ln 100)/(\ln 40{,}000 - \ln 100).$$

Thus, the GDI uses the same formula for combining the different component as in HDI except that here the EDE value of each component is found by taking gender into consideration.

III) Measurement of GEM

Symbolically we can write.

$$GEM = (PRI + CAMPTI + PCGDPI_{ede})/3.$$

This is again the simple arithmetic mean of three components, but the components are different from those of HDI and GDI.

The first component (PRI) of GEM

The concerned variables are women's and men's percentage share of parliamentary seats. Suppose PR_m and PR_f are percentage shares of parliamentary representations for men and women, respectively. We first find EDE measure by the following formula:

$$PR_{ede}{}^{1-\varepsilon} = p_m \cdot PR_m{}^{1-\varepsilon} + p_f \cdot PR_f{}^{1-\varepsilon}.$$

The parliamentary representation is indexed as

$$PRI = PR_{ede}/50.$$

The Second Component (CAMPTI) of GEM

It is again a combination of two indices, namely index of administrative and managerial positions and the index of professional and technical positions.

$$CAMPTI = (AMI + PTI)/2,$$

where, $AMI = AM_{ede}/50$ and $PTI = PT_{ede}/50$.
We use the same formula for EDE measures to get

$$AM_{ede}{}^{1-\varepsilon} = p_m \cdot AM_m{}^{1-\varepsilon} + p_f \cdot AM_f{}^{1-\varepsilon}, \text{ and}$$
$$PT_{ede}{}^{1-\varepsilon} = p_m \cdot PT_m{}^{1-\varepsilon} + p_f \cdot PT_f{}^{1-\varepsilon}$$

where, AM_m and AM_f are percentage share of administrative and managerial positions for men and women, respectively and PT_m and PT_f are percentage share of professional and technical positions for men and women, respectively.

The Third Component (PCGDPI) of GEM

Here we first calculate $PCGDP_f$ and $PCGDP_m$ as given in the case of GDI. But we do not take logarithms to get the indexes. We simply get:

$$PCGDPI_m = (PCGDP_m - 100)/(40,000 - 100), \text{ and}$$
$$PCGDPI_f = (PCGDP_f - 100)/(40,000 - 100).$$

The EDE measure is found by the same formula.

$$PCGDPI_{ede}^{1-\varepsilon} = p_m \cdot PCGDPI_m^{1-\varepsilon} + p_f \cdot PCGDPI_f^{1-\varepsilon}.$$

IV) The Duncan and Duncan (1955) Index of Segregation

The Duncan and Duncan (1955) Index is defined as:

$$I_D = \tfrac{1}{2}\sum T_i \, |F_i/T_i - P_f|/(TP_f(1-P_f)),$$

where $P_f = F/T$, the proportion of female employees in the population, T and F being the total number of employees and female employees respectively. T_i and F_i are the number of employees and female employees, respectively for the ith category. This is the weighted sum of deviation of female proportion from its overall proportion. At first it may seem that the measure is not symmetric and has a female bias in the definition itself. This is not true, which can be seen from the following simplified form:

$$I_D = \tfrac{1}{2}\sum T_i \, |F_i/F - M_i/M|,$$

where M_i and M are the number of male employees in the ith category and all categories. The constant ½ is taken just to make the measure lie in between 0 and 1.a

(En)gendering Poverty Policy in India

BINA FERNANDEZ[*]

1

INTRODUCTION

The word 'engendering' has acquired a new meaning in the feminist vocabulary of the past decade: it is used to signify the idea of incorporating a gender analysis and/or mainstreaming women's concerns within an institution or a discourse. The word in this chapter is used with this connotation as well as in the dictionary definition:[1] *to produce, give existence to*. These two definitions are explored through a gender analysis of the production of anti-poverty policy in India, specifically the Swarnajayanti Gram Swarozgar Yojana (SGSY). The objective is to understand how anti-poverty policy is produced or brought into existence, how this process is gendered, and following from this, what the implications are for mainstreaming gender concerns in the anti-poverty policy discourse.

There have been some evaluatory studies of the precursors to SGSY—the Integrated Rural Development Programme (IRDP) and Development of Women and Children in Rural Areas (DWCRA),

*I would like to thank Barbara Harriss-White, for attentive feedback that constantly pushed me to clarify my ideas, and for shutting down the post-structuralist linguistic 'escape hatches'. Professor Rajeswari Sunder Rajan and Cathie Lloyd, for their insightful comments and encouragement; Joy Wang, for much needed editorial help; Shubada Deshmukh, for sharing her deep knowledge of the field, and for her hospitality during data collection; Gomathy Balasubramanian for discussions that contributed to my understanding of processes that impoverish; Sheila Allcock, for advice on the references; and Laila Hirani Trust and Wolfson College for financial support to conduct fieldwork. The errors and omissions are, of course, mine.
[1] Oxford English Dictionary, the third entry: Engender—of both parents, also vaguely of ancestors, and transf. of countries, situations, conditions, etc.; to produce, give existence to (living beings). In pass., to be produced, begotten (const. between, of); to be descended.

including recent studies of their impact specifically on women.[2] 'The common finding of all these studies is that state programmes, either as a result of their very design or through their implementation, rarely fulfil their goal of alleviating poverty' (Purushothaman 1998, p. 215).

These studies list a predictable litany of reasons why these programmes fail. Some of the oft-repeated ones are: the high levels of 'leakage' of resources due to corruption, 'targeting errors',[3] excessive target orientation,[4] the 'absence of forward and backward linkages',[5] the low participation of the poor, particularly women, and political interference. Given these failures, what are the prospects for poor women in the SGSY, the 'new-old' anti-poverty policy of the State?

Translated from Hindi, SGSY reads as *Golden Jubilee Village Self-employment Programme*.[6] It is necessary to clarify at the outset that SGSY is one among several Central and state[7] government programmes which, taken together would comprise the welfare component of the poverty alleviation policy.[8] Introduced in 1998, SGSY aims to facilitate poor people's self-employment in micro-enterprises, through the provision of a grant and low-interest credit. Two significant features distinguish it from its predecessor, the IRDP: a commitment to ensure that 40 per cent of the coverage is of poor women and an emphasis on channelling the funds for micro-enterprises to Self-help Groups (SHGs), rather than individuals.

The field work for this study was conducted in the Gadchiroli district of Maharashtra state. This is commonly perceived as one of the

[2] There have been four major official all-India studies of IRDP (by NABARD in 1984, the Planning Commission in 1985, the RBI in 1984, and again in 1993), as well as several state specific studies by the Planning Commission. A few of the academic studies include (Pulley 1989; Copestake 1992; and Vyas and Bhargava 1995). Studies analysing the impact on women include those by Purushothaman (1998), Ghosh (1998), and Galab and Rao (2003).

[3] That is, the inclusion of the ineligible, and the exclusion of the eligible.

[4] That is, the bureaucratic pursuit of quantitative programme targets, which is often at the cost of the quality of the programme intervention.

[5] That is, the absence of adequate and co-ordinated training, raw material supply, storage, and marketing facilities.

[6] The Golden Jubilee referred to is the 50th anniversary of Indian independence.

[7] I follow the convention here of referring to federal governments with an initial lower case, that is as state.

[8] Other components of anti-poverty policy include macroeconomic policy measures that affect prices and employment (as discussed further).

most 'backward' districts in the state, primarily because its large tribal population rates low on development indicators of income, health, and literacy (see Appendices for data).

The second, third, and fourth sections of this chapter are organized as a nested sequence of interrelated layers: anti-poverty policy, the administration of poverty, and the SHG–State encounter. The word 'nested' was used to indicate not only that the three sections are organized in a schema of macro, meso, and micro levels for analytical purposes, but also to indicate that these levels are not mutually exclusive and are inseparable in actuality.

The concluding section integrates the analysis in these sections and summarizes the evidence on how the construction of poverty policy is gendered; and how and why there are persistent policy failures.

ANTI-POVERTY INTERVENTIONS

Post-independence, the national consensus on the imperative of poverty alleviation (Vyas and Bhargava 1995, p. 2559) resulted in three broad policy approaches. The first was the *dirigiste* model of planned development in which rapid economic growth was considered necessary for poverty reduction (Patnaik and Patnaik 2001, pp. 33–4). The second approach was a *structural, redistributive* approach to poverty through land ceiling legislation and redistribution programmes; which was propelled in part by widespread peasant unrest (Desai 1979). Third, a *total rural development initiative* addressing health, education, and infrastructure needs was undertaken in the Community Development Programme[9] (CDP) of the First Five Year Plan (FYP) (1951–6).

Each of these approaches failed to make a substantial dent in the levels of poverty. The focus of the development plans on infrastructure and the public sector did not generate the expected levels of economic growth necessary to stimulate mass employment. Despite positive results in a few blocks, the CDP was abandoned, and its failures are attributed to problems of 'poor design', (Mathur 1996, p. 180), a social structure dominated by class hierarchies, and rent-seeking tendencies of the bureaucracy (Vyas and Bhargava 1995, pp. 2559–60).

[9] Based on a highly successful Ford Foundation pilot project in Etawah (Mathur 1996).

The primary asset endowment scheme[10] which provided credit for self-employment to the rural poor was the IRDP, introduced in 1978. It was the largest anti-poverty programme in the world,[11] and the mainstay of anti-poverty policy for two decades. The companion scheme introduced in 1982, DWCRA,[12] reflected policy recognition of WID concerns. Evaluations of IRDP have documented the exclusion of the poorest, and the inclusion of between 25–35 per cent of the 'non-poor'.[13] Rates of loan repayment are also abysmally low and are reflected in the 'overdues' or 'non-performing assets' of the banks.[14]

Introduced in April 1998, the SGSY[15] was proclaimed as an improved, rationalized version of IRDP, amalgamated with several rural development schemes.[16] Arguably,[17] SGSY is the brainchild of the Bharatiya Janata Party (BJP) government that gained power in 1997, the name change signalling not only its programmatic differences, but also IRDP's identification with the preceding Congress governments[18] (Mooij and Dev 2002, p. 47).

[10] Other asset endowment and training schemes introduced in the 1980s were the Million Wells Scheme (MWS), the Supply of Tools to Rural Artisans (SITRA), and Training of Rural Youth for Self-employment (TRYSEM).

[11] It reached over 50 million beneficiaries since its inception, and disbursed over Rs 30,000 crores (Das 1998, p.182).

[12] A revolving fund of initially Rs 15,000 and in later years, Rs 25,000 was provided to women's SHGs to undertake micro-enterprises, and in certain areas where NGOs were involved, showed positive results.

[13] Planning Commission studies document the inclusion of the non-poor to the extent of 29.8 per cent in Uttar Pradesh (c. 2001), 24 per cent in Bihar (c. 2001, p. ix); 26 per cent in Andhra Pradesh (2002, p. 52), and 37 per cent in Maharashtra (2000, p. 21).

[14] The RDD recognizes that IRDP 'loan recovery performance has been of the order of 30–35 per cent' in Annexure IV Agenda: Meeting of the CLCC, Mumbai, 25 June 1999.

[15] Translated from Hindi: Golden Jubilee Village Self-employment Scheme. The Golden Jubilee referred to is the 50th anniversary of Indian independence in 1998

[16] These include IRDP, DWCRA, SITRA, MWS, TRYSEM, and GKS.

[17] The 'rationalization of IRDP' is not a new idea of the BJP; it had been advocated for a long time by several internal Planning Commission studies and reviews. Further, the general trend of liberalization of the economy begun by the Congress in the early 1990s, was continued by the BJP regime with no major differences and only token anti-liberalization rhetoric.

[18] See 'Centre Unveils Old Schemes in Saffron Bottle', New Delhi 23 March, http://www.lib.virginia.edu/area-studies/SouthAsia/bihar/0324nat.htm

Similar to IRDP, SGSY offers a credit and subsidy package to promote micro-enterprises; and similar to DWCRA, the formation of SHGs is central (see Table A1.2.1 for a comparison of the two schemes). Other key features include: a substantial upward revision of the amount of credit and subsidy to be made available,[19] and a concomitant increase in bankers' decision-making power. The scheme aims at 40 per cent coverage of women, 50 per cent for scheduled castes/scheduled tribes (SCs/STs), and even a 3 per cent quota for the disabled. However, in the amalgamated SGSY, the content of the other schemes appears to have evaporated, leaving in effect a revised version of IRDP and DWCRA.

Counting the Poor and the Cost of the Poor

Estimates of the extent and degree of poverty are a classic example of a deeply political issue that is cloaked in contentious technical debates. While it is not possible here to engage in the debates on measurement of poverty, the trends in the levels of poverty can be outlined. The percentage of rural poverty stagnated between 45 per cent to 55 per cent in the first three decades of post-independence, and the first unambiguous decline in the poverty ratio dates from the early 1980s. This can be attributed to the increase in public expenditure, particularly in rural areas, including the expenditures on specific poverty alleviation programmes such as IRDP and the wage employment programmes (Patnaik and Patnaik 2001, pp. 39–44). The multiplier effects of government expenditure were increases in the real wages of rural and urban unskilled labour, the growth of employment in non-agricultural sectors, and relative stability in food prices (Ghosh 1998).

This trend of poverty reduction was temporarily reversed after the liberalization of the economy in 1991 (see Table A1.2). The Indian Government, however, denies the post-liberalization increase in poverty, and on the contrary claims that the poverty ratio has declined from 36 per cent in 1993–4 to 26 per cent in 1999–2000 (Saxena, c. 2001). However, the use of new methodology in the 55th Round of the National Sample Survey (NSS) makes the results non-comparable with previous NSS poverty estimates (Patnaik and Patnaik 2001, p. 58). Indeed, the new methodology is arguably a convenient statistical sleight

---

[19] Whereas IRDP was Rs 15,000 per family, the norm in SGSY is set at Rs 25,000 per family. An SHG is entitled to a maximum of Rs 2.5 lakh.

of hand, since parallel independent evaluations of the same period show overall rural poverty ratios have increased (see Table A1.2.2), though the state-wise trend is varied. For example, Maharashtra, which had witnessed considerable reduction in poverty ratios in the 1980s, saw an increase during the 1990s (see Table A1.2.3).

Shariff et al. (2002) document the overall decline in the budget for poverty alleviation programmes in the 1990s. They also draw attention to the disparities between allocated and actual expenditures, and suggest that 10–12 per cent of the allocated expenditure is never spent.

Zones of Authorization and Allocation

First, we will examine the labels and constructs constituting the *zone of authorization* (Schaffer 1984). Inherent in the label 'swarozgar' is the shift from the construct of 'beneficiaries' (deployed in IRDP) to an emphasis on the construct of the 'self-employed', and implicitly self-reliant entrepreneur. Whereas in the wage employment schemes and IRDP, the State was the provider or benefactor, in SGSY, there is a shift in rhetoric towards absolving the State of this role. Following Wood (1985, p. 23), we could say that *swarozgari* has been cast in the image of the self-employed entrepreneur in whom the State invests. The expectation that the 'self-employed', 'self-reliant entrepreur should no longer be dependent on the State for handouts was reinforced in the original guidelines. In these guidelines, there was a compulsion that swarozgaris must earn Rs 2000 per month (net of repayment of the loan) after three years, so that 'family income is above the probable poverty line of the next plan period' (para 1.1 of the *SGSY Guidelines*, 1999). This unrealistic expectation[20] was modified to 'ensuring appreciable sustained level of income over a period of time' in the *Amended Guidelines* (2002).

The presumption is that markets will operate neutrally in the interests of the swarozgari entrepreneur, enabling straightforward project formulation and profit/loss calculations. The swarozgari is thus abstracted from the segmented, complex, and highly gendered social relations of family, community, caste, and market, and the

[20] The 'unrealism' of this expectation was pointed out by bankers seeking clarifications from the RBI, see Repayment of Loan, point No.4, SGSY Clarifications, Annexe 1(1) RBI Circular: RPCD.SP.BC. 14/09.01.01/2001–02, 17 August 2001.

corresponding systems of exchange and obligations. These obligations include the agricultural (or other wage) labour and the domestic and subsistence labour of the woman, as well as constraints on women's mobility, and access to markets. Following Wood (1985, p. 23), these constraints necessitate a level of behavioural adjustment to the swarozgari label which automatically restricts women's demand for SGSY benefits, or produces quiescence and conformity among them.

A related new label is SHG. This label simultaneously invokes both a tradition of co-operation, and the new compulsions to shake off dependence by promoting self-reliance. Despite the wide variety of traditional, voluntary forms of self-help, the SHG form to be promoted has been specified in detail.[21] Although it is a gender neutral institution, in practice, the majority of the groups promoted are of women.

Indicative of the only partial transition to the construct of self-reliance is the fact that 'swarozgari' is a label of official, usually written usage. The older labels of 'beneficiary' or Below Poverty Line 'BPL' are still common oral usage, an indicator of their defining power. 'BPL' in particular is a powerful label, used as a noun, as well as adjective, thus collapsing distinctions between the person, and a (State-imposed) descriptive category. It is an acronym for 'below poverty line', a status determined through an ostensibly technical[22] survey of consumption expenditure.

'Willful defaulter' is another new label, used in conjunction with BPL as an eligibility criterion, disqualifying those who have not repaid IRDP loans. The 'defaulter' label is used to discipline non-performance, by enforcing repayment, or by exclusion from SGSY. The presumption of malfeasance leaves unaddressed the question of the non-willful defaulter: those who defaulted because they never benefited from IRDP. As the Block Development Officer (BDO), Korchi and the

---

[21] The amended SGSY guidelines identify phases of formation, stabilization, micro-credit, and micro-enterprise development that all SHGs will move through; as well as detailed criteria to assess its functioning (*Amendments in the Guidelines of SGSY*, para 3.3).

[22] Each state government determines an annual consumption expenditure amount as the poverty line. Household surveys are conducted (by teachers and other field level government officers) to determine eligibility. Gram sabhas (village councils) are supposed to ratify the lists generated, and they can pass resolutions for amendments (usually addition rather than deletion of names) to the list.

APO (SGSY) both pointed out, a large percentage of the IRDP default in the block and district is because the 'beneficiary' never benefited, due to substantial bribes paid, or third party appropriation of the loan. Further, loan repayment capacity is also affected by failure of the enterprise, or instability of their poverty status. Here again, women are affected by the definition of the 'BPL Family', since individual women are not eligible if male family members (husband/father) are willful defaulters.

The ironic practice of poverty alleviation policy is the incremental exclusion of the poor. First, studies have shown that often the extremely poor (migrants and those vulnerable to temporary/cyclical poverty) are not included in the BPL lists; while the non-poor with political clout manipulate their names onto the list. Second, in the original guidelines, there was an ambitious objective that 30 per cent of BPL population in each block should be covered within the first five years, 'subject to the availability of funds'. The *Amendments* (2002) have dropped this stipulation (para 1.4), not necessarily due to the 'unavailability' of funds. Third, there is an explicit strategy of assisting those in the upper layers of the poverty pyramid to cross over the poverty line. It is formally detailed (para 1.4) in the amended guidelines that priority loans will be provided to those BPL with land, followed by loans to artisans, and finally to the poorest who are 'asset-less and skill-less' and require 'small doses of multiple credit'. Fourth, 'defaulters' (willful or otherwise) as pointed out, are forcefully excluded from the scheme. Fifth, the amended guidelines have a provision for the 'inclusion' of non-BPL members in SHGs. Consequently, the policy practices of exclusion form an inverse pyramid, which reaches only a fraction of the poorest at the bottom of the poverty pyramid.

These practices of excluding the poor have the greatest negative impact on women and SC/STs, since they constitute the majority of the 'poorest' at the base. They are in an unequal competition for policy resources against the 'non-poor' and the 'better-off' poor. They rarely have independent titles to land, which eliminates them from priority consideration. Further, they often do not have independent access to other productive resources that would enable artisan skill development.

Turning now to the zone of allocation, SGSY is supposed to be a more efficient management of resources because of a single-window approach, and concentration of resources for maximum effect. The claim is that more resources have been allocated for poverty alleviation. On the face of it, the 8th Plan allocation of Rs 4049 crores for the forerunners of SGSY was increased to Rs 4690 crores for SGSY (see Table A1.2.4). This is a relatively marginal increase, and more importantly, the rhetoric masks a first, a substantial 9 per cent decrease in the total amount allocated to poverty alleviation programmes. Second, as Shariff et al. (2002) show, it also masks the fact that revised budget estimates (based on utilizations) show a drastic decline in the SGSY budget from 18.6 per cent in 1990–1 to 4.2 per cent in 2001.

The Central Government provides 75 per cent of the funds for SGSY, while state governments are expected to contribute the balance of 25 per cent. The total government funds are divided as follows: 60 per cent for subsidy, 20 per cent for infrastructure, and 10 per cent each for training and the revolving fund. The disbursement of subsidy at the end of the first two years was found to be lower than the targets set.[23]

Credit is supposed to match subsidy in a 1:3 ratio; however, the mobilization of credit has been less than 30 per cent of the target; thus making the ratio 1:2. This low rate is accounted for by the banker's fear of non-repayment. Some banks appear to have deliberately underfinanced the swarozgaris. In few cases, the entire amount of loan sanctioned is released and shown so in the loan account ledger. Half the amount of the loan sanctioned, however is retained by each concerned bank and deposited in the bank itself by opening a separate savings bank account in the name of the swarozgaris. The swarozgaris are, on the other hand, never allowed to draw any amount from these accounts.

A second significant banking practice introduced is the back-end subsidy,[24] which was introduced during IRDP, based on the recommendation of the Mehta Expert Committee. The subsidy will be forfeited in the event of non-repayment. Ironically, the subsidy is also forfeited if the repayment is before time to ensure that the beneficiaries do not make the repayments by selling off assets.[25]

---

[23] RBI Circular: RPCD.SP.BC.113/09.01.01/2002–03.

[24] RDD Circular No.I. 12011/1/95-IRD Credit, dated 4 June 1996; Recommendation of the Expert Committee on the IRDP system of Back-end subsidy (with reference to RPCD. No.SP.BC.89/09.01.01/95–96 13 February 1996).

[25] RBI Circular: RPCD.SP.BC.113/09.01.01/2002–03.

The good news for women appears to be the significant six-fold increase in budgetary allocation for women entrepreneurs in SGSY[26] compared to DWCRA. Further, although initially lagging, the target of 40 per cent coverage of women was achieved by 2002.[27]

THE ADMINISTRATION OF POVERTY

The 'Black Box' of the Bureaucracy

'It is as though the behaviour of those manning the state apparatus is like a "black box" (a device with known performance but unknown constituents and means of operation)' (Das 1998, p. 5).

In this assessment, the focus is on two key determinants of bureaucratic functioning: first, the role of bureaucrats in disbursing state resources; and second, the absence of formal accountability of bureaucrats to political processes.

In the post-independence era, the path of planned development charted by the leaders of the Indian National Congress necessitated the continuation of the earlier form and structure[28] of the bureaucracy, with, however, two crucial differences from the colonial bureaucracy. The first difference is that in the State's path of planned development, there is an elaboration of the state function of allocation of resources for development and the elimination of poverty, which is distinct from the revenue extraction and law enforcement roles of the colonial state.[29]

---

[26] The budget for DWCRA in the 8th Plan was Rs 150 crore, the utilization was Rs 189.54 crore. The SGSY budget in the 9th Plan is Rs 4690 crore, 60 per cent is towards the subsidy, and 40 per cent of that amount is the subsidy for women; that is Rs 1125.6 crore.

[27] CLCC Agenda Notes, 3 June 2002, Agenda No.3B. Physical Achievements, p. 7.

[28] With, of course the difference that members are Indians at all levels. Vitthal (1997) identifies the three levels of the bureaucratic hierarchy: at the lowest end are the non-gazetted employees, followed by the gazetted officers (both of which are state specific cadres), and the highest level are the covenanted services (all-India cadres of the administrative and diplomatic services).

[29] The First FYP 1951–6 clearly states this: 'From the maintenance of law and order and collection of revenue, the major emphasis now shifts to development of human and material resources and the elimination of poverty....' (cited in Mathur 2001, p. 124). Resource allocations now include subsidies and welfare programmes for the agrarian and urban poor, infrastructure for the public sector, licences/tariffs for the private sector.

The second difference is the weak articulation of formal accountability of the bureaucracy to the political process.[30]

The allocation of State resources through planned development has implications for the role of the bureaucracy in disbursal. These implications can be mapped into three inter-related areas that define the parameters of the policy processes: the proliferation of rules, the determination of targets, and the allocation and utilization of budgets.

Zone of Establishment

Before examining the SGSY 'black box', it would be useful to begin by identifying the endemic administration problems of IRDP, in order to understand what (if any) have been the changes. The several reviews of IRDP, both official and academic,[31] invariably catalogue the following as problems: excessive target-orientation, targeting errors, loan non-repayment, lack of decentralized planning, and corruption.

The strongest criticism of target-orientation has emerged from those directly responsible for implementing the targets—the extension officers (EOs), bank managers (BMs) and non-governmental organizations (NGOs). Target-orientation is at best a sanction and at worst a mechanism for misutilization, since the imperative to fulfil targets means that little or no attention is paid to the question of who benefits. The mechanical herding together of women into groups to achieve targets can result in targeting errors—where the ineligible may be included, and the neediest eligible may be excluded. There is a conflict between the disbursal targets of the Rural Development Department (RDD) and the recovery targets of the bankers.

On the front lines, BMs and EOs have a range of strategies to deal with the conflict between 'target achievement' for the District Rural Development Agency (DRDA) and the threat of 'non-performing

---

[30] Das' observation that the civil service reform requires the enforcement of the political accountability of the bureaucracy is an implicit recognition of the same point (Das 1998, p. 226).

[31] Major all-India official studies include the RBI study of 1984, the NABARD study of 1984, the Planning Commission study of 1985, and, more recently, in 1994 the Expert Committee review chaired by D.R. Mehta (cited in Das 1998, p. 183). There have also been state-specific official studies conducted by the Planning Commission. Academic studies include those by Pulley (1989), Copestake (1992), Vyas and Bhargava (1995), and Ghosh (1998).

assets' for the banks. Whether it is a 'collaborative' strategy depends to some extent on the individuals, and the equation they have with each other. These strategies include the following:

+ disbursal to individual beneficiaries, rather than groups, since they are easier to control/influence on repayment;
+ sanctioning the amount, but releasing only the subsidy and not the credit component to the groups;
+ disbursement of the financial target in smaller loans to more groups rather than as a big loan to one group (that is, increase the physical target), thus spreading the 'risk' of non-repayment; and
+ delaying the processing (that is, long gaps between receipt of applications, sanction, and disbursal of installments).[32]

If none of these strategies work, the 'never fail' escape hatches include blaming the SHGs or NGOs for non-repayment and group failure.

A large proportion of the overdue IRDP loans are explained by 'leakage': that is, substantial portions of the IRDP loans were pocketed either by the bank officers and/or the DRDA staff or by the local elite. Evaluations of IRDP have documented rampant corruption, where over 60 per cent of the beneficiaries paid some amount of bribe in order to obtain the scheme.[33] The 'beneficiaries' may benefit partially, or not at all; however the loan repayment is still their responsibility, regardless of whether their capacity to repay has improved.

A specific measure that SGSY has incorporated as a means of addressing the problem of loan non-repayment due to corruption is the back-end subsidy. The checks against corruption in SGSY that were commonly mentioned both by bankers and bureaucrats were first, the greater levels of awareness and vigilance among people.

Second, and more emphatically, several argued that the SHG itself was a mechanism to prevent corruption. The rationale given was that the SHGs maintained verifiable records and had collective decision

---

[32] RBI Circular No. RPCD.SP.BC.113/09.01.01/2002-03, 4 July 2002 took note of these delays, and instructed bankers to minimize it.

[33] The Planning Commission studies documented that bribes varied between 7 per cent of the loan paid by 60 per cent of beneficiaries in Andhra Pradesh (2002, p. 53), 10–20 per cent of the loan paid by 60 per cent of the beneficiaries in Maharashtra (2002, p. 26); and 5–35 per cent of the loan paid by beneficiaries in Uttar Pradesh (c. 2001).

making. Further, while corruption is easy with individual beneficiaries, they argued that it is difficult to cheat a group of women.

However, it is now apparent that, where government officials are responsible for group formation and promotion, the SHGs are sometimes formed after taking money. The co-ordinator of one of the NGOs complained that the groups promoted by the NGO were deliberately sidelined in the gradation process, precisely because the officials could not take bribes from them. There is usually no way of tracing these transactions,[34] since it is not in the interest of either party to admit to the same.

It was also observed that several new NGOs had been formed in the Gadchiroli district. For instance, the new NGOs of a local teacher and a political party had received contracts for group formation under SGSY. It appeared that these organizations had a better 'collaborative' (rent-sharing?) relationship worked out with the local officials.

'Non-policy' Practices and 'Escape Hatches'

The arena of 'non-policy' which will be outlined here includes what (Bacchi 1999) and (Schaffer 1984) call the 'foreclosures', or the areas that should be, but are not, within policy practices.

Although SGSY has designated 40 per cent of resources for women, women officers are few and generally at the upper levels of the bureaucracy and bank hierarchies.[35] SGSY ignores the gender division of labour in social reproduction. The policy ignores the reality of women's double labour burden, and the fact that self-employment would further increase this burden. It is almost inevitable then, that men take over the management of the enterprise. There are also no mechanisms to safeguard the interests of weaker members of the group against the appropriation of resources by a few within the group.

---

[34] In an amusing anecdote of an exception, the NGO 1 co-ordinator described how the bribe paid by an SHG in Pauni village, Dhanora block came to light because they had recorded it in their accounts ledger.

[35] Only two of the officials interviewed in this study were women, and they were at the state level. Women constituted only 7.5 per cent of the higher civil services in 1997, according to the GoI, Department of Women and Child Development (2000) Report to CEDAW.

Ethnic identity, in particular, is an important variable in Gadchiroli. It is a district with 38.7 per cent tribal population,[36] who constitute a disproportionately higher percentage of the poor, representing 43.7 per cent the BPL population (see Table A1.1.3). Like many other tribal pockets of the country, as noted already, this district is characterized by 'backwardness' on key development indicators (see Tables A1.1.1 and A1.1.2). The SGSY has a provision that 50 per cent of the beneficiaries should be from ST and SC populations. This 'target' has been 'achieved' in the district, however, in interviews, the Assistant Project Officer (APO) and PD of the DRDA discussed how the strategy in the remote tribal blocks of Etapalli and Bhamragad was to identify individual beneficiaries, rather than form SHGs. These individuals are more likely to be men, which operates to the disadvantage of tribal women.

The foreclosures that operate in the arena of ethnic identity are first, the policy non-recognition of the local self-governance powers conferred on tribal communities by the provisions of the Panchayats Act of 1996.[37] The second foreclosure is the possibility of linking SGSY 'key activities' and 'cluster' enterprises to the tribal livelihood strategy of collection of non-timber forest produce.[38] Although this was suggested by NGO representatives at the state level meeting on SGSY,[39] it remains un-operationalized.

Let us now turn to the 'escape hatches' used by government officials to avoid consideration of the specificities of gender and ethnic identity. In interviews, when officials discussed reasons for women's 'non-participation', 'exit', or 'implementation failures', the paternalistic explanations they invariably offered were: women's illiteracy, their lack

[36] The main tribal groups in the district are the Gond, Pradhan, Madia, and Kolam.

[37] The Provisions of Panchayats (Extension to Scheduled Areas) Act or PESA, 1996 was based on the detailed and insightful recommendations of the Bhuria Committee. It not only guarantees the 1993 Panchayati Raj (local self government) provisions of the 73rd Amendment, but also gives *adivasis* living in scheduled areas additional self-governance rights and privileges, particularly over the natural resources in their villages.

[38] As a district with 70 per cent forest cover, forest produce is a major revenue source both for the district government, as well as private contractors. The tribal (particularly women) collectors, however, are paid a fraction of what the produce is worth.

[39] See RDD circular SGSY-1000/428/43, 16 August 2000.

of experience, their domestic responsibilities, and traditional social customs that restrict their mobility in public space. However, this is a circular argument, since if these 'preconditions' for SGSY success were indeed in place, there would not be a need for the policy!

Escape hatches vis-à-vis tribal communities are typically their 'backwardness', the difficulties of communication because their languages are different, and the remoteness of villages in forested areas.

THE SHG–STATE ENCOUNTER

State Programmes for Women

The history of development planning for women can be considered to have begun in 1938 with the pre-independence Sub-Committee on Women's role in the Planned Economy.[40] Chaudhuri's recent study (1995) shows that the radical economic vision of the Sub-Committee demanded recognition of women's rights to property and recognition of women's role as workers, significantly including the value of household labour. The Sub-Committee's radical impetus was reversed in the community development programmes of the First FYP (1951–6), which identified women's role as: 'a good wife, a wise mother, a competent housewife, and a responsible member of the village community'.[41]

This period of relative quiescence was broken by the report 'Towards Equality' produced by the Government of India Committee on the Status of Women in 1974, which documented the deteriorating condition of women in all spheres. The report compelled initiatives for the integration of women in development (the WID approach) policy and academic research.

Parallel to the WID initiatives for women's economic self-reliance through SHGs, the late 1980s and 1990s also witnessed major feminist incursions[42] into state programmes designed explicitly with a GAD

[40] This was one of the 29 sub-committees of the National Planning Committee under the chairmanship of Jawaharlal Nehru.

[41] Statement of the Director of the Women's Programme, 1959 (cited in John 1999, p. 109).

[42] Feminists were consultants in the design of the programmes, and feminist organizations such as Jagori in New Delhi were involved in training women, especially the village-level *sathins* (activists).

agenda of consciousness-raising and empowerment of women.

Despite these bleak assessments of both WID and GAD state programmes, 'empowerment of women' is now a mobilizing metaphor (Apthorpe 1996) for the State. For instance, the Ninth FYP (1997–2002) identified the empowerment of women as a key strategy for development, a parliamentary committee on empowerment of women was established in 1997, and the Prime Minister's Office directed a review be made of the impact of gender mainstreaming in ministries and departments.

Micro-practices of SHGs

Within the mandate of SGSY, SHGs are formed by, and come into regular contact with, the frontline staff of the DRDA (Gram Sevaks [GSs], EOs and the BDO) and the banks (Bank Field Officers [BFOs], and BMs). These interactions are structured by the procedural requirements of SGSY, as well as the dynamics of gender, class, and caste. Women of SHGs also have to negotiate informally with local men, who are outside the structures of SGSY, and include their husbands/male relatives, local moneylenders, and local elite. The following subsections detail SHG interface with the DRDA, banks, and local men. Although SHGs also had interactions with NGOs at all stages of SGSY, these processes have not been considered here because the significant difference in this interaction is that at the 'gate-keeping' decision points (gradation and release of funds) NGOs had little or no control.

The procedural requirements of SGSY that structure this interface are SHG formation, gradation, training, and enterprise asset verification. The formation of SHGs is primarily the responsibility of the DRDA, except where NGOs have been contracted to do the job. Initially, however there was considerable overlap of area and competition over groups claimed between the various agents to whom the DRDA had assigned the task of group formation, that is, the EOs, GS, Anganwadi Sevikas (AS), the NGOs, and in some places, the Bank Field Officer (BFO).

In 1999–2000, since new group formation would take time, DRDA staff began by re-constituting the existing SHGs in the villages in order to fulfil the annual targets. Some of these were old DWCRA groups, others were SHGs established by NGOs, and some were the residual groups of a plethora of transient state programmes for women.[43] The reconstitution of old groups was necessary to ensure that all the members were BPL according to the ninth Plan BPL lists. The *Amended Guidelines* (2002) formalized the participation of non-BPL membership up to 20 per cent of total membership. However, the problem with this general inclusion is that it allows easier manipulation of the group by the village elite.

Gradation is a critical gate-keeping function that is performed by the EO and the BM to determine the eligibility of the SHG to SGSY finance. The first gradation is an exercise to determine eligibility for the Rs 25,000 revolving fund, and assesses the level of group functioning.[44] The primary 'tangible' indicator is the maintenance of records and it is presumed that SHGs' record-keeping capacity is equivalent to the 'intangible' capacities to manage a group enterprise. In practice, 'adjustments' in the records are made by EO/BDO to ensure that selected SHGs 'fit' the gradation requirements. For instance, the Korchi EO quite casually 'created' back-dated records for an SHG while I waited to interview him. The second gradation is supposed to assess the utilization of the revolving fund, and determine eligibility for the loan component. However, since there is no pro forma for the second gradation, it is controlled even more by the subjective perceptions and priorities of the concerned officers.

The BM's stamp of approval on the gradation of the SHG is critical (unlike the signature of the sarpanch, which is treated as a technicality), since it is a signal for the release of funds. However, BMs have been releasing only the subsidy component of the revolving fund,[45] to the extent that at the aggregate level, this is reflected as an issue of 'under financing', that is, lower disbursal of credit relative to subsidy.[46] The

---

[43] These include SHGs formed under the aegis of the Maharashtra Rural Credit Programme (MRCP), the Indira Mahila Yojana (IMY), the SHG–Bank Linkage Programme of NABARD, and watershed development programmes.

[44] Scores are given based on these evaluation criteria: regularity of meetings, attendance, savings, internal lending, leadership, and decision making.

[45] The break up of the Rs 25,000 revolving fund is Rs 10,000 interest free subsidy from the DRDA, and Rs 15,000 loan at 12.5 per cent interest per annum from the bank.

[46] Under financing has been a persistent problem at the CLCC meetings in May 2001 and June 2002. See RBI Circulars: RPCD.SP.BC.113/09.01.01/2002–03, 4 July 2002, and RPCD.SP.BC. 19/09.01.01/2001–02, 30 August 2001.

release of the larger loan (Rs 1.25 lakh) ostensibly occurs after the second gradation; however, some banks have released the amount without a second gradation format, in order to show minimal target achievement. Further, as in the case of the Korchi Bank Manager, they were engaging in 'discretionary practices' of releasing only part of the loan, for instance, Rs 50,000 in the first instance.

Poor women's powerlessness and dependence on men in the public domain is constructed through the complicity of officials, and local male elite. A classic (though unsurprising) example is *Saraswati* SHG (in Waddha village, Armori block), which was proclaimed by the CEO to be a success story, since they were running a mini rice-mill. However, the rice-mill was being managed entirely by a local 'doctor', who was also a member of the Gram Panchayat. The ten illiterate women who were members of the SHG had no control over the enterprise (run by hired workers), or information about the accounts (they did not even have their SHG bank pass book). They were nevertheless liable for the repayment of not only the Rs 1.25 lakh SGSY loan, but an additional loan of Rs 1 lakh that had been sanctioned by the bank.

The Gadchiroli district administration is very satisfied with its achievement of 47 per cent coverage of women under SGSY in 2001–02, given the guideline specification of 40 per cent. This trend is replicated in the aggregate data for the state. In WID terms, this represents a significant advance over the IRDP marginalization of women. The figures conceal the fact that this was achieved only in the last year. More important is the marked division of individual SGSY sanctions for men, and group SGSY sanctions for women (a trend that is repeated in the Maharashtra State data). As Figures 1.1 and 1.2 show, individual men are by far the largest category of beneficiaries, and individual women constitute less than a third of the total individual beneficiaries.

This recognition of the men as individual beneficiaries has to be viewed in conjunction with the emphasis on household level definition of 'BPL family', in which women's eligibility as individuals is contingent on whether male family members are defaulters. This skewed policy treatment of male and female entitlements is also reflected in cases of loans above Rs 50,000. Since bankers unofficially require land mortgage for loans above Rs 50,000 (a 'discretionary practice', to use Schaffer's term), women's lack of independent title to land necessitates dependence on male land title deeds.

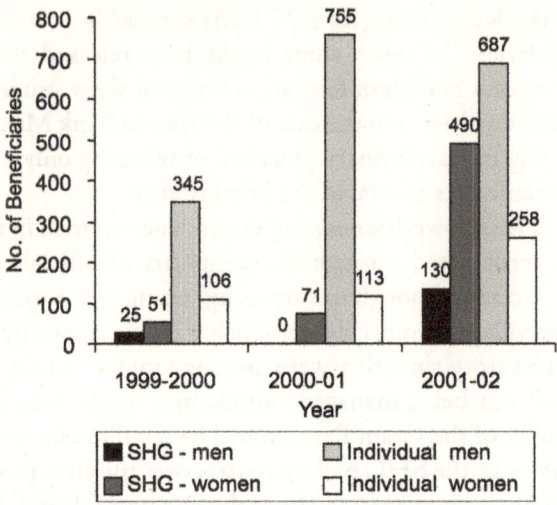

Figure 1.1: SGSY beneficiaries, Gadchiroli District

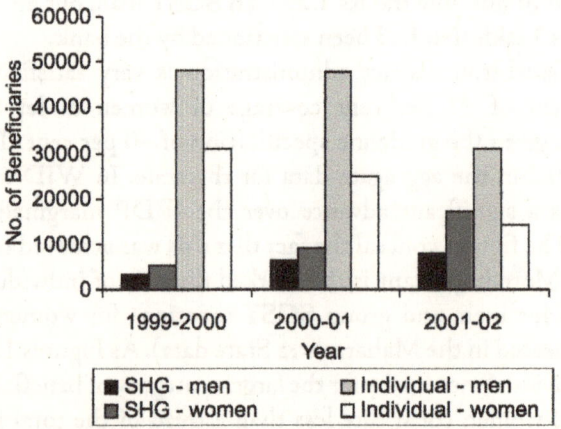

Figure 1.2: SGSY beneficiaries, Maharashtra

CONCLUSION

The objective in this chapter has been to interrogate the gendered processes of anti-poverty policy production and to understand how and why there are persistent policy failures. Such an understanding is a vital precondition to sharpen strategies for making policy more accountable, particularly to poor women. In the preceding sections, Schaffer's (1984) conceptualization of contingent zones of authorization, allocation, and establishment has been used to scrutinize the practices of SGSY policy.

The Gendered Production of Anti-poverty Policy

The core representation of the problem in SGSY is that poor people's lack of access to non-exploitative credit hinders their entrepreneurial capacity and consequently their capacity to increase their incomes. While this was also the perspective of IRDP, in SGSY there is a critical shift in the representation that is signalled by the use of the labels swarozgari (the self-employed), and SHGs to promote the concept of self-reliance. The emphasis on self-reliance contains the unstated policy objective of reducing the perceived 'dependence' of poor people on State resources.

Following Fraser (1989) juridically, women are primarily viewed as members of a household. Their structural position of dependence within the household is thus reinforced by the policy. A range of administrative practices reinforce women's dependence in the public domain: corrupt practices of officials (and/or their collusion in corruption with local elite), paternalist attitudes of protection, the absence of women-friendly administrative initiatives (such as women staff), and the targeting of SHGs for other 'women's welfare' programmes. Therapeutic practices subject the functioning of SHGs to normalization (through training) and surveillance (through gradation). The net effect of these practices is to diffuse the transformatory potential of SHGs, or indeed of the policy, for women.

Let us now focus on how and why policy failures persist. The oft-stated reasons for failure of the programme are namely: 'targetting errors', target orientation, the 'absence of forward and backward linkages', the high levels of 'leakage'/corruption, loan non-repayment, the low participation of the poor, particularly women, and political interference.

However, the representation of the problem of poverty as a lack of access to credit forecloses other explanatory factors that produce and maintain gendered poverty. These include women's unequal access to land and other resources, exploitative labour markets, macroeconomic policies of structural adjustment, and the social relations of caste and class that perpetuate poor women's dependence and powerlessness vis-à-vis men in their households, and vis-à-vis men in the public domain (local elite, government officials etc.). These factors are not seriously considered within the SGSY domain. There is no recognition that women's agency, the redistribution of assets, or improvement in the conditions of wage work have relevance to poverty alleviation. The low participation of poor women is justified through 'gender escape hatches'. These are predictable arguments about the conditions of women's poverty (illiteracy, lack of mobility or entrepreneurial experience) and their 'domestic responsibilities'.

Implications for GAD Mainstreaming

SGSY is a policy in the WID mould and, therefore, can be subjected to the typical GAD analysis of the gender specific effects of policy assumptions and areas that remain outside the policy boundaries. For instance, the assumption of the 'family' as a unit, and the assumption of the 'normative male subject' of policy is fundamental to GAD analyses (see Agarwal 2000).

The point is not to devalue what has been achieved by GAD gender mainstreaming initiatives, but to argue for a methodology that brings into sharper analytical focus not only the 'problem' but also the process of problematizing gender and poverty policy and actual policy practices.

As has been attempted in this study, such an analysis would include the following considerations:

+ Constitutive contexts: what are the contexts of state and society that define the parameters of policy?
+ Problem representation: how is the policy 'problem' represented? What are the labels and frames used?
+ Identities and agency: how is the normative subject of policy constructed? How are identity differences treated in policy? How do policy subjects gain agency?
+ Practices: what are the practices of:
  a) Determining access to the policy?
  b) Allocating and utilizing policy resources?
+ How are these practices deployed vis-à-vis the representations?
+ Institutions: what are the institutional imperatives, and how do these operate to shift the representations and practices? What are the points of leverage that can be used?
+ Foreclosures: what alternative representations and practices are excluded from the policy arena?

* Escape Hatches: what are the 'known failures', and what are the justifications for allowing them to persist? What are the mechanisms to prevent such justifications?

Any feminist intervention in State programmes has to adopt a nuanced understanding not only of State and society hierarchies, but also of how alternative policy foreclosures and escape hatches (specifically 'gender escape hatches') are deployed by these hierarchies. That is, the input should plan for resistance, and this plan should include a repertoire of collaborative, conflictual, and/or subversive strategies, appropriate to the specific context.

REFERENCES

Primary Sources

Government of India, Ministry of Rural Development
Government of India, Planning Commission
Government of Maharashtra, Rural Development and Water Conservation Department
Reserve Bank of India

Secondary Sources

Agarwal, B. (2000), *The Family in Public Policy: Fallacious Assumptions and Gender Implications*, National Council of Applied Economic Research, New Delhi.

Amendments (2002), Press release as on 31 December 2002, Ministry of Rural Development, Government of India, available at: *http://pib.nic.in/archive/Ireleng/lyr2002/rdec2002/31122002/r311220029.html*

Apthorpe, R.J. and D. Gasper (1996), 'Reading Development Policy and Policy Analysis: On Framing, Numbering and Coding', in R.J. Apthorpe and D. Gasper (eds), *Arguing Development Policy: Frames and Discourses*, Frank Cass in Association with the European Association of Development Research and Training Institutes (EADI), London and Geneva.

Bacchi, C.L. (1999), *Women, Polity and Politics: The Construction of Policy Problems*, Sage Publications, London; Thousand Oaks, California.

Chaudhuri, M. (1995), 'Citizens, Workers and Emblems of Culture: An Analysis of the First Plan Document on Women', *Contributions to Indian Sociology* (n.s.), Vol. 29, Nos. 1 and 2, pp. 211–35.

Copestake, J. (1992), 'The Integrated Rural Development Programme: Performance During the Sixth Plan, Policy Responses and Proposals for Reform', in B. Harriss-White, et al. (eds), *Poverty in India: Research and Policy*, Oxford University Press, Bombay.

Das, S.K. (1998), *Civil Service Reform and Structural Adjustment*, Oxford University Press, Delhi and Oxford.

Desai, A.R. (1979), *Peasant Struggles in India*, Oxford University Press, Bombay.

Fraser, N. (1989), *Unruly Practices: Power, Discourse and Gender in Contemporary Social Theory*, Oxford, Polity.

Galab, S. and C. Rao (2003), *Women's Self-Help Groups, Poverty Alleviation and Empowerment*, Economic and Political Weekly, March, Vol. 22, No. 29, pp. 1274–83.

Ghosh, J. (1998), *Assessing Poverty Alleviation Strategies for Their Impact on Poor Women: A Study with Special Reference to India*, United Nations Research Institute for Social Development, Geneva.

John, Mary (1999), 'Gender, Development and the Women's Movement', in R.S. Rajan (ed.), *Gender Issues in Post-Independence India*, Kali for Women/Rutger's University Press, New Delhi and New Brunswick, New Jersey.

Mathur, K. (1996), 'Designing Poverty Alleviation Programmes: International Agencies and Indian Politics', in K. Mathur (ed.), *Development Policy and Administration*, Sage Publications, New Delhi; Thousand Oaks, California.

———(2001), 'Strengthening Bureaucracy: State and Development in India', in N.G. Jayal and S. Pai (eds), *Democratic Governance in India: Challenges of Poverty, Development, and Identity*, Sage Publications, New Delhi and London.

Mayoux, L. (1995), *From Vicious to Virtuous Circles?: Gender and Micro-enterprise Development*, United Nations Research Institute for Social Development, Geneva.

Mooij, J. and M. Dev (2002), 'Social Sector Priorities, An Analysis of Budgets and Expenditures in India in the 1990s', IDS Working Paper No. 164, Institute of Development Studies, Sussex.

Patnaik, U. and P. Patnaik (2001), 'The State, Poverty and Development in India: Challenges of Poverty, Development and Identity', in N.G. Jayal and S. Pai (eds), *Democratic Governance in India: Challenges of Poverty, Development, and Identity*, Sage Publications, New Delhi and London,

Pulley, R.V. (1989), 'Making the Poor Creditworthy: A Case Study of the Integrated Rural Development Program in India', World Bank Discussion Paper 58, World Bank, Washington, D.C.

Purushothaman, S. (1998), *The Empowerment of Women in India: Grassroots Women's Networks and the State*, Sage Publications, New Delhi and London.

Rogaly, B. and S. Johnson (1997), *Microfinance and Poverty Reduction*, Oxfam and Action Aid, Oxford.

Saxena, N.C. (c. 2001), *Poverty Alleviation During the 10th Plan—Policy Issues*, Planning Commission, Government of India, New Delhi, Available from: <http://planningcommission.nic.in/reports/articles/artf.htm> (Accessed on 30 April 2003).

Schaffer, B. (1984), 'Towards Responsibility: Public Policy in Concept and Practice', in E.J. Clay, and B. Schaffer (eds), *Room for Manoeuvre: An Exploration of Public Policy in Agricultural and Rural Development*, Heinemann Educational Books, London.

Schaffer, B. and E. Clay (1984). 'Introduction—Room for Manoeuvre: the Premise of Public Policy', in: E. J. Clay and B. Schaffer (eds.) *Room for Manoeuvre : An*

Exploration of Public Policy in Agricultural and Rural Development, Heinemann Educational Books, London.

Shariff, A., P. Ghosh, and S.K. Mondal (2002), 'State-Adjusted Public Expenditure on Social Sector and Poverty Alleviation Programmes', *Economic and Political Weekly*, 23 February, pp. 767–87.

United Nations, Division for the Advancement of Women (2000). *Consideration of reports of States parties, India Initial report*. Committee on the Elimination of Discrimination against Women, Twenty-second session, 17 January–4 February 2000. Accessed on 30 April 2002 at: *http://www.un.org/womenwatch/daw/ cedaw/ indiaclu.htm*

Vyas, V.S. and P. Bhargava (1995), 'Public Intervention for Poverty Alleviation: an Overview', *Economic and Political Weekly*, 14–21 October, pp. 2559–72.

Wood, G.D. (1985), 'The Politics of Development Policy Labelling', in G.D. Wood (ed.), *Labelling in Development Policy: Essays in Honour of Bernard Schaffer*, Sage development studies, Sage Publications/Institute of Social Studies, London/ The Hague.

Appendix A1.1: Data on Gadchiroli District

Table A1.1.1: Socio-demographic profile

	India	Maharashtra	Gadchiroli
Population (millions)	839	79.8	0.79
Sex ratio (women per 1000 men)	927	934	976
Fertility rate (children per woman)	4.3	3.7	4
Infant mortality rate (deaths per 1000 births)	77	74	106
Female literacy (per cent)	39	52	29
Female mean age at marriage (years)	17.7	17.9	18

Source: Census of India (1991).

Table A1.1.2: Rural infrastructure profile

(all figures in percentages)

Inhabited villages	India	Maharashtra	Gadchiroli
Having access to any medical facility	33.0	30.0	24.2
Having access to drinking water from tap	18.1	32.9	21.0
Having electricity for domestic purpose	63.6	93.1	44.9
With a telephone connection	5.6	6.1	2.5
Having bus stand	33.7	62.8	22.6
Having pucca roads	36.9	42.7	17.0

Source: Census of India (1991).

Table A1.1.3: Below Poverty Line (BPL) population in Gadchiroli district

(figures in brackets are percentages)

	Total	ST	SC
Total population (1991 census)	969,960	304,535 (38.70)	95,996 (12)
BPL families (1997–8)	99,392	43,486 (43.7)	14,875 (14.9)
BPL population (1997–8)	499,869	218,442	74,480

Source: Gadchiroli district website *http://district.mah.nic.in/gadchiroli/* and district documents.

Table A1.1.4: New estimates of BPL population

	India	Maharashtra
% BPL in 1993–4	35.97	36.86
% BPL in 1999–2000	26.1	25.02

Source: Planning Commission (2001).

Appendix A1.2

Table A1.2.1: Differences between IRDP and SGSY

IRDP	SGSY	In Practice
IRDP credit-cum-subsidy programme Linkages between groups formed under DWCRA and trainees of TRYSEM and IRDP not strong	Holistic programme covering all aspects of self-employment	Still viewed as credit and subsidy programme Single window 'holistic' approach → reduction in total resources
No time frame for the assisted BPL families to cross the poverty line	3-year time frame	Dropped in the amended guidelines
No estimate regarding the coverage of target groups	Plans to cover 30 per cent of the BPL families in each block (this is subject to availability of funds) in 5 years	Dropped in the amended guidelines
Dispersed Activities	Activity cluster identification	No actualization of concept of 'activity clusters'
Groups given maximum of 25 per cent coverage	Focus on group approach	Initial focus on individuals, due to time taken for group formation
Procedure of selection of beneficiaries by the gram sabha	Selection of beneficiaries by 3-member team, by visiting each habitation	2 member team, not necessarily by visiting habitation
No specific role of Panchayats	Greater role of Panchayats: List of swarozgari families selected by bankers would be placed before gram sabha Panchayat monitors performance Responsibility for recovery Panchayat Samiti to finalize activity clusters	Little or no gram sabha involvement in selection of beneficiaries, key activity clusters or monitoring Panchayat 'responsibility' for recovery to be enforced by disqualifying panchayat if there is non-repayment
No provision for technology and marketing	Provision exists for linkages	On paper, and in 'trainings'

(Contd.)

(Table A1.2.1 *Contd.*)

Did not envisage specific role of NGOs	NGOs role emphasized	NGO as 'yes boy' implementer or 'whipping boy' New 'NGOs' formed by members of political parties and lower level government officials
Bank role mostly confined to sanction of loans	Banks' role integral to all aspects	Now bank driven programme: conflict with the Rural Development Department
Recovery of loan not given due weightage	SGSY lays stress on recovery Recovery to be monitored Specific provisions of disincentives	Promotion of subsidy at the field level Expectation that women's SHGs have a higher track record of repayment

Table A1.2.2: Poverty estimates for 1978–98

(percentage of poor in total population, headcount)

NSS Round	Period	Rural Headcount Poverty	Urban Headcount Poverty			
32	July 77–June 78	50.60	40.50			
38	Jan. 83–December 83	45.31	35.65			
42	July 86–June 87	38.81	34.29			
43	July 87–June 88	39.60	35.65			
44	July 88–June 89	39.06	36.60			
45	July 89–June 90	34.30	33.40			
46	July 90–June 91	36.43	32.76			
47	July 91–December 91	37.42	33.23			
48	January 92–December 92	43.47	33.73			
50	July 93–June 94	38.74	30.03			
43*	July 87–June 88	39.23	36.20			
50*	July 93–June 94	36.66	30.51			
		Gupta	Datt	T-S	Datt	
51	July 94–June 95	38.0	41.0	43.6	33.5	
52	July 95–June 96	38.3	37.2	40.1	28.0	
53	January 97–December 97	38.5	35.8	38.3	30.0	
54	January 98–June 98	45.3	NA	44.9	NA	

Notes: * The surveys based on large samples are at five-year intervals, in rounds 32, 38, 43, 50, and 55. There is an alteration in the reference period in the latest round 55 in 2000, making it non-compatible with earlier rounds, therefore, the results have not been included here. Other rounds are based on thin samples which are however adequate for making overall all-India estimates reproduced above.
Source: Patnaik and Patnaik (2001), p. 39.

Table A1.2.3: Percentage reduction in poverty ratio in states
(grouped by initial poverty levels)

(percentage change)

States grouped by initial (1977–8) poverty levels	Phase I 1977–8 to 1987–8	Phase II 1987–8 to 1993–4	Overall Reform Period	
			1977–8 to 1993–4	1990 to 1993–4
High Poverty (Over 60 per cent)				
Bihar	16.9	−10.2	08.4	−25.3
Orissa	20.4	13.4	31.1	−36.7
West Bengal	29.3	16.6	41.0	18.6
Madhya Pradesh	32.9	2.6	34.7	03.8
Maharastra	36.3	5.4	39.7	−7.5
Medium High Poverty (45 to 60 per cent)				
Uttar Pradesh	13.7	−03.6	10.5	−22.4
Assam	34.1	−14.2	24.8	−33.5
Tamil Nadu	20.6	28.8	43.5	13.1
Karnataka	32.0	14.0	41.5	19.2
Kerala	43.4	22.4	56.1	24.4
Medium Low Poverty (30 to 40 per cent)				
Andhra Pradesh	45.1	23.4	58.0	27.6
Gujarat	31.3	22.6	46.9	−2.8
Rajasthan	07.5	17.2	23.4	−6.2
Low Poverty (Below 30 per cent)				
Haryana	41.5	−77.2	03.6	−47.2
Punjab	23.2	00.8	23.8	−34.4
Rural India	26.4	4.1	29.4	−7.1

Notes: Percentage reduction in poverty ratio (improvement) is denoted as a positive number and percentage rise in poverty ratio (deterioration) has a minus sign.
Source: Patnaik and Patnaik (2001), p. 40.

Table A1.2.4: Plan expenditure on poverty alleviation

Name of the Scheme	7th Plan		8th Plan		9th plan
	Outlay	Actual	Outlay	Actual	Outlay
IRDP	1186.79	1548.08	3350.00	2921.06	
Training rural youth for self-employment (TRYSEM)		24.29	300.00	85.38	
DWCRA	20.30	36.63	150.00	189.54	
SITRA			149.07	120.08	
GKY			100.00	55.66	
Million wells scheme				394.83	
National rural employment programme (NREP)*	1250.81	2027.74			
Rural landless employment guarantee programme*	1743.78	2797.21			
Employment assurance Scheme				5242.94	8690.00
JRY*		2100.76	18400.00	14712.71	7095.90
SGSY#					4690.00
Total (poverty alleviation and employment schemes)	4,201.68	8,534.71	22,449.07	23,722.20	20,475.90

Notes: * NREP and RLEGP merged with JRY from 1989–90.
IRDP, TRYSEM, DWCRA, SITRA, GKY merged with SGSY in ninth Plan.
Source: Ministry of Rural Development tables on budget estimates and outlays; data for SITRA and GKY from Annual Report 1998–9 of RDD at http://rural.nic.in/annual.htm

Women and Agriculture in India
Work and Wages

MADHURA SWAMINATHAN _____ 2

INTRODUCTION

Women engaged in different types of agricultural activity in India constitute a large and significant section of our population. At the time of the Census of 2001, there were 111 million women workers in rural India and 89 million women working in agriculture. Women working in agriculture in India outnumbered the total population of Germany (82 million). Clearly the socio-economic status of women in Indian agriculture is a matter of widespread concern. This chapter concentrates on women as workers. In the next section of the chapter, I examine the changing occupational structure of women workers in rural areas with data from secondary sources. In this context, I bring out problems such as the lack of diversification out of agriculture among women workers, the feminization of the agricultural labour force, and the casualization of the rural workforce. I then turn to some aspects of wages and earnings in agriculture, and particularly, the gender gap in wages in the third section. I also discuss the impact of modern technology on women's labour use in agriculture. To fill out the picture obtained from national trends, in the fourth section, I present some findings from a detailed study of a village in Tamil Nadu. Some concluding remarks are made in the fifth section.

WOMEN WORKERS IN AGRICULTURE: 1901–2001

With the initiation of regular decennial population censuses in the late nineteenth century, we have a statistical base for capturing the extent of participation of women in agricultural activity.[1] For the discussion

---

[1] For a discussion of the kind of historical sources that can provide information on the nature of work performed by women in rural society in the nineteenth century, see Mitra (1982).

here, I have divided the period into two parts: 1901–51 and 1961–2001. Note that work participation refers to the ratio of workers to the total population but labour force participation refers to the ratio of persons either employed/working or 'seeking or available for work' to the total population.[2]

1901–51

Data from the Censuses of India for the period 1901–51, reported in Table 2.1, have been compiled by Krishnamurty (1982).

Table 2.1. Share of cultivators and agricultural labourers in the workforce, all-India, 1901–51

(per cent)

Year	Cultivators	Agricultural labourers	Others	All workers
Females				
1901	43.6	30.2	26.2	100
1911	41.0	32.5	26.5	100
1921	48.1	28.0	23.9	100
1931	30.4	43.8	25.8	100
1951	45.7	34.5	19.8	100
Males				
1901	53.2	14.3	32.5	100
1911	53.5	15.4	31.1	100
1921	56.1	14.4	29.5	100
1931	49.8	19.5	30.7	100
1951	54.4	16.4	29.2	100

Source: Krishnamurty, 1982.

If we exclude the Census of 1931 (because of problems of change in definitions),[3] then the first impression from data in Table 2.1 is that of

[2] This chapter uses a narrow definition of the term 'work': it refers to work at hired labour, salaried employment, and self-employment other than at tasks within a person's own household. While all work by women, whether paid or unpaid, whether for domestic consumption or for the market, should be measured and valued, work for domestic consumption alone has to be analytically distinguished from work that gains a woman an outside income, as the two have different implications for the socio-economic status of women and for their emancipation. The socio-economic status of a woman depends crucially on the extent to which she participates in economic activities outside the purview of unpaid domestic work (see, in this context, Nagaraj 1989 and the references therein).

[3] See Duvurry (1989).

constancy in the occupational structure of men and women workers. A more careful look, however, shows that there was a rise in the share of cultivators and agricultural labourers between 1901 and 1951, and this was more marked among women than men. Second, in every Census, a higher proportion of women workers were engaged in agricultural activity (as cultivators and agricultural labourers) than male workers. In short, occupations were less diversified among women, who tended to be mainly occupied in agriculture. In 1951, for example, over 80 per cent of women workers were classified as agricultural labourers or cultivators while the corresponding proportion among men was 70.8 per cent. Third, while the majority of men occupied in agriculture were reported to be cultivators, among women, a relatively higher proportion was agricultural labourer.

To sum up, during the period 1901 to 1951, the majority of women workers were in agriculture, and there was a tendency towards further concentration in agriculture over this period (with the exception of 1931). This process was accompanied by a rise in the ratio of agricultural labourers to cultivators among women workers.

Table 2.2: Work participation rates for women in rural India, 1961– 2001 (Census of India)

| Year | Females | | |
	Total	Main	Marginal
1961	31.4		
1971	15.5	13.1	2.4
1981	23.2	16.0	7.2
1991	26.8	18.7	8.1
2001	30.9	16.7	14.2

Notes: For Census of India data, the work participation rate is defined as the ratio of total workers (main and marginal) to the total population. Main workers are those involved in the economic activity for more than six months (183 days) of the year. Marginal workers are those who worked for some time during the preceding year but not for the major part of the year.
Source: Unni (1989) for 1961 and 1971, Sinha (2001) for 1981 and 1991, and Census (2001).

1961–2001

For the post-Independence period, there are three major national sources of data on participation of women in economic activity in rural India:

Table 2.3: Share of cultivators and agricultural labourers in the rural workforce, all-India, 1961–2001

(per cent)

Year	Cultivators	Agricultural labourers	Others	All workers
Females				
1961	58.9	27.7	13.4	100
1971	32.6	54.4	13.0	100
1981	40.8	47.7	11.5	100
1991	38.9	48.5	12.6	100
2001	36.5	43.4	20.1	100

Notes: In 1991, the distribution is among main workers only.
Source: Unni (1989), and Census of India (1991, 2001).

Table 2.4: Women's labour force participation rates in rural India (NSS), 1977–8 to 2004–05

(per cent)

Year	Labour force participation rate	
	Principal status	All workers (principal and subsidiary status)
1977–8	26.3	33.8
1983	25.2	34.2
1987–8	25.4	33.1
1993–4	23.7	33.0
1999–2000	23.5	30.2
2004–05	24.9	33.3

Notes: Labour force participation rates from the NSS, for comparability with the Census, are based on the usual status criterion (that is, with a reference period of one year). The labour force participation rate covers 'principal status' workers (whose principal status is that of a worker) and 'subsidiary status' workers (who pursued some economic activity in a subsidiary capacity during the reference period).
Source: Vaidyanathan (2001), Table 17, p. 229 and NSSO Report No. 515: *Employment and Unemployment Situation in India*, 2004–05.

+ the decennial population Censuses;
+ successive rounds of Employment and Unemployment Surveys conducted by the National Sample Survey Organization (NSSO); and
+ the *Rural Labour Enquiries* published by the Labour Bureau (which are based on data collected by the NSSO).

There is now general agreement that the censuses of India and the NSS underestimate women's work participation. Among the reasons for the underestimation are problems with the definition of 'work' used by the Census of India and the NSS (although these have improved), and empirical problems associated with the measurement of work in a subsistence economy where much work is unpaid and is undertaken at home or on a person's own premises.[4] There are also practical problems such as how the question is asked, who responds in the family, and so on.[5] Over the years, interviewer bias may have changed as the training of enumerators has improved. Many scholars have argued that in respect of women's work participation, the NSS is superior to the Census both on grounds of methodology (by, for example, including non-marketed activity) and on grounds of better data collection (due to better training of enumerators).

Given these differences, it is not surprising, as we shall see below, that the Census of India and the NSS yield different results on women's work participation. The rate of women's work participation is consistently lower in the Census of India than the rate given by the NSS (see Tables 2.2 and 2.4). The gap between the two, however, appears to have closed. Further, since there have been changes in concepts and definitions over time, it is not very easy to gauge whether the reported changes in work participation are on account of changes in definition and improvements in methods of data collection (including increased sensitivity to the nature of women's work) or on account of real changes in participation rates. While official sources of large-scale data have the merit of wide coverage, they are less than satisfactory in respect of methods of collecting and processing data and in respect of the socio-economic details they provide on conditions of work in rural India, particularly women's work.

Results from the Census, 1961–2001

If we exclude 1971, a year in which there were major changes in the Census questionnaire, the following features emerge from the Census data on work participation (Table 2.2). First, the work participation rate among women is low: in most years, less than one-third of rural women were reported to be workers. This is a low work participation rate relative to men but also relative to women in other Asian countries.

---

[4] See, for example, the discussion in Bannerjee (1989), Jose (1989), Krishnaraj (1990), Nayyar (1987), and Unni (1989).

[5] See Sinha (2001) on various aspects of this problem such as women's self-perception about work, their responses in front of a male family member, and the sensitivity to the sex and social class of the enumerator.

In China, for instance, the female work participation rate is around 73 per cent. Second, there was a decline in work participation between 1961 and 1981 but this has been reversed in the last two decades and work participation in 2001 is similar to the levels observed in 1961. However, and this is a noteworthy point, the rise in women's work participation between 1981 and 2001 has been mainly on account of a rise in marginal workers and, in fact, there has been a small decline in main workers in the 1990s.[6] In other words, women are entering the workforce but not as full-time or year-round workers. This phenomenon could be on account of several factors including a lack of appropriate work opportunities (on the demand for labour side), and on account of constraints on women's full time work participation (such as stemming from the obligations of domestic labour). The reasons for this pattern of work participation require further investigation.

Turning to the occupational structure (Table 2.3), and again excluding 1971, there is a very clear pattern of change. First, the share of women engaged in agriculture has declined, from almost 87 per cent of all workers in 1961 to 80 per cent in 2001, but the decline has been very slow and the overwhelming majority of rural women workers are still employed in agriculture. Second, the share of cultivators has declined steadily: between 1961 and 2001, the share fell by 20 percentage points. Third, the share of agricultural workers among women workers rose till 1991 and then fell slightly in the last decade of the century. The latter decline is associated with an increase in women engaged in other occupations. Fourth, from 1981 onwards, in every Census, women agricultural labourers have outnumbered women cultivators. It is worth pointing out here that this pattern does not hold among male workers. In 2001, for example, 42 per cent of male workers were reported to be cultivators and only 27.5 per cent were agricultural labourers. Among women workers in 2001, 43.4 per cent were agricultural labourers and 36.5 per cent were cultivators.

If we review data from the Census over the entire century, there are two overriding observations. The first feature of note is the continued dominance of agriculture among women workers, or to put it differently, the lack of diversification of employment among women workers in

---

[6] Main workers were defined as those who were engaged in an economic activity for more than 183 days a year whereas marginal workers were those who worked for some time during the preceding year but not for the major part of the year.

rural areas. Second, within agriculture, there is a near-reversal of the share of cultivators and agricultural labourers over the century—the ratio of women cultivators to labourers was 1.5:1 in 1901 and 0.8:1 in 2001.

Results from the National Sample Survey, 1972–3 to 2004–05

Let me begin with the labour force participation rate reported by different rounds of the NSS. When all workers (principal and subsidiary status) are considered, 33.8 per cent of women were in the labour force in 1977–8; the participation rate fell to 30.2 per cent in 1999–2000 but has recovered to 33.3 per cent in 2004–05.

Since these figures refer to all females from the age of five onwards, I next examine labour force participation rates disaggregated by age (Table 2.5). As expected, labour force participation is higher in the age group 30–49 as compared to all other ages in all the survey years. However, there are two interesting age-wise trends. First, a welcome feature is the sharp fall in labour force participation among children (ages 10 to 14), from over 14 per cent in 1993–4 to 7.5 per cent in 2004–05. Second, between 1993–4 and 1999–2000, labour force participation declined in all age groups. This suggests that the fall in

Table 2.5: Women's labour force participation rate by age group in rural India (NSS), 1993–4 to 2004–05

(per cent)

Age Group	1993–94	1999–2000	2004–05
5–9	1.4	0.7	0.3
10–14	14.2	9.6	7.5
15–19	37.1	31.4	33.1
20–24	47.0	42.5	43.5
25–29	52.8	49.8	53.0
30–34	58.7	55.7	59.3
35–39	61.0	57.9	64.2
40–44	60.7	58.6	62.7
45–49	59.4	56.6	61.6
50–54	54.3	51.5	56.2
55–59	46.8	45.0	50.9
60	24.1	21.8	25.4
All	33.1	30.2	33.3

Source: NSS Report No. 515: *Employment and Unemployment Situation in India, 2004–05.*

participation in the 1990s cannot be explained, as is done by some scholars (Sundaram 2001), mainly by a rise in school enrolment and participation in other educational institutions.

I now turn to the variation in worker-population ratios among women with different levels of educational attainment (Table 2.6). The relation between labour force participation and educational attainment follows a U shape: the participation rate is relatively high at the two ends of the spectrum, among non-literate women and women with graduate or higher qualifications. The participation rate is lowest for women with secondary and higher secondary school education. In other words, in rural areas, women tend to withdraw from the labour force when they have a school education but return to the labour market at high levels of education.

Table 2.6: Worker population ratio for women (15 years and above) [usual status] by level of education in rural India, 1993–4 to 2004–05

(*in per cent*)

Level of education	1993–4	1999–2000	2004–05
Non-literate	54.0	51.3	55.0
Literate and up to primary school	41.6	40.3	44.9
Middle school	29.0	29.0	37.1
Secondary school	25.8	25.7	30.5
Higher secondary	23.4	20.6	25.2
Diploma/certificate	–	–	52.3
Graduate and above	36.6	31.0	34.5
All	48.6	45.2	48.5

Source: NSS Report No. 515: *Employment and Unemployment Situation in India, 2004–05.*

Let us turn to what the NSS tells us about the occupations in which rural women participate. Data in Table 2.7 are unambiguous on this issue: agriculture is the principal occupation of women workers in rural India even today. While 88 per cent of women worked in agriculture in 1977–8, more than 25 years later, 83 per cent continue to work in agriculture. There has been a small rise in the share of workers in manufacturing, construction, and services. Nevertheless, agriculture dominates all other occupations.

Finally, the NSS categorizes workers into three types: the self-employed, regular employed, and casual labour. According to the NSS,

Table 2.7: Sectoral distribution of women workers in rural India, 1977–8 to 2004–05

(percentage share of total workers)

Sector	1977–8	1983	1987–8	1993–4	1999–2000	2004–05
Agriculture	88.1	87.5	84.7	86.2	85.4	83.3
Mining	0.2	0.3	0.4	0.4	0.3	0.3
Manufacturing	5.9	6.4	6.9	7.0	7.6	8.4
Electricity, gas and water	–	–	–	0.1	–	0
Construction	0.6	0.7	2.7	0.9	1.1	1.5
Trade	2.0	1.9	2.1	2.1	2.0	2.5
Transport	0.1	0.1	0.1	0.1	0.1	0.2
Services	3.0	2.8	3.0	3.4	3.7	3.9
All	100.0	100.0	100.0	100.0	100.0	100

Source: Vaidyanathan (2001), Annex Table 11, p. 247 and NSS Report No. 515: *Employment and Unemployment Situation in India, 2004–05.*

a casual wage labour is a worker who receives wages according to a daily or periodic work contract; a regular salaried or wage employee is a worker who receives wages on a regular basis. Self-employed persons are those who operate their own farm or non-farm enterprise or work independently in a profession or trade. If we examine the distribution of women workers in rural areas by these three status categories (Table 2.8), the most important category emerges as that of the self-employed. Next come casual labourers and finally, there are a small proportion of regular employed workers. In terms of changes between 1977–8 and 1999–2000, the main feature of note, and of concern, is the rise, particularly during the 1990s, of the proportion of casual labour. This

Table 2.8: Distribution of women workers by type of work status in rural India, 1977–8 to 2004–05

(percentage share of total workers)

Work status	1977–8	1983	1987–8	1993–4	1999–2000	2004–05
Self-employed	62.1	61.9	60.8	58.6	57.3	63.7
Regular employed	2.8	2.8	3.7	2.7	3.1	3.7
Casual labour	35.1	35.3	35.5	38.7	39.6	32.6
All	100	100	100	100	100	100

Note: See text for definitions.
Source: Vaidyanathan (2001), Annex Table 10, p. 246 and NSS Report No. 515: *Employment and Unemployment Situation in India, 2004–05.*

evidence supports the hypothesis of a 'casualization' of the workforce following the introduction of policies of structural adjustment and liberalization.[7] The latest round of the NSS, however, shows a reversal of this trend.

Feminization of Labour Force in Agriculture[8]

In the literature and public discussion on women workers in rural India, one of the significant issues raised has been about the extent of feminization of the agricultural workforce.[9] This issue is important since agricultural labour is the single largest occupation among women workers in India (with over 48 million workers in 2001); and at the same time, it is an occupation of last resort, an occupation with low wages, and limited opportunities for mobility. Evidence of increased feminization of the agricultural labour workforce can be an indicator of enduring or even worsening occupational segregation.

Three measures taken together have been regarded as indicative of the 'feminization' of the agricultural workforce (Duvurry 1989). These are as follows.

1. An increase in the proportion of female agricultural workers in the female workforce.

2. An increase in the ratio of female agricultural workers to male agricultural workers.

3. An increase in the proportion of female workforce in the female population.

At the all-India level, there was a significant increase in the proportion of female agricultural workers in the female work force (indicator i) over the 1960s and 1970s (by Census data, from 25.6 per cent in 1961 to 49.6 per cent in 1981).[10] Data from later Censuses of India (see Table 2.9) show a small fall in this indicator between 1981 and 2001. However, the two other indicators show a sharp rise; indicator ii, for example, rose from 80 per cent in 1981 to 88 per cent in 2001. In

---

[7] See also, Unni (1999).

[8] This section draws on Ramachandran, Swaminathan, and Rawal (2001).

[9] See, for example, AIDWA et al. (1995), da Corta and Venkateswarlu (1999), Duvurry (1989), Jose (1989), and Nagaraj (1989).

[10] The increase in female workers between 1971 and 1981, as has been widely noted, is on account of gross underestimation of female workers in 1971. Agricultural labourers, however, were least affected as they are more visible as workers compared to women engaged in self-employment at the farm or household.

Table 2.9: Indicators of the feminization of the agricultural labour force,
India, 1981–2001

Indicator	Rural India		
	1981	1991	2001*
Number of female AL (in million)	27.4	28.4	48.4
Ratio of female AL to total female workers (%)	47.7	46.4	43.4
Ratio of female AL to male AL(%)	80.7	84.0	88.0
Ratio of female AL to total female population (%)	11.1	12.4	13.4

Notes: AL is agricultural labourer. * The figures for 2001 refer to main and marginal
workers whereas the figures for earlier Censuses refer to main workers alone.
Source: Census of India, different volumes.

absolute terms, of course, there has been an increase in the number
of female agricultural workers during the 1990s. (Note that there is a
small problem of comparing the numbers given for 2001 with earlier
Censuses since the former includes marginal workers. Nevertheless,
the broad trend is likely to be reflected in these comparisons.)

To summarize, the 'feminization' of the agricultural labour force in
India over the 1960s and 1970s that was noted by scholars, on the
basis of Census of India data, has continued through the 1980s and
1990s.

Number of Days of Employment

The Rural Labour Enquiry (RLE) reports the average number of
days of employment per worker in rural labour households separately
for men and women, by agricultural and non-agricultural activity as
well as by wage employment (hired labour) and other employment.
According to the RLE, the total days of employment available to a
woman worker in a rural labour household in India has risen, on
average, from 179 days in 1974–5 to 264 days in 1993–4 (Table 2.10).
The days of employment in agriculture, however, have fallen steadily
and correspondingly, the days of employment in non-agricultural
tasks have risen. The reports indicate further that this is primarily on
account of a rise in the days of wage employment. These estimates of
employment availability per worker, as discussed in the fourth section,
appear to be exaggerated.

WAGES AND EARNINGS

On trends in real wages, there are three sources of official statistics.
The NSS and RLE provide data on earnings. The serial publication

Table 2.10: Days of employment for women of rural labour households, all-India, 1974–5 to 1993–4

(in days a year)

Year	Total days of employment
1974–5	179
1977–8	227
1983	230
1987–8	253
1993–4	264

Source: Sharma (2001), Table 3, p. 32.

Agricultural Wages in India (*AWI*) has data on wage rates for different operations at selected centres in all parts of the country. The NSS data show a rise in real wages for men and women workers in agricultural activities between 1983 and 1993–4: according to the NSS, male wages rose 90 per cent while female wages rose 85 per cent (Unni 1999). There was a similar rise in real wages for non-agricultural employment. According to some scholars, wages in agriculture have risen rapidly between 1993–4 and 1999–2000 (Sundaram 2001). For example, wages for women casual labour in agriculture have risen at the rate of 2.9 per cent per annum during this period. Unlike earlier, in the 55th round of the NSS, questions were asked about overtime wages. It is possible that persons working on piece rates for more than 8 hours a day reported additional earnings as overtime earnings. In this way, the estimate of wages could be higher than actual.

Table 2.11: Wages for agricultural operations, rural labour households, India, 1974–5 to 1993–4

(in rupees at 1980–1 prices)

Year	Agricultural operations	
	Real wages for women workers	Ratio of female to male wage (%)
1974–5	2.52	70.0
1977–8	3.36	56.1
1983	3.04	57.9
1987–8	4.40	77.9
1993–4	5.42	60.1

Source: Sharma (2001), Table 4, p. 34.

The average daily wage earned by women, roughly doubled between 1974–5 and 1993–4 according to the RLE (Table 2.11). The rise was observed for agricultural and non-agricultural occupations, and occurred mainly in the 1980s. The AWI data present a slightly different picture of wage changes. The AWI provides monthly information on wage-rates at the state level, as well as for selected villages in each district. There are serious problems of quality with regard to the collection, processing, and presentation of AWI data (Jose 1988); nevertheless, they do give us something of a first take on trends in wage rates in India. Recent computations of real wages in terms of rice equivalents from 1964–5 to 1994–5, based on AWI data, indicated the following trends.[11] Real wages stagnated till the late 1970s, rose in the early 1980s (with a dip in 1983) and peaked in the mid- to late-1980s. Real wages fell in the early 1990s but rose again from 1993, although they remained below the peak of the 1980s.

This picture is confirmed by a detailed study of data from different rounds of the RLE between 1964–5 and 1999–2000 by Chavan and Bedamatta (2006). The authors find that after a period of high growth, growth of real wage earnings for female agricultural labourers slumped between 1987–8 and 1993–4, and remained low between 1993–4 and 1999–2000. During the period of slowdown in growth of earnings, inter-state disparities increased as did the gap between male and female earnings (Chavan and Bedamatta 2006).

Gender Differentials in Wages

It is not easy to compare the wages that men and women receive, as there are only a few agricultural operations that are performed by both men and women. There is also much diversity in the level and form of payments for different operations. Nevertheless, data from different rounds of the RLE show that the ratio of female to male wages deteriorated during this period of rising wages. The ratio of female to male wages was, for instance, 70 per cent in 1974–5 and 60 per cent in 1993–4 (Table 2.11).

[11] This is based on papers for an assignment on trends in real wages undertaken by the students of the course titled 'Land and Labour in Rural India' at the Indira Gandhi Institute of Development Research, Mumbai, August-December 1999 (see Chavan 1999; Misra 1999; Ramakumar 1999; Sinha 1999; and Thomas 1999). Nominal wage rates from the AWI were converted to real wages using the retail price of rice as deflator.

Figures from the AWI indicate a worsening of the gender gap in wages in the immediate post-1991 period (Unni 1999). To illustrate, let me take the case of Tamil Nadu; Table 2.12, computed from AWI data, shows the ratio of female wages to male wages in three districts of Tamil Nadu (Ramakumar 1999). In North Arcot and Coimbatore, the gender gap widened between 1964–5 and 1994–5. In both districts, the male-female differential was highest in the 1980s. In Thanjavur, women earned only a quarter of male wages in 1964–5; the relative wage rate for women improved until the early 1980s, when it again began to worsen. Table 2.12 has two notable features. First, even in the 1990s, wages for women were typically around one-half of wages for men, a very large disparity indeed. Second, the period of rising wages, the 1980s, was associated with a widening of the gender gap in wages.

Table 2.12: Ratio of female to male wage rates, selected districts, Tamil Nadu, 1964–5 to 1994–5

Year	North Arcot	Coimbatore	Thanjavur
1964–5	0.95	0.87	0.25
1970–1	0.70	0.5	0.55
1979–80	0.80	0.65	0.51
1983–4	0.44	0.5	0.96
1988–9	0.36	0.6	0.56
1990–1	0.53	0.67	0.68
1991–2	0.43	0.61	0.53
1992–3	0.43	0.59	0.52
1993–4	0.33	–	0.58
1994–5	0.50	0.75	0.57

Note: For men and women, the wage rate for 'field labour' was used if available. Otherwise the wage rate for the category 'other agricultural labour' was taken for men, and the wage rate for weeding was taken for women. The annual wage is a simple 12-month average. The centre selected in each district was the one for which the longest continuous time series was available.
Source: From Ramakumar (1999).

A Village Study: Gokilapuram 1977 to 1999[12]

This is a case study of a village located in Theni district (erstwhile Madurai district) of Tamil Nadu. Gokilapuram is in the Cumbum

---

[12] This section is based on Ramachandran et al. (2001, 2002), and I am grateful to V.K. Ramachandran and Vikas Rawal for permission to utilize the material.

Valley, a fertile, irrigated, and relatively advanced agricultural region of Tamil Nadu. In 1977, a census type socio-economic survey of the village was conducted in Gokilapuram (see Ramachandran 1990); the village was resurveyed in 1999. This provides an opportunity to examine aspects of change at the micro-level over two decades. In this section, I focus on one group of households in the village in 1999, the set of landless households dependent on incomes from manual labour, termed landless labour households. For comparisons with 1977, the data for the class of landless agricultural labour households have been used. In this section, I report some findings on the days of employment, wages, and earnings among women workers.

Days of Employment

The major sources of official data and micro-studies differ substantially in respect of statistics on the average number of days of employment that a worker receives in a year and trends in annual employment per worker. The number of days of employment estimated by scholars from village studies—for both men and women—is substantially lower than the days of employment reported by the RLE (Mukherjee 1998; Ramachandran 1990). This is confirmed by the findings below.

First, the average number of days of employment available to a woman worker is low, and has remained almost stagnant between 1977 and 1999. In 1976–7, the average days of employment were estimated to be 158 days and the corresponding figure for 1998–9 was 162. Thus, women were employed for less than six months in a year. In short, the work calendar of a woman worker is characterized by chronic underemployment and employment-insecurity.

Second, there has been a major change in the composition of employment, with a clear decline in agricultural employment. In 1977, women obtained 103 days of employment in agriculture and 55 days at non-agricultural tasks. The shares were almost reversed in 1999, as on average, women received 61 days of employment at agricultural tasks and 101 days at non-agricultural tasks.

In respect of wages, non-agricultural work is of two types. There are some activities in which the daily wage is higher than the wage rate for daily-rated, cash-paid tasks in agriculture. Such employment included plantation work, construction work, work at brick kilns, road-construction, and work at other public works projects. The second category comprises tasks that are paid at average wage rates that are lower than the wage rate for daily-rated, cash-paid operations in agriculture. The main job here is processing tamarind (the category also includes domestic work). Thus, while the average number of days of employment for a woman from a hired labour household remains almost the same, that number conceals a change in the composition of a working-woman's year. Women now have to spend more time than before in a relatively low-paid, non-agricultural task in order to survive. This shift shows that women workers have to increasingly seek employment in low-paid non-agricultural work.

Third, in 1976–7, there were three main types of cultivation in the village: on canal-irrigated land on which two crops of paddy a year were grown; on unirrigated land on which a crop of traditional cereals was grown; and on groundwater-irrigated land (or land irrigated by wells fitted with motor pumps), on which a wide variety of crops, including cotton, vegetables, and bananas were grown. In the period between the two surveys, two major changes have occurred. First, unirrigated land was converted to lift-irrigated land; second, cropping patterns on lift-irrigated land have changed. There has been an expansion in crops such as banana, coconut, and grape, all of which are less female-labour-absorbent than the cotton and vegetable crops they have replaced. The stagnation in women's employment despite the overall intensification of cultivation in the region is thus a consequence of the increase in the supply of women workers (caused particularly by an accelerated process of differentiation among the peasantry) as well as changes in cropping patterns. In fact, the days of employment in agriculture halved, from 103 to 61 days. The decline has occurred even in the case of traditionally female-labour-intensive crops such as paddy: the average days of employment on paddy fell from 65 days in 1977 to 36 days in 1999.

Wages and Earnings

The modal wage rate paid to women at cash-paid, daily-rated operations in the village in 1998–9 was Rs 25. To examine real wages, we deflated the nominal wage by the retail price of second-sort rice in Gokilapuram. By this method, the rice purchasable with a day's wage was 2.5 kg in 1999; the corresponding quantity in 1977 was 1.31 kg. While wages are low, the real wage rate has risen over these 22 years. A woman worker in Gokilapuram earned an average of Rs 4778 a year (or roughly US$ 111 a year) in 1998–9. This equalled only 42.7

per cent of a man's earnings. This is indeed a large gender disparity in earnings.

To put these earnings in perspective, the wage of the lowest-paid worker in a textile mill in Coimbatore or Chennai was Rs 3596 a month or Rs 43,156 a year in 1998–9 (GoI 2000). The average woman manual worker in Gokilapuram thus earned only 11 per cent of the earnings of such an urban worker.

CONCLUDING REMARKS

To sum up, women's work participation, that is, participation in work involving production of goods and services for the market, is low, and lower than in countries of East and South-east Asia. This is partly due to problems in the definition and measurement of work. Research and intense debate on this issue have highlighted the fact that women's work is often concealed work and women workers are under-counted. Both the Census of India and the NSS seriously underestimate levels of women's work participation. A recent pilot study of time use conducted by the NSS in six states of India reports estimates of employment that are five per cent higher than those reported in NSS surveys (CSO 2000).[13]

Of the three sectors of the economy namely primary, secondary, and tertiary, the majority of workers in India, particularly women workers are concentrated in the primary or agricultural sector of the economy and they are, in large part, unskilled manual workers. Over time, the proportion of women agricultural labourers in total workers has increased, and agricultural labour is undoubtedly the single largest occupation of women workers in the country today.

Two tendencies that have been observed with respect to the rural female labour force are the growing casualization of the workforce and the feminization of the agricultural workforce. Both tendencies have been strengthened in the 1990s, the era of neo-liberal economic reform.

The most striking feature of wages for women in agriculture is how low they are, in absolute terms, in relation to male wages, and in relation to minimum wages for urban industrial workers. This is despite a rise in real wages over time. Another marked feature of

[13] This large-scale study, the first of its kind in India, was conducted in 1998–9 and covered 18,380 households in 52 districts (CSO 2000).

wages is the disparity between men and women. The gender division of labour often conceals wage disparities. Occupations in which women are concentrated tend to be paid poorly. Nevertheless, the data indicate that wage disparities did not improve in rural India in a period of rising wages.

Historically, women have been credited with the origins of field agriculture. In rural India today, the majority of women continue to be engaged in agriculture and related activities. In fact, as men move away from agriculture and diversify their occupations, women are being further concentrated in agriculture. There is thus an urgent need to focus on the concerns of women in agriculture. For women agricultural labourers, who are growing in both absolute and relative terms, the major issues of concern are the abysmally low level of wages for tasks that women perform, insecurity of employment, and lack of adequate days of employment.

REFERENCES

All India Democratic Women's Association (AIDWA) et al. (1995), *Towards Beijing: A Perspective from the Indian Women's Movement*, New Delhi.

Banerjee, Nirmala 1989, 'Trends in Women's Employment, 1971–81: Some Macro Level Observations', *Economic and Political Weekly* Vol. 24, No. 17, pp. WS10–WS22.

Census of India (1991), Registrar General of India, New Delhi.

———(2001), *www.censusindia.net/results/wrk_statement1.html*

Central Statistical Organization (CSO) (2000), *Report of the Time Use Survey*, Government of India, Ministry of Statistics and Programme Implementation, New Delhi.

Chavan, Pallavi (1999), 'A Study of Real Agricultural Wages in Gujarat, Maharashtra and Karnataka', IGIDR Class Assignment, November.

Chavan, Pallavi and Rajshree Bedamatta (2006), 'Trends in Agricultural Wages in India: 1964–65 to 1999–2000', *Economic and Political Weekly*, Vol. 41, No. 38, pp. 4041–51.

da Corta, Lucia and Davuluri Venkateswarlu (1999), 'Unfree Relations and the Feminisation of Agricultural Labour in Andhra Pradesh, 1970–95', *Journal of Peasant Studies*, Vol. 26, Nos 2 and 3, pp. 71–139.

Duvurry, Nata, (1989), 'Work Participation of Women in India: A Study with Special Reference to Female Agricultural Labourers, 1961 to 1981', in A. V. Jose (ed.) *Limited Options: Women Workers in Rural India*, ILO-ARTEP, New Delhi; pp. 63–107.

Government of India (2000), Ministry of Labour, and Employment, Labour Bureau, *Indian Labour Journal*, Shimla.

———(2006), 'Employment and Unemployment Situation in India 2004-05', Report No. 515, Ministry of Statistics and Programme Implementation, National Sample Survey Organization, *www.mospi.nic.in*.

Hirway, Indira (1999), 'Estimating Workforce using Time Use Statistics in India and its Implications for Employment Policies', paper presented at the International Seminar on Time Use Studies, Ahmedabad, 7–10 December.

Jose, A. V. (1988) 'Agricultural Wages in India', *Economic and Political Weekly*, Vol. 23, No. 26 A46–A58.

———— (1989), 'Female Labour Force Participation in India: A Case of Limited Options', in A. V. Jose (ed.) (1989), *Limited Options: Women Workers in Rural India*, ILO-ARTEP, New Delhi.

Krishnamurty, J. (1982), 'The Occupational Structure' in D. Kumar (ed.) *The Cambridge Economic History of India*, Vol. 2, *1757–1970*, Orient Longman and Cambridge University Press, UK.

Krishnaraj, Maithreyi, (1990), 'Women's Work in Indian Census: Beginnings of Change', *Economic and Political Weekly*, Vol. 25 pp. 2663–72.

Misra, N (1999), 'A Study of Real Agricultural Wages in Haryana, Rajasthan and Punjab', IGIDR Class Assignment, November.

Mitra, M., (1982), 'Women and Work from Historical Data in India', in Papers presented at the Golden Jubilee Symposium on Women, Work, and Society, Indian Statistic Institute, New Delhi.

Mukherjee, A. (1998), 'Labour' in P. Lanjouw and N. Stern (eds), *Economic Development in Palanpur over Five Decades*, Oxford University Press, Delhi.

Nagaraj, K. (1989), 'Female Workers in Rural Tamil Nadu—A Preliminary Study' in A. V. Jose (ed.), pp. 108–202.

Nayyar, Rohini (1987), 'Female Participation Rates in Rural India', *Economic and Political Weekly*, Vol. 24, No. 17, pp. 2207–16.

Ramachandran, V. K. (1990), *Wage Labour and Unfreedom in Agriculture: An Indian Case Study*, Clarendon Press, Oxford.

Ramachandran, V. K., Madhura Swaminathan, and Vikas Rawal (2001), 'How Have Hired Workers Fared? A Case Study of Women Workers from an Indian Village, 1977 to 1999', Centre for Development Studies, Working Paper No. 323, December.

———— (2002), 'Agricultural Workers in Rural Tamil Nadu: A Field Report' in V. K. Ramachandran and Madhura Swaminathan (eds) *Agrarian Studies*, Tulika Books, New Delhi.

Ramakumar, R. (1999), 'Agricultural Wages in Kerala, Tamil Nadu and Andhra Pradesh', IGIDR Class Assignment, November.

Sharma, H. R. (2001), 'Employment and Wage Earnings of Agricultural Labourers: A State-wise Analysis', *Indian Journal of Labour Economics*, Vol. 44, No. 1.

Sinha, S. (1999), 'A Study of Real Agricultural Wages in Assam, West Bengal and Orissa', IGIDR Class Assignment, November.

———— (2001) 'Female Work Participation in Rural India: A Case Study of Rural West Bengal, 1961 to 1991', M.Phil Thesis, submitted to the Indira Gandhi Institute of Development Research, Mumbai.

Sundaram, K. (2001), 'Employment-Unemployment Situation in the Nineties: Some Results from NSS 55th Round', Souvenir of the 43rd Annual Conference of the Indian Society of Labour Economics, Nagarbhavi, Bangalore.

Thomas, J. J. (1999), 'Real Wages in Agriculture: A Study of the States of Bihar, Madhya Pradesh and Uttar Pradesh', IGIDR Class Assignment, November.

Unni, Jeemol (1989), 'Changes in Women's Employment in Rural Areas, 1961-83', *Economic and Political Weekly*, Vol. 24, No. 17, pp. WS23–WS31.

———(1999), 'Women Workers in Agriculture: Some Recent Trends', in T. S. Papola and Alagh Sharma (eds) *Gender and Employment in India*, Vikas Publishing House, New Delhi.

——— (2000), *Sustainable Development and Social Security, Role of the Non-Farm Sector*, Vikas Publishing House, New Delhi.

Vaidyanathan, A. (2001), 'Employment in India, 1977-78 to 1999-2000: Characteristics and Trends', *Journal of Indian School of Political Economy*, Vol. 13, 2 April-June, pp. 217–54.

Visaria, Pravin (1997), 'Women in the Indian Working Force: Trends and Differentials', *Artha Vijnana*, Journal of the Gokhale Institute of Politics and Economics, Vol. 39, No. 1.

Gender, Religion, and the Age at Marriage in India

SRIYA IYER _____ 3

'Many girls are married off as young as ten in India, though the law says they should be 18. Now some Muslims want the legal right to wed girls at puberty.'

—Reported in *The Times* newspaper, 28 August 2002, London, pp. 4–5.

INTRODUCTION

The impact of gender and religion on the age at marriage in India is the subject of popular and academic debate. The legal age at marriage in India is 18 years for women and 21 years for men, but in recent years the All-India Muslim Personal Law Board has been to India's Supreme Court to demand exemption from the law for Muslim women in India. The Board argued that the legal age should not apply to Muslim women as the *Shariat* allows marriage at puberty for girls. This move did not, however, reflect widespread Muslim public opinion in India, bringing sharply into focus the whole question of the role of gender and religion in influencing the age at first marriage in India.

The interactions between gender, religion, and marriage need to be understood carefully. One feature of this interaction is women's preference with respect to marriage; the other is women's preference with respect to religion. Women's preferences both with respect to the desire to marry and to profess religious faith may influence the decision to marry, but the timing of women's marriage is not always dictated by individual choice. More frequently, it is dictated by the circumstances in which women are raised. Norms encouraging marriage and religious institutions which articulate these norms may encourage early marriage, affecting the constraint structure that women face; thereby altering the age at which women marry. More significantly, the circumstances or constraint structure faced by women of different religions may be different, depending upon the textual theology of the religion that they profess (Olmsted 2002). Not all women of the same religious persuasion, however, marry at the same age. This is because the ability of women to adhere to religious precepts on marriage will depend upon factors other than religion, such as their education or employment. Often, these economic factors contribute to a later age at marriage for women. These ideas suggest key questions: first, how does the constraint structure defined by textual theology, differ for different religions in India and does this affect the age at which individuals marry? Second, to what extent is the constraint structure affected by socio-economic characteristics? Third, do religion or socio-economic characteristics explain why age at marriage differs for Hindu and Muslim women and men in India?

GENDER, RELIGION, AND THE AGE AT MARRIAGE IN INDIA

Gender differentials in the age at marriage have important implications for women's well-being. A low age at marriage entails reproductive costs for women in terms of higher fertility in the future and higher levels of unwanted fertility, coupled with negative effects on women's health (Brien and Lillard 1994). Women's limited control over resources and their allocation within the household may also be affected if there is a large age gap between spouses. A low marriage age for women compared to men has implications for women's employment opportunities and their mobility. A combination of low marriage age, high wanted and unwanted fertility, limited opportunities for employment, and limited control over the distribution of economic resources, food, and health care, will have implications not only for the women themselves, but also for their children, especially their girls. Hence the question of gender differentials in the age at marriage is an important one. There is a large literature which has examined gender differentials in marriage in India and marriage-related issues such as dowry (Anderson 2003; Deolalikar and Rao 1998). Gender issues have also been investigated more widely in the context of Indian demography and development (Krishnaraj, Sudarshan, and Shariff 1998; Murthi, Guio, and Drèze 1995).

Gender differences in decision making about marriage are influenced both by preferences for marriage and the constraint structure that bounds decision making. A combination of factors, both economic and religious, may lead to observed differences in the age at marriage between men and women, and between individuals of different religions. Unlike the issue of gender, the role of religion in Indian demography is less extensively analysed (Iyer 2002; Jeffery and Jeffery 1997). A few studies have explicitly concentrated on the socio-economic characteristics of religious groups (Iyer 2002; Aruga 2003). There is a small existing literature on marriage age in India which focuses on explaining the rise in the age at first marriage over the last century or so (United Nations 1961; Caldwell, Reddy, and Caldwell 1983; International Institute of Population Sciences 1995). Research conducted on other societies has examined religious or ethnic differences and marriage age (Brien and Lillard 1994; Sander 1995). However, in India, religious differences in marriage age in the context of gender have not been explored systematically.

Historically in India, early marriage and child marriage were recognized as social problems and social reformers were involved in campaigns to increase male and female marriage age. In 1872, the Civil Marriage Act was passed, and the Infant Marriage Prevention Regulation was passed in 1894, prohibiting the marriage of girls below 8 years and boys below 14 years. This policy did have some impact as demonstrated by the Mysore Population Study conducted in 1961, which found that the percentage of women marrying under the age of 13 had fallen from 34 per cent for women in the birth cohort 1893-1902, to 18 per cent for women in the birth cohort 1928–32 (United Nations 1961, p. 93). For men, only 4 per cent in the 1893–1902 cohort had married before age 18; this fell to 1 per cent for the cohort 1923-27 (United Nations 1961, p. 96). This study also found that the age at first marriage in erstwhile Mysore state increased from 14.0 years for women in the birth cohort 1893-1902 up to 15.5 for women in the birth cohort 1928–32 (United Nations 1961, p. 91); the corresponding figures for men were 22.6 to 24.9 years (United Nations 1961, p. 95). But it was only later in British India that the Sarda Act of 1929 fixed the legal marriage age for men at 18 and for women at 14. After the Sarda Act was passed, Mysore state also enacted a legislation fixing the minimum age at marriage for girls at 14 years, and for boys at 18 years. In 1949, the minimum age at marriage for girls was raised to 15. In 1955 a revision of the Hindu Marriage Law, which was valid throughout India, established the minimum age at marriage for girls at 15 years and for boys at 18 years. In independent India, the Child Marriage Restraint Act was passed in 1978 fixing the legal age at marriage for women at 18 years and for men at 21 years. Where the 1978 Child Marriage Restraint Act differed from past legislation was that child marriage was now made an offence punishable by law. More recently, the National Family Health Survey (NFHS) has found that between 1961 and 1993, the female age at first marriage in Karnataka rose from 16.4 years to 19.6 years (International Institute of Population Sciences 1995, p. 47). But these trends have not been replicated in India more widely—the median age at first marriage for women aged 20–49 is 16.7 years, still well below the legal age.

Aside from differences between women and men, there are also religious differences in marriage age in India. Demographic indices for India as a whole show that Hindus form over 80 per cent of India's population and Muslims form 15 per cent of the population. Age-specific fertility rates depict that Muslims are bearing larger numbers of children at earlier ages than Hindus, attributed to lower ages at first marriage among them (Office of the Registrar General 1995; *The Times* 2002). In the 7th Round of the NSS undertaken in 1953-54, it was found that Muslim women in Karnataka were marrying a year later than Hindu women, while Muslim men were marrying nearly 1.5 years later than Hindu men (Caldwell, Reddy, and Caldwell 1983, p. 344). In the cross-section of 173 ever-married Hindu and Muslim couples studied in Ramanagaram, the mean age at first marriage for Hindu and Muslim women taken together is 17 years; it is 23 years for Hindu and Muslim men. The age at marriage is also higher for Muslims considered separately, at 17.6 years for women and 24.4 years for men, than it is for Hindus at 16.9 years for women and 22.4 years for men (Iyer 2002).

Hinduism and Islam on Marriage

Men and women's preferences and the constraint structure affecting their age at marriage may be affected by religion. A pure religious effect on marriage can operate in terms of norms about the 'proper' age to marry, polygyny, religious vows and practices of celibacy, and practices related to divorce.[1] The Sharia was made applicable to all Muslims in India in 1937. Islam is hypothesized to affect the age at marriage directly by its theological prescriptions on marriage,

---

[1] A substantial body of research has concerned itself with the normative values associated with Islam (Coulson and Hinchcliffe 1978; Youssef 1978; Qureshi 1980; Gellner 1981; Obermeyer 1992).

polygyny, and divorce (Qureshi 1980, p. 564). In the Koran all Muslim males are encouraged to marry; the universal remarriage of widowed and divorced women is also highly encouraged (Youssef 1978, p. 88; Coulson and Hinchcliffe 1978, pp. 37–8). Other features of Islamic marriage contracts is the control of parents and guardians over the selection of marriage partners; the dower, which is paid to the bride or her guardian; and strict seclusion before marriage (Youssef 1978, p. 78). For a Muslim marriage to be legally valid, it needs to meet four conditions–proposal by one; acceptance by the other; the presence of sufficient witnesses (two in Sunni law); and both the proposal and the acceptance need to be expressed formally at the same meeting (Azim 1997). But classical Islamic law treats men and women differently; it does not require a husband to obtain permission from a court or from current wives in order to contract another marriage. But a Muslim woman in India can legally have only one husband; if she marries a second she is liable for bigamy under the Indian Penal Code, and the offspring of such a marriage are also deemed illegitimate (Azim 1997).[2] Moreover, evidence from some Arab countries, and from India, shows that the theological toleration for polygyny is not practised empirically because supporting more than one wife is costly (Obermeyer 1992). The Indian Census of 1961 showed that polygyny was practised least by Muslims, and the most by tribal communities in northern India (Iyer 2002). In the fieldwork conducted for this study (discussed later), only four out of the 173 marriages were polygynous unions.

Similar to the Koranic view, the Hindu view of marriage encourages all Hindus to enter married life. For example, Shakuntala, a princess from Hindu mythology tells Dushyanta her beloved that 'when a husband and wife are carrying on smoothly, then only pleasure, prosperity and piety are possible' (Deshpande 1978, p. 91).[3]

---

[2] It is interesting in India though that not all aspects of the classical provisions in Islamic law for the sanction of polygyny are implemented in practice. As pointed out by Azim, a demographic fact of 12th century Arabia—frequent tribal wars that left many widows and orphaned daughters–led the 4th Sura and III verse of the Koran to counsel: 'If ye fear that ye shall not be able to deal justly with the orphans, marry women of your choice, two, or three, or four' (Azim 1997, p. 171). The provision for polygyny therefore may have been motivated primarily by economic circumstance.

[3] The importance of marriage is also indicated by Hindu gods who are always depicted as being married or with at least one consort, which in itself may provide evidence for the sanction of polygyny (Radhakrishnan 1947, p. 149).

Unmarried Hindu goddesses in Indian mythology are often portrayed as dangerous and violent, while married goddesses are reputed for their tranquility and obedience (Kinsley 1988, p. 203). However, the perfect marriage repeatedly idealized in the Hindu scriptures, is the monogamous one, epitomized by the relationship between the gods Rama and Sita.[4] Polygyny is tolerated in Hindu scriptures as well, but only in the absence of male offspring. But in scriptural Hinduism, as in Islam, women and men are viewed differently. For example, Vyasa argues in the *Mahabharata* that 'A woman is supposed to have one husband, a man many wives. ... A woman may have a second husband for progeny in case of difficulty' (Deshpande 1978, p. 90). In contrast, the *Ramayana* highlights the evils of polygamy. Polygyny became illegal for Hindus in India in 1955 with the Hindu Marriage Act legislation.

Differences between men and women are particularly marked when it comes to issues such as divorce. Studies of the Islamic marriage contract point out that Islam permits a man to divorce his wife, in some situations, unilaterally (Coulson and Hinchcliffe 1978). In addition, a divorced or widowed woman retains custody of children only for a limited period, after which custody passes to a male relative. The provision for unilateral divorce by the husband is an aspect of the *Sharia* which is particularly important in India, because there has been considerable debate over the Muslim woman's right to maintenance after divorce.[5] In scriptural Hinduism divorce is permitted in certain circumstances. As Kautilya argues in the *Arthashastra*, 'if the husband is of bad character, or is long gone abroad, or is guilty of high treason, or is dangerous to his wife, or has become an outcast, or has lost virility, he may be abandoned by his wife' (Radhakrishnan 1947, pp. 181–2). Correspondingly, a husband also has sanction to terminate a marriage: Vyasa argues in the *Mahabharata* that 'A husband also can abandon a wife who is free of the husband (self-willed), acts as she pleases, who is sterile or gives birth only to daughters or whose children die young' (Deshpande 1978, p. 93). Therefore, the differences between Hinduism and Islam on marriage leave room for different interpretations of

[4] This view is also popularly reflected in Indian folktales such as the *Silappadiharam* in which the heroine Kannagi's faithfulness guarantees her husband's life (Kinsley 1988, p. 201).

[5] Some Islamic scholars in India have argued that a woman in Islam is also allowed to initiate a 'delegated divorce', in which the husband authorizes the wife to divorce herself from him (Azim 1997).

scriptural content by individual Hindus and Muslims and by religious institutions such as the clergy.

Socioeconomic Determinants of the Age at First Marriage

There are many economic and social factors which may alter both individuals' preferences and the constraint structure that influence age at marriage. Theoretically, the educational level of men and women can increase the age at marriage as there may exist more opportunities outside marriage, especially for the woman, in terms of higher education or employment. Education may also enable a woman to obtain a better-educated husband or one with an urban job, increasing the search time for finding a suitable partner and delaying marriage. In Indian society, women's schooling enhances a woman's prospects in the marriage market and the discharge of 'status production' duties (Jeffery and Jeffery 1997). Empirical evidence is available from India and from many other countries that education and marriage age are causally related (Brien and Lillard 1994; Caldwell, Reddy, and Caldwell 1983; Singh 1992). The educational level of her husband is another variable which may influence a woman's age at marriage (Sander 1995).[6]

Another potential influence on marriage age is income (Ermisch 1981). A greater income earned by a woman herself may reduce her expected gains from marriage, thereby increasing her marriage age. However, increased income earned by a man may enable him to afford the expenses of supporting a wife and children, thereby enabling him to marry earlier.[7] Where a dowry system still operates, as in South Asia, the ability of parents to meet dowry payments may influence the daughter's age at marriage (Rao 1993). If parents expect dowry demands to become even higher in the future, they may decide that if they can afford it, it is better to marry daughters as soon as possible.

---

[6] The way in which this influence might work would be that a better educated man prefers to marry a woman who is older because: he wants a better educated spouse, or he believes that it is better to marry someone who is more mature, or he believes that a better educated wife will earn more, or he believes that she will cause their children to be better educated.

[7] It is this reasoning which lies behind the claim that in pre-industrial Europe, wealth and income were negatively associated with marriage age, with richer farmers and the nobility marrying younger than poorer ones or landless people.

Social norms are significant in the context of who makes the decision about men and women's marriage (Dasgupta 2000). In societies where parents exercise considerable influence over the choice of marriage partners for their children, we may expect a lower age at marriage as parents may not want to delay marriage for their children once a suitable spouse has been found. Alternatively, parents may choose to have their children married early because they expect that other parents in their society will behave similarly. Identifying changes in norms about marriage age, changes in who takes the marriage decision, and distinguishing them from changes in marriage behaviour, is difficult. One possible way to measure changes in norms is to examine changes over time empirically, by comparing the year of marriage across women and men.

For women, the age at menarche may exert an autonomous effect on the female age at marriage (Caldwell, Reddy, and Caldwell 1983). The Mysore Population Study found that 42 per cent of women born in Karnataka between 1893 and 1902 were married before the age of 13 (United Nations 1961, p. 93). Traditionally in north India as well, marriage shortly after menarche is popular though there is normally a gap of several months between marriage and cohabitation (Jeffery and Jeffery 1997). In the present study, a linear trend which examined the gap between menarche and marriage against the year of marriage showed that for the women of the Ramanagaram sample, the gap between the age at menarche and the age at marriage increased from about 2 years for women who married in the 1940s to almost 5 years for women who married in the late 1990s (Iyer 2002).

In Karnataka, consanguineous unions between men and women are quite common even today (Bittles, Cobles, and Appaji Rao 1993). The NFHS estimated that 37 per cent of ever-married Hindu women in Karnataka and 31 per cent of ever-married Muslim women had married a relation (International Institute of Population Sciences 1995, pp. 54-5).[8] The existence of consanguinity between spouses can be attributed to the reduced need for dowry payments in such unions (Do, Iyer, and Joshi 2006; Govinda 1988); improvements in public health which ensure increased numbers of children surviving to marriageable

---

[8] In Karnataka, the nature of the consanguineous relationship also varies between religious communities. For example, Muslims have traditionally married first cousins while Hindu women have traditionally married their maternal uncles (Bittles, Cobles, and Appaji Rao 1993).

age; and the desire to exercise better control over ancestral property. Marriage between relatives was widely prevalent in the Ramanagaram sample, where 38 per cent of Hindu couples and 41 per cent of Muslim couples were related by blood before marriage. The average coefficients of inbreeding (a statistical measure of consanguinity) were 0.03 for the Hindus and 0.03 for the Muslims, which are high when compared to the standards of other populations.

Data and Methods

A detailed micro-level data set was collected in Ramanagaram *taluk* in the south Indian state of Karnataka (Iyer 2002). Ramanagaram taluk was chosen for conducting fieldwork for several reasons. First, the religious distribution of the population in the taluk facilitates comparison between religious groups. Second, Ramanagaram has been exposed to family planning (FP) and literacy programmes since the early 1950s. Educational infrastructure in Ramanagaram is poor: it consists of only six primary schools, reflected in the low mean level of education for the women and men in the sample (5.5 years for women and 5.7 years for men). The Integrated Child Development Services Programme (ICDSP) provides supplementary education and health services for women, children under six, and adolescent girls. In terms of health infrastructure, there is only one public hospital, staffed by two doctors. Catholic missionaries run one health centre. The facilities in Ramanagaram for health care are about average for an Indian town of its size. The sample chosen covered Ramanagaram town and five other villages that were intimately connected with the small-scale economy of Ramanagaram taluk. The sampling procedure adopted was a two-stage quota sampling technique. The five villages will be referred to as villages A, B, C, D, and E. Depending on the size of the town or village, a proportional sample size was selected. Among the total of 201 households surveyed, there were 173 Hindu and Muslim households with ever-married men and women. The analysis here discusses these households only, because this is the more interesting contrast for this region.

Qualitative Evidence: Interpretation of Hinduism and Islam

The Ramanagaram women were asked several questions about the manner in which their religious beliefs and practice were related to marriage decisions in a local context. In the Ramanagaram sample, 'God's will' was not an important direct reason for marriage and it was cited by less than 2 per cent of Hindu or Muslim women. A more important influence was prevailing social norms concerning marriage. For example, Nagamma, age 36 and a mother of four daughters, from village D, remarked, 'I will marry my daughters at 15. I know it is wrong, but I do it because it is expected, we live in a "society", though personally I want to improve them'. Another woman, Laxmiamma, age 29, from village A, remarked, 'Marriage at 15 is the norm here. I feel I have suffered enough, why should I make her suffer? But, society matters too'. However, women were reluctant to marry their daughters before menarche. Of the women in the sample, 52 per cent said that daughters would definitely be sent to school after puberty rather than be kept home to be married. However, particularly in light of the current debate, it is interesting that the Ramanagaram women considered 15 years to be the 'normal' age of marriage, even though national legislation in the form of the Child Marriage Restraint Act of 1978 sets the minimum female age of marriage at 18 years. In the Ramanagaram sample, an average of 54 per cent of the women who married after 1978 did so after the age of 18, compared to an average of 27 per cent for those who married before 1978. Although the law is still not wholly complied with, it does appear to have exerted some influence on people's behaviour. For example, Sardamma of village C said 'My daughter can study as much as she wants to for now, and she must get married only at 18'. On the other hand, the law is certainly still being violated, as illustrated by Chandramma of village B who said that for her daughter 'it is best that she should get married at 15–16. As she is currently that age, I am looking out for an alliance for her'. Some women were not hesitant to delay their daughters' marriage, provided that they could obtain a better-educated bridegroom or one with an urban job. A Muslim woman, Sofia Banu, age 40, remarked, 'I have given my daughter an education so that she can find employment and find a good husband—it is a better investment than jewellery'. Economic considerations thus interacted with religious reasons to determine the timing of marriage.

Parents exercised a considerable degree of power in the choice of a suitable spouse. For example, one woman Padmavatamma from village B remarked that it would be considered 'highly irresponsible' if parents did not look after the matrimonial interests of offspring, especially daughters. However, she acknowledged that 'they are influenced by what they see at the cinema. It gives them ideas that they should choose for themselves'. These findings suggest that while religion may be playing an implicit role in influencing social norms that affect the timing of marriage, there are also changes occurring in these norms that have less to do with religion and more to do with modernity and the spread of information. While it is acknowledged that identifying these changes in social norms concerning marriage is difficult, we do find some qualitative evidence in women's views concerning their daughters' age at marriage. Women who had married daughters were asked at what age their daughters had been married, and, for those who had unmarried daughters, at what age they desired their unmarried daughters to be married. Interestingly, the mean age at marriage for daughters already married (17.2 years) was considerably lower than that proposed for unmarried daughters (18.7 years). Both these figures are higher than the mean age at marriage for Hindu and Muslim ever-married women in the sample as a whole (17 years), again indicating that 'normal' female marriage age may be rising. This difference, amounting to nearly two years, was particularly marked for the Hindus.

The question of divorce was raised in group discussions by asking the Ramanagaram women if there were any instances observed locally of husbands abandoning their wives. The discussions around this issue implied that men usually left wives for other relationships; it was less common for a woman to leave her husband. In the case of one Muslim woman who was a second wife, the husband divided his time between the two households. Remarriage was also not regarded as a feasible course of action by either Hindu or Muslim women, even those widowed at a very young age. This suggests that the textual theology of Islam and Hinduism is irrelevant, because women in this region are guided by social norms that did not encourage remarriage or divorce.

QUANTITATIVE EVIDENCE: A MODEL OF THE AGE AT MARRIAGE BY GENDER AND RELIGION

Regression models of marriage age were estimated to capture the decision-making of women and men separately. For men, six variables were identified as being potential influences on the age at first marriage. These were: the education of the man, total household expenditure (as a proxy for income), the year in which the man's marriage took place, the religion in which the man was brought up, whether his marriage was a consanguineous union or not, and his primary occupation. Age at marriage is measured as the man's age at the time of his first marriage for Hindu and Muslim ever-married men in the sample ($N = 173$).

For women, eight variables were identified as being potential influences on the age at first marriage. These were the education of the woman, the education of her spouse, total household expenditure (as a proxy for income), the woman's age at menarche, the year in which the woman's marriage took place, the religion in which the woman was brought up, whether her marriage was a consanguineous union or not, and the primary occupation of the woman's husband. Age at marriage is measured as the woman's age at the time of her first marriage for Hindu and Muslim ever-married women in the sample ($N = 173$).

In the models, education was measured by the number of years of education attained, for both men and women. Consumption measured by total expenditure was chosen as the most relevant measure of income because it was correlated with other income measures, and it was the variable for which the households were best able to provide information accurately. Husband's occupation was measured so as to take a value 1 if the husband was employed in a skilled occupation and 0 if he was employed in an unskilled occupation. Marital consanguinity was measured by a dummy variable which took the value 1 if the woman (or man) had married a relation and 0 otherwise. In order to assess the influence of religion exerting a shift effect on the age at marriage, a dummy variable was created which took a value 1 if the woman (or man) was Muslim. In order to assess whether religion also exerted slope effects, that is, whether the effect of various socio-economic variables on age at first marriage varied across religious groups, Muslim interaction terms were created. Successive variable deletion tests, using a joint F-test of zero restrictions on the coefficients of groups of variables, were imposed on this general model, yielding the specification shown in Tables 3.1 and 3.2.

In order to compare the behaviour of the Hindus with that of Muslims, restrictions were imposed on the parameters of the model and Wald tests were performed to test the validity of these restrictions. The first hypothesis tested whether the effect of education on female marriage age differed between Hindus and Muslims. A Wald test rejected the restriction that there was no difference in the effect of education on marriage age between the two religious groups. Thus,

Table 3.1: Interaction model of the determinants of women's age at first marriage, Ramanagaram sample

(Base category: Hindus)

Regressor	Coefficient	Standard error	Tratio [Prob]
Intercepts			
Constant (CONST)	−366.76 ***	64.57	−5.68 (0.000)
Muslim religion dummy (MUSLIM)	290.47 ***	89.56	3.24 (0.001)
Woman's education			
Woman's education (EDU)	0.22 ***	0.08	2.63 (0.009)
Education for Muslim women (MEDU)	0.04	0.13	0.30 (0.762)
Husband's education			
Husband's education (EDUSP)	−0.05	0.07	−0.65 (0.515)
Education for Muslim husband (MEDUSP)	0.14	0.12	1.17 (0.244)
Age at menarche			
Age at menarche (AGEMEN)	0.55 **	0.23	2.37 (0.019)
Age at menarche for Muslims (MAGEMEN)	−0.03	0.39	−0.07 (0.947)
Income			
Total expenditure (EXPN)	0.00	0.00	0.93 (0.353)
Total expenditure for Muslims (MEXPN)	0.15	0.12	1.17 (0.244)
Husband's occupation is skilled			
Husband's occupation is skilled (SKILL)	3.00 ***	0.97	3.11 (0.002)
Muslim husband's occupation is skilled (MSKILL)	−0.08	1.36	−0.06 (0.955)
Consanguinity			
Woman married a relative (RELATION)	0.07	0.65	0.12 (0.908)
Muslim woman married a relative (MRELATION)	0.81	0.99	0.81(0.417)
Year of marriage			
Year of marriage (YRMAR)	0.19 ***	0.03	5.77 (0.000)
Year of marriage for Muslims (MYRMAR)	−0.15 ***	0.05	−3.22 (0.002)
R-Bar-Squared	0.5191		

Notes: *** = Significant at 0.01 level; ** = Significant at 0.05 level; * = Significant at 0.10 level. Dependent variable is AGEMAR: the woman's age at first marriage in years. Sample: 173 ever-married Hindu and Muslim women

Table 3.2: Interaction model of the determinants of men's age at first marriage, Ramanagaram sample

(*Base category: Hindus*)

Regressor	Coefficient	Standard error	Tratio [Prob]
Intercepts			
Constant (CONST)	−553.74 ***	124.75	−4.44 (0.000)
Muslim religion dummy (MUSLIM)	338.55 *	178.29	1.90 (0.059)
Man's education			
Man's education (EDUSP)	0.09	0.14	0.67 (0.505)
Education for Muslim men (MSEDUSP)	0.29	0.22	1.36 (0.176)
Income			
Total expenditure (EXPNRS)	0.00	0.00	0.94 (0.348)
Total expenditure for Muslims (MEXPN)	0.00	0.01	0.11 (0.911)
Man's occupation is skilled			
Man's occupation is skilled (SKILL)	2.66	1.93	1.38 (0.169)
Muslim man's occupation is skilled (MSKILL)	−3.87	2.77	−1.40 (0.164)
Consanguinity			
Man married a relation (RELATION)	0.97	1.37	0.71 (0.476)
Muslim man married a relation (RELATION)	−0.74	2.06	−0.36 (0.720)
Year of marriage			
Year of marriage (YRMAR)	0.29 ***	0.06	4.59 (0.000)
Year of marriage for Muslims (MYRMAR)	−0.17 *	0.09	−1.89 (0.060)
R-Bar-Squared	0.2091		

Notes: *** = Significant at 0.01 level; ** = Significant at 0.05 level; * = Significant at 0.10 level. Dependent variable is AGEMAR: the man's age at first marriage in years. Sample: 173 ever-married Hindu and Muslim men

the theoretical expectation that education would increase women's marriage age was borne out, particularly for the Hindus. Education was unimportant in the model of men's marriage age, for both Hindu and Muslim men. Husband's education is also theoretically supposed to affect women's marriage age, but in the model estimated it did not have a significant effect. One reason for this finding may be that the effect of men's education is being picked up by other variables such as husband's skilled occupation, which did emerge as a significant influence on female marriage age. A Wald test showed that husband's occupation being skilled had a significantly different effect on age at marriage for Hindus than for Muslims. This variable affects Hindus significantly more than Muslims, probably because there were more Hindu men employed in skilled occupations.

The next hypothesis tested concerned the effect of age at menarche. In light of the recent debates about Muslim marriage age, a Wald test showed that there is a difference in the effect of menarche on marriage between Hindus and Muslims. There are several possible reasons for why the age at menarche may have had a positive effect on Hindu marriage age. First, menarche may be a sign of a woman being 'grown up' enough to marry 'soon'. Second, it may be a sign that a girl is now reproductively fertile and needs to be married off to prevent illegitimate pregnancies.[9] The positive relationship between age at marriage and age at menarche may also exist because menarche is a good proxy for a woman's health and nutritional status and hence her desirability in the marriage market (Iyer 2002). The total expenditure and marital consanguinity variables were insignificant for both religious groups in both models.

The year of marriage was included in the marriage models as a possible proxy for changes in social norms and/or legislation over time, both of which are theoretically postulated to increase marriage age. The econometric findings showed that for both women and men, a one-year later year of marriage was associated with a significant increase in marriage age for both religious groups. A Wald test in both models showed that the effect of the year of marriage on age at marriage for Hindus is not significantly different from its effect for Muslims. One possible reason for the importance of the year-of-marriage variable might be legislation concerning the age at marriage in Karnataka. According to the Child Marriage Restraint Act of 1978, the minimum

---

[9] The qualitative evidence collected during my fieldwork suggests that both of these factors may have been at work. Most important, however, was that two key desired characteristics in a potential bride in Ramanagaram were physical strength and long hair, which are directly related to better nutrition and health, which in turn are medically known to be reflected in early menarche.

legal age for marriage in India is 18 years for women and 21 years for men. However, the NFHS documented that for Karnataka as a whole in 1995, 51 per cent of women in the 20–24 age group had married at 18 or younger. If we consider mean age at marriage alone, many women in the Ramanagaram sample appear also to not have followed the legal prescription of 1978. The mean age at marriage for Hindu and Muslim women taken together was 17 years, which is clearly lower than the legal age. More interestingly, for those women marrying after 1978 the mean age at marriage was 18.4 years, while the mean age at marriage for those marrying before 1978 was 15.5 years.

In contrast to women, the mean age at marriage for men, at 23 years, did appear to follow the legal prescriptions. The implications of the significant effect exerted by the year of marriage variable must be considered more carefully. With the imposition of the Child Marriage Restraint Act in 1978, there has been a change in the practice of child marriage. Although the law is still not wholly complied with, it appears to have exerted some influence on people's behaviour. The fact that we see the 'time' effect operating on age at marriage even after controlling for variations in other factors such as education, income, and occupation may mean that the 1978 law is being better enforced, among Hindus as well as Muslims. However, it is more likely to be followed for men than for women.

Finally, in the models for men as well as for women, a Wald test accepted the restriction that the intercept for Hindus is not significantly different from the intercept for Muslims. This result suggests that membership of the Hindu instead of the Muslim religion does not have a significant effect on female (and male) age at marriage, independently of socio-economic differences between the two religious groups. However, in the context of a model of the age at marriage, in which the dependent variable and all of the explanatory variables take values strictly greater than zero, it is not possible to draw interpretative conclusions from the size of the intercept coefficient.

CONCLUSION

This chapter examines the interactions between gender, religion, and the economic determinants of marriage age in a cluster of communities in India. Qualitative evidence on the norm-enforcing strength of the textual theology of Islam and Hinduism shows that women and men are treated differently with respect to marriage, polygyny, and divorce. However, the extent to which rural Indian women interpret textual theology to influence their preferences about the age at marriage is important. In Ramanagaram taluk, among both Hindus and Muslims, marriage was dictated by prevailing local norms that encouraged early marriage. Remarriage and divorce, although sanctioned by the religion, were not regarded as feasible options for women. What is striking is that the women in the sample did not blindly accept religious prescriptions on marriage. However, they still appear to hesitate in translating their personally-held views fully into actual practice. This is because the age at marriage for women here may be influenced more by economic circumstances. Consequently, multiple regression interaction models of the age at first marriage were estimated separately for women and men. The factors that influenced female marriage age were the educational level of the woman; whether the woman's husband had a skilled occupation; the woman's age at menarche; the year in which the marriage took place; and religion. Men's marriage age was influenced mainly by the year of marriage and religion. After controlling for other socio-economic variables, although religion by itself had a significant effect on Hindu and Muslim male and female marriage age, the effect of religion was not significantly different between the two religious groups. There were also differences between Hindus and Muslims in the socio-economic factors affecting marriage age and considerable gender differences among both religious groups specifically in the economic factors that affected male and female marriage age. These findings provide little empirical support for concerns which have been put forward in India since the 1990s about the so-called 'Islamic' effects on marriage. The findings suggest that there are significant gender differentials among both religious groups: both Hindu and Muslim women's decisions to marry are being affected by the economic circumstances in which they are placed, and significantly more so compared to their husbands. This makes the current debate in India about enforcing a Muslim woman's right to marry at puberty, all the more complex. Both women's and men's interpretation of textual theology may be significant for marriage decisions. However, this factor does not vary substantially between Hindu and Muslim women and men in rural south India. Women's ability to enforce their views is determined by their access to socio-economic characteristics, which does vary considerably across religious groups. Therefore, until the links between gender, Hinduism and Islam, and women's and men's economic circumstances are better understood, the debates about enforcing the Shariat's prescriptions on the age at first marriage, will continue to recur.

REFERENCES

Anderson, S. (2003), 'Why Dowry Payments Declined with Modernization in Europe but Are Rising in India', *Journal of Political Economy*, Vol. 111, No. 2, pp. 269–310.

Aruga, K. (2003), 'Differences in Characteristics of Religious Groups in India: As Seen from Household Survey Data', Centre for Energy Policy and Economics Working Paper 26, Zurich.

Azim, S. (1997), *Muslim Women: Emerging Identity*, Rawat Publications, New Delhi.

Becker, G.S. (1974), 'A Theory of Marriage', in T.W. Schultz (ed.), *Economics of the Family: Marriage, Children and Human Capital*, National Bureau of Economic Research, The University of Chicago Press, Chicago, pp. 299–351.

Bittles, A.H., J.M. Cobles, and N. Appaji Rao (1993), 'Trends in Consanguineous Marriage in Karnataka, South India, 1980–89', *Journal of Biosocial Science*, Vol. 25, pp. 111–16.

Brien, M.J. and L.A. Lillard (1994), 'Education, Marriage and First Conception in Malaysia', *Journal of Human Resources*, Vol. XXIX, No. 4, pp. 1167–1204.

Caldwell, J.C., P.H. Reddy, and P. Caldwell (1983), 'The Causes of Marriage Change in South India', *Population Studies*, Vol. 37, No. 3, pp. 343–61.

Coulson, N. and D. Hinchcliffe (1978), 'Women and Law Reform in Contemporary Islam', in L. Beck and N. Keddie (eds), *Women in the Muslim World*, Harvard University Press, Cambridge, pp. 37–49.

Dasgupta, P. (2000), 'Population and Resources: An Exploration of Reproductive and Environmental Externalities', *Population and Development Review*, Vol. 26, No. 4, pp. 643–89.

Deolalikar, A.B. and V. Rao (1998), 'The Demand for Dowries and Bride Characteristics in Marriage: Empirical Estimates for Rural South-Central India', in M. Krishnaraj, R. Sudarshan, and A. Shariff (eds), *Gender, population and development*, Oxford University Press, Delhi, pp. 122–40

Deshpande, C.R. (1978), *Transmission of the Mahabharata Tradition, Vyasa and Vyasids*, Institute of Advanced Study, Simla.

Do, Q., S. Iyer, and S. Joshi (2006), 'The Economics of Consanguineous Marriages', World Bank Policy Research Working Papers, No. 4085, The World Bank, Washington DC, December.

Ermisch, J.F. (1981), 'Economic Opportunities, Marriage Squeezes and the Propensity to Marry: An Economic Analysis of Period Marriage Rates in England and Wales', *Population Studies*, Vol. 3, pp. 347–56.

Gellner, E. (1981), *Muslim Society*, Cambridge University Press, Cambridge.

Ghallab, M. (1984), 'Population Theory and Policies in the Islamic Model', in J. Clarke (ed.) *Geography and Population: Approaches and Applications*, Pergamon, Oxford, pp. 232–41.

Govinda Reddy, P. (1988), 'Consanguineous Marriages and Marriage Payment: A Study Among Three South Indian Caste Groups', *Annals of Human Biology*, Vol. 15, No. 4, pp. 263–8.

International Institute of Population Sciences, Mumbai and Institute of Social and Economic Growth, Bangalore (1995), *National Family Health Survey 1992–93: Karnataka*, Bombay.

Iyer, S. (2002), *Demography and Religion in India*, Oxford University Press, Delhi.

Jeffery, R. and P. Jeffery (1997), *Population, Gender and Politics: Demographic Change in Rural North India*. Cambridge University Press, Cambridge.

Kinsley, D.R. (1988), *Hindu Goddesses*, (Second edition), University of California Press, Berkeley and Los Angeles.

Krishnaraj, M., R. Sudarshan, and A. Shariff (1998), *Gender, Population and Development*, Oxford University Press, Delhi.

Murthi, M., A-C Guio, and Dreze (1995), 'Mortality, Fertility, and Gender Bias in India: A District-Level Analysis', *Population and Development Review*, Vol. 21, No. 4, pp. 745–82

Obermeyer, C.M. (1992) 'Islam, Women and Politics: The Demography of Arab Countries', *Population and Development Review*, Vol. 18, No. 1, pp. 33–60.

Office of the Registrar General, Demography Division (1995), *Census of India 1991: Paper 1 on Religion*, Registrar General, New Delhi.

Olmsted, J.C. (2002), 'Assessing the Impact of Religion on Gender Status', *Feminist Economics*, Vol. 8, No. 3, pp. 99–111.

Qureshi, S. (1980), 'Islam and Development: The Zia Regime in Pakistan', *World Development*, Vol. 8, pp. 563–75.

Radhakrishnan, S. (1947), *Religion and Society*, George Allen and Unwin, London.

Ragab, I.A. (1980), 'Islam and Development', *World Development*, Vol. 8, pp. 513–21.

Rao V. (1993), 'The Rising Price of Husbands: A Hedonic Analysis of Dowry Increases in Rural India', *Journal of Political Economy*, Vol. 101, pp. 666–77.

Sander, W. (1995), *The Catholic Family*, Westview Press, Boulder.

Singh M. (1992), 'Changes in Age at Marriage of Women in Rural North India', *Journal of Biosocial Science*, Vol. 24, No. 1, pp. 123–30.

The Times newspaper (2002), Report on 'A mum at 11, a great grandmother at 38', 28 August, pp. 4–5.

United Nations (1961), *Mysore Population Study*, Department of Social and Economic Affairs, New York.

Youssef, N.H. (1978), 'The Status and Fertility Patterns of Muslim Women', in L. Beck and N. Keddie (eds) *Women in the Muslim World*, Harvard University Press, Cambridge, pp. 69–99.

Invisibility and Ordeal of Women Workers in India

AMAL MANDAL ————————————— 4

INTRODUCTION

Since the publication of provisional figures of 2001 Census, manifold commentaries have been harping on 'significant improvement' in women's workforce participation. Gainful employment is indubitably one primary desiderate for ensuring gender equality, emancipation from poverty, ignorance, for freeing women from domestic clutches, for giving them autonomy of action and choice, and ultimately for improving overall status. This is particularly indispensable when women's entity is shrouded in subordination and dependency syndrome. The gender difference in workforce participation rate in India is about 26 per cent (Mukhopadhyay 2005). The moot question is whether the increasing work participation rates are uniform over all the states and over organized and unorganized sectors and whether the gainful employment led to economic empowerment of women.

A number of studies exist in the literature on workforce participation of women. Dev (2004) examines female workforce participation and finds that inter-state disparities in workforce participation rates are much higher for rural females than urban females. His analysis is based on NFHS, NSS, and Census data. Thus female labour participation is low in some states and high in some other states. Low female labour participation may be a crude predictor of female seclusion and segregation, but high female labour participation may not mean that women are secluded in those states (Miller 1982). There has been a big shift for urban women workers to the manufacturing industries. However, the share of women's employment in hotels and restaurants has fallen compared to 1999–2000 (Chandrasekhar and Ghosh 2007).

Also, there is a conceptual and measurement related problem on the workforce participation rates of men and women (Agarwal 1985).

Over the years, women's work participation rate has been improving. Yet three-fourths of total women are still recorded as non-workers. Does this imply that the vast majority of women are sitting idle and living on a platter provided by others, in other words, are non-working women merely dependent on male breadwinners, and thus economically inconsequential? When the work and working ambience of Indian women are examined in a generic sense it transpires that women's economic contribution to the family survival, sustenance, and consequently to national development has been grossly underestimated and undervalued. Women workers have consistently been confined to low paid, unskilled manual, seasonal, casual, flexible, and above all leftover occupations and they encounter flagrant discrimination and outright abuses. Subsistence struggle and growing shrinkage of employment opportunities are putting enormous pressure on women. Modernization and technological advances in production processes are either pushing women out from their traditional occupations or pushing them down the job hierarchy. The unfolding trends in the labour market do not attest to instant escape from the entrapment. For women, all-round discrimination and debasement at the employment front is seen to be related to, and coterminous with, their general social status.

Women's Workforce Participation

Workforce participation rate—that is the percentage of women workers to their total population—returned by Census figures is a convenient indicator for comprehending the employment status of women as the Census figures are based on exhaustive enumeration and provide detailed break-ups. The latest 2001 Census figures in fact divulge disconcerting dimensions including disparities for women workers.[1] The work participation rate may have improved somewhat 'remarkably', from 14.2 per cent in 1971 to 19.7 per cent in 1981, 22.3 per cent in 1991, and 25.7 in 2001, but the advancement is not robust especially in urban areas. The increase is mainly due to about a two-

---

[1] NSS returns, 55th Round (1999) for instance, are not fundamentally different from Census figures.

fold surge in marginal works in both rural and urban areas. Such an increase may lead one to be contended but it is important to note that a massive number of women—total 120 million or 74.3 per cent—are still out and out non-workers. In the same vein, compared to males the proportion of women workers is extremely iniquitous.

Most of the women are working in rural areas—110 million or 87.7 per cent of total—in contrast to 72 per cent males. Work participation rate of women in rural areas has now improved from 26.7 in 1991 to 31 per cent in 2001. Higher work participation rates of rural women essentially evince that the more poor the women, the greater the work participation. Another disquieting dimension is that women workers abound in marginal works. The share of men in marginal works in rural areas is decreasing while for women it is increasing, from 6.3 per cent in 1991 to 11 per cent in 2001.

For the nature of occupations in which main workers are distributed, it is discernible that 32.5 per cent of total women are cultivators, 39.4 per cent agricultural labourers, 6.4 per cent work in household industries, and the rest in the category of 'other works'. Agriculture

Table 4.1: **Work participation, workers and activities,**
women and men, 2001   (*per cent*)

Category of Work/Worker	Women	Men
Work participation rate	25.7	51.9
Work participation rate–rural	31.0	52.4
Work participation rate–urban	11.6	50.9
Total non-worker	74.3	48.1
Main worker	14.7	45.4
Main worker–rural	16.8	44.5
Main worker–urban	9.1	47.5
Marginal worker	11.0	6.6
Marginal worker–rural	14.2	7.9
Marginal worker–urban	2.4	3.4
Cultivator	32.5	31.3
Cultivator–rural	36.5	42.2
Agricultural labourer	39.4	20.8
Agricultural labourer–rural	43.4	27.5
Household industries	6.4	3.0
Other workers	21.7	41.8

Source: Census of India, 2001 (provisional figures).

has all through been the single largest employment provider for the Indian population. At present it accounts for 58 per cent of total employment. Thus, it may not be surprising that among total workers, 52 per cent of men and 72 per cent of women are engaged in agricultural activities alone. In rural areas, 76 per cent women workers are attached to agriculture whereas the corresponding male figure is 63 per cent. In the category of cultivators in rural areas, males may still surpass females but women outnumber men in agricultural labour class (43.4 per cent women and 27.5 per cent men) which has obvious ramifications. Women's share in household industries is about two-fold more in rural and three-fold in urban areas.

The only other category employing more than 5 per cent of working women is the service sector, which includes occupations such as social work, receptionists, clerks, and teaching. About 80 per cent women workers in urban area are employed in sectors such as household industries, petty trades and services, buildings and construction work. Furthermore, higher levels of education do not directly imply a higher proportion of main workers for women. The 1991 Census Report revealed that 18 per cent illiterate women were employed as main workers and just 11 per cent educated were employed as such.

Over 95 per cent of total women workers are engaged in agriculture, animal husbandry, beedi rolling, labelling, and packing, building and construction, collection of raw hides and skins, handlooms weaving, brick kilns, stone quarries, saw mills, and oil mills etc. These income earning activities of women fall in the broader category of unorganized sector of the economy.[2] They are 'the most vulnerable' section of workers because these works are insecure, irregular, under-waged, and are unregulated by any public policy framework. Cycles of excessive seasonality of employment, lack of security, and strenuous nature of work with longer working hours are some of the features of those activities. These women are coerced into a trap of vicious circle and

---

[2] Institutional theory visualizes the labour market as consisting of primary and secondary sectors. The primary sector is regarded as the organized sector and secondary sector as unorganized sector. The unorganized sector is variously termed as informal, traditional, or unregulated sector. Sometimes the unorganized sector can further be typified into institutional and non-institutional segments. However, the unorganized sector with its overwhelming number of workers, range, and complexity of problems is not amenable to any statistical accuracy and precision in the same sense as the organized sector.

are victims of a lopsided labour market. Long and arduous working hours impair their health and fertility. Poor housing conditions, worse form of sanitation, and absence of childcare services compound oppressive social practices to add to their burden (Mazumdar 1989). Casual nature of employment, ignorance and illiteracy, and small and scattered size of the establishments prevent such workers from organizing themselves in pursuit of common interests such as job security and social amenities.

The proportion of women workers in the organized sector is only microscopic—not more than 6 per cent of the total. The workers here may be fortunate because they are covered by protective labour legislation, fixed rate of wage, and somewhat permanent employment etc. Yet, the women herein are not in an enviable position. Employers frequently exploit women's weak bargaining power by paying lower wages than males, and women are clustered in occupations which have lower wage rates. Women are also deprived of statutorily available amenities and securities like maternity benefits, crèches etc. There remains a huge gap between statutorily available welfare provisions and those that are readily available. When relatively secure and protected employment in the organized sector can not enlist or win much, it testifies to what awaits the vast majority women in the unprotected sector. And this also tends to vindicate that denigration of women in the unorganized sector is unlikely to be ameliorated easily or instantly.

Underestimation of Women's Work

We have realized that women's work participation rate is substantially higher than the official estimates. The Census and NSS figures do not disclose the complete extent of women's work participation. No definition of work—both Census and a somewhat broader conceptualization of NSS—has ever been able to capture the factual extent of women's work participation. This is because attention is singularly directed to those whose end product of labour reaches the market. To one estimate at least 83 million Indian women workers are still to be accounted for (Omvedt 1992). To other appraisals underreporting in Census data varies at least between 30 to 40 per cent. Women carry out multi-dimensional functions of production and reproduction. Persistent recording failures have devalued women's work participation,[3] underestimated their overall role in the family and economy, and helped in entrenching the perception that women's economic role is only incidental. Greater injustice is thus being meted out by the social invisibility of their constant and concrete contributions.

There are basically two kinds of work: with payment and without payment. Men are engaged in those tasks where payment is inherent, in other words, they are concentrated in the market-oriented side of the continuum of work. Hence, there will not be much variation in the estimatation of men as workers, irrespective of the methodology employed. For women, a combination of domestic drudgery and economic activities is the special feature and they are caught in 'non-monetized' subsistence production and domestic duties. Even when women assume a wage-earning role they cannot skip but spend several hours doing work for which no payment is forthcoming.

Work without payment has two categories: (i) some tasks are necessary for survival but these are simply not recognized as economic activities—domestic work like cooking, cleaning, childcare may be fundamental for maintaining a family and have a clear productive value but are not regarded as economic activities per se; (ii) a few tasks with categorical productive value are also not considered as economic activities when performed within and for the family. Subsistence activities in post-harvest processing, feeding of farm hands, livestock maintenance, labour on the family farm, and a host of similar activities fall into this stereotype. Ironically, most women are invariably engaged in such activities and there seems no respite from such work. All in all, unpaid household labour of a woman is virtually ignored because what she creates on this front has 'use value'. Women, who produce 'use value' are considered unemployed and not contributing to the economic development, slighting the fact that hours of work put into household chores are much higher than paid employment.

---

[3] For details see Krishnaraj, M. (1990), 'Women's Work in Indian Census', *Economic and Political Weekly*, 17 January; Premi, M.K. and Raju (1994), *Gender Issue in Workforce Participation in 1991 Census in India*, IASP, New Delhi; Mehta, B.C. (1999), 'Gender and Regional Pattern of Work Participation in Rural Rajasthan', *Manpower Journal*, July–September; and Mehta, Aasha Kapur (2000), 'The Invisible Workers: Women's Unrecognised Contribution to the Economy', *Manushi*, November–December.

The conceptual conundrum notwithstanding, earnest effort is lacking in locating and recording women workers, in evaluating their work load and time-disposition either in family farming or in household economic occupation.[4] The enumerators/serveyors generally meet only male members of the households. As the status-conscious male respondents are not positive in their replies to questions on economic activities of the family women, the enumerators tend to conclude that the women are mainly active in domestic chores; they are simply housewives and their economic activity, if any, is only casual. More often, male 'breadwinning ethics' and 'housewification' prevail and predominate in the recording process.

Gender Discrimination

Indian women workers are found in a few specific occupations, most of which are manual, insecure, part-time or uncertain works, and are characterized by informality, flexible hours; and location of work which can be carried out from home and can easily be combined with domestic duties. Men monopolize the better-paid and secure jobs and women predominate in unskilled, arduous operations down the ladder.

The labour market is highly sex-segregated and biased. Women perform different works and their labour is perceived and valued differently. The sexual division of labour determines the kinds of work, the earning potential, promotion prospect, and general status in terms of the gender of the workforce. A few gender differentials dominate the labour market. The gender composition of the workforce is subject to male/family decision making. Male employer/supervisor's notion of what kind of work is appropriate for women ascertains the facets of women's employment. Both employers and husbands are said to have a common interest in confining women to homes while at the same time earning an income.

---

[4] A good example of the enumerator's perception is highlighted by one survey commissioned by the United Nations Development Fund for Women, India (UNIFEM), which found that 98 out of 100 enumerators did not even put questions regarding work to women, it was simply assumed that women did not work. Out of the 2002 women in the 1000 households covered, only four women were asked about any work that they had done in the previous year. Enumerators depended solely on information supplied by male members of the family (cited in *The Report of the National Commission on Labour* 2002, p. 938, Ministry of Labour, Government of India).

From recruitment to remuneration, occupational segregation, and at times of lay-offs women workers of all categories face discrimination and deprivation almost uniformly and universally.[5] Because of socio-economic and locational exclusivities, women workers are not a homogeneous group. But what is absorbing and at the same time unfortunate is that the denigration is common to all; an exception here and there does not matter much. Lowly paid occupations have disproportionately larger proportion of women. Even in the organized sector of the Indian economy about 90 per cent women workers are engaged in semi-skilled and unskilled jobs. Men and women tend to work in different sectors and hold different positions within the same occupational group. Women are victims of restricted job opportunity (Mazumdar 1990), they have a narrower range of occupations than men, and are more likely to work part time or in short spells. Women encounter more barriers in career advancement. Gender differentials are also stark in emerging areas of work—the information and communication technology once hailed as the window of equal opportunity and treatment has largely failed to act as a leveller.

Women undertake multiple employment ranging from unpaid family work to wage earning, contractual work to independent work, rendering services in exchange of goods and services. Women contribute more than men in total labour energy expenses.[6] But they are surely getting much less in return. Even when men and women are doing the same type of work, women get about 30 per cent less wage. Compared to men, Indian women agricultural labourers are usually paid at least 30–40 per cent less.[7] Moreover, the wages are usually given

[5] Women are by far the largest discriminated group. Today many more women earn an income than before, but they are restricted to low-skilled jobs. In countries where women are equally or even more educated than men, the 'glass ceiling' often blocks their ultimate rise to the top. Coupled with the glass ceiling, the 'pay gap' between women and men is explicit in most countries (ILO 2003). Compared to men, women workers get on average one-third wage worldwide.

[6] A poor woman's average work per day ranges between 14–18 hours in contrast to 8–10 hours for men (Mazumdar 1989; Banerjee 1995). Banerjee, Narayan (1995), 'Women's Participation & Development', Occasional Paper no. 5, Centre for Women's Development Studies, New Delhi. According to the *Human Development in South Asia, 2002* (UNDP) a working class village woman in South Asia works for 12–16 hours a day. In Nepal, women on an average work for 12.07 hours, 47 per cent higher than men.

[7] Three occupational wage surveys by the Labour Bureau found that average daily wage earning of women workers was 30 to 100 per cent lower than males in all 30

to the male head of the family and women do not necessarily have the autonomy to spend their income according to own preferences or priorities. Partly due to varying standards of work and partly due to personal outlook of employers there is widespread scepticism about the comparative efficiency of women workers and this is buttressed by a lower wage structure for women.

However, micro studies have documented that women are not inefficient and lower wage rate is not related to their low productivity. In almost all the main occupations where both men and women are working, women are as efficient as men or even more efficient in some specific cases. A recent study has shown that in the more developed district of Karnal in Haryana women received Rs 12 a day for weeding whereas men got Rs 28. During threshing season, women received Rs 20–25 in contrast to Rs 40–60 by men. The low wages paid to women are not because of their low inefficiency or output. On the contrary, it was found that the picking rate per labourer per minute was 1.6 for men and 5.2 for women (Sridhar 2003).

Women workers suffer not only economically but also because of gender. The *Shramashakti* Report (1988) revealed the extent of non-payment, irregular payment, signature on false amount, and harassment/exploitation by employers/contractors. The Report divulged that women's earnings were misused by husband/family. The study of women workers of a brick factory—a typical example of unorganized sector works—in Cooch Behar district (Mandal 2004) shows that survival struggle drags women to multiple engagements, and women's work is solely for the family sustenance. Furthermore, most conspicuous is the absence of maternity benefits, crèches, insurance, and other minimum social security provisions.

For women workers, gender divides are present in every occupation. Women workers in brick factories are exclusively confined to two types of work—brick carrying (*Rejin*) and brick making (*Pathera*), they do not have single representation in dock or other skilled works. The weekly wage drawn by those piece-rated women also attests that they earn on average Rs 103 less than male workers in the same category of works. Similarly, in the garment industry, men undertake tasks like master cutter and machine operation while women are

industries. Cited in *The Report of the National Committee on Rural Labour* (1991, p. 133), Ministry of Labour, Government of India.

concentrated in assembly lines. In construction works, men usurp all skilled operations and women dig earth, mix mortar, carry bricks/bags, and act as helpers. In the tea plantations, women are engaged in the 'inhuman' task of plucking tea leafs. Planters adjudge women as best and fast pluckers (Roy 2001). By such branding women get the ascribed status, they are a cheap labour force with natural rather than professional skills. Accordingly, wage differentiation and discrimination are perpetuated.

Constitutional law may have provided for equal remuneration and equal status in employment, and statutory provisions may have elaborate protective measures but real equality is yet to descend upon women workers evenly and uniformly. Our study in brick factories shows that the wage rate of daily workers is less for women— Rs 50 for men and Rs 47 for women. This rate is modified each year after the bipartite meeting between the trade union and owners' association, the rate is also circulated in print form but the variance in the rate has been persisting for decades. What is amazing is that even in public policy, gender discrimination is not covert.[8] As one Government of India report (1986) documented, wages fixed by many state governments under Minimum Wage Act 1948 were much lower for women than men workers. During 1963, the State Acts of Andhra Pradesh, Madhya Pradesh, Kerala, Maharashtra, and West Bengal prescribed much lower rate of minimum wage for women in rice and dal mills and match factories (in West Bengal, the maximum rate for men was Rs 1.49 and for women Re 1 only).

The discrimination stems partly from women's unconcerned outlook towards their employment, as they are ready to work at whatever wage rate for supplementing the family income. Thus employers find it easy to exploit the situation. Somehow or the other, the employers have a preconceived notion that women workers are not as efficient as men. The common thread is that some employers are against employing women because of their perceived inefficiency. Some employers are apprehensive that by engaging women they will have to incur additional expenditure as on crèches. Some fear that the very presence

[8] Gender differentials are an almost universal phenomena. To cite one example, the Chinese Constitution envisions gender equality as its basic national policy, yet Chinese women workers do not enjoy the right to work as long as men, and get lower retirement benefits than their male counterparts. Women civil servants and government employees have to retire at the age of 55, five years earlier than men.

of women would breed unnecessary trouble on the labour front. Almost as a rule, women are employed as and when they come comparatively cheap and are ready to work in harsher conditions.

Apart from the wage discrimination, women have to confront sexual abuse. For the brick factories in Bihar and West Bengal it has been documented (Saran and Sandhwar 1990) that during working hours rebuking, beating, threatening, and molestation are not infrequent. Women are sometimes treated as private property of the owner/manager. Women cannot resist sexual exploitation. If they refuse they are gang raped or thrown out of factory work. They are kept naked during the night and their children are kept hostage so that they do not flee. The invidious extent of abuse in unorganized, seasonal, contractual employment is largely accounted for by the fact that in these sectors employers enjoy an unassailable position and often women workers have to satisfy the demands of employers.

The sexual abuses are partly due to the vulnerable position of women workers, they have to continue work under all constraints otherwise food security for their families will be at stake. Both employers and male workers nurture an antagonistic outlook towards women; the ingrained attitude perceives women as intruders in the job market who are taking away the employment opportunities (especially when the employment scope is gradually reducing). The outburst of such perceptions is sexual assault.

Another disconcerting trend is that with the modernization of economy and establishment of big industrial enterprises, women are being exposed more to the 'road to ruin' (literally). Sociological studies discern that cash crop export and high income lead to increasing number of wives (Nelson 1999). Dharmalingam (1995) documented yet another grim trend. With newly acquired wealth, brick factory owners resort to marrying more than once and also pursue illicit relationships with factory girls. The friends and followers of factory owners indulge in affairs with girls and abandon them subsequently. Because of money power owners and their cronies disregard the verdict of panchayat on illegal relations with girls. If any extramarital relation is reported they bribe the police to suppress the case.

TECHNOLOGICAL ADVANCEMENT AND EVICTION

Phenomenal changes in the production process due to technological improvements, globalization, and liberalization have precipitated a direct onslaught on the types of work and working conditions. More ominous is the fact that such adversities will probably become more intensified. Technological advancement has evicted women from their traditional jobs and put them in entirely new work environment, and technologies themselves have subverted women's concerns.

Studies have documented the nature and extent of expulsion of women from their conventional employment (that is, thrashing, fodder cutting etc.). The alternative job opportunities have not opened up at the same rate of displacement. While development endeavours have intensified the inequality between sexes (Giriappa 1988) mechanization has thrown out women because they in general do not have the required training and handling skill/expertise (Rao 1986). Women have disproportionately been vulnerable to the quantitative and qualitative impact of technological sophistication because of their low skill, and concentration in relatively small number of low-skilled and labour intensive jobs. Modernization of production process may have made the production task easier, reduced time spent on it and increased the output, but for women it has more nagging impacts. All skilled jobs and those associated with machines have become the preserve of males (Chowdhury 1993), in the process leaving the harder drudgery in the traditional sector to women. Thus women are being exploited both on conditions of work and on wage.

Eviction of women from their traditional occupations is no less considerable due to technological advancement (Kumari 1989). When a new technology is introduced to automate specific manual labour, women tend to lose the job—rice mills appropriate means of livelihood of women who used the traditional husking mechanism, mechanization in textile and garment industry has displaced a huge number of women workers. When grinding machines replace wheat grinding and weeding, women get evicted from those works. When bucket system of irrigation makes way for tube well and canal water, women are pushed out. In paddy cultivation, mechanization of operations like weeding and combined operation of harvesting, threshing, winnowing, and shelling displace women labourers (Rani and Mukherjee 1991).

Emerging employment opportunities including their technological part are more often dangerous for women. Construction work is a case fit for substantiation. The mixing machine may have lessened the labour of mixing mortar and facilitated more output in lesser time but women 'helpers' have to carry such mortar to higher levels of skyscrapers and act as helpers to masons on dangerously higher levels. Being thrown in the whirlwind of casual labouring, they have come under increasing control of masons and contractors. In the same vein, proliferation of small-scale chemical industries of various hues is one example where women workers have been exposed to hazardous work environment, unknown a few decades earlier.

Because of technological sophistication, cottage industries are becoming non-viable and redundant. Obsolescence of craft skill is forcing men to migrate to other jobs and move away from the family. For the men migration is not so difficult but for women lack of skill, capital, and steadfast gender division of labour prevent them from embarking on self-employment or venturing into activities like hawking—common to poor men. At the same time, migration of men delegates the responsibilities of the family and its survival struggle to the women.

Modernization of agriculture has transformed the economy by generating additional agricultural produce and raw materials for a growing number of agriculture-based industries. Introduction of modern methods in cultivation has resulted in gradual displacement of women, mechanization has squeezed their activities, and in fact shunted women workers. It has increased the extent of seasonal fluctuation in women's employment. 'Green revolution' and consolidation of landholdings force small landholders to casual wage labouring by dispossessing the land. And women bear the brunt. The conspicuous trend is that employment options for women agricultural workers are dipping and many women are forced to seek casual work in other sectors, having the tag of low wages and low productivity. It has also been substantiated that the thrust of technology has no concern for women. In agriculture, subsistence crops are the concern of women but sufficient research attention has not been paid to such crops (Chambers 1982).

Women's workforce participation rate is increasing not essentially because of their higher educational attainment or changing work attitude but because of transformation in the overall production process, including the technological and organizational framework. Because of globalization and liberalization, new employment opportunities have opened up. The location of enterprise and labour use pattern have been transformed drastically. Rising transaction cost of labour is forcing relocation of operations and a shift of the labour intensive part of production to countries with cheap labour. With the setting up of new units of production, low skill jobs are available and in this category women worker abound. The readiness of poor women to do any kind of work for the sheer survival of their family is precisely the cause of the availability of cheap women labour or a vast 'reserve army of labour' that Third World countries offer. Flexible, least organized labour is the prerequisite of these units and women are being absorbed precisely because they fit into the scheme of things.

New units are being run on cost effectiveness and unregulated marker conditions—higher working hours, piece rate or contract work without any attention to working condition or social security. Uncertain employment, exploitative wage, oversight to working conditions, low income syndrome, flexible labour laws, and unorganized trade unions are some features of the unfolding production process. Flexible labour market with unfettered power of the employers to hire and fire workers according to the vagaries of market is likely to create problems for millions of Indian workers particularly when India has a high degree of labour surplus.

With globalization women may get more jobs but what they are really getting are more casual in nature or jobs that men do not prefer. Moreover, job squeeze, retrenchment, and casual employment are a few emerging dimensions of the labour market. When the male breadwinner loses his secure employment, the economic condition of family will worsen and this will sooner or later aggravate the plight of women. As women bear the brunt of poverty and are more concerned with maintaining the living standard of the family, any impoverishment of the family will affect women more adversely than men.

Incessant Ordeal

In a sense, the sordid saga of the Indian women workers is not surprising. The invisibility, undermining on the employment front is an index of their social status. Much of the agony is the extension or replication of their subjugated social life.

Domestic and social values ensconce Indian womenfolk into the four walls of family. A well entrenched socio-cultural milieu reiterates that women should only undertake household chores. In taking up wage earning activities they have been compelled to, not eke out their own livelihood but to safeguard the family 'fortune'. They begin to work when the economic conditions of the family demand so and they are withdrawn when affluence returns. Particularly for rural women, there tends to be a closer correlation between economic conditions of the family and women's employment. Survival of the poorest of poor households depends on the concrete economic contribution of women members. They enter the job market when the men's earning becomes inconsistent, inadequate, or is suspended. Family control over their entry and exit limits women's flexibility in the labour market. Women thus become flexible workers more for the family than for the employer.

Between the sexes, given the option, employment is always preferred for men. Women's employment is seen largely in a complementary sense, with the objective of meeting the shortfall in the earnings of the family. Women are not considered as primary earning members, but merely as a back-up for emergencies. Their contribution may be crucial for the family, yet they are regarded as supplementary earners and temporary entrants into the labour market (Banerjee 1995). When a family can survive without women's contribution, women are withdrawn from the labour market. Such withdrawal tends to be an indicator of the economic status and a demonstration towards observance of higher caste norms, which is expected to help the family in moving upward in the caste hierarchy.

Domesticity ethos controls and constricts women's work. The normative values insist and often glorify the worth and entity of women only within the confines of family and this is buttressed and accentuated by the nature and scope of women's employment. There are different standards of behaviour for men and women in the social sphere and this is also carried on and reflected in the working world of women. Women are expected to be chaste, modest, and submissive and all these attributes colour and curb their ability to perform in the workplace on an equal footing as men.

Domestic responsibilities being sacrosanct, women tend to land in conflicting and often perplexing no-win positions. As women have primary obligations to the family, employment—outside employment in particular—puts irreconcilable pressures on them. They have to be good wives and good employees as well. Torn between two incompatible roles women suffer. As and when women devote time and energy to the demands of employment they find less time to pay attention to family liabilities which will invite the wrath of family members. If they are preoccupied with family responsibilities they will surely neglect career demands thus being dubbed negligent and inefficient employees. Reconciliation between the two conflicting roles is treacherous and whether and how women workers balance domestic and career demands will indicate their role and position on both fronts.

Career women have not been freed from, nor they can forgo their primary family responsibilities. There has not been any significant attitudinal change among husbands, family members, and the community towards working women. Social receptivity to women workers is still to come by (Bhoite 1987). There is also little change in the attitude towards women in and around the working place. Not surprisingly thus, women workers are being defeated by the dichotomous roles they play.

Being overburdened and by and large beaten, any expectation of positive results that employment can facilitate remains elusive for women. Because of non-responsive and non-accommodative family gesture, disparaging social reception, antagonistic work environment, and compulsion to join work for the cause and sake of family, women in general are far away from developing a rational, impersonal, formal, utilitarian world view, and from shaping an assertive personality and independence that the employment opportunity is capable of endowing. The net result is that gainful employment has not brought about any significant transformation in the lives of women, rather, it has dragged women to yet more stress.

A clear off-shoot of the domesticity ethos is the lower level of educational attainment of the womenfolk, which in essence bounds them to the lower rung of occupations. For girls, education is considered a mere means for increasing their value in the matrimonial market. Thus, skill attainment, which is imperative for modern and professional employment takes a backseat and this in turn restricts women to unskilled and manual work. Lack of required education and skill is pushing women towards agricultural wage labouring. The massive concentration of women in agricultural activities is not because of their deliberate preference but simply because they do not have any other option. An obvious lack of education, expertise, and the prevalent 'social ideology' debar women from competing for the few skilled or better opportunities up for grabs in modern industrial units. However, the mere attainment of higher education or professional skills is not likely to ameliorate their overall woes as the fructification of it depends in part on the available employment opportunities. Given the nature of the emerging employment scenario—'jobless growth', unregulated and informal employment—women have to bear the brunt of what all these imply. The Indian job market is most unlikely to cater to all job seekers, thus marginal works and subsistence struggle will remain inescapable for the vast majority of women.

Even when women's economic contribution is indispensable for family survival, they are regarded as second-rate workers, only helping the breadwinner. Employment may offer to males assertiveness, autonomy, or affluence but for women it is more abasement. Women have to confront all the odds at the workplace, including sexual harassment for the sake of their family. Modern employment has displaced them from the family-centred enterprises and thrown them into the vagaries of the 'world market'. They have come under increasing control of employers/contractors who practically dictate the place and type of work. Also the hard day's toil is subject to deduction as commission by those who help in arranging the employment. A new set of problems has besieged women. The work environment tends to be unsuitable for healthy living. Employers/mangers/contractors have found it easy to exploit and abuse women (particularly younger women) and women find it generally infeasible to resist because without employer's/contractor's will they can not earn wages and thus sustain living.

References

Agarwal, Bina (1985), 'Work Participation of Rural Women in Third World—Some Data and Conceptual Biases', *Economic and Political Weekly*, 21–28 December.

Banerjee, Nirmala (1995), 'Sexual Division of Labours; Myth and Reality in the Indian Context', in Josodhara Bagchi (ed.) *Indian Women, Myth and Reality*, Sangam Books, Hyderabad.

Bhoite, Anuradha (1987), *Women Employees and Rural Development*, Gian Publishing, New Delhi.

Chambers, Robert (1982), *Rural Development, Putting the Last First*, Orient Longman, New York.

Chandrasekhar, C.P. and Jayati Ghosh (2007), 'Recent Employment Trends in India and China: An unfortunate convergence?', Paper presented at ICSSR–IHD–CASS Seminar on Labour markets in India and China: Experiences and emerging perspectives, 28–30 March 2007, New Delhi.

Chowdhury, Prem (1993), 'High Participation, Low Evaluation, Women and Work in Rural Haryana', *Economic and Political Weekly*, 25 December.

Dev, S. Mahendra (2004), 'Female Work Participation and Child Labour: Occupational Data from NFHS', *Economic and Political Weekly*, 14 February.

Dharmalingam, A. (1995), 'Conditions of Brick Workers in South Indian Village', *Economic and Political Weekly*, 25 November.

Giriappa, S. (1988), 'Decision Roles of Women in Different Rural and Semi-urban Activities', *Journal of Rural Development*, April.

Government of India, Ministry of Labour (1986), *Socio-Economic Conditions of Women Workers in Manufacture of Chemicals and Chemical Products and Food Products Industries*, Labour Bureau, Chandigarh.

International Labour Organization (ILO) (2003), *Time for Equality at Work—Global Report under the Follow-up to the ILO Declaration on Fundamental Principles and Rights at Work*. Geneva.

Kumari, Sudha (1989), 'Women Workers in Unorganised Sector in India', *Yojana*, 1–15 July.

Mazumdar, Vina (1989), 'Peasant Women Organise for Empowerment. Bankura Experiment', Occasional Paper no.13, Centre for Women's Development Studies, New Delhi.

———(ed.) (1990), *Women Workers in India*, Chankya Publications, New Delhi.

Mandal, Amal (2004), *Women Workers in Brick Factory*, Northern Book Centre, New Delhi.

Miller, B. Barbara (1982), 'Female Labur Participation and Female Seclusion in Rural India: A Regional View', *Economic Development and Cultural Change*, Vol. 30, No. 4, pp. 777–94.

Mukhopadhyay, I. (2005), 'Economic Empowerment', in Jashodhara Bagchi (ed.) *The Changing Status of Women in West Bengal, 1970–2000: The Challenge Ahead*, Sage Publications, New Delhi, pp. 71–80.

National Commission on Labour (2002), *Report of The National Commission on Labour*, Ministry of Labour, Government of India, New Delhi, India.

Nelson, J. (1999), 'The Cultural Impact of Literacy', *Notes on Literacy*, Vol. 25, No. 3–4, pp. 1–10.

Nelson and Chowdhury (eds) (1999), *Women & Politics—World-wide*, Oxford University Press, New York.

Omvedt, Gail (1992), 'The Unorganised Sector and Women Workers', *Gurunanak Journal of Sociology*, April.

Rani, S. and A. Mukherjee (1991), ' Farm Mechanisation and Women in Paddy Cultivation', in R.K. Puniah (ed.) *Women in Agriculture*, Northern Book Centre, New Delhi.

Rao, Amiya (1986), 'Cost of Development Project: Women Among Willing Evacuees', *Economic and Political Weekly*, 21 December.

Roy, Debesh (2001), 'Role and Status of Women Workers in an Agro-industrial Context', *Man in India*. Vol. 81, No. 1 and 2.

Saran A.B. and A.N. Sandhwar (1990), *Problems of Women Workers in Unorganised Sector*, Northern Book Centre, New Delhi.

'Shramashakti', (1988), Report of the National Commission on Self Employed Women and Women in Informal Sector, Ministry of Human Resource Development, Government of India.

Sridhar, Lalitha (2003), 'Women Work the Land, but Do not Inherit It', *Info Change News and Features*, May.

Will Increasing Women's Power Reduce Discrimination against Girl Children in South Asia?

LISA C. SMITH and
ELIZABETH M. BYRON

5

INTRODUCTION

South Asia is the region with the most severe anti-female gender discrimination in the world. Among adults, it is manifested in strong gender differences in education levels, employment, and earnings (World Bank 2001). The region's high rates of maternal mortality (Adamson 1996) indicate a neglect of women's health care. While not all studies agree, many find that males are favoured in the allocation of food within households, especially when it comes to diet quality (Haddad et al. 1996; Chen et al. 1981; Bouis and Novenario-Reese 1997; Del Ninno et al. 2001; DeRose et al. 1998; Miller 1992).

Gender-based discrimination in the region is not limited to adults. Among children, boys are treated for illness more often than girls and immunization rates are higher for boys, indicating a relative neglect of girls' health needs (Haddad et al. 1996; Filmer et al. 1998; Arnold 1997; Ryland and Raggers 1998; Hazarika 2000). The most extreme son preference in the world is found in South Asian countries, whether stemming from economic considerations, such as sons' greater abilities to provide old-age economic support to parents or from deeply engrained traditions, such as dowry, which makes daughters a considerable cost at the time of marriage (Arnold 1997; Alderman and Gertler 1997; Rosenzweig and Schultz 1982). Perhaps the most disturbing manifestations of son preference are female infanticide (relatively rare) and an increasingly common 'high-tech' form of discrimination—sex-selective abortion—leading to 'natality inequality' between the genders (Sen 2001; Miller 2001). With these practices, girls' rights are violated before they are even born or shortly after, times when they are most vulnerable and innocent.

The end result of gender discrimination among both adults and children in South Asia is a high rate of excess female mortality, unnaturally low life expectancies for females relative to males, and population sex ratios skewed disproportionately in favour of males, the latter which documents at an aggregate level evidence of millions of 'missing women' in the region's population (Sen 1992; Klasen and Wink 2001).

Poor health among girls and women leads to low birth weight babies and continued health problems for both men and women, including increased incidence of cardiovascular disease later in life. Further, gender inequalities slow the pace of development by stalling economic growth and poverty reduction (Sen 2001; World Bank 2001). Reducing gender discrimination is not only a legitimate development outcome for equity reasons, it would benefit the regions' overall social and economic development in many ways.

While women's decision making power within the households, where most of the decisions about care for children take place, is known to be lower than that of their husbands, women are the main caretakers of children in South Asia as across the developing world. Past studies have demonstrated that when this power is increased women use it to direct household resources towards improving their caring practices for, and the health and nutritional status of, their children (for example Smith et al. 2003; Thomas 1997; Doss 1997; Kishor 2000; and Mencher 1988).

This study asks if increasing South Asian women's power is an effective force for reducing discrimination against girls. Will women use increased power to direct household resources towards equalizing the well-being of girls and boys? The measure used for examining gender discrimination among children is girl–boy comparisons of the nutritional status of 0–3 years old children. Nutritional status is the outcome of a child's nutrient intakes and health status, both of which are strongly influenced by the quality of care for children (UNICEF 1998).[1] The objective of the chapter is to determine whether increases

---

[1] 'Care' is defined as 'the provision in household and communities of time, attention, and support to meet the physical, mental, and social needs of the growing child and other household members' (ICN 1992). Examples of caring practices

in women's decision-making power relative to their husband's, will lead to greater improvements in a daughter's nutritional well-being than a son's, evidence that increasing women's power would serve to reduce gender inequalities not only among adults but in the next generation as well. The data employed are from nationally representative Demographic and Health Surveys (DHS) conducted in Bangladesh, India, Nepal, and Pakistan.

The next section reviews previous studies of the effects of parental power on investment in female and male children. In the following section, the data sets, measures of child nutritional status and women's power, and methods employed are discussed. Finally, the empirical results are presented and discussed, followed by concluding comments.

PARENTAL POWER AND GENDER DISCRIMINATION AMONG CHILDREN

Power is the ability to make choices. It is the ability of a person or group of people to define goals and pursue them, even in the face of opposition from others. It is exercised through decision making and can take the form of actual decisions made on one's own or made jointly with another person through a process of bargaining and negotiation. It can also take the form of deception and manipulation, resistance, violence, coercion, threat, or even 'non-decision making,' in which a person or group accepts the status quo as given without reflection or allows others to make a decision for them (Kabeer 1999; Riley 1997; Safilios-Rothschild 1982; Sen 1990). A person's control over resources, including economic resources, human resources, and social resources,[2] enhances her/his ability to exercise choice (Quisumbing and Maluccio 2003; Kabeer 1999; Sen and Batliwala 2000).

The question this study explores is whether increasing the power of women, relative to men, within households will bring about a reduction in discrimination against girls in South Asia. There are at least three circumstances under which such a reduction might be expected. First, if women's basic preferences are inherently altruistic

---

include breastfeeding, complementary feeding, and the utilization of health services and facilities to attend to health needs.

[2] Example of human resource is education; example of social resource is membership in groups.

towards all, regardless of gender, we would expect them to strive to provide equitable care to boys and girls given the ability to do so. Second, such a reduction might be expected if exposure to education, employment, and time spent outside of the home, which are common instigators of power shifts, bring increased consciousness on the part of women of gender inequalities and a subsequent growing sense of responsibility for reducing them among their own children. Finally, it might be expected if women and men have same-sex preferences, in which case women would actually favour their own gender and thus tend to allocate increased resources under their control towards girls.

While some may think it inevitable that women will take action to reduce gender discrimination against girls as their power increases, Sen (2001) questions this assumption. Pointing to Indian women's choices to use sex-selective abortion, he writes 'This face of gender inequality cannot ... be removed, at least in the short-run, by the enhancement of women's empowerment and agency, since that agency is itself an integral part of the cause of natality inequality' (p. 11). He points to the examples of East Asian countries, such as Singapore, Taiwan, China, and South Korea, where two traditional paths to reducing gender inequality, increased female education, and economic participation, do not appear to have reduced natality and mortality inequalities that favour males. These countries have even more male-skewed population ratios than those of South Asia.

Turning to the evidence from past empirical studies, most have explored parental investment patterns in children and have focused on control over resources as an indicator of power. Among these, a few have looked specifically at differences in parental investment, disaggregating both between resources controlled by mothers and fathers as well as investments in daughters and sons. Those that have undertaken these gender disaggregations have found mixed results.

Hallman (2000) finds that parental resource control, measured as control over current and premarital assets as well as transfers of assets at marriage, has different effects on child health in Bangladesh depending on the gender of the parent and of the child. Mothers' resources reduce morbidity of pre-school age girls while fathers' resources reduce morbidity of pre-school boys. The study thus detects same-sex preferences in the effect of parental resource control, suggesting that increasing women's power would reduce discrimination against girls.

Using data from four developing countries, Quisumbing and Maluccio (2003) test for differences in educational attainment of school-aged girls and boys associated with their mother's and father's education or assets controlled at the time of marriage. They find a pattern of same-sex preferences in Bangladesh, Ethiopia, and among households of Indian origin in South Africa. They find no evidence of gender preferences in Indonesia, but of opposite-sex preferences among African households in South Africa.

Similarly, while some earlier studies from across the developing world, as reviewed by Hallman (2000), find a pattern of same-sex preferences, others do not. Analysing data from urban Brazil, (Thomas 1997) finds that parents' individual non-labour income is associated with larger positive effects on the nutritional status of children of their same gender. Similarly, in Zambia, Wang (1996) finds that mothers' income improves infant girls' nutritional status while fathers' income improves that of infant boys. However, a study by Haddad and Hoddinott (1994) concludes that increases in women's share of household cash income in Côte d'Ivoire result in greater improvements in boys' nutritional status than in girls', evidence of opposite-sex preferences.

Godoy et al. (2003) test whether parents invest a variety of resources consistently in favour of children of one sex using panel data from an Amerindian group living in the Bolivian Amazon. The conclusion reached is that mothers and fathers do not invest resources consistently in favour of children of either sex. For example, fathers' cash earnings are found to benefit boys' nutritional status more than girls', but fathers' schooling and wealth benefit girls more than boys. In the Philippines, Quisumbing et al. (2004) find that parents invest resources differently by gender of their children, directing greater investment in education towards daughters and land inheritance toward sons.

In sum, a clear global pattern of gender discrimination in investment in children by mothers and fathers does not emerge from existing research. This is to be expected as the relative returns to parents from investing in boys and girls, for example, in the form of old-age support, as well as the degree of patriarchy in kinship systems, differ substantially across cultures and societies. With respect to South Asia in particular, while the two studies from Bangladesh, and that of households of Indian origin in South Africa, suggest same-sex preferences, no strong hypothesis as to the direction of the effect of women's power on discrimination among girls and boys can be advanced given the dearth of studies. The rest of this chapter attempts to fill this knowledge gap using a broad set of data covering multiple countries in the region.

DATA, MEASURES, AND METHODS

Data

This study employs data from DHS conducted in the 1990s in Bangladesh, India, Nepal, and Pakistan. These countries represent 97 per cent of the population of South Asia. The sample includes 33,316 children under three years of age and 30,334 women–husband pairs, usually the children's parents.[3] The country with the largest sample size, by far, is India (see Table 5.1). The DHS data sets are from nationally representative surveys of households with at least one woman 10 to 49 years of age.[4] Due to similar survey instruments and data collection methodologies, the data are largely comparable across countries.

Table 5.1: **Data sets and sample sizes**

	Name of survey	Year of collection	Number of children (< 3 years of age)	Number of women/ husbands
Bangladesh	DHS III	1997	2767	2633
India	NFHS II	1998	24,360	22,149
Nepal	DHS III	1996	3692	2349
Pakistan	DHS II	1991	2497	2203
Total from all countries			33,316	30,334

Source: Demographic and Health Survey during 1990s.

[3] Only children living in households containing both their mother and her husband are included, as is necessary for construction of the measure of women's relative decision making power. The percentage of women dropped from the sample because they did not meet this criteria is 1.2 per cent.

[4] The surveys are based on two-stage sample designs. In the first stage, enumeration units or 'clusters' are selected from larger regional units within countries. Following this, households are randomly selected within clusters (Macro International, Inc. 1996). The data are collected by various in-country research and statistical agencies with technical assistance from Macro International, Inc. and major funding from the United States Agency for International Development.

Table 5.2: Means of indicators and index of women's decision-making power relative to men

	Whether woman works for cash	Woman's age at first marriage	Age difference of woman and husband	Education difference of woman and husband	Index of women's relative decision-making power
	(yes=1)	(years)	(per cent)	(years)	(0–100)
India	0.165	17.6	-17.40	-2.48	34.5
Bangladesh	0.200	14.3	-26.39	-1.16	28.6
Nepal	0.071	16.2	-13.26	-3.17	33.7
Pakistan	0.107	17.9	-16.97	-3.11	35.8
South Asia	0.154	17.1	-17.98	-2.45	34.0

Source: Demographic and Health Survey during 1990s.

Measure of Child Nutritional Status

The measure of nutritional status employed is a child's height-for-age (HAZ), a long-term measure of nutritional well-being reflecting linear growth achieved both in-utero and during early childhood. Children who have a HAZ two standard deviations below the median (HAZ ≤ −2) of the National Centre for Health Statistics/World Health Organization (WHO) international growth reference (WHO 1995) are considered to be 'stunted.' A stunted child has likely suffered from long-term inadequate nutrition or poor health, or both.

Measure of Women's Relative Decision-making Power

The measure of women's decision-making power relative to their husbands used in this study is based on four indicators that are combined into an index using factor analysis. The indicators were chosen as part of a broader global study investigating the influence of women's status on child nutritional status in developing countries (Smith et al. 2003) and based on their conceptual relevance, their applicability across cultures, and their availability for a large number of developing countries.[5]

[5] The sample for creation of the index includes 133,555 women and their husbands from 40 countries in four developing regions: South Asia, sub-Saharan Africa, Latin America and the Caribbean, and the near East and North Africa.

In keeping with the multi-dimensionality of the concept of women's empowerment or status (Mason 1986; Jejeebhoy 2000; Sen and Batliwala 2000), one of the indicators is in the area of employment, one in the area of marriage, and two in the area of human capital (education and experience). A detailed discussion of the rationale for including each in the index of women's status is presented in Smith et al. (2003). The indicators are as follows:

+ whether the woman works for cash income (*workcash*, a dummy variable);
+ the woman's age at first marriage (*agemar*);
+ the percentage difference in the woman's and her husband's age (*agedif*); and
+ the difference in the woman's and her husband's years of education (*educdif*).

Table 5.2 reports the mean of each indicator by country. In the study sample, 15.4 per cent of women work for cash.[6] The average age at first marriage of the women in this study is 17.1 years, with the lowest in Bangladesh at 14.3 years.[7] In all the countries the typical woman is at an age and education disadvantage relative to her husband, with the average percentage difference in age being around 20 per cent[8] and with women having on average 2.5 less years of education than their husbands.

The factor analysis[9] yields an index of women's status (denoted *dm_index*) that is a linear combination of the four indicators as follows:

---

[6] Note that because the large majority of sample men do so, this indicator essentially captures women's cash earning *relative* to men's.

[7] Men's ages at first marriage are not reported in the DHS surveys so it is not possible to construct a relative measure of this indicator.

[8] The per cent difference (rather than the difference itself) controls for the age of the woman's husband, so that the same difference is given a higher value the lower the husband's age, basically giving this factor more importance for younger couples.

[9] Factor analysis is a 'data reduction' technique that reduces a set of observed variables that are hypothesized to be related to one another to a smaller number of unobserved, more fundamental constructs called 'factors'. It does so by detecting structure in the relationships among the observed variables as represented by their correlation matrix. For each identified factor, the analysis produces 'loadings', one for each variable, that are estimated drawing only on the *shared* variance of the variables. The loadings are the correlation between the observed variables and the factor. If, after examining the loadings, the hypothesis is borne out, then new variables (indices, or factor scores) that

$$dm\_index = 0.0701 * workcash + 0.3645 * agemar + 0.2832$$
$$* agedif + 0.1540 * educdif$$

where the values of the indicators are standardized values. Accordingly, *agemar* is given the greatest weight, followed by *agedif*, *educdif*, and lastly *workcash*. The final index is placed on a 0–100 scale for ease of interpretation in the regression analysis. The sample mean of the index is 34 (Table 5.2). It is the highest for Pakistan, followed by India and Nepal, and lowest for Bangladesh. Note for reference that the index value for Norway, in which women and men are amongst those with the highest degree of equality in power in the world today according to the above indicators, is 59.2 (Smith et al. 2003).[10]

Empirical Methodology

The central empirical task of this chapter is to investigate whether women's relative decision-making power has a different effect on child nutritional status for girls and boys. The technique used is to test for structural differences in the determinants of child nutritional status and their strength of association for girls and boys employing multivariate regression analysis. A country fixed-effects regression model is specified (Greene 1997).[11] In addition to the index of women's relative decision-making power, the independent variables, commonly included in studies of the socio-economic determinants of child nutritional status, are as follows:

+ the child's age (whether in the 1–2 or 2–3 years age group);
+ the woman's and her husband's education, measured as ordered

are linear combinations of the observed variables are estimated, based on the loadings. Note that the original observed variables are standardized before analysis so that their ranges and variations do not affect their index coefficients (Sharma 1996).

[10] Note also that a factor analysis index based only on the four South Asian countries of this study assigns roughly the same index numbers to women, having a correlation with the 40-country index of 0.97 (p=0.000).

[11] While a household or 'maternal' fixed effects analysis (Alderman, Hoddinott, and Kinsey 2003) would control for factors influencing child nutritional status at the household level other than those directly included as explanatory variables here, it is not possible to implement this approach. This is because even though a sufficient number of cases exist where a woman has two or more children of opposite sex under three years of age (N=2982 children), the explanatory variables employed, and most particularly women's status, do not vary across children in the same household.

dummy variables, with 'no education' being the reference category and indicator dummies for both primary and secondary education;

+ type of water use, with the reference category being surface water and dummy variables for well and piped water, reflecting increasingly safe water;
+ type of latrine use, with the reference category being no latrine and dummy variables for pit latrines and flush toilets indicating more sanitary facilities;
+ economic status, with households classified into four groups—destitute, poor, middle, and rich—based on consideration of two factors: the degree to which a household is able to satisfy the basic needs of its members using its own investments as opposed to public resources, and ownership of various assets;[12]
+ the child's parents' ages;
+ household age-sex composition; and
+ country of residence.

[12] The variables used to reflect whether basic needs are met are: a home with a finished floor, a home with a toilet facility of some kind, and access to water piped into the home. The assets are broken into two groups, those that are relatively cheap (radio, television, and bicycle) and those that are relatively expensive (refrigerator, motorcycle, and car). The classification is based on *numbers* of basic needs satisfied and cheap or expensive assets owned rather than on any specific type of need or asset in order to maintain cross-country comparability. The four groups and their definitions are as follows:

Destitute	Owns no assets and satisfies either none or only 1 basic need.
Poor	Owns no assets but satisfies 2 basic needs; or
	Owns only cheap assets and satisfies either none or only 1 basic need.
Middle	Owns only cheap assets and satisfies either 2 or 3 of the basic needs; or
	Owns at least one expensive asset but satisfies either none or 1 basic need.
Rich	Owns at least one expensive asset and satisfies 2 or 3 of the basic needs.

Here a 'destitute' household owns no luxury items at all and has an unfinished floor, no toilet facility, and water that is not piped into the home, or has satisfied just one of these needs. By contrast, a 'rich' household owns an expensive luxury asset, such as a refrigerator or motorized vehicle, and has satisfied all or almost all of the basic needs. The poor and middle groups fall in between (see Smith et al. 2003 for additional information).

All explanatory variables are assumed to be contemporaneously exogenous (that is, the model is a reduced-form model).[13]

The dependent variable, child nutritional status (denoted Y), is hypothesized to be determined by the child's sex and K explanatory variables, denoted X and indexed $k=1...K$, whose effects are possibly dependent on the child's sex. The cross-country model takes the form:

$$Y_{i_c} = \alpha + \beta_0 sex + \sum_{k=1}^{K} \beta_k X_{k,ic} + \mu_c + \sum_{k=1}^{K} \gamma_k X_{k,ic} sex + \mu_c sex + \upsilon_{ic}, \upsilon_{ic} \sim N(0, \sigma^2),$$

$$i = 1,....,n \; c = 1,....C$$

where i denotes children and c denotes countries. The μc are unobservable country-specific, household-invariant effects and the υ_{ic} are stochastic. Unbiased and consistent estimates of the β_k and γ_k can be obtained using ordinary least squares (OLS) estimation if the error term does not contain components that are correlated with an explanatory variable. The country effects are included to avoid any such bias emanating from country-specific factors that may be correlated with included explanatory variables.[14]

In the above equation, the coefficient of each explanatory variable for boys is given by β_k. That for girls is given by $(\beta_k + \gamma_k)$. If γ_k is statistically significant (at least at the 10% level), a significant difference in effect between girls and boys is detected. To determine whether the girl and

[13] While they are of course important determinants of child nutritional status, more 'proximal' determinants, such as caring practices and mother's nutritional status, are not included in the regression model. Including them would lead to biased estimation of the regression coefficients of the socio-economic determinants because they are themselves pathways through which the socio-economic determinants influence child nutrition. To illustrate, if we include mother's body mass index (BMI) in the regression equation, the coefficient on women's education would no longer represent the full association between education and child nutrition because of the presence of another independent variable (BMI) that is partially influenced by education.

[14] Because of the two-stage sample design of the DHS surveys, more than one household is sampled for each cluster. Thus the possibility that the error term will not be independently and identically distributed arises. Unobserved cluster-specific attributes will influence the outcome variables similarly for households living in the same cluster, leading to biased estimates of the parameter covariance matrix. Additionally, a Cook–Weisberg test (STATA 2001) indicates strong heteroskedasticity. Thus a robust covariance matrix is used to compute standard errors (and thus t-statistics).

boy coefficients are individually statistically significant, we estimate the following equation using the data only for girls and then only for boys:

$$Y_{ic} = \alpha + \sum_{k=1}^{K} \beta_k X_{k,ic} + \mu_c + \upsilon_{ic}.$$

The above regression analysis is conducted first for the entire four-country sample of children and then for the four countries individually, followed by a set of regressions run by age groups of children (0–1 year olds, 1–2 year olds, and 2–3 year olds) within countries.

EMPIRICAL RESULTS

In this section we first lay out the evidence on gender differences in child nutritional status and discuss their implications for the existence of gender discrimination. We then present the results of the regression analysis examining the relationship between women's power and gender discrimination among children.

Evidence on Gender Differences in Child Nutritional Status

Because of biological differences between girls and boys, gender bias—a behavioural phenomenon—as manifested in measures of physical well-being, often reveals itself not in comparing girls and boys directly, but in comparing differences between them to some norm. Boys are inherently more vulnerable to illness than girls as infants, even in an optimal health environment. Therefore, the first year of life (infancy), is characterized by excess male mortality. However, empirical evidence shows that in the 1–4 age group, gender differentials in mortality are normally insignificant. Thus, inferring gender bias in the 0–1 age group from mortality data requires examination of whether girl–boy mortality differentials are higher than the norm of a health-neutral environment (a differential less than zero), while inferring it in the 1–4 age group requires examination of whether the differentials are higher than (roughly) zero (Agnihotri 1999).

Inferring gender bias using anthropometry data requires the same sensitivity to (i) the comparison of gender differences with some norm; and (ii) differences in norms across age groups. To be sure, the measure employed in this study, the HAZ, already incorporates a comparison to a reference norm that takes into account biologically-based gender differences in growth. But in developing countries, even those without evidence of sex bias, similar to the pattern with mortality data, we see

Table 5.3: Nutritional status of girls and boys in South Asia, SSA, and LAC

(mean HAZ score)

	0–3 year olds		0–1 year olds		1–2 year olds		2–3 year olds	
	Girls	Boys	Girls	Boys	Girls	Boys	Girls	Boys
Developing Regions								
South Asia	−1.86	−1.81	−1.11	−1.15 ***	−2.21	−2.19	−2.26	−2.12 ***
SSA	−1.33	−1.44 ***	−0.60	−0.75 ***	−1.71	−1.84 ***	−1.82	−1.88 ***
LAC	−0.61	−0.69 ***	−0.32	−0.47 ***	−0.90	−0.97 ***	−0.61	−0.62
South Asian countries								
Bangladesh	−1.91	−1.93	−1.08	−1.11	−2.32	−2.33	−2.40	−2.34
India	−1.86	−1.79	−1.13	−1.16 **	−2.21	−2.18	−2.23	−2.07 ***
Nepal	−1.98	−1.93	−1.21	−1.26	−2.25	−2.21	−2.51	−2.34 **
Pakistan	−1.74	−1.81	−0.87	−1.03	−2.13	−2.16	−2.29	−2.31

Notes: *** and *** indicate that a two-sided t-test of the girl-boy difference is significant at 10% and 5% levels, respectively. Countries in SSA include: Benin, Burkina Faso, Cameroon, Central African Republic, Chad, Comoros, Côte d'Ivoire, Ghana, Kenya, Madagascar, Malawi, Mali, Mozambique, Namibia, Niger, Nigeria, Rwanda, Senegal, Tanzania, Togo, Uganda, Zambia, and Zimbabwe. Countries in LAC include: Bolivia, Brazil, Colombia, Dominican Republic, Guatemala, Haiti, Nicaragua, Paraguay, and Peru.
Source: Demographic and Health Survey during 1990s.

infant boys doing worse off than girls in nutritional status.[15] Given the above, the presence of anti-female gender bias in care for children, as reflected in gender differentials in nutritional status, would be detected when girls are doing the same or worse than boys, especially in the 1–4 age group. This is indeed the pattern revealed by the data from South Asia used in this chapter.

Table 5.3 first compares the children of South Asia with those of two other developing regions, sub-Saharan Africa (SSA) and Latin America and the Caribbean (LAC), both of which have been found to be sites of little gender discrimination among children (Arnold 1997). It shows that among 0–3 year olds as a group, boys have slightly lower long-term nutritional status than girls in both SSA and LAC. In comparison, while not statistically significant, the opposite pattern is found for South Asia: girls have slightly lower measures of nutritional status, on average, than boys.

The gender differences are more starkly revealed when examined by age group. Among 0–1 year olds of SSA and LAC we find a fairly strong difference in HAZ in favour of girls (the difference is 0.15 for both); for South Asia we also find a statistically significant difference in favour of girls, but it is much smaller (0.04). This suggests the presence of gender discrimination even among infants. For 1–2 and 2–3 year olds, SSA and LAC exhibit continued differences in favour of girls. However, in contrast, South Asia exhibits a pattern favouring boys. In the 2–3 years old group, the average HAZ for girls is less than that for boys by 0.14 a statistically significant difference.

Figure 5.1 illustrates the above, showing the relationship between age and the girl–boy HAZ difference graphically for South Asia, SSA, and LAC. In all regions we see a pattern where the girl advantage begins to drop off near the end of the first year. This is consistent with a reduction with age in the importance of the biological factors driving gender differences. What stands out is that in South Asia the girl–boy HAZ difference stays near zero and far below the other regions over most of the 0–3 age range, and actually drops below zero at 19 months. Curiously, in LAC the difference drops below zero as well, at 26 months.

---

[15] The latter is perhaps due to harsher living conditions than those facing the reference population, which exaggerates the gender difference attributable to biological male vulnerability.

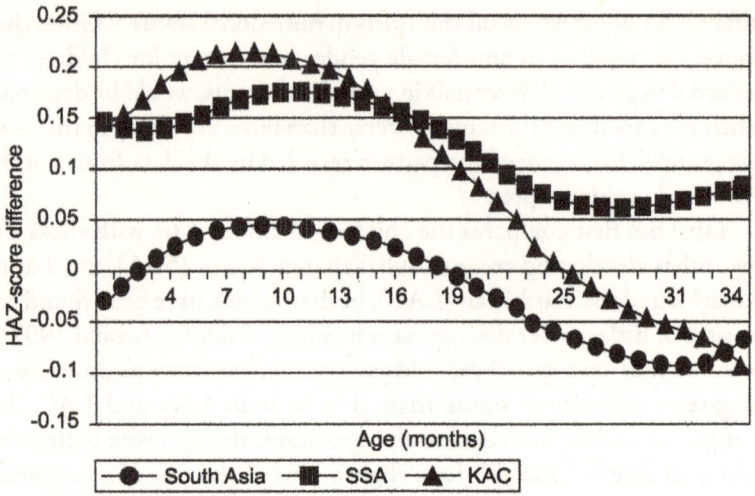

Notes: Generated using lowess smoothing of the average girl-boy difference in HAZ score over all sample children in the region-specific data sets (see notes to Table 5.3 for a list of countries).
Source: Authors' calculations.

Figure 5.1: Girl–boy difference in HAZ score
by developing country region and age

Returning to Table 5.3, the lower panel presents the mean HAZ for girls and boys from the four study countries. Among 0–1 year olds, the mean z-score for boys is consistently less than that for girls, though the difference is only statistically significant for India. Among 1–2 year olds, boy and girl z-scores are roughly equal. By 2–3 years of age, mean z-scores for girls are lower than for boys in Bangladesh, India, and Nepal, with the latter two countries displaying the biggest differences (0.16 and 0.17 z-scores, respectively), indicating the presence of anti-girl gender bias in caring practices. Pakistan stands out from the other three countries, displaying a particularly strong girl–boy difference in favour of girls among 0–1 year olds (0.16 z-scores) and no significant difference among 1–3 year olds, a pattern more consistent with those of SSA and LAC.[16]

---

[16] Note that this result is not consistent with the cultural patterns described in Hazarika (2000) and Miller (2001), who characterize Pakistan to be similar to North and West India when it comes to women's status and son preference.

The Relationship between Women's Power and Gender Discrimination among Children

Regression Results

Table 5.4 presents the results of regressions exploring the determinants of child nutritional status for girls and boys using the entire sample of children in the four countries combined while controlling for country of residence. Both boys' and girls' nutritional statuses are influenced by the major socio-economic determinants in the expected, positive direction: the child's mother's decision-making power relative to her husband, the child's parents' educations and ages, and the economic status, sanitary conditions, and size of the child's household. The only exception is for safe water use. The use of well and piped water (as opposed to surface water) appears to have a weak association with children's nutritional status. This brings into doubt the cleanliness of water, perhaps due to inadequate protection from human and animal waste or, as appears to be the case in Bangladesh, from groundwater toxins such as arsenic. The regression coefficients on the age dummy variables bring out the reduction in nutritional status after one year of age, typical in developing countries. Note that the pattern has a fairly strong gender difference: the age-related reduction for the 2–3 years old group is substantially greater for girls than boys (1.12 vs 0.95 z-scores).

Our main interest is in determining whether there is a gender difference in the effect of women's relative decision-making power on children's nutritional status. The test for parameter stability does indeed pick up on such a difference. Although it is not strongly statistically significant ($p=0.074$), its magnitude is fairly large. The estimated girl coefficient on the index of women's relative decision-making power is 50 per cent higher than the boy coefficient (0.018 vs 0.012). To give a sense of the practical significance of the regression coefficients and their difference, Figure 5.2 plots out the predicted HAZ for girls and boys as the index of women's relative decision-making power increases over its range. The increase in HAZ is large for both boys and girls, confirming that this variable has a strong influence on child nutritional status in the region, as found by Smith et al. (2003). In terms of the girl–boy difference, an increase in the index of women's decision-making power, relative to men, from its current level of 34 points to 61 points, almost double, would be required to bring about a girl–boy

Table 5.4: Determinants of child HAZ scores in South Asia:
girl–boy differences

Variable	Girls		Boys		p-value for difference (if significant)*
	coefficient	t-stat	coefficient	t-stat	
Women's relative decision-making power	0.018	7.45 ***	0.012	5.30***	0.074
Mother's education: primary	0.154	4.76 ***	0.160	5.11***	
Mother's education: secondary	0.275	6.22 ***	0.358	8.71***	
Father's education: primary	0.108	3.34 ***	0.151	4.72***	
Father's education: secondary	0.264	7.19 ***	0.269	7.95***	
Well water used	−0.098	−1.95 *	0.037	0.79	
Piped water used	−0.049	−0.94	0.071	1.46	0.083
Pit latrine used	0.169	4.70 ***	0.087	2.51**	
Flush toilet used	0.254	5.57 ***	0.205	4.85***	
Poor	0.064	2.18 ***	0.072	2.60***	
Middle	0.192	4.45 ***	0.183	4.42***	
Rich	0.383	6.79 ***	0.367	6.86***	
Child aged 1–2	−1.080	−37.98 ***	−1.018	−37.88***	
Child aged 2–3	−1.120	−37.09 ***	−0.951	−33.90***	0.000
Mother's age	−0.020	−4.30 ***	−0.016	−3.67***	
Father's age	0.019	5.63 ***	0.015	5.05***	
Household size	−0.011	−3.30 ***	−0.008	−2.31**	
Per cent females 15–55	0.006	3.99 ***	0.004	2.56**	
Per cent females 55+	0.003	1.50	0.003	1.62	
Per cent males 0–15	0.000	0.47	0.000	−0.01	
Per cent males 15–55	0.002	1.70 *	0.001	1.00	
Per cent males 55+	0.000	−0.01	−0.001	−0.86	
Bangladesh	−0.003	−0.06	−0.030	−0.62	
Nepal	0.067	1.67 *	0.117	2.99***	
Pakistan	−0.011	−0.21	−0.021	−.040	
Number of observations	15,967		17,349		
R-squared	0.185		0.159		

Notes: *, **, *** indicate that the coefficient is statistically significant at 10 per cent, 5 per cent and 1 per cent levels, respectively. All p-values are based on white-corrected standard errors and are robust to intra-cluster correlation. For variables constructed using more than one term (ordered dummy variables), the reported p-values are for a test of a jointly significant difference.

Source: Authors' calculations.

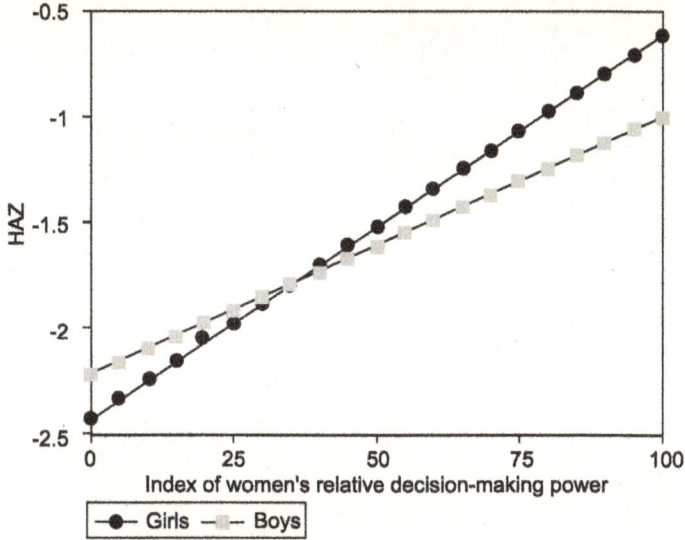

Source: Authors' calculations.

Figure 5.2: Predicted HAZ scores of girls and boys by index of women's relative decision-making power

difference roughly on par with that of SSA, for instance (which is 0.11 z-scores). Thus, for the South Asian region as a whole, the regression results imply that an increase in women's relative decision-making power—if quite substantial—would be an effective force for reducing gender discrimination against girls.

The top panel of Table 5.5 reports the regression results for the index of women's relative decision-making power for 0–3 year olds by country. The lower panel gives the results broken down by age group. Bold coefficients signify that the coefficient is statistically significant at the 10 per cent or lower level. For the 0–3 year olds as a group, the regression coefficients for Bangladesh and Nepal are not statistically significant. This could either indicate that women's relative decision-making power has no impact on child nutritional status in these countries, that the variation in this independent variable is not strong enough to pick up an impact if one indeed exists,[17] or that statistically

---

[17] An examination of the standard deviations of the index of women's relative decision-making power reveals that Bangladesh and Nepal have the lowest within-country variance. The standard deviations are:

India: 7.2, Bangladesh: 6.4, Nepal: 6.8, and Pakistan: 8.2.

Table 5.5: Girl–boy differences in the effect of women's relative decision-making power on children's HAZ scores by country and age group

Variable	Bangladesh			India			Nepal			Pakistan		
	Girl	Boy	p-value for difference (if significant)	Girl	Boy	p-value for difference (if significant)	Girl	Boy	p-value for difference (if significant)	Girl	Boy	p-value for difference (if significant)
0–3 years olds	−0.001	−0.000		0.018	0.016		0.008	0.007		0.025	0.005	0.064
Number of observations	1,372	1,395		11,574	12,786		1,800	1,892		1,221	1,276	
R-squared	0.262	0.237		0.175	0.147		0.238	0.208		0.249	0.212	
0–1 years olds	−0.015	0.027	0.027	0.006	0.011		0.013	0.004		0.042	0.012	
1–2 years olds	0.014	−0.030	0.022	0.028	0.018		−0.002	0.014		0.018	0.010	0.094
2–3 years olds	0.007	−0.010	0.022	0.019	0.020		0.014	0.008		0.014	0.003	

Notes: All p-values are based on White-corrected standard errors and are robust to intra-cluster correlation; Bold coefficients signify that the coefficient is statistically significant at 10% level of significance or lower level.
Source: Demographic and Health Survey during 1990s.

significant impacts among some population groups within these countries (for example, age or ethnic groups) are cancelling each other out at the aggregate level. In the case of Nepal, either of these could apply, and it is not possible to tell which.

For Bangladesh, after examining the results broken down by age group, it appears that the latter reason is applicable. For 0–1 and 1–2 year olds, we find that there is a significant difference ($p=0.022$) between the influence of women's relative decision-making power for girls and boys. Specifically, in the 0–1 group, the effect is strongly positive for boys but not significant for girls, indicating that improvements in women's power relative to men will lead to a worsening of gender discrimination against girls among infants. By contrast, in the 1–2 year group the effect is strongly negative for boys, remaining statistically insignificant for girls, suggesting that improvements in women's power will reduce discrimination against girls. However, the reduction would be brought about not through greater improvements in girl-child nutrition than boy-child, but through reductions in boy-child nutritional status. Of course this is not a desirable pathway for reducing discrimination against girls in a population group for which the average HAZ for both boys and girls is already below stunting classification (see Table 5.3).

The data from India reveal strong positive effects of women's relative decision-making power on children's nutritional status for both boys and girls but, for the country as a whole, no significant difference was seen between them for any of the age groups. The only country for which a significant gender difference in the influence of women's relative decision-making power can be detected is Pakistan, where anti-girl discrimination is weakest and women's relative power highest. Here the effect for girls 0–3 years is very strong and that for boys not statistically significant. The greater positive influence for girls is most apparent in the 0–1 age group.

Conclusion

The general conclusion reached from the empirical analysis of this chapter is that for the South Asia region as a whole, an increase in women's relative decision-making power—if substantial—would indeed be an effective force in reducing gender discrimination against girls. However, this finding is certainly not applicable everywhere and for all children in the region. Pakistan is the only country of the four studied for which there is strong evidence that an increase in women's power would benefit girls more than boys. While the finding does not apply for Bangladesh at the country level, it does apply for 1–2 years old Bangladeshi children. Furthermore, we find evidence that increases in women's relative decision-making power can be expected to worsen discrimination against infant (0–1 year old) girls in Bangladesh. Future research is needed to examine intra-country regional differences that may be masked by this national analysis, especially in India, where there is wide variation in cultural norms.

The lesson for policy makers and development practitioners is that while increasing women's power is likely to improve the well-being of children, it will not necessarily diminish the anti-girl discrimination that violates human rights and undermines the region's economic development and the health of its population. At the root of gender preference in favour of males are long-standing, deeply embedded, cultural and social influences, such as customs regarding marriage, caregiving, and inheritance (Sen 2001; Quisumbing and Maluccio 2003). These influences act as constraints to reducing discrimination against females which increases in women's power may not be sufficient to overcome. Writes Sen (2001, p. 15): 'When anti-female bias ...reflects the hold of traditional masculinist values from which mothers themselves may not be immune, what is needed is not just freedom of action, but also freedom of thought—in women's ability and willingness to question received values'. The challenge for policy makers wishing to reduce discrimination against girls through increasing women's power, then, is to combine empowerment with interventions that address the underlying cultural constraints and promote and protect such freedom of thought.

REFERENCES

Adamson, P. (1996), 'A Failure of Imagination. (Comment on Women: Maternal Mortality)', in *The Progress of Nations*, United Nations Children's Fund, New York, pp. 10–21.

Agnihotri, S.B. (1999), 'Inferring Gender Bias from Mortality Data: A Discussion Note', *Journal of Development Studies*, Vol. 35, No. 4, pp. 175–200.

Alderman, H. and P. Gertler (1997), 'Family Resources and Gender Differences in Human Capital Investments: The Demand for Children's Medical Care in Pakistan', in L. Haddad, J. Hoddinott, and H. Alderman (eds), *Intrahousehold Resource Allocation in Developing Countries: Models Methods, and Policy*, Johns Hopkins University Press, Baltimore, pp. 231–48.

Alderman, Harold, John Hoddinott, and Bill Kinsey (2003), 'Long-term Consequences of Early Childhood Malnutrition', Food Consumption and Nutrition Division Discussion Paper No. 168, International Food Policy Research Institute. Washington DC.

Arnold, F. (1997), 'Gender Preferences for Children', Demographic and Health Surveys, Comparative Studies No. 23, Macro International Inc., Calverton, MD.

Bouis, H. and M.J.G. Novenario-Reese (1997), 'The Determinants of Demand for Micronutrients: An Analysis of Rural Household in Bangladesh', Food Consumption and Nutrition Division Discussion Paper No. 32 International Food Policy Research Institute, Washington, DC.

Chen, L., E. Huq, and S. D'Souza (1981), 'Sex Bias in Family Allocation of Food and Health Care in Rural Bangladesh', *Population and Development Review*, Vol. 7, pp. 55–70.

Das Gupta, M. , J. Zhenghua, L. Bohua, X. Zhenming, W. Chung, and B. Hwa-Ok (2003), 'Why is Son Preference so Persistent in East and South Asia? A Cross-Country Study of China, India, and the Republic of Korea', *The Journal of Development Studies*, Vol. 40, No. 2, pp. 153–87.

Del Ninno, C., P.A. Dorosh, L.C. Smith, and D.K. Roy (2001), 'The 1998 Floods in Bangladesh: Disaster Impacts, Household Coping Strategies, and Response', *IFPRI Research Report* No.122, International Food Policy Research Institute, Washington, DC.

DeRose, L., E. Messer, and S. Millman (1998), 'Who's Hungry? And How Do We Know?: Food Shortage, Poverty, and Deprivation', United Nations University, Tokyo.

Doss, C. (1997), 'The Effects of Women's Bargaining Power on Household Health and Education Outcomes: Evidence from Ghana', Economics Department, Williams College Williamstown, MA.

Filmer, D.E., M. King, and L. Pritchett (1998), 'Gender Disparity in South Asia: Comparison Between and Within Countries', Policy Research Working Paper 1867, Development Research Group, Poverty and Human Resources, The World Bank, Washington, DC.

Godoy, R., W.R. Leonard, E. Byron, V. Reyes-García, V. Vadez, T. Huanca, and K. Patel (2003), 'Do Parents Use Investment Resources Consistently to Favour Children of One Sex? A Methodological Contribution to the Measure of Intra-Household Girl-Boy Discrimination with Data from an Amazonian Society', Draft Paper, Brandeis University, Waltham, MA.

Greene, W.H. (1997), *Econometric Analysis*, Third edition, Prentice-Hall, Upper Saddle River, NJ.

Haddad, L. and J. Hoddinott (1994), 'Women's Income and Boy-Girl Anthropometric Status in the Côte d'Ivoire', *World Development*, Vol. 22, No. 4, pp. 543–53.

Haddad, L. C. Peña, C. Nishida, A. Quisumbing, and A. Slack (1996), 'Food Security and Nutrition Implications of Intrahousehold Bias: A Review of Literature', Food Consumption and Nutrition Division, Discussion Paper No. 19, International Food Policy Research Institute, Washington, DC.

Hallman, K. K. (2000), 'Mother–Father Resource Control, Marriage Payments, and Girl–Boy Health in Rural Bangladesh', Food Consumption and Nutrition Division Discussion Paper No. 93. IFPRI, Washington, DC.

——(2003), 'Mother–Father Resources, Marriage Payments, and Girl–Boy Health in Rural Bangladesh', in A. R. Quisumbing (ed.), *Household Decisions, Gender, and Development: A Synthesis of Recent Research*, IFPRI, Washington DC.

Hazarika, G. (2000), 'Gender Differences in Children's Nutrition and Access to Health Care in Pakistan', *The Journal of Development Studies*, Vol. 37, No. 1, October, pp. 73–92.

ICN (International Conference on Nutrition) (1992), Caring for the Socioeconomically Deprived and Nutritionally Vulnerable, Major Issues for Nutrition Strategies', Theme Paper No. 3. ICN/92/INF/7, Food and Agricultural Organization of the United Nations and World Health Organization, Rome.

Jejeebhoy, S. (2000), 'Women's Autonomy in Rural India: Its Dimensions, Determinants, and the Influence of Context', in H. Presser and G. Sen (eds), *Women's Empowerment and Demographic Processes*, Oxford University Press, Oxford.

Kabeer, N. (1999), 'Resources, Agency, Achievements: Reflections on the Measurement of Women's Empowerment', *Development and Change*, Vol. 30, pp. 435–64.

Kishor, S. (2000), 'Empowerment of Women in Egypt and Links to the Survival and Health of Their Infants', in H. Presser and G. Sen (eds), *Women's Empowerment and Demographic Processes*, Oxford University Press, Oxford.

Klasen, S. and C. Wink (2001), 'A Turning Point in Gender Bias in Mortality?: An Update on the Number of "Missing Women"', Discussion Paper 2001–13, October, Department of Economics, University of Munich.

Macro International, Inc. (1996), *Sampling Manual*, DHS III Basic Documentation No. 6, Macro International, Inc., Calverton, MD.

Mason, K. (1986), 'The Status of Women: Conceptual and Methodological Issues in Demographic Studies', *The Eastern Sociological Society*, Vol. 1, No. 2, pp. 284–300.

Mencher, J. P. (1988), 'Women's Work and Poverty: Women's Contributions to Household Maintenance in South India', in D. Dwyer and J. Bruce (eds), *Women at the Center: Development Issues and Practices for the 1990s*, Stanford University Press, Stanford, CA, pp. 99–119.

Miller, B. (1992), 'Gender Discrimination in Intrahousehold Food Allocation in South Asia: Debates and Dilemmas', Paper Presented at the 1992 Meetings of the American Anthropological Association, 2–6 November, San Francisco, CA.

——(2001) 'Female-Selective Abortion in Asia: Patterns, Policies, and Debates', *American Anthropologist*, Vol. 103, No. 4, pp. 1083–95.

Murthi, M., A. Guio, and J. Drèze (1995), 'Mortality, Fertility, and Gender Bias in India: A District-Level Analysis', *Population and Development Review*, Vol. 21, No. 4, December, pp. 745–82.

Pal, S. (1999), 'An Analysis of Child Malnutrition in Rural India: Role of gender, Income, and Other Household Characteristics', *World Development*, Vol. 27, No. 7, July, pp. 1151–71.

Quisumbing, A.R. and J.A. Maluccio (2003), 'Resources at Marriage and Intrahousehold Allocation: Evidence from Bangladesh, Ethiopia, Indonesia, and South Africa', *Oxford Bulletin of Economics and Statistics*, Vol. 65, No. 3, pp. 283–328.

Quisumbing, A.R., J.P. Estudillo, and K. Otsuka (2004), *Land and Schooling: Transferring Wealth Across Generations*, Johns Hopkins University Press for IFPRI, Baltimore, MD.

Riley, N. (1997), 'Gender, Power, and Population Change', *Population Bulletin*, Vol. 52, No. 1, pp. 2–46.

Rosenzweig, M.R. and T.P. Schultz (1982), Market Opportunities, Genetic Endowments, and Intrafamily Resource Distribution: Child Survival in Rural India', *The American Economic Review*, Vol. 72, No. 4, pp. 803–15.

Ryland, S. and H. Raggers (1998), 'Childhood Morbidity and Treatment Patterns', Demographic and Health Surveys Comparative Studies No. 27, Macro International Inc., Calverton, MD.

Safilios-Rothschild, C. (1982), 'Female Power, Autonomy and Demographic Change in the Third World', in R. Ankar, M. Buvinic, and N. Youssef (eds), *Women's Roles and Population Trends in the Third World*, Croom Helm, London.

Sen, A. (1990), 'Gender and Cooperative Conflicts', in I. Tinker (ed.), *Persistent Inequalities: Women in World Development*, Oxford University Press, Oxford, pp. 123–49.

———(1992), 'Missing Women', *British Medical Journal*, Vol. 304, pp. 586–7.

——— (2001), 'Many Faces of Gender Inequality', *Frontline*, Vol. 18, Issue 22, 27 October–9 November, Available at *http://www.flonnet.com/f11822/18220040.htm*.

Sen, G. and S. Batliwala (2000), 'Empowering Women for Reproductive Rights', in H. Presser and G. Sen (eds), *Women's Empowerment and Demographic Processes*, Oxford University Press, Oxford.

Sharma, S. (1996), *Applied Multivariate Techniques*, John Wiley & Sons, Inc., New York.

Smith, L.C., U. Ramakrishnan, A. Ndiaye, L. Haddad, and R. Martorell (2003), 'The Importance of Women's Status for Child Nutrition in Developing Countries', IFPRI Research Report No. 131, International Food Policy Research Institute, Washington, DC.

STATA (2001), Stata Statistical Software: Release 7.0 Stata Corporation, College Station, TX.

Thomas, D. (1997), 'Income, Expenditures, and Health Outcomes: Evidence on Intrahousehold Resource Allocation', in L. Haddad, J. Hoddinott, and H. Alderman (eds), *Intrahousehold Resource Allocation in Developing Countries: Models, Methods, and Policy*, Johns Hopkins University Press, Baltimore, MD pp.142–64.

United Nations Children's Fund (UNICEF) (1998), *The State of the World's Children 1998*, Oxford University Press, New York.

Wang, M. (1996), 'Gender Differences in Intrahousehold Resource Allocations: An Empirical Analysis of Child Health in Zambia', Department of Economics, George Washington University, Washington, DC.

World Bank (2001), 'Engendering Development Through Gender Equality in Rights, Resources, and Voice', World Bank Policy Research Report, The World Bank, Washington, DC.

World Health Organization (WHO) (1995), 'Physical Status: The Use and Interpretation of Anthropometry'. WHO Technical Report Series No. 854, World Health Organization, Switzerland.

Maternal Literacy and Child Malnutrition in India

VANI K. BOROOAH _____ 6

INTRODUCTION

A recurring theme in the literature on the welfare of children in developing countries is the importance of having literate parents and, in particular, of having a literate mother. There is a body of evidence to suggest that the number of children born to a woman is inversely related to her level of education (Borooah 2000, 2002). Furthermore, there is considerable evidence to suggest that children's health (including the likelihood of their surviving infancy and childhood), nutritional status, and educational attainments are enhanced by having better educated parents, particularly the mother (Behrman and Wolfe 1984; Thomas, Strauss, and Henriques, 1991; Sandiford et al. 1995; Lavy et al. 1996; Ravallion and Wodon 2000; Gibson 2001). Evidence also suggests that a farm-household's total income depends upon the highest education level reached by a household member rather than by the mean educational level of the household or by the educational level of the household head (Foster and Rosenzweig 1996). To add to this litany, education also raises the wages of both men and women (Kingdon and Unni 2001).

Overlaying this theme is another, more recent, theme relating to the nature of literacy. This argues that some of the disadvantages to a person of being illiterate may be mitigated if he/she lives in a household in which other members are literate since, for many activities, having access to the ability of the literate members to read and write may serve as a form of 'surrogate' or 'proximate' literacy. In that sense, an illiterate person living with a literate person(s) may not, by virtue of his/her illiteracy, be so badly off as an illiterate person living in a household in which all are illiterate since, in the former situation, he/

she is 'proximate literate' while in the latter situation, he/she is illiterate (Basu and Foster 1998).

A final twist to the concepts of 'literacy', 'proximate literacy', and 'illiteracy' is provided by Basu, Narayan, and Ravallion (2002) who argue that the fact that literate household members are able to confer the benefit of 'proximate literacy' on their illiterate cohabitants gives them a certain 'power' in the process of decision-making within the household. Consequently, while household income might be higher when some household members are literate, than when all the members are illiterate, the intra-household distribution of income may be more to the disadvantage of the illiterate members when there are literate members present than when all in the household are illiterate. Consequently, whether proximate literacy benefits the illiterate household members depends on the trade-off between the size of household income and its distribution between the members.

Against this background, the purpose of this study is, first, to use unit-record data on over 50,000 rural children, from 16 major states of India, to analyse the determinants of malnutrition. The data provide anthropometric measures (height-for-age and weight-for-age) for each of the children and relate this information to inter alia: the household circumstances of the children, including the quality of living conditions of the household and the birth order of the children; the circumstances of the mothers; the quality of the relevant infrastructure available to the households in which the children live, with particular reference to the quality of the water supply and the availability of hospitals and mother-and-child centres (known in India as *anganwadis*); and the degree of 'food security' that the children's households enjoy.

These data are based on unit record data from a survey of 33,000 rural households—encompassing 195,000 individuals—spread over 1765 villages in 195 districts in 16 states of India. This survey, commissioned by the Indian Planning Commission and funded by a consortium of United Nations agencies, was carried out by the National Council of Applied Economic Research (NCAER) over January–June 1994 and most of the data from the survey pertain to the year prior to the survey, that is to 1993–4. Details of the survey, hereafter referred to as the NCAER Survey, are to be found in Shariff (1999), though some of the salient features of data from the NCAER Survey, insofar as they are relevant to this study, are described here.

The importance of studying the determinants of malnutrition, particularly in the context of children in India, derives from the fact that the prevalence of under-nourishment in India, even relative to other poor countries, is shockingly high. Thus in the 1990s, 36 per cent of children in India below the age of five, compared to 21 per cent in SSA were severely stunted;[1] and 49 per cent of women between the ages of 20–29 years in India, compared to 21 per cent in SSA had a body mass index (BMI) of less than 18.5[2] (Svederberg 2001). Compounding the suffering that underlies statistics such as these is the 'silence with which it is tolerated, not to mention the smugness with which it is sometimes dismissed' (Sen 2001). This study, therefore, represents an attempt to disturb this quietude.

The second feature of this study obtains from Caldwell's (1993) observation—made in the context of the cultural, social, and behavioural determinants of health in developing countries—that the educational attainments of women of maternal age had the strongest correlation with health success (measured in terms of life expectancy and rates of infant mortality) and that the task of health transition research was to 'explore the mechanics whereby good health was achieved in poor countries and to suggest interventions in other countries based on this knowledge'.

In conjunction with this precept, this study explores, in the context of India, the mechanics whereby parental literacy in general, but maternal literacy in particular, affects the likelihood of children being malnourished. It does so by allowing the effects of some of the variables, which influence the likelihood of children being malnourished, to vary according to the literacy status of the mothers. Children, in this study, were distinguished according as to whether their mothers were:

+ literate;
+ 'proximate' literate, that is mother illiterate but father literate;
+ illiterate, that is mother and father illiterate.

An important feature of this study is an examination of whether the channels of influence, running through a particular determinant of

[1] Meaning that their HAZ was below three standard deviations of the WHO norm.
[2] The BMI for a person is defined as the weight (in kilograms) divided by the square of the height (in metres). Adults with a BMI of less than 18.5 are considered to be chronically energy deficient.

malnutrition, were different for these three different types of maternal literacy.

In so doing, this study follows in the footsteps of Thomas, Strauss, and Henriques (1991), who studied the relation between maternal education and the height of children in Brazil; Sandiford et al. (1995), who studied the interaction between maternal literacy and access to health services affecting the health of children in Nicaragua; Lavy et al. (1996) who examined the relation, for Ghana, between the quality and accessibility of health care, on the one hand, and, child survival and child health outcomes, on the other; and Gibson (2001), who measured the size of the intra-household externality, arising from the presence of literate members in the household, on height-for-age outcomes for children in Papua New Guinea.

However, this study differs in at least three essential respects from this corpus of work. First, and most obviously, it is a study of India—perhaps, the first study of child malnutrition in India based on unit record data—where, as noted above, the incidence of child malnutrition, both in terms of severity and in terms of numbers involved, is particularly acute. Indeed, as Shariff (1999) observes, 'there is scope to undertake a comprehensive analysis of the determinants of malnutrition among children in India' (p. 96). Second, it examines the relationship between the circumstances of mothers and the likelihood of their children being undernourished. This resonates with the argument, recently made by Osmani (2001), that the undernourishment of children in India begins in the womb and can be traced to discrimination against women. Third, it focuses on the influence of household food security—as measured by the size of a household's food stocks and its access to fair price shops—on child malnutrition. This issue is particularly important today in India because there has been a progressive dismantling of the fair price shop system where households could buy food at subsidized prices. Indeed, it is ironical that the very system of higher producer prices that has resulted in a record stockpile of 62 million tonnes of food grains in India has kept food away from the reach of poorer consumers.

The fact that children from different (parental) literacy backgrounds had different health outcomes could be due to the beneficial effects of literacy per se but it could also owe to the fact that inter-children differences in (parental) literacy backgrounds were reflected in differences between the children in the quality of their 'health-friendly' environment. If, for example, household income was a significant determinant of health outcomes and literate persons were more likely to have higher incomes than illiterate persons, then one would expect to see differences in health outcomes between children with literate and illiterate parents without any appeal to the role of literacy in influencing these outcomes. Call this the 'attribute effect'. On the other hand, children, faced with the same health-related environment, might have different health outcomes simply because literate parents were better at turning a specific environment to their children's advantage than were parents who were illiterate. Call this the 'literacy effect'. The health outcome for children is, of course, the consequence of an amalgam of both effects. The crucial task is then to estimate, after disentangling the two effects, the relative contributions of attribute and literacy effects on the health outcomes of children in India.

MODEL SPECIFICATION

As Thomas, Strauss, and Henriques (1991) have observed, models of child health outcomes have attempted to integrate the biomedical approach—which views health outcomes in terms of a production process into which several factors enter as inputs—with a model of the family (Becker 1981). This results in reduced form of child health functions being estimated. Underlying these reduced forms is the assumption that households maximize a quasi-concave utility function—which depends on consumption, leisure, and the quantity and quality of children—subject to a household budgetary constraint, individual time constraints, and the constraint of the child health production function (Behrman and Deolalikar, 1988). The inputs entering into the production function are inter alia: the child's diet (including the length of breastfeeding and the age at which the child is introduced to supplementary foods); the quality of health-related infrastructure (including the quality of the water supply and the availability of medical attention and dietary advice); and the level of sanitation in the home.

In this model, the demand for child health (H_i) will depend upon the vector of child characteristics (X_i); the vector of household or parental characteristics pertaining to the child (W_i); and the relevant community characteristics vector (V_i). Consequently,

$$H_i = H(X_i, W_i, V_i)$$

$$(6.1)$$

The NCAER Survey provided data on two anthropometric measures for the health outcomes of children (between the ages of 0–12 years) in the sample.

1. Height-for-Age defined as: $S_i^* = (h_i - \mu_h)/\sigma_h$ where h_i is the height of the child; μ_h is the age and sex specific reference median height;[3] and σ_h is the standard error of the distribution of heights.

2. Weight-for-Age defined as: $R_i^* = (w_i - \mu_w)/\sigma_w$ where w_i is the weight of the child; μ_w is the age and sex specific reference median weight;[4] and σ_w is the standard error of the distribution of weights.

Following from these measures, a child is regarded: as 'severely stunted' when $S_i^* < -3$ and 'mildly stunted' when $-3 \le S_i^* \le -2$; as 'severely underweight' when $R_i^* < -3$ and 'mildly underweight' if $-3 \le R_i^* \le -2$ (World Health Organization 2000).

Using the anthropometric data, the binary variables, S_i and R_i were defined as follows:

1. $S_i = 1$ if $S_i^* < -3$ (child is severely stunted), $S_i = 0$, otherwise.
2. $R_i = 1$ if $R_i^* < -3$ (child is severely underweight), $R_i = 0$, otherwise.

Hereafter, the terms 'stunting' and 'underweight' are used in this chapter to mean 'severe stunting' and 'severely underweight'.

Next, the bivariate probit model was specified as:

$$S_i = \alpha_0 + \alpha_0^P + \alpha_0^L + \sum_{j=1}^{J} \alpha_j z_{ij} + \sum_{j=1}^{J} \alpha_j^P (PX_i * z_{ij}) + \sum_{j=1}^{J} \alpha_j^L (ML_i * z_{ij}) + \varepsilon_i^h$$

$= 1$ if $S_i^* \le -3$, $S_i = 0$, otherwise;

$$R_i = \beta_0 + \beta_0^P + \beta_0^L + \sum_{j=1}^{J} \beta_j z_{ij} + \sum_{j=1}^{J} \beta_j^P (PX_i * z_{ij}) + \sum_{j=1}^{J} \beta_j^L (ML_i * z_{ij}) + \varepsilon_i^w$$

$= 1$ if $R_i^* \le -3$, $R_i = 0$, otherwise;

(6.2)

where:

- z_{ij} is the value of the jth determining variable for the ith child ($j = 1...J$, $i = 1...N$);

---

[3] National Centre for Health Statistics (NCHS) standards.
[4] NCHS standards.

$PX_i=1$, if the child's mother is illiterate, but the father is literate (that is, the mother is proximate literate), $PX_i=0$, otherwise;

+ $ML_i=1$, if the child's mother is literate, $ML_i=0$, otherwise;
+ ε_i^b and ε_i^w are the error terms, such that:

$$E(\varepsilon_i^b) = E(\varepsilon_i^w) = 0;\ \text{Var}(\varepsilon_i^b) = \text{Var}(\varepsilon_i^w);\ \text{cov}(\varepsilon_i^b) = \text{cov}(\varepsilon_i^w) = \rho\ .$$

The specification of the model as a bivariate probit allows the error terms to be correlated within the context of a binary dependent variable.

The coefficients α_j and β_j in equation (6.2) are the coefficients on the jth determining variable for children whose both parents are illiterate; the coefficients α_j^P and β_j^P in equation (6.2) represent the additional effect (over α_j and β_j) of the jth variable that arises for children whose mother is 'proximate' literate; and the coefficients α_j^L and β_j^L in equation (6.2) represent the additional effect (over α_j and β_j) of the jth variable that arises for children whose mothers are literate.

Measuring Literacy Effects

Three scenarios were constructed in order to quantify the effects of community on the likelihood of children being stunted and underweight. In the first, 'all illiterate' (I), scenario: all the N children in the stunting and underweight equations were assumed to have illiterate parents. In the second, 'all proximate literacy' (P) scenario: all the N children were assumed to have illiterate mothers and literate fathers and in the third, 'all-literate' scenario (L): the mothers of all the N children were assumed to be literate. If p_i^k and q_i^k ($k= I, P, L$) represent the (estimated) probabilities of a child being, respectively, stunted and underweight, then the difference between the p_i^k (and between the q_i^k) across the scenarios is entirely due to differences in maternal literacy status since nothing was changed between the three scenarios except the literacy status of the mothers.

The mean values of the p_i^k and q_i^k, denoted respectively as p^k and q^k, may be termed the average 'literacy-determined' probabilities of being, respectively, stunted and underweight and $\lambda^k = p^I - p^k$ and $\mu^k = q^I - q^k$ may be termed as the 'literacy determined' probability surpluses (of being, respectively, stunted and underweight) of children with illiterate mothers over children with mothers who are literate ($k=L$) or who are 'proximate literate' ($k=P$). If $\bar{p}^k$ and $\bar{q}^k$ are the observed proportions of children, with mothers in literacy status k

$(k=I, P, L)$ who are, respectively, stunted and underweight, then the observed probability surpluses (of children with illiterate mothers over children whose mothers are literate or proximate literate) of being stunted (Ωk) and underweight (Φ^k) can be decomposed as:

$$\Omega^k = \bar{p}^I - \bar{p}^k = \bar{p}^I - p^I + p^I - p^k + p^k - \bar{p}^k$$

$$= p^I - p^k + [(\bar{p}^I - p^I) - (\bar{p}^k - p^k)] = \lambda^k + \pi^k \text{ where: } k = P, L$$

$$\Phi^k = \bar{q}^I - \bar{q}^k = \bar{q}^I - q^I + q^I - q^k + q^k - \bar{q}^k$$

$$= q^I - q^k + [(\bar{q}^I - q^I) - (\bar{q}^k - q^k)] = \mu^k + \psi^k \text{ where: } k = P, L \tag{6.3}$$

The terms π^k and ψ^k in equation (6.3) can be interpreted as the 'attribute-determined' probability surpluses of children with illiterate mothers over children with mothers who are either literate $(k=L)$ or 'proximate literate' $(k=P)$. If $\pi^k = 0$, then $\Omega^k = \lambda^k$ and the observed probability surplus (of being stunted) is equal to the 'literacy-determined' surplus. But if $\pi k \neq 0$, then $\Omega^k \neq \lambda^k$: interposing between the observed and the 'literacy-determined' surpluses is the effect of differences between children with illiterate mothers and children with mothers who are literate/proximate literate in their respective endowments of the other factors which affect the likelihood of being stunted. If $\Omega^k > \lambda^k$ (that is, $\pi k > 0$), these attribute differences add to the literacy-determined surplus; on the other hand, if $\Omega^k < \lambda^k$ $(\pi^k < 0)$, these differences subtract from the literacy-determined surplus.

THE DATA AND EQUATION SPECIFICATION

The data used for estimating the bivariate probit equations, whose dependent variables were described above, were obtained from the NCAER survey, referred to earlier.

As observed earlier, the vector of determining variables z_i for the ith child $(i=1...N)$ could be partitioned into those which related to: the child's characteristics (X_i); the child's household or parental characteristics (W_i); and the characteristics of the community within which the child lived (V_i).

The child's characteristics were specified in terms of the following variables.

1. sex=1 if the child was female.
2. age and age². Even though, the dependent variable controls for the age of children, Gibson (2001) and Thomas and Strauss (1992)

have pointed to the importance of including age as an explanatory variable. The square of age was included in order to allow for possible non-lineararity in the effect of age on the likelihood of being stunted/underweight.

3. The age (in months) at which the child had been introduced to solid foods (*sfa*). The expectation was that the later the age, the higher the probability of being stunted/underweight.
4. The age (in months) till which the child had been breastfed (*bmk*). The expectation was that the later the age, the lower the probability of being stunted/underweight.

The household parental characteristics were specified in terms of the following characteristics.

1. Whether the child's mother was literate (*ML*), proximate literate (*PX*), or illiterate.
2. The spacing of the mother's pregnancies (*spg*), defined as the number of years married divided by the number of pregnancies.
3. The age of the mother at marriage (*agm*).
4. The birth order of the child (*bod*).
5. The sex of the head of household (*hsex*=1, if head was female).
6. Whether women in the household were empowered: *emp*=1, if a female member of the household, at least 1–2 days per week: read a newspaper, or listened to the radio, or watched television.
7. Whether the household was a poor household: *pov*=1, if household income was BPL.[5]
8. The size of the household's food stocks in kgs (*fst*).
9. Whether the household had access to a fair price shop: *fps*=1, if it did.
10. The existence and quality of a toilet in the house: *tol*=1, if there was either no toilet in the house or it was manual.
11. The quality of housing condition of the household: *phs*=1, if housing conditions were poor, defined as an absence of a separate kitchen, with no ventilation while cooking, with food being cooked on an open charcoal/wood burning stove (*chula*).

The community level characteristics were defined in terms of the following:

---

[5] The NCAER Survey provided information on the incidence of household poverty.

1. Whether the household had access to safe drinking water: *water*=1, if it was not safe.[6]
2. Whether the household had easy access to a hospital or a sub-station: *hsp*=1, if it did have such access.[7]
3. Whether there was an anganwadi in the village: *angw*=1, if there was. Anganwadis are village-based early childhood development centres. They were devised in the early 1970s as baseline village health centres, their role being to: (i) provide government-funded food supplements to pregnant women and children under five; (ii) work as an immunization outreach agent; (iii) provide information about nutrition and balanced feeding, and provide vitamin supplements; (iv) run adolescent girls' and women's groups; and (v) monitor the growth, and promote the educational development, of children in a village.

Table 6.1 shows the distribution of some of these characteristics across the 53,207 children analysed. Of the 53,207 children, between the ages of 0–12 years, that were analysed, 43 per cent were stunted and 9 per cent were underweight (that is their z-scores<−3). Of the children that were underweight, 81 per cent were stunted and, of the children that were stunted, 16 per cent were underweight. The incidence of stunting and of being underweight was lower for girls than it was boys: 42 per cent versus 44 per cent for stunting and 7 per cent versus 10 per cent for being underweight.

The incidence of stunting and of being underweight was also lower for children with literate mothers (40 per cent and 7 per cent) than it was for children whose mothers were illiterate or proximate literate. However, there was no difference in the incidence of stunting and of being underweight between children whose mothers were illiterate and those whose mothers were proximate literate. Of the total number of children, 27 per cent had literate mothers, 30 per cent had mothers who were proximate literate, and the remainder (43 per cent) had illiterate mothers.

In addition to benefiting from having literate a mother, children also benefited from living in households where at least one of the women

[6] If the household's source of drinking water was from ponds, running streams, or wells.

[7] Defined as a hospital within 5 km of the household's village and/or a sub-station within the village.

Table 6.1: Selected data for severely stunted and severely underweight children (0–12 years)

	% children stunted	% children underweight
All children (53,207)	43	9
All boys (27,765)	44	10
All girls (25,442)	42	7
Mother literate	40	7
Mother proximate literate	44	9
Mother illiterate	44	9
Households with poor toilets	43	9
Households with adequate toilets	40	6
Households with poor cooking facilities	44	10
Households with adequate cooking facilities	42	7
Household head female	38	6
Household head female	43	9
Households with empowered females	42	8
Households with not empowered females	44	10
Poor household	44	9
Non-poor household	42	8
Households with access to fair price shops	42	8
Households without access to fair price shops	47	9
Households with unsafe water	44	10
Households with safe water	42	8
Hospital within 5 km	42	8
No hospital within 5 km	45	9
Anganwadi in village	42	8
No Anganwadi in village	44	9

Source: NCAER Survey.

was empowered (in the sense defined earlier) and, in particular, they benefited from living in households headed by a female. Women were empowered in 47 per cent of households and 4 per cent of households were headed by a woman. Living in a poor household (22 per cent of children lived in poor households) also raised the incidence of being stunted and of being underweight. However, the fact of living in a household without access to a fair price shop made an even bigger impact on these two incidences than did living in a poor household: the incidence of stunting was 47 per cent among children living in households without access to a fair price shop, as compared to 42 per cent for children living in households that did have access to such shops.

Differences in living conditions were reflected in differences in the incidence of stunting and being underweight: a higher proportion of children living in households with poor toilet facilities and with poor cooking facilities were stunted and underweight than children who did not live in similarly handicapped households.[8]

The provision of infrastructure—by way of safe drinking water, hospitals, and anganwadis—reduced the incidence of both stunting and being underweight, safe drinking water had the biggest impact on the incidence of being underweight while the presence of anganwadis in villages and relatively easy access to hospitals had the biggest impact on the incidence of stunting.

ECONOMETRIC RESULTS

The results from estimating the bivariate probit model (set out in equation [6.2]), using as determining variables those delineated in the previous section, are shown in Table 6.2 with the equation statistics shown in Table 6.3. The first thing to note from Table 6.3 is that the null hypothesis, of no correlation between the error terms of the stunting and the underweight equations, could not be accepted; the correlation coefficient was estimated to be 0.48. This suggests that it was, indeed, more appropriate to estimate the equations as a system of seemingly unrelated equations rather than to estimate them individually.

Table 6.2: Bivariate probit estimates of the stunting and underweight equations

	Stunting	Underweight
Age	−0.1466115	−0.564651
	(19.42)	(4.44)
Age2	0.0067737	−0.0158592
	(12.23)	(11.53)
Sex	−0.0534501	−0.3194747
	(4.83)	(17.57)

(*Contd.*)

[8] Eighty-eight per cent of children lived in households with poor toilet facilities and 50 per cent of children lived in households with poor cooking facilities.

(Table 6.2 *Contd.*)

Birth order	0.0109082	0.0241039
	(3.20)	(4.95)
Birth order * milt	−0.0111094	−
	(1.83)	−
Sex of hoh	−0.0828648	−0.1057504
	(2.88)	(1.95)
Age at solid foods intake	0.0136627	0.0434836
	(2.88)	(8.71)
Age till given breast milk	−0.0373337	−0.0225344
	(6.42)	(3.62)
Poor household	0.0160976	0.0451513
	(1.18)	(2.10)
Unsafe drinking water	0.0196769	0.0624639
	(1.58)	(3.17)
Easy hospital access	−0.0260958	−
	(2.02)	−
Easy hospital access * ml	−0.0547708	−0.0910527
	(2.43)	(3.21)
Anganwadi in village	−0.0224904	−
	(1.76)	−
Anganwadi in village*px	−	−0.0714305
	−	(2.77)
Anganwadi in village*ml	−0.063942	−
	(2.78)	−
Stock of food grains	−0000242	−
	(2.02)	−
Access to fair price shop	−0.0810994	−
	(4.14)	−
Poor housing	−	0.074794
	−	(4.01)
No vaccination	0.0326996	−
	(1.15)	−
Females empowered	−0.031174	−0.0633504
	(2.65)	(3.29)
Mother's spacing of pregnancies	−0.0068982	−
	(2.31)	−
Mother's age at marriage	0.0026539	−
	(1.28)	−
Intercept	0.51055	−0.7175276
	(9.93)	(19.06)

Notes: z-values in parentheses. Birth order * denotes the interaction effect of birth order and mother's literacy status.
Source: NCAER Survey.

Table 6.3: Equation statistics—stunting and underweight equations

Number of Observations	53,207
Wald Test: $\chi 2(34)$	5509.29
Estimate of ρ	0.4818963
LR test of $\rho=0$: $\chi 2(1)$	1871.84

Source: NCAER Survey.

A positive coefficient estimate in Table 6.2 indicates that the likelihood of being stunted/underweight increases, while a negative coefficient estimate in Table 6.2 indicates that the likelihood of being stunted/underweight decreases, for an increase in the value of the associated variable. A variable, which was not an interaction term (that is, was of the form, z_i), was included in the estimated equation if the z-score associated with its coefficient was greater than 1; on the other hand, interaction terms (of the form: $z_i \times PX_i$ or $z_i \times ML_i$) were included only if they were significantly different from zero at a 10 per cent level of significance.

The main conclusions that emanate from the estimated bivariate probit model (Table 6.2) may be summarized as follows, all the results being reported on a ceteris paribus basis.

1. The likelihood of being stunted and underweight was lower for girls than for boys. In this connection, Lavy et al. (1996) also reported that the height-for-age and the weight-for-age were lower for male children in Ghana; on the other hand, Gibson (2001) did not find any significant gender difference between the height-for-age of children in Papua New Guinea.

2. The higher the birth order of a child, the greater the likelihood of it being stunted/underweight. To the best of our knowledge the importance of birth order to child malnutrition has not been previously considered in the literature.

3. Children living in female-headed households were less likely to be stunted/underweight than children living in male-headed households. Again, Lavy et al. (1996) reported that the height-for-age and the weight-for-age of children were higher for female-headed households.

4. The later a child was introduced to solid foods, the greater the likelihood of it being stunted/underweight; on the other hand, the longer it was breastfed, the smaller the likelihood of it being

stunted/underweight. As Bellamy (1998) concludes 'a child must have complementary foods at the six-month point ... delaying the switch-over [from breast milk] can cause a child's health to falter' (p. 28). On the other hand, as she goes on to say, 'exclusive breast feeding for the first six months provides the best nourishment and protection from infection' (p. 29).

5. Household poverty had no significant effect on the likelihood of a child from that household being stunted, but it did significantly raise the likelihood of a child from that household being underweight. This is consistent with some studies but not with others: Lavy et al. (1996) reported that in Ghana 'expenditure as a measure of resource availability is not a significant determinant of child height' though Gibson (2001) found there to be a significant relation between per capita household expenditure and children's height-for age in Papua New Guinea.

6. The size of a household's stock of food-grains and its access to a fair price shop were inversely related to the likelihood of a child from that household being stunted, but neither variable had an effect on the likelihood of being underweight. Smith and Haddad (2000) in a cross-country analysis using country-level data emphasized the role of food security for ensuring good nourishment. Our results confirm, but also refine, this result in the Indian context.

7. Poor housing conditions—in the sense of poor cooking conditions—affected the likelihood of being underweight but not the likelihood of being stunted. Thomas et al. (1991) also emphasized the importance of housing conditions for child malnutrition in Brazil and argued that 'children are shorter in communities which rely on rudimentary sewage systems' (p. 207).

8. Children from households with one, or more, 'empowered' females, defined earlier, were less likely to be stunted and to be underweight than children from other households. Again, Thomas et al. (1991), in the context of Brazil, emphasized the importance of women's access to information through reading newspapers, watching television, and listening to the radio. This is equally true in India.

9. The greater the spacing of a mother's pregnancies, the less likely it would be that her children were stunted. Most studies do not (cannot) relate children's nutritional outcomes to the medical

history of the mother. This study is a small exception: even though data on the medical past of the mother is sketchy, the results are able to point to the importance of foetal malnutrition (caused by births following each other too closely) on child development.

Among these effects, there were three instances where the influence of a variable varied according to the literacy of the mother.

1. Although the likelihood of a child being stunted/underweight increased with its birth order, the effect of birth order on stunting, compared to a situation in which the mother was illiterate, was moderated when the mother was literate, though not when the mother was proximate literate.

2. The presence of anganwadis in a village and the easy access to hospital facilities both reduced the likelihood of stunting, even when the mothers were illiterate; however, the reduction in this likelihood, flowing from the presence of these facilities, was particularly marked when the mothers of the children were literate.

3. Easy access to hospitals only reduced the likelihood of children being underweight when their mothers were literate; the presence of village anganwadis only reduced the likelihood of children being underweight when their mothers were literate or proximate literate, the influence of literacy being stronger than that of proximate literacy.

Findings (2) and (3), above, are consistent with, and indeed, corroborate, Caldwell's (1993) observation that, in the context of developing countries, three areas are of critical importance to a child's health. First, an educated mother assumes the responsibility of taking a sick child to a health centre; by extension, educated mothers, more than illiterate mothers, take advantage of the advice and information on child care and health available from anganwadis. Second, the time that mothers spend discussing their child's illness with a doctor is almost directly proportional to their level of education: in consequence, illiterate women (and their sick children) get much less out of visiting a doctor than do literate women. Last, when a currently prescribed course of treatment for a child proves to be ineffective, illiterate mothers, relative to literate mothers, are less inclined to report this to their doctor. Collectively, these observations imply that the effectiveness of health care organizations to child health is enhanced when their services are complemented by mothers who are literate.

THE EFFECT OF MATERNAL LITERACY ON STUNTING AND LOW WEIGHT

Table 6.4 shows the effect of maternal literacy on the likelihood of children being stunted and being underweight. The first column of Table 6.4 suggests that if all the 53,207 children in the sample had had literate mothers, then the likelihood of their being stunted and being underweight would have been, respectively, 40 per cent and 7 per cent. In terms of the notation of the third section, these are the estimated values of p^L and q^L of equation (6.3). The observed sample proportions of children with literate mothers who were stunted and who were underweight are shown parenthetically in Table 6.4. The numbers in parentheses are the $\bar{p}^k$ and $\bar{q}^k$ of equation (6.3). As Table 6.4 shows, $p^L = \bar{p}^L$ and $q^L = \bar{q}^L$, the conclusion is that children with literate mothers did not have any 'attribute' advantage over other children.[9]

Table 6.4: Likelihood of children being severely stunted and underweight under different maternal literacy scenarios

Literacy Scesnario→ Probability of ↓	Mother Literate	Mother Proximate Literate	Mother Illiterate
Stunted	40	44	44
	(40)	(44)	(44)
Underweight	7	8	9
	(7)	(8)	(9)

Note: Figures in parentheses represent sample proportions.
Source: NCAER Survey.

In the notation of equation (6.3), $\pi^L = \psi^L = 0 \Rightarrow \Omega^L = \lambda^L; \Phi^L = \mu^L$. If children with literate mothers had had an attribute advantage/ disadvantage over the other children, then their 'maternal literacy' advantage would have been boosted/dampened by their attribute advantage/disadvantage leading to, in the case of attribute advantage, the observed likelihoods $\bar{p}^k$ and $\bar{q}^k$ being less than the corresponding 'synthetic' likelihoods, p^L and q^L.

A similar conclusion holds with respect to children whose mothers were, respectively, proximate literate and illiterate. In both instances,

---

[9] 'Attribute' here means the collective of non-literacy related attributes.

the sample proportion of children, in these categories, who were stunted and underweight were the same as the likelihoods that would apply when all the children had mothers who were proximate literate/illiterate. In the notation of the third section: $p^P = \bar{p}^P$ and $q^P = \bar{q}^P$; $p^I = \bar{p}^I$ and $q^I = \bar{q}^I$ so that: $\pi^k = \psi^k = 0 \Rightarrow \Omega^k = \lambda^k; \Phi^k = \mu^k, k = P, I.$

However, as Table 6.4 indicates, children whose mothers were illiterate had a literacy-determined surplus (in their likelihood of being stunted/underweight) over children whose mothers were literate: this surplus amounted to 4 percentage points (pp). By contrast, children whose mothers were illiterate did not suffer any disadvantage, relative to children whose mothers were proximate literate: since $p^I = p^P$, the literacy-determined surplus of children with illiterate mothers, over children with proximate literate mothers, was zero.

This last finding harks to the trade-off—to which Basu, Narayan, and Ravallion (2002) drew attention—that illiterate persons in households containing literate individuals could face, between higher family income but lower individual shares. Basu, Narayan, and Ravallion (2002) found a positive externality associated with proximate literacy—after controlling for other variables, an illiterate household member earned significantly more in the non-farm sector in Bangladesh when there were literate household members present than when there were not. So indeed did Gibson (2001), in the context of children's HAZ in Papua New Guinea: he concluded that the size of the externality provided by literate, to illiterate, members through proximate literacy was large. By contrast, this study's conclusion is that while, in general, the empowerment and the position of women in the household and, in particular, the literacy of mothers, was important for reducing the risk of children being stunted or underweight, maternal illiteracy exercised the same degree of influence, whether or not the father of the child was literate.

THE PROVISION OF HEALTH CARE FACILITIES AND THE RISK OF STUNTING AND LOW WEIGHT

Earlier, the point was made that the effectiveness of the supply of health care facilities, on reducing the likelihood of children being stunted and being underweight, depended upon whether or not the mothers of these children were literate. This issue is quantified in this section. The basic counterfactual situation considered was one in which every village had both an anganwadi and also easy access to hospital facilities.

This basic counterfactual situation was then combined with three possible counterfactual scenarios relating to maternal literacy: (i) all the mothers were literate; (ii) all the mothers were proximate literate; and (iii) all the mothers were illiterate as shown in Table 6.5.

Table 6.5: Effects of health care facilities on stunting and low weight

	All Villages Have an Anganwadi and Also Easy Access to Hospital Facilities		
	All mothers literate	All mothers proximate literate	All mothers illiterate
Likelihood of children being stunted	38	43	43
Likelihood of children being underweight	6	8	9

Source: NCAER Survey.

Table 6.5 shows the likelihood of children being stunted and being underweight when the supply-side counterfactual scenario was combined with each of three demand-side scenarios. This shows that when all mothers were literate, the universal provision, to every village, of an anganwadi and of easy access to hospital facilities would lower the risk of stunting to 38 per cent (from the sample average of 43 per cent) and the risk of being underweight to 6 per cent (from the sample average of 8 per cent). This reduction is the consequence of improved health care facilities meeting universal maternal literacy. When, however, improved health care facilities were met by universal maternal proximate literacy or by universal maternal illiteracy, the likelihood of being stunted was 43 per cent (which coincidentally was also the sample proportion). The benefits of improved facilities were negated by losing the advantage in having (some) literate mothers when they were universally replaced by mothers who were proximate literate or illiterate. (The likelihood of being underweight was slightly lower when all mothers were assumed to be proximate literate than when they were assumed to be illiterate because of the presence, in the underweight equation, of the interaction term between anganwadis and proximate literacy).

CONCLUSION

This chapter employed a bivariate probit model to estimate equations for risk of rural children in India being stunted and being underweight.

Estimating the equations as a system, allowed the estimation process to take account of the correlation between the unobserved error terms of the two equations, as was seen, this correlation was considerable. In so doing, this study of child malnutrition in India—employing unit record data for over 50,000 children—represents a rare, if not the only, countrywide analysis for India based on individual data.

A particular feature of interest was the role of maternal literacy in reducing the risk of child malnutrition and, more specifically, the channels through which this risk reduction might operate. The results indicated that literate mothers made more effective use of health care institutions than illiterate mothers. This national finding is conceptually consistent with an earlier result from Caldwell et al. (1983) that young mothers in South India, who had been to school, were more likely to demand of their husbands and mothers-in-law that a sick child be treated. This finding, it was argued, meant that the effectiveness of supply-side factors (more hospitals, more anganwadis) also depended upon the effectiveness with which the users employed such institutions. In particular, the value of such institutions to children would be considerably enhanced if the end-users, in the form of the children's mothers, were literate.

More generally, the study pointed to the importance of the role that women played within the household. Households that were headed by women or those in which the women had access to information—through newspapers, radio, and television—would have better-nourished children than households in which women were not empowered. Sadly, the study reported that, when it came to the nutritional well-being of the children, the literacy of the father was a poor substitute for the literacy of the mother. In order to reduce the risk of children in India being stunted or underweight it was far more important that the mothers be actually literate than simply have literate husbands. This is the central conclusion of this chapter.

REFERENCES

Basu, K. and J. Foster (1998), 'On Measuring Literacy', *Economic Journal*, Vol. 108, pp. 1733–49.

Basu, K., A. Narayan, and M. Ravallion (2002), 'Is Literacy Shared between Households?', *Labour Economics*, Vol. 8, pp. 649–65.

Becker, G. (1981), *A Treatise on the Family*, Harvard University Press, Cambridge.

Behrman, J.R. and B.L. Wolfe (1984), 'The Socioeconomic Impact of Schooling in a Developing Country', *Review of Economics and Statistics*, Vol. 66, pp. 296–303.

Behrman, J. and A. Deolalikar (1988), 'Health and Nutrition', in H. Chenery and T.N. Srinivasan (eds), *Handbook of Development Economics*, North-Holland, Amsterdam.

Bellamy, C. (1998), *The State of the World's Children, 1998*, Oxford University Press, Oxford.

Borooah, V.K. (2000), 'The Welfare of Children in Central India: Econometric Analysis and Policy Simulation', *Oxford Development Studies*, Vol. 28, pp. 263–87.

——(2002), 'Births, Infants and Children: An Econometric Portrait of Women and Children in India', *Development and Change* (forthcoming).

Caldwell, J.C. (1993), 'Health Transition: The Cultural, Social and Behavioural Determinants of Health in the Third World', *Social Science and Medicine*, Vol. 36, pp. 125–35.

Caldwell, J.C., P.H. Reddy, and P. Caldwell (1983), 'The Social Component of Mortality Decline: An Investigation in South India Employing Alternative Methodologies', *Population Studies*, Vol. 37, pp. 185–205.

Foster, A.D. and M.R. Rosenzweig (1996), 'Technical Change and Human Capital Returns and Investments: Evidence from the Green Revolution', *The American Economic Review*, Vol. 86, pp. 931–53.

Gibson, J. (2001), 'Literacy and Intra-household Externalities', *World Development*, Vol. 29, pp. 155–66.

Kingdon, G.G. and J. Unni (2001), 'Education and Women's Labour Outcomes in India', *Education Economics*, Vol. 9, pp. 173–95.

Lavy V., J. Strauss, D. Thomas, and P. de Vreyer (1996), 'Quality of Health Care, Survival and Health Outcomes in Ghana', *Journal of Health Economics*, Vol. 15, pp. 333–57.

Osmani, S.R. (2001), 'Hunger in South Asia: A Study in Contradiction' *The Little Magazine*, Vol. 2, pp. 35–40.

Ravallion, M. and Q. Wodon (2000), 'Does Child Labour Displace Schooling? Evidence on Behavioural Responses to a Enrolment Subsidy in Bangladesh', *Economic Journal*, Vol. 110, pp. 158–76.

Sandiford, P., J. Cassel, M. Montenegro, and G. Sanchez (1995), 'The Impact of Women's Literacy on Child Health and its Interaction with Health Services', *Population Studies*, Vol. 49, pp. 5–17.

Sen, A.K. (2001), 'Hunger: Old Torments and New Blunders', *The Little Magazine*, Vol. 2, pp. 9–13.

Shariff, A. (1999), *India Human Development Report*, Oxford University Press, New Delhi.

Smith, L.C. and L. Haddad (2000), *Explaining Child Malnutrition in Developing Countries*, International Food Policy Research Institute, Washington, DC.

Svederberg, P. (2001), 'Hunger in India: Facts and Challenge', *The Little Magazine*, Vol. 2, pp. 26–34.

Thomas, D., J. Strauss, and M-H Henriques (1991), 'How Does Mother's Education Affect Child Height', *The Journal of Human Resources*, Vol. 26, pp. 183–211.

Thomas, D. and J. Strauss (1992), 'Prices, Infrastructure, Household Characteristics and Child Height', *Journal of Development Economics*, Vol. 39, pp. 301–31.

World Health Organization (2000), *Nutrition in South-East Asia*, WHO, New Delhi.

Gender, Poverty, and HIV Transmission in India[†]

KOUMARI MITRA _____ 7

INTRODUCTION

The HIV/AIDS pandemic is broader than a mere health issue: it is more a symptom of poverty, inequity between the rich and poor, high incidence of illiteracy, and a general lack of access to social services (CIDAs HIV/AIDS Action Plan 2001). Earlier, the expert consensus was that India had the most HIV cases in the world at a staggering 5.7 million and that numbers could rise further in the absence of effective intervention strategies. More recently, the National AIDS Control Organization (NACO) in India, with support from national and international experts including the United Nations Programme on HIV/AIDS (UNAIDS) and the WHO, have developed new and improved data collection techniques to produce revised AIDS estimates for the country. The revised estimates show that in 2006, some 2.5 million people were living with the virus and that HIV prevalence among adults was around 0.36 per cent. In addition, estimates for previous years (since 2002) have also been revised to give a more accurate picture of the trend of the epidemic in India over the past few years (UNAIDS 2008; NACO 2007a). According to these reports, the revised estimates have been possible primarily because of three main factors: (i) a new population-based survey, which included

[†] This chapter is based on my research project 'Women's Reproductive Health and Poverty: A Qualitative Study of the Prevalence of Sexually Transmitted Diseases Among Populations Living in Selected Slum Areas of New Delhi, India', which received funding from the University of New Brunswick, Fredericton, New Brunswick Canada, and a seed grant award from the Social Sciences and Humanities Research Council of Canada (SSHRC).

an important HIV component; (ii) expanded sentinel surveillance which included groups at higher risk of HIV infection, and (iii) revised methodology to make the best use of the new data sources. With the help of improved methodologies, these estimates now provide a more realistic understanding of how India's AIDS epidemic has spread and are very useful for developing suitable intervention strategies. The current estimates clearly demonstrate that there is still a window of opportunity left to prevent HIV/AIDS from reaching escalating proportions, and it lies in scaling up local prevention efforts, and targeting the most vulnerable groups.

With nearly one billion people and a large diversified economy, India is the largest democracy and a growing economic and political power in Asia (USAID 2007). Ironically, India is also slated to be the epicentre of HIV/AIDS in Asia, and there are increasing rates of HIV infection stemming from people who are involved in risky behaviour. About half of India's population is in the sexually active age group of 15 to 49 years (Scambler and Paoli 2008; NACO 2007a; Cornman et al. 2007; Pallikadavath et al. 2004; Bharat and Aggleton 1999). The percentage of the population infected with HIV in India may seem relatively low at 0.36 per cent in the age group 15–49 years, compared with rates of 20 per cent and more in South Africa, Zimbabwe, and Botswana (UNAIDS 2007; NACO 2007a; Bryan et al. 2001). But given the immense proportion of the population in the sexually active age group, a mere 0.1 per cent increase in the prevalence rate would increase the numbers living with HIV by over half a million. Consequently, intervention strategies that address the needs of vulnerable populations in controlling the HIV/AIDS epidemic are urgently required (USAID 2007; Rao Gupta 2004; O'Neil et al. 2004).

Epidemiological analyses of reported AIDS cases have shown that AIDS is increasingly affecting young people. For instance, the majority of the HIV infections (87.7 per cent) are in the age group of 15–44 years. The overwhelming mode of transmission is predominantly heterosexual (85.69 per cent), followed by injection drug use (2.2 per cent), blood transfusion and blood product infusion (2.6 per cent), perinatal transmission (2.7 per cent), and others (6.8 per cent). According to the HIV sentinel surveillance carried out in 2006, women account for around one million out of 2.5 million estimated number of people living with HIV/AIDS in India. Nationally, the prevalence rate for adult females is 0.29 per cent, while for males it is 0.43 per cent. So, for every 100 people living with HIV and AIDS (PLHAs), 61 are men and 39 are women respectively and the numbers are rising steadily for women. The most predominant opportunistic infection among AIDS patients is tuberculosis, indicating a potential spread of an HIV–TB co-infection (NACO 2007a).

Recent NACO fact sheets show that HIV prevalence among the general population is 0.36 per cent but is much increased among the high-risk groups. For instance, among injecting drug users (IDUs), it is as high as 8.71 per cent, it is 5.69 per cent among men who have sex with men (MSM) and 5.38 per cent for female sex workers.

It is well established that the presence of other ulcerative sexually transmitted diseases (STDs) including gonorrhea and syphilis greatly increase the HIV transmission rate. In India, low levels of condom use and inadequate knowledge regarding sexual health, and reproductive functioning have also been identified as important contributing factors (Bharat and Aggleton 1999; Trollope-Kumar 2001; Hawkes and Santhya 2002; Chatterjee 2004; Bhatia et al. 2005). In particular, abstinence and condom use are often very difficult for women as social and cultural norms dictate that women remain sexually 'naïve and innocent'. The problem is compounded for sex workers who are not only stigmatized but also marginalized (NACO 2007a; Finn and Sarangi 2008; Scambler and Paoli 2008).

Social factors such as population mobility from rural to urban areas in search of employment, combined with poverty, and inadequate access to the basic amenities such as health care, and educational facilities, have clearly been implicated in the transmission of STDs and HIV infections (Soloman et al. 2004; Ghosh 2002; Upadhyay 2000; Shreedhar and Colaco 1996; DeSircar and Tewari 1996).

The WHO, UNAIDS, and the Centres for Disease Control and Prevention (CDC) are citing India as a high priority for prevention (WHO 2005; UNAIDS 2005). The infection has now spread to all states and union territories and is no longer confined to vulnerable groups such as sex workers and transport workers, or to urban areas. The practice of risky sexual behaviour among high-risk groups such as commercial sex workers and truck drivers makes them vulnerable to HIV infection; the consequences of their high-risk behaviour are of utmost concern. This is because the high-risk group individuals do not belong to a localized category. Instead their sexual contacts, with primary and secondary partners contribute towards making the general population highly susceptible to HIV transmission (Bryan et al. 2001; Pandev et al. 2002; O'Neil et al. 2004; Pallikadavath et al. 2005; Mitra and Basu 2004). Furthermore, HIV infections and cases of AIDS in India often go unrecognized and unreported, mainly due to inadequate testing facilities and systems for diagnosis and reporting (Chatterjee 2004; Shreedhar and Colaco 1996).

Epidemiological studies have shown that over time, HIV infection shifts from high-risk groups to the general population. Based on sentinel surveillance data, the HIV epidemic has become generalized in six states of India; other states are also highly vulnerable and in many of these states there is insufficient data available. In the absence of effective intervention strategies, all states can go through stages of low, concentrated, and finally generalized epidemic (NACO 2004). In the Indian context, however, it is difficult to estimate the exact prevalence of HIV because of the varied cultural characteristics, traditions, and values with special reference to sex related risk behaviours (NACO 2004). It is likely that more than 90 per cent of people living with HIV/AIDS do not know they are infected. Strong cultural taboos towards pre-marital sex leading to a culture of secrecy and silence, gender norms and gender-based inequality, and cultural inhibitions, are among the various reasons for the rapid spread of this infection in India (Nag 1996; Soloman et al. 2004). Awareness of HIV/AIDS and HIV transmission is quite low particularly for women; gender inequalities and stigma against people living with HIV are common. In many cases, public discussions of sexuality and risk of infection are still very rare.

Recent estimates indicate that HIV/AIDS cases are present throughout India with a wide variation in prevalence across the nation. Earlier Tamil Nadu and other southern states had reported high HIV burden in comparison to other states. However, HIV prevalence has since begun to decline or stabilize in these states due to extensive intervention strategies that have been in place for several years. On the other hand, HIV continues to emerge in new areas. The surveillance data from 2006 have identified selected pockets of high prevalence in the northern states. Currently, there are 29 districts with high prevalence, particularly in the states of West Bengal, Orissa, Rajasthan, and Bihar (UNAIDS 2007). Furthermore, the 2006 surveillance figures show an increase in HIV infection among vulnerable groups. For instance, HIV prevalence rate among IDUs has been found to be significantly high in metropolitan cities of Chennai, New Delhi, Mumbai, and Chandigarh. In addition, the states of Orissa, Punjab, West Bengal, Uttar Pradesh, and Kerala also show high HIV prevalence among IDUs. Although revised reports indicate that HIV prevalence rates are declining among sex workers in the southern states, overall prevalence levels among this group still continue to be high (UNAIDS 2007).

Several factors put India in danger of experiencing a rapid spread of the virus if effective prevention and control measures are not scaled up and expanded throughout the country (World Bank 2006). Many researchers, however, criticize the practice of placing primacy on risk while ignoring other structural features with respect to HIV transmission (Farmer 2001; Karnik 2001; O'Neil et al. 2004). According to Farmer, poverty and gender inequality are the strongest enhancers of risk exposures to HIV, a subject that has been largely neglected in both the biomedical and the social science literature on HIV transmission (Farmer 2001).

Impact of Impoverished Environment on HIV Transmission

The rapid growth of India's urban centres without a proper infrastructure has given rise to slum colonies lacking access to adequate housing, drinking water, food, and health care (Dhar Chakrabarti 2001; Sivam 2003). An expanding population of migrant workers in search of better quality of life, proliferations in slum colonies, and extreme conditions of poverty are greatly increasing the spread of STDs and HIV infections. Slums reflect very poor living conditions with sub-standard housing and lack of civic amenities leading to unhygienic conditions (Dhar Chakrabarti 2001; Sivam 2003; Kumar and Awasthi 2006). Perhaps, the magnitude of urban poverty can be best understood when one considers the appalling conditions of life offered in the slum environment with regard to basic services such as clean water, adequate nutrition, proper housing, access to health care, as well as steady income, and employment.

Existing studies have revealed that STDs are high among populations living in slum areas, and several cases of HIV infections have been reported (Kumar and Awasthi 2006; ACTION AID 1998; Chatterjee 1999). The prevalence of STDs and HIV particularly for women can become worse under slum conditions due to prevailing unhygienic conditions and inaccessible medical care. For instance, case studies of specific slum areas conducted in many cities have found that health conditions, and health facilities for slum dwellers are grossly inadequate (Mitra et al. 1998; Bhattacharya 1996; Mulgaonkar 1996). These conditions when combined with lack of access to adequate food and water supplies or to medical care, add up to inadequate or no treatment for STDs for both men and women, as well as an increased susceptibility to HIV/ AIDS (Doyal 1995, p. 81). Therefore, recent studies have begun to document the association between gender, impoverished environment, and the prevalence of STDs (UNDP 2000; Upadhyay 2000).

Feminization of Poverty and HIV Transmission

Medical anthropologists have long contended that poverty and inequality (including gender-based discrimination) combined with powerlessness are a significant risk enhancer for most STDs including HIV/AIDS (Farmer 2001). The World Bank analysis reports that social conditions, including poverty, inequality of income across households, and low status for women contribute to the spread of HIV (World Bank 2006; Upadhyay 2000). The *feminization* of poverty is a term used to describe the overwhelming representation of women among the poor (Jackson 1996, p. 491). Consequently, this feminization of poverty, combined with the social, political, and economic conditions has largely contributed to the deterioration of health status and provision for health care in developing nations since poor women often lack access to medical services for the treatment of chronic and acute conditions (Jackson 1996; Mitra and Pool 2000).

Though HIV infection is not confined only to the poor, poverty has contributed to its spread by creating yet another situation of vulnerability. Poverty and powerlessness can serve as powerful co-factors in the spread of HIV (Farmer 2001). Existing research studies indicate that the interrelationship between HIV transmission and poverty is complex and has to be understood in relation to the detailed history of individual countries or regions (Doyal 1995; Mitra 2003; Pallikadavath et al. 2005). Poverty, low social status, and lack of equal economic rights and opportunities make girls and women susceptible to sexual trafficking and exploitation by 'sugar daddies', thereby exchanging sexual favours for necessities and goods (UNFPA 2002;

Ratliffe 1999). Earlier research studies have also shown that women in high-risk relationships perceive the short-term costs of leaving the relationship much higher than the potential long-term health costs (Rao Gupta 2005).

Rural poverty has often forced unskilled labour populations to move to cities in search of better economic opportunities. These migrant populations are more likely to be socially marginalized, with restricted access to economic assets, information, and services (World Bank 2004; Pandev et al. 2002; Rao Gupta 2002). For instance, lack of training in case of women and especially young girls makes them ill-prepared for employment, and renders them vulnerable to prostitution as a survival strategy (Mitra and Basu 2004).

Poverty also controls access to information such that women and men who are economically disadvantaged are less likely to have information about HIV/AIDS. Moreover, the biological vulnerability of young women living under impoverished conditions is increased by poor nutrition and calorie wastage, which acts to delay menarche and prevents the development of the lower reproductive tract. As a result, young girls are more vulnerable to HIV transmission because malnutrition is known to depress immunological competence, making infection easier to establish and harder to suppress in women (Bailey 1997; Mitra 2003).

Why are Women More Vulnerable to HIV/AIDS?

Women's vulnerability to HIV/AIDS and other STDs is inextricably linked to their biological and social roles, including their socio-economic status, prevailing sexual practices and behaviours, and the access to health care services (NACO 2008; Rao Gupta 2005; Mulgaonkar 1996). Early marriage, violence, and sexual abuse against women are the major socio-economic reasons of their vulnerability to HIV infection (NACO 2008). Biomedical research has convincingly demonstrated that susceptibility of women, particularly young women, to HIV cannot be explained only by examining cultural, social, and economic conditions under which women have intercourse. There is a definite possibility of physiological and biological vulnerability that needs to be added to the growing list of contributory factors (Reid and Bailey 1992; Kumar et al. 2001). Women's biological construct makes them more susceptible to HIV infection in any given heterosexual encounter (NACO 2008). For example, adolescent girls, particularly early adolescents (10–12), are at an even greater risk for contracting HIV infection through intercourse prior to menstruation when the lower reproductive tract is still developing (UNAIDS 1999; Bailey 1997; Kumar et al. 2001).

The rate of HIV infection in women is as much as two to four times higher than that in men, not only due to physiological factors but also due to the nature of HIV transmission (Kumar et al. 2001). Further, semen infected with HIV contains a higher concentration of the virus than female sexual secretion (Kumar et al. 2001). While many men and women have no symptoms, men with STDs are more likely than women to have symptoms. Therefore, men are also more likely to seek treatment in comparison to women. And most sexually transmitted infections, such as gonorrhoea and chlamydia, are transmitted more easily from men to women, than vice versa because of differences in the anatomy of the male and female reproductive tracts (Epstein 1996; Kumar et al. 2001). However, biological factors act in combination with socio-economic influences such that HIV infection rates are the highest in adolescent women, particularly in the developing world (Bailey 1997).

Gender Norms and HIV Transmission

In India and in other developing countries HIV/AIDS is primarily transmitted heterosexually. Therefore, an understanding of gender relationship and sexual practices is necessary for designing and implementing effective HIV/AIDS prevention and control programmes (UNFPA 2002; Long and Messersmith 1998). Research studies have amply demonstrated the need to go beyond the 'high risk' groups as targeting solely the members from the 'high risk group' has proven to be inadequate (Long and Messersmith 1998). Accordingly, HIV/AIDS must be understood within broader socio-cultural and economic contexts. Further, a comprehensive prevention strategy also requires a better understanding of gender relationships, roles, and responsibilities in all aspects of life (Rao Gupta 2005; UNFPA 2002; Long and Messersmith 1998).

Socio-cultural norms, beliefs, and practices that apply to, and affect, women and men differently have a direct effect on vulnerability to HIV infection (UNFPA 2002; Helman 2000). While sex is biological, gender is socially ascribed. It determines how individuals and society perceive what it means to be male or female, influencing one's roles, attitudes, behaviours, and relationships. However, discrimination against girls and women based on socio-cultural norms often relegates them to lower status and value. This often places them at considerable disadvantage in terms of their access to resources and goods, decision-making power, choices, and opportunities across all spheres of life. Therefore, gender based inequality has a direct bearing in sexual decision making and the HIV/AIDS pandemic (UNFPA 2002; Helman 2000).

In many cases, women have feared reprisals from their partners and others, as being identified as promiscuous, immodest, or unfaithful, if they raise issues related to sexuality and sexual health including STD/ HIV prevention. In particular, many women suffering from STD-related problems accept these as a normal part of 'being a woman', and do not seek medical treatment. Conversely, boys and men are expected to be sexually knowledgeable and experienced and may express sexual prowess to prove their manliness through casual and multiple partners (including sex workers), infidelity, and dominance in sexual relations. Consequently, this deters many men from asking questions or seeking STD and HIV/AIDS services (UNFPA 2002; Hawkes and Collumbien 2001).

Many factors account for why vulnerability and risk differ for men and women, including life-cycle differences at different stages (Rao Gupta 2002). Women are especially at high risk of contracting HIV because of the interplay of biological, economic, and social factors. As mentioned earlier, biological reasons or the risks of contracting HIV through unprotected sex are higher for women than men. However, the high rates of HIV infection among women and young girls often have less to do with biology, and more to do with fundamental issues of power and control between women and men. More significantly, differences in power relations between men and women, largely grounded in economic inequality and vulnerability, have primarily been implicated in the spread of HIV/AIDS (Rao Gupta 2004). This unequal power balance in gender relations favours men, and translates into an unequal power balance in heterosexual interactions, in which men have greater control than women over when, where, and how sex takes place. Hence, crucial to this analysis is an understanding of gender norms of sexuality as constructed by a complex interplay of social, cultural, and economic forces that determine the distribution of power (Rao Gupta 2000; 2005).

Because women's vulnerability to HIV infection is increased by economic or social dependence on men, there are situations where women's ability to insist on condom use becomes particularly difficult. Abstinence and condom use are usually not the options available to women since social norms dictate that women remain sexually naïve and inexperienced (NACO 2008). When women refuse sex or request condom use, they may experience abuse or suspicion of infidelity. They may even be abandoned or forced to leave home. Indian social values surrounding fertility and motherhood often prevent women from using condoms, and often HIV-positive mothers refrain from using infant replacement formula for fear of stigmatization (UNFPA 2002; Rao Gupta 2004).

Sexual violence, including rape and sexual molestation, poses a significant threat to the reproductive health of women and girls, and increases the risk of HIV infection. Most research on sexual coercion shows that deeply rooted gender norms can contribute to sexual coercion. Often social norms contribute to a perception that controlling women is a sign of masculinity. Sexual coercions in childhood and adolescence have grave consequences, including adverse impact on reproductive health and HIV-related outcomes; not to mention subsequent experience of violence at the hands of intimate partners, and mental health problems. Forms of coercion and violence against women include physical, verbal persuasion, blackmail, and deception. Research indicates that in such settings, men forced sexual encounters either singly or in groups, and victims included girlfriends, intimate partners, sex workers, or strangers. Moreover, encounters are more often perpetrated under the influence of alcohol or drugs; coercion has also been reported in transactional sex (Population Council 2004; Bott and Jejeebhoy 2003).

Recent studies, however, have challenged the common assumption that only women are victims of violence, and have helped to shed light on the experiences of young males as victims of sexual coercion (Population Council 2004). In many cases, perpetrators of violence on young male victims are older males, and are known persons not strangers. Studies have found that among schoolboys in India, the most common male perpetrators were older students or friends. But a smaller number of young men also reported sexual coercion by experienced older females. As coercion is a violation of a person's rights, leading to serious consequences, it is imperative that intervention programmes consider patterns of coerced sex when addressing reproductive health, HIV prevention, and other needs (Youth Lens 2004; Population Council 2004).

In India men's behaviour is contributing substantially to the spread and impact of HIV, and may put men themselves on the 'front line of risk'. In most cases, existing data show that men have more sex partners than women, and are more likely to be the clients of sex workers (Hawkes and Collumbien 2001). Furthermore, HIV is more easily transmitted sexually from men to women than vice versa. In addition, HIV-positive drug users are predominantly male, and can transmit the virus to both their drug partners and sex partners (UNAIDS 2000; 2004). What is perhaps less often recognized is that cultural beliefs and expectations also heighten men's vulnerability. For instance, men are less likely to seek health care than women, less likely to pay attention to their sexual health and safety, and are much more likely to engage in behaviour that puts their health at risk. Therefore, engaging men as partners in the effort against AIDS can be the most strategic means to change the course of this epidemic (Badrud Duza 2001; Mitra and Basu 2005).

STDs and HIV Transmission

India has a high incidence of STDs in both urban and rural areas, with an annual incidence rate of 5 per cent, translating to an average of 40 million new cases every year (De Sircar and Tiwari 1996; Gangakhedkar et al. 1996; Mulgaonkar 1996; ACTION AID India 1998; FAITH Health Care Draft Report 2001). In addition, more than a million women in India suffer from reproductive tract infections due to the infections acquired during unsafe child birth, illegal and unsafe abortions as well as unprotected sex and poor reproductive hygiene, accounting for 25 per cent of the reproductive tract infections between the ages of 15-44 (ACTION AID India 1997). This situation is worse under slum conditions because of prevailing unhygienic conditions and inaccessible medical care.

Research studies have long established that STDs act as co-factors in the heterosexual spread of HIV infection (Wasserheit 1990; Farmer 2001). We know that women are more susceptible to STDs including HIV infection, as a result of their social and biological circumstances.

But scant attention has been given to other causes of female genital lesions, including infections and inflammation that are equally plausible pathways for HIV transmission (McNamara 1991). These causes include intravaginal insertion of foreign objects for contraception or abortion, early initiation of sexual activity and childbearing, trauma during sexual intercourse, lower reproductive tract infections and infibulation, among others (McNamara 1991). The vaginal epithelial mucosa is the female's normal protection against infection; if it is not intact, susceptibility is increased (McNamara 1991; Bailey 1997).

All infections that occur in the genital tract are reproductive tract infections (RTIs) but only some are sexually transmitted (Schmid 1999; Epstein 1996; McNamara 1991). Further, not all infections result in a disease, therefore, sexually transmitted infections (STIs) need to be identified and treated because they are capable of ultimately causing a disease, either in the person infected or in someone who might be infected by that person (Schmid 1999). Thus, reproductive tract infections fall into three categories: (i) STDs including gonorrhea, syphilis, and HIV infections; (ii) infections acquired as a result of badly performed medical procedures such as unhygienic insertion of an intrauterine contraceptive device (IUD) and unsafe child birth practices or illegal abortions; and (iii) infections that result from overgrowth of micro-organisms that normally inhabit the reproductive tract and are not sexually transmitted (Epstein 1996; ACTION AID India 1998).

Reproductive tract infections including STDs and STIs produce ulceration and discharge of pus, which facilitates the transmission of HIV virus most efficiently (Gangakhedkar et al. 1996; ACTION AID 1997; Datta Ghosh 2002). Both ulcerative and non-ulcerative STIs are known to enhance the transmission efficiency of HIV. Specifically, presence of ulcers on genitalia due to STIs presents a raw area through which the entry of HIV in the body is facilitated. In particular, STDs weaken the body's defences against HIV by causing bleeding and inflammation of the soft tissues of the genitalia (Epstein 1996; Datta Ghosh 2002). Consequently, untreated STDs can increase the risk of becoming infected with, or transmitting HIV, sometimes as much as ten-fold (Epstein 1996; Kumar 2001).

A research study from New Delhi found the following relationship between STDs and increased susceptibility to HIV infection, among populations living in slum areas of the city: (i) most STD affected persons rely on informal, traditional sources of health care for treatment of STDs or resort to self medication; (ii) female STD patients have very limited awareness of RTIs or STDs. Even in the presence of signs and symptoms, women generally ignore the problem. This is also attributed to the social stigma attached to STDs, and fear restrains women from seeking appropriate care; and (iii) women with STD problems generally try to avoid male doctors to examine them because of cultural inhibitions. In the absence of female doctors in most STD clinics, they avoid treatment (FAITH Health Care Draft Report 2001).

Culture of Silence and Suffering

In many parts of the world, women's reproductive health is surrounded by a 'culture of silence', and often very little information has been available about the scale of the problem of RTIs. In India, inhibitions about drawing attention to the body can be so great that even female health workers must rely upon verbal accounts of the symptoms of women who will not subject themselves to a physical examination (ACTION AID 2007; Ramasubban 1992; McNamara 1991; Hawkes and Santhya 2002).

This culture of silence surrounding STDs exists due to the stigma and taboos associated with such infections, and a belief among many that symptoms of pain and discomfort are a part of being a woman (Dixon-Mueller and Wasserheit 1991). As a result, women often do not seek clinical treatment because of fear or embarrassment, or the lack of appropriate care, particularly in a slum environment (Rice and Manderson 1996; ACTION AID India 1997). Because of cultural inhibitions, communication between partners on sexual matters, including morbidity is at times restricted. Women are often, as noted by Ramasubban, 'too afraid and confused to bring these (symptoms) to the notice of the family..., both because they are not supposed to have such problems in the first place and also because they are socially deemed to be polluters, the originators of sexual problems' (Ramasubban 1992; cited in Hawkes and Santhya 2002, p. 134). Accordingly, studies have found that women do not inform their husbands about their gynaecological symptoms (Hawkes and Santhya 2002).

Women are also burdened by many other factors surrounding STDs such that fear of stigmatization forces them to suffer in silence. For instance, an association of STDs with promiscuity, popular representation of STDs as the 'women's disease' and the common use of the term 'reservoirs of infection' to describe the commercial sex workers, place the onus solely on females, regardless of the male's multiple relationships (McNamara 1991). Therefore, counselling women about prevention and the need for treatment of their partners may presume incorrectly that they are free to discuss sex and condoms without jeopardy (McNamara 1991; Rao Gupta 2002).

Domestic violence is not uncommon in India, but is exacerbated by many folds under impoverished conditions (Ratnathicam 2001; UNAIDS 2000). When coupled with the stigma associated with HIV infection, the fear of violence deters many women from getting tested, revealing their HIV status, or seeking treatment (Ratnathicam 2001, p. 257).

ADOLESCENCE AND THE RISK OF HIV TRANSMISSION

The WHO defines 'adolescence' as the period of life between 10–19 years, 'youth' as between 15–24 years and 'young' people, as those between 10–24 years. Problems of interchanging the definition of youth and adolescence have also been countered by accepting that the dynamic transitions of this stage of life have as much to do with biological aspects as with socio-cultural conditions. Therefore, the health of youth and adolescents are often considered together (WHO 2004).

There are more than 280 million young people in India, forming a significant quarter of the country's population base. More significantly, over 35 per cent of all reported AIDS cases in India occur among young people in the age group 15 to 24 years, indicating that young people are at high risk of contracting HIV infection (NACO 2004). While adolescents (aged 10–19 years) represent almost one quarter of the Indian population, their sexual and reproductive health needs are not adequately addressed (Ministry of Welfare, Department of Women and Child Development 1990; cited by Jejeebhoy 1998, p. 1286; Gupta 2003). Recent studies have established beyond a doubt that there is a lack of knowledge and awareness among adolescents about health issues and problems (CARE-India 2004; UNFPA 2003; ICRW 2001). In particular, knowledge and awareness about puberty, menstruation, physical changes in the body, reproduction, contraception, pregnancy, childbearing, RTIs, and STIs including HIV are low among girls and boys, especially in younger adolescents (ages 10–14). During this transitory period, lack of knowledge and awareness about reproductive organs, physiological changes, or sexuality can promote psychological stress (Gupta 2003). Therefore, awareness programmes and related services must make special efforts to reach this vulnerable group (Canadian Office of the Minister for International Cooperation 2003; CIDA 2003).

ACCESS TO HEALTH CARE FACILITIES AND ANTI-RETROVIRAL THERAPY (ART)

Apart from cultural factors, the obstacles many women face in access to health care are caused by poverty, lack of education, inferior position in society, and inadequate health systems, among others (NACO 2007b; Kumarasamy 2007; Ratnathicam 2001; Kusum 2002; McNamara 1991). Moreover, women usually have poor mobility, which inhibits access to information and services (NACO 2007b).

It is important to acknowledge that effective diagnosis and treatment of STDs not only makes a significant contribution towards reducing the associated impact of these diseases, but also reduces the risk of HIV transmission (Kusum 2002). Nevertheless, diagnosis and treatment of STDs are possible only when women have access to health care providers with the skills and means to identify their condition correctly and supply appropriate medication (McNamara 1991; Ratnathicam 2001; Kusum 2002).

Treatment seeking in India is determined by a number of variables, among which are: perceived seriousness and causality of symptoms; availability of health care; costs (including opportunity costs) of treatment; perceived and actual quality of care; and beliefs about the appropriate provider to consult (Hawkes and Santhya 2002, p. 134). For instance, in India, DHS data show that many women, especially those from the poorer sections, and those in rural areas, receive no prenatal care and very few deliver with trained assistance (Ratnathicam 2001; Kusum 2002). In particular, distances to health facilities in both urban and rural areas can be very great, and women often lack autonomy and money (McNamara 1991; Mulgaonkar 1996).

Again, the culture of silence built around sex and sex-related diseases operates strongly as a barrier to informed health promoting communication with respect to STDs and HIV/AIDS. Like other STDs in India, HIV/AIDS has also come to occupy the status of *gupt rog* (private disease), and women are reluctant to seek advice and counselling. This is further exacerbated in a slum environment, where access to medical facilities is restricted or non-existent.

Since 2004, the Government of India has launched free anti-retroviral (ARV) drugs at eight government hospitals in six high prevalence states and the National Capital Territory of Delhi (NACO 2007; Kumarasamy 2007). While this is being scaled up in a phased manner, by 2006 there were 107 ART centres providing free ART to 60,000 people living with HIV and AIDS (PLHAs) in 31 states and union territories of the country. Additionally, a significant number of about 10,000 patients are receiving free ART at NGOs/inter-sectoral ART centres. The National AIDS Control Programme (NACP) Phase III plans to provide at least 300,000 patients with access to free ARV drugs distributed by 250 ART centres by 2010.

At present, the goal of NACP III is to provide comprehensive ART services to eligible persons with HIV/AIDS such that there is: (i) prevention of new infections in high-risk groups and general population; (ii) increase in proportion of people living with HIV/AIDS who receive care, support, and treatment; and (iii) strengthened infrastructure, systems, and human resources in prevention and treatment programmes at the district, state, and national levels. Specifically, the ART centres aim to: (i) identify eligible persons with HIV/AIDS requiring ART through laboratory services (HIV testing, CD4 count, and other required investigations); (ii) provide free ARV drugs to eligible persons with HIV/AIDS continuously; (iii) provide counselling services before and during treatment for ensuring drug adherence; (iv) educate persons and escorts on nutritional requirements, hygiene, and measures to prevent transmission of infection; (v) refer patients requiring specialized services or admission; and (vi) provide comprehensive package of services including condoms and prevention education (NACO 2007, p. 3).

There are a number of challenges associated with implementing the programme, particularly with respect to continuous supply of ARV drugs, infrastructural problems at various ART centres and the quality of care being offered to the patients. While the current focus is on distribution in high prevalence states, the need for access to ARV free of charge is present everywhere. In a recent monitoring and evaluation survey carried out by NACO, it was observed that there are a number of operational problems at ART centres, which vary across the region. Therefore, a need for a set of uniform operational guidelines for

ART centres was deemed necessary for developing better patient care strategy, and for facilitating proper health care delivery by providing uniform guidance to centres on various administrative, financial, and operational issues.

The NACO operational guidelines are very useful in describing the functions of the ART centres, facilities required in terms of physical infrastructure, general and medical equipments, human resources, and linkages including the roles and responsibilities of different categories of health care providers (Rao 2007). However, the operational guidelines do not provide adequate information on the criteria for selection of patients who qualify for ARV therapy or the status of HIV positive women and mothers with respect to access and adherence to ART. Women still face a number of hurdles as adequate information is often not provided and very little education or counselling is provided to HIV positive women for taking care of their children.

CONCLUSION

Anthropological research is especially concerned with highlighting the voices of vulnerable groups and sufferers, their needs and concerns to policy makers, so as to provide assistance in implementing prevention strategies in a culturally sensitive and locally competent manner.

For women, cultural conditions and inadequate health services compound the disadvantages of sexual and social inequality, which not only increase their vulnerability to infection but also limit their resources for treatment. Moreover, barriers to diagnosis and treatment of STDs including HIV/AIDS are often specific to women, varying in different cultures but with common themes: lack of information, differential access to health care, violation of norms of personal modesty, including ignorance or denigration of women's needs. However, these barriers can be lowered with education, economic opportunities, better and more available health services, including preventive methods that women can control themselves (McNamara 1991; Epstein 1996; Ratnathicam 2001; Rao Gupta 2005; NACO 2008).

Prevention strategies that place the burden solely on women frequently ignore the subordinate position of the majority of women, who are economically and emotionally dependent on their male sexual partners (Worth 1989; McNamara 1991; Rao Gupta 2002). Women are seldom in a position to discuss, let alone negotiate sexual decisions

(Hankins 1997; NACO 2008). In particular, the decision to use a condom is not only a stand taken for not getting infected, but also for not reproducing. As a result, women must constantly address the issue of sexual decision making and sexual control, and each time this is done they are emotionally, sexually, physically, and economically rendered vulnerable (Worth 1989; McNamara 1991; Rao Gupta 2002).

The stereotypical notions of gender roles should not dictate HIV/ AIDS intervention strategies. Rather, these intervention strategies must focus on data based on women and men's lives in a particular community or setting. This implies understanding and responding to the specific challenges faced by women and men, young girls and boys, in decision making and in negotiating safer and voluntary sex, as well as fostering open discussions on sexual health and challenging negative gender norms (UNFPA 2002; WHO Report 2003; Mitra 2006).

The basic source of power for individuals in a society is access to information, education, and skills. Access to information is crucial for HIV/AIDS prevention and for reducing myths, fear, stigma, and discrimination against people living with HIV/AIDS. Providing women with information and access to economic resources and assets reduces gender inequality, which will ultimately reduce women's risk and vulnerability to the infection (WHO Report 2003). More specifically, empowerment of women is about providing information, education, economic opportunities and assets, social support, services, technologies and political participation, all of which help them to take control of their lives (Ford Foundation Report 2002).

References

ACTION AID India (1997), 'Strategy for Prevention and Control of STD/HIV/ AIDS in India', Draft Report for Internal Discussion within Action Aid India.
———(2003), 'The Sound of Silence: Difficulties in communicating on HIV/AIDS in schools—Experiences from India and Kenya', Action Aid, London.
———(2007), 'Empower Women. End Poverty'. Available at www.actionaid.org.
Asthana, Sheena (1995), 'Variations in Poverty and Health between Slum Settlements: Contradictory Findings from Visakhapatnam, India', Social Science and Medicine, Vol. 40, No. 2, pp. 177–88.
Badrud Duza, M. (2001), 'Capacity Building in Reproductive Health Programs Focussing on Male Involvement: A South-to-South Framework', in Programming for Male Involvement in Reproductive Health, Report of the WHO Regional Advisers in Reproductive Health.
Bailey, M. (1997), 'Young Women and HIV: The Role of Biology in Vulnerability', in José Catalán Lorraine Sherr and Barbara Hedge (eds), The Impact of AIDS:

Psychological and Social Aspects of HIV Infection, Harwood Academic Publishers, Netherlands.

Bharat, S. and P. Aggleton (1999), 'Facing the Challenge: Household Responses to HIV/AIDS in Mumbai, India', *AIDS Care*, Vol. 11, No. 1, pp. 31–44.

Bhatia, V., H.M. Swami, A. Parashar, and T.R. Justin (2005), 'Condom-promotion Programme among Slum-dwellers in Chandigarh, India', *Public Health*, Vol. 119, pp. 382–84.

Bhattacharya, A. (1996), 'Problems of Urban Slums and Possible Solutions', *Nagarlok*, Vol. 28, No. 3, pp. 13–21.

Bhattacharya, B. (2001), 'AIDS in South and Southeast Asia. HIV/AIDS: Perspective on India', *AIDS Patient Care and STDs*, Vol. 15, No. 6, pp. 433–35.

Bott, S. and S. Jejeebhoy (2003), 'Adolescent Sexual and Reproductive Health in South Asia: An Overview of Findings From the 2000 Mumbai Conference', in S. Bott, S. Jejeebhoy; I. Shah, and C. Puri (eds), *Towards Adulthood: Exploring the Sexual and Reproductive Health of Adolescents in South Asia*, World Health Organization, 2003. ISBN 92 4 156250.

Bryan, A., J.D. Fisher, and T. Joseph Benziger (2001), 'Determinants of HIV Risk Among Indian Truck Drivers', *Social Science and Medicine*, Vol. 53, pp. 1413–26.

Canadian International Development Agency's (CIDAs) HIV/AIDS Action Plan (2001), available at *http://www.acid-cida.gcCI.ca/aids*

——— (2003), 'Canada Contributes to HIV/AIDS Awareness Program For Adolescents In India', 2003-31, News Release, available at *http;//www.acid-cida. gc.ca/cida_ind.nsf*

Care-India (2004), 'Program for Urban Slum Dwellers in India', available at *www. popcouncil.org/pdfs and http://www.careindia.org.*

———(2006), 'Reproductive and Child Health, Nutrition and HIV/AIDS', Available at *http://www.careindia.org.*

Chatterjee, N. (1999), 'AIDS-related Information Exposure in the Mass Media and Discussion Within Social Networks among Married Women in Bombay, India', *AIDS Care*, Vol. 11, No. 4, pp. 443–46.

Chatterjee, P. (2004), 'HIV/AIDS Prevention Carries On In Rural India', *The Lancet Infectious Diseases*, Vol. 4, p. 386.

Cornman, D.H., S. J. Schmiege, A. Bryan, T. J. Benzinger, and J. D. Fisher (2007), 'An Information-motivation-behavioral Skills (IMB) Model-based HIV Prevention Intervention for Truck Drivers in India, *Social Science and Medicine*, Vol. 64, pp. 1572–84.

Datta Ghosh, M. (2002), *Indian Infections Soar*, available at *www.napwa.org.au/ node/311.*

DeSircar, Debashree and H.R. Tewari (1996), 'Migration, Mobility and HIV Infection', *Social Action*, Vol. 46, pp. 467–80.

Dhar Chakrabarti, P.G. (2001), 'Urban Crisis in India: New Initiatives for Sustainable Cities', *Development In Practice*, Vol. 11, No. 2 and 3.

Dixon-Mueller, R. andd J. Wasserheit (1991), *The Culture of Silence: Reproductive Tract Infections Among Women in the Third World'*, International Women's Health Coalition, New York.

Doyal, L. (1995), 'What Makes Women Sick: Gender and the Political Economy of Health', Rutgers University Press, New Brunswick, New Jersey.

Epstein, H. (1996), 'The Silent Pandemic: Reproductive Tract Infections', *Panos Briefing*, Vol. 21, No. 9, p. 9.

FAITH Health Care Draft Report (2001), 'Communication Needs Assessment and Planning of the IEC Component in the AIDS Prevention Program', Sponsored by Delhi AIDS Control Society; FAITH Health Care Private Limited, New Delhi; Educational Consultants of India Limited, NOIDA, India. *Personal Communication.*

Ford Foundation Report (2002), 'Gender and the Epidemic', article by Kott, available at *http://www.fordfound.org/publications*

Epstein, Helen (1996), 'The Silent Pandemic: Reproductive Tract Infections', Panos Briefing No.21/December 1996.

Farmer, Paul (2001), *Infections and Inequalities: The Modern Plagues*, University of California Press, Berkeley and Los Angeles, CA.

Fauci, Anthony S. (1999), 'The AIDS Epidemic: Considerations for the 21st Century', *New England Journal of Medicine*, Vol. 341, No. 14, pp. 1046–50.

Finn, M. and S. Sarangi (2008), 'Quality of Life as a Mode of Governance: NGO talk of HIV "positive" health in India', *Social Science and Medicine*, Vol. 66, pp. 1568–78.

Gangakhedkar, R.R., M. Bentley, A.M. Rompalo, M.E. Shepherd, S.M. Mehendale, S.M. Thilakavathi, A. Amin, D.A. Gadkari, R.C. Bollinger, and T.C. Quinn (1996), 'STD and HIV Infection among Female Non-commercial Sex Workers Attending STD Clinics in Pune, India', International Conference on AIDS, July.

Gnaneshwar, V. (1995), 'Urban Policies in India—Paradoxes and Predicaments', *Habitat International*, Vol. 19, No. 3, pp. 293–316.

Ghosh, J., V. Wadhwa, and E. Ralipeni (2009), 'Vulnerability to HIV/AIDS among Women of Reproductive Age in the Slums of Delhi and Hyderabad, India', *Social Science and Medicine*, Vol. 68, No. 9, pp. 638–42.

Ghosh, J. (2002), 'A Geographical Perspective on HIV/AIDS in India', *Geographical Review*, Vol. 92, No. 1.

Ghose, T., D. Swendeman, S. George, and D. Chowdhury (2008), 'Mobilizing Collective Identity to Reduce HIV Risk Among Sex Workers in Sonagachi, India: The Boundaries, Conciousness, Negotiation Framework', *Social Science and Medicine*, Vol. 67, No. 2, pp. 311–20.

Grown, C., G. Rao Gupta, and R. Pande (2005), 'Taking Action to Improve Women's Health through Gender Equality and Women's Empowerment', *The Lancet*, Vol. 363, pp. 541–43.

Guha, Sapir (1996), 'Health and Nutrition of the Urban Poor: The Case of the Calcutta Slums', in Monica Das Gupta, Lincoln C. Chen and T.N. Krishnan (eds), *Health, Poverty and Development in India*, pp. 172–202, Oxford University Press, New Delhi.

Gupta, S.D. (2003), 'Adolescent and Youth Reproductive Health in India: Status, Issues, Policies, and Programs', in Policy Project USAID.

Hankins, Catherine (1997), 'Recognizing and Countering the Psychological and Economic Impact of HIV on Women in Developing Countries', in José Catalán, Lorraine Sherr, and Barbara Hedge, *AIDS: Psychological and Social Aspects of HIV Infection*, Harwood Academic Publishers, Netherlands.

Hawkes, S. and M. Collumbien (2001), 'The Sexual Health of Men in India and Bangladesh: What are men's Concerns?' in *Programming for Male Involvement in Reproductive Health*, Report of the WHO Regional Advisers in Reproductive Health.

Hawkes, Sarah and K.G. Santhya (2002), 'Diverse Realities: Sexually Transmitted Infections and HIV in India', *Sexually Transmitted Infections*, Vol. 78 (suppl1), pp. 131–39.

Helman, Cecil G. (2000), *Culture, Health and Illness*, Reed Educational Publishing, Oxford.

Hull, Valerie, Widyantoro and Tamara Fetters (1996), 'No Problem: Reproductive Tract Infections in Indonesia', in Pranee Liamputtong Rice, and Lenore Manderson (eds), *Maternity and Reproductive Health in Asian Societies*, Harwood Academic Publishers, Netherlands.

International Centre For Research on Women (ICRW) 2001, 'Youth, Gender, Well-Being and Society: A Contextual Approach to Adolescent-Health in India'. Available at *http://www.icrw.org*.

Jackson, Cecile (1996), 'Rescuing Gender from the Poverty Trap', *World Development*, Vol. 24, No. 3, pp. 489–504.

Jejeebhoy, S.J. (1998), 'Adolescent Sexual and Reproductive Behavior: A Review of the Evidence from India', *Social Science and Medicine*, Vol. 46, No. 10, pp. 1275–90.

Karnik, N.S. (2001), 'Locating HIV/AIDS and India: Cautionary Notes on the Globalization of Categories'. *Science, Technology and Human Values*, Vol. 26, No. 3, pp. 321–49.

Kumar, N, J. Larkin, and C. Mitchell (2001), 'A Gender, Youth and HIV Risk', *Canadian Women Studies*, Vol. 21, No. 2, pp. 35–43.

Kumar, Y., and I.C. Awasthi (2006), 'Globalization and Urban Powerty: Issues and Challenges', in *Managing Urban Poverty*, Council For Social Develoment, pp. 40–70, Uppal Publishing House, New Delhi.

Kumarasamy N. (2007), 'ARV Access and Challenges in India', YRG Centre for AIDS Research and Education, VHS, Chennai, India.

Kusum, B.S. (2002), 'Early Diagnosis and Treatment of STDs May Be An Important Factor in Reducing HIV Infection Among Tribal Sex Workers: An Experience of Rural Areas in Rajasthan State in India', in News and Abstracts: The XIV International AIDS Conference, Barcelona.

Long, Lynellyn D. and Lisa J. Messersmith (1998), 'Reconceptualizing Risk: A Feminist Analysis of HIV/AIDS', in *Women in the Third World: An Ongoing Encyclopedia of Controversial Issues*, Garland, NY, pp. 157–64.

McNamara, Regina (1991), 'Female Genital Health and the Risk of HIV Transmission', UNDP Issues Paper No. 3. Available at *http://www.undp.org/hiv/publications/issues/english/ issue03e.htm*

Mitra, K. (2003), 'Anthropological Perspectives on HIV/AIDS in India', *South Asian Anthropologist*, Vol. 3, No.1, pp. 79–87.

——— (2006), 'Can Globalization Facilitate HIV Transmission in India?' *South Anthropologist*, Vol. 6, No. 2, pp. 107–113.

Mitra, K. and K. Basu (1998), 'An Eco-health Study in Urban Slums of Delhi', *Journal of Human Ecology*, Vol. 9, No. 2, pp. 153–57.

Mitra, K., K. Basu, and S. Basu (1998), 'Health Problems and Practices of Slum Women of Delhi', *South Asian Anthropologist*, Vol. 19, No. 1, pp. 37–44.

Mitra, K. and S. Basu (2004), 'The Impact of Globalization on Gender and HIV/AIDS in India', in *The Globalization, Gender and Health Research Policy Interface*, The Centre for Research in Women's Health (CRWH) in Partnership with Canadian Institute of Health Research Institute of Gender and Health.

——— (2005), 'The Unintended Consequences of Globalization: Strategies for Effective Management of Urban Poverty in India' (eds.) M.D. Asthana and Sabir Ali, Council for Social Development, New Delhi, India, Uppal Publishing House.

Mitra, K. and G. R. Pool (2000), 'Why Women Stay Poor: An Examination of Urban Poverty in India', *Social Change: Journal of the Council for Social Development*, Vol. 30, No. 102, March–June, Special Issue, pp. 153–78.

Mulgaonkar, Veena B. (1996), 'Reproductive Health of Women in Urban Slums of Bombay', *Social Change: Journal of the Council for Social Development*, Vol. 26, Nos. 3 and 4, September–December, pp. 137–56.

Mutatkar, R. K. (1995), 'Public Health Problems of Urbanization', *Social Science and Medicine*, Vol. 41, No. 7, pp. 977–81.

Nag, M. (1996), 'Sexual Behaviour and AIDS in India', Vikas Publishing House Private Ltd, New Delhi.

NACO [National AIDS Control Organization] (2002, 2004, 2006), *Country Scenario, An Update*, October 2002, 2004, 2006, Ministry of Health and Family Welfare, Government of India.

——— (2007a), 'HIV Data', Ministry of Health and Family Welfare, Government of India.

——— (2007b), 'Operational Guidelines for ART Centres', Ministry of Health and Family Welfare, Government of India.

——— (2008), Woman: India Scenario, Ministry of Health of Family Welfare, Government of India.

O'Neil, J. Treena Orchards, R.C. Swarankar, J.F. Blanchard, K. Gurav, and S. Moses (2004) 'Dhandha, Dharma, and Disease: Traditional Sex Work and HIV/AIDS in Rural India', *Social Science and Medicine*, Vol. 59, No. 9, pp. 851–60.

Pallikadavath, S., A. Sanneh, J.M. McWhirter, and R.W. Stones (2005), 'Rural women's Knowledge of AIDS in the Higher Prevalence States of India: Reproductive Health and Sociocultural Correlates' *Health Promotion International*, Vol. 20, No. 3, pp. 249–59.

Pallikadavath, S., L. Garda, H. Apte, J. Freedman, and R. William Stones (2004), 'HIV/AIDS in Rural India: Context and Health Care Needs', *Journal of Biosocial Science*, Cambridge University Press, pp. 1–15.

Pandev S., A. Chatterjee, and A.S. Abdul Quader (eds), (2002), *Living with the AIDS Virus: The Epidemic and the Response from India*, Sage Publications, New Delhi.

Population Council's Frontiers in Reproductive Health Program and CARE India (2004), in *Integrating Adolescent Livelihood Activities within a Reproductive Health Program for Urban Slum Devellers in India*, available at the Population Council website.

Population Council of India (2003), 'HIV/AIDS In India: The Hard–Hit States', available at *www.popfound.org*; and *www.prb.org*

Ramasubban, R. (1992), 'Sexual Behaviour and Conditions of Health Care: Potential Risks for HIV Transmission in India', in T. Dyson (ed.) *Sexual Behaviour and Networking: Anthropological and Socio-cultural Studies on the Transmission of HIV*, Derouaux-Ordina, Liege, pp. 175–202.

Ramasundaram, S. (2002), 'Can India Avoid Being Devastated By HIV?', *British Medical Journal*, Vol. 324, pp. 183–4.

Rao Gupta, G. (2002), 'How Men's Power Over Women Fuels the HIV Epidemic?', *British Medical Journal*, Vol. 324, pp. 182–3.

——— (2004), 'Globalization, Women and the HIV/AIDS Epidemic', *Peace Review*, Vol. 16, No. 1, pp. 79–83.

——— (2005), 'Luncheon Remarks on Women and AIDS', International Center for Research on Women (ICRW), 2 June 2005, Washington, D.C.

Rao Sujatha, K. (2007), 'Operational Guidelines for ART Centres', National AIDS Control Organization of India.

Ratliff, Eric A. (1999), 'Women as "Sex Workers", Men as "Boy Friends": Shifting Identities in Philippine Go-Go Bars and Their Significance in STD/AIDS Control' *Anthropology and Medicine*, Vol. 6, No. 1, p. 101.

Ratnathicam, Anita (2001), 'AIDS in India: Incidence, Prevalence, and Prevention', *AIDS PATIENT CARE and STDs*, Vol. 15, No. 5, pp. 255–61.

Reid, E. and M. Bailey (1992), 'Young women: silence, susceptibility and the HIV epidemic', Issues paper, UNDP HIV and Development Programme.

Rice, Pranee Liamputtong and Lenore Manderson (ed.) (1996), *Maternity and Reproductive Health in Asian Societies*, Harwood Academic Publishers, Netherlands.

Scambler, Graham and Frederique Paoli (2008), 'Health Work, Female Sex Workers and HIV/AIDS: Global and Local Dimensions of Stigma and Deviance as Barriers to Effective Interventions', *Social Science and Medicine*, Vol. 66, pp. 1848–62.

Schmid, G. (1999), 'Thinking About Sexually Transmitted Diseases', *American Family Physician*, Vol. 60, No. 5, pp 1335–6.

Shreedhar, Jaya and Anthony Colaco (1996), *Broadening the Front: NGO responses to HIV and AIDS in India*, UNDP and ACTION AID, New Delhi, India and United Kingdom.

Sivam, Alpana (2003), 'Viewpoint: Housing Supply in Delhi', *Cities*, Vol. 2, No. 2, pp. 135–41.

Solomon, S., A. Chakraborty, and R. D'Souza Yepthomi (2004), 'A Review of the HIV Epidemic in India', *AIDS Education and Prevention*, Vol. 16, Supplement A, pp. 155–69.

Trollope-Kumar, K. (2001), 'Cultural and Biomedical Meanings of the Complaint of Leukorrhea in South Asian Women', *Tropical Medicine and International Health*, Vol 4, pp. 260–6. Available at *http://www.unaids.org*

UNAIDS (1999), *Global HIV/AIDS and STD Surveillance: Epidemiological Fact Sheets by Country*.

—— (2000), 'AIDS Epidemic Update', UNAIDS/00.44E-WHO/CDS/CSR/EDC/2000.9, (English original, December 2000).

—— (2004), 'Treat Millions By 2005: India Epidemiological Fact Sheets on HIV/AIDS and Sexually Transmitted Infections', Available at *http://www.unaids.org*

—— (2005), 'Asia Epidemic update: December 2005', Available at *http://www.unaids.org*

—— (2007), '2.5 Million People Living with HIV in India', Available at *http://www.unaids.org*

—— (2008), UNGASS Country Progress Report 2008: India, Available at *http://www.unaids.org*

United Nations Development Programme (UNDP) (1992), 'Young Women: Silence, Susceptibility and the HIV Epidemic', UNDP, New York, *http://www.us.unaids.org/highband/ document/epidemio/ june99/fact_sheets/index.html*

—— (2000), *Human Rights and Human Development*, UNDP Report, available at *http://hdr.undp.org/en/reports*

UNFPA (United Nations Populations Fund) (2002), 'HIV Prevention Now', available at UNFPA website, *http:// www.unfpa.org/aids/index.htm*

—— (2003), 'Adolescent Reproductive Health'. UNFPA Technical Report. Available at *http://www.unfpa.org*

Upadhyay, Ushma D. (2000), 'India's New Economic Policy of 1991 and Its Impact on Women's Poverty and AIDS', *Feminist Economics*, Vol. 6, No. 3, pp. 105–22.

USAID (2007), *www.usaid.gov/in*

Wasserheit, Judith N. (1990), 'Reproductive Tract Infections', in *Special Challenges in Third World Women's Health: Presentations at the 117th Annual Meeting of the American Public Health Association*, Chicago, October 1989, International Women's Health Coalition, New York.

Women's International Network News (2001), 'Powerlessness of Women Increases Their Risk of Rape and AIDS', *Women's International Network News*, Vol. 27, No. 2, p. 73.

World Bank (2000), *World Development Report 1999/2000: Entering the 21st century*, Oxford University Press, New York.

—— (2004), *Understanding Poverty*, The World Bank Group, available at *http://worldbank.org*

—— (2006), *Preventing HIV/AIDS in India*, The World Bank Group, available at *http://go.worldbank.org*

World Health Organization [WHO] (2003), 'Integrating Gender Into HIV/AIDS Programs: A Review Paper', Department Of Gender and Women's Health, Family, and Community Health, World Health Organization, Geneva.

—— (2005), *India: Summary Country Profile for HIV/AIDS Treatment Scale–UP*, available at *www.who.int/hiv*

World Health Organization Report (2004), 'Adolescent Health', available at *www.who. int/topics/adolescenthealth/en/*

Worth, D. (1989), 'Sexual Decision-making and AIDS: Why Condom Promotion among Vulnerable Women is likely to Fail ?', *Studies in Family Planning*, Vol. 20, No. 6, pp. 297–307.

Youth Lens (2004), 'Non-Consensual Sexual Experience of Young People in Developing Countries', available at *www.fhi.org*

Gender Differences in Early Childhood Feeding Practices
Rural West Bengal

APARNA PANDEY* ————————————————— 8

INTRODUCTION

Children below five years of age constitute approximately 12 per cent of India's population (Census of India 2001). Rapid growth and development during this period make these children vulnerable to nutritional deficiencies and increased susceptibility to morbidities (Ministry of Human Resource Development 2002; Gove 1997). It has been observed that malnutrition during this phase of life is mostly due to faulty feeding practices rather than lack of resources (Ghosh 1998; ICMR Bulletin 2000). Feeding practices have also been shown to be discriminatory by the sex of the child (Chen et al. 1981; Das Gupta 1987; Sen and Sengupta 1983, and Frongillo and Begin 1993). Indirect evidence like the dwindling child sex ratio, poor health and nutritional status, and greater risk of dying among girls are pointers to gender discrimination (Census of India 2001; Ghosh 1991; Cowan 1990; Chen 1982; and Balkrishnan 1994).

The objective of this study is to ascertain the gender differences in feeding practices and nutritional status of pre-school children and to identify the underlying socio-cultural factors affecting feeding

* Financial assistance for the project was provided by UNICEF, Kolkata. I express my gratitude to the Director National Institute of Cholera and Enteric Diseases (NICED) for providing necessary help for successful completion of the study. I am thankful to the faculty members, senior research fellows, and field staff of NICED and the surveillance workers, who helped in data collection. My thanks extended to all children and their family members specially mothers, without whose active participation it would not have been possible to complete the study.

and nutrition of children. A cohort of 530 (273 boys and 257 girls) pre-school children from four demarcated villages of West Bengal was followed over a period of one year from June 1998 to May 1999. Information was recorded on existing breastfeeding, weaning, and child feeding practices. Data were also recorded on anthropometric measurements (weight, height, and mid-arm circumference) and relevant cultural practices and customs.

MATERIALS AND METHODS

This chapter reports findings from a collaborative project of Indian Council of Medical Research (ICMR) and UNICEF Kolkata. This was a community based observational study, in which a cohort of children under five years of age was followed up for a period of one year from June 1998 to May 1999.

Study Settings and Study Population

The study was carried out in four demarcated villages of North 24 Parganas of West Bengal. These villages constitute the practice field of the National Institute of Cholera and Enteric Diseases (NICED), Kolkata. The area has a population of 7000, distributed into 1500 families. Pre-school children constitute 10.3 per cent of population. The area has one surveillance worker for every 1000 population. The surveillance workers, locally recruited by NICED, carry out surveillance of diarrhoeal diseases by undertaking weekly visits in each family. These surveillance workers have a minimum education of class VIII and are trained in surveillance methodology by NICED. Detected diarrheoa cases are offered first line of treatment by surveillance workers and NICED staff. Serious cases are referred to nearby health facility. Children between 0 to 48 months of age constituted the study population.

Data Collection

At the outset, children between 0–48 months were enlisted and their socio-demographic characteristics recorded.

Exploratory Survey

To collect first hand information of prevailing feeding practices and customs having a bearing on feeding, an explorative survey was undertaken. Information was gathered from 40 randomly selected

(10 from each village) children. These identified feeding practices and customs were subsequently studied in detail during follow-up.

Follow up Monthly Visits

These were organized to follow each child for a period of one year to record information regarding the following.

1. Qualitative diet composition of the child during the last 24 hours was noted by interviewing the mothers/care providers.
2. Children aged 6–18 months were also kept under observation, at the time of feeding for an average period of two hours.
3. In-depth interview of mothers and other family members was undertaken during last follow-up visit by a social scientist. The interview covered various aspects such as breastfeeding, weaning, top feeding, complementary feeding, and initiation age for different types of food. Information was also collected regarding customs having a bearing on feeding.

Feeding during Illness

Acute diarrhoeal episodes were studied using existing surveillance system.

Weight and Height/Length

These were recorded at four-monthly intervals. Mid-arm circumference of children aged >12 months was also recorded during the last visit.

Mother's Attitude

Mother's attitude towards use of colostrum, breastfeeding, and top feeding was recorded by a social scientist using a Likert's five point scale. For this, a sub-sample of 145 mothers having a child less than one year of age was identified. Both positive and negative questions were administered to respondents and their responses were recorded and coded. Reliability of these questions was checked and suitable modifications were made before finally administering them to the care providers.

On completion of data collection, health education was imparted to all mothers covering various components of child feeding practices (WHO 1997). Senior research fellows (SRFs) both medical and non-medical (social scientist), trained field investigators, and surveillance workers helped in data collection. To minimize inter- and intra -

observer variations, the whole process of data collection was monitored by independent observers and supervised by the investigators. Ten per cent of data were crosschecked for validity. Information thus collected was recorded on semi-structured interview schedules and observation sheets specially prepared for the study. These schedules were thoroughly validated and pre-tested in the field before actual use.

Data Analysis

Breastfeeding and top feeding indicators were calculated by summarizing child-wise information, recorded during monthly follow-up visits and in-depth interviews. Sex-wise proportion and means were calculated. Qualitative information about food composition of children aged 6–18 months recorded during monthly follow-up visits was clubbed and treated cross-sectionally. Proportions were calculated for different food items present in the diet of boys and girls. Nutritional data were recorded longitudinally but treated cross sectionally for the purpose of analysis. Standard Statistical methods were used for calculating weight for age (WFA) and height for age (HFA) for particular age groups using NCHS standards.

Data were entered into the computer using suitable software. Variables were categorized and responses coded wherever possible. Analysis was done sex-wise using pre-identified indicators. Suitable statistical test like Chi Square for proportions and Student's t test were used for significance testing wherever required. Non-parametric tests were used for asymmetrical distribution. For analysis, Epi Info V.06 and SPSS V.10 were used.

RESULTS

Out of 640 eligible children enumerated initially, 585 were chosen for follow-up. Fiftyfive children were either temporary residents or visitors, hence were not considered. A total of 530 (273 boys and 257 girls) children followed for a year. Rest 55 could followed for a varying period of 6 to 11 months.

Socio-economic Information

Study children belonged to low socio-economic class with mean per capita income of Rs 475.50 per month and median of Rs 500 per month. Majority of children (82.8 per cent) came from the families where heads were daily wage labourers or employed in low end jobs such as boating, fishing, or vendoring etc. Mothers of 93.8 per cent of children were housewives. Rest 6.2 per cent were engaged in some type of full time or part time jobs like household maids, vendors etc. With regard to parental education, 38.5 per cent of mothers and 36.9 per cent of fathers were illiterate. Children came from the families with mean family size of 4.5 (± 1.8) members. Mean ages of fathers and mothers were 29.6 (± 6.3) years and 21.4 (± 3.9) years, respectively.

Feeding Practices

Breastfeeding Practices

Breastfeeding was initiated early for boys (3.2 ± 1.8 hours) in comparison to girls (5.8 ± 2.1 hours). Boys received prelacteal feeds less often (70.0 per cent) than girls (93.3 per cent). These feeds were given within half an hour to six hours after birth. Common prelacteal feeds were tap water, given to 7.7 per cent boys and 30.4 per cent girls, boiled water to 76.9 per cent boys and 65.9 per cent girls, mineral water to 3.9 per cent boys and 0.0 per cent sugar, candy, or glucose water to 46.2 per cent boys and 43.2 per cent girls and honey to 3.9 per cent boys and 13.0 per cent girls.

Table 8.1: Breastfeeding practices by child's gender

Breastfeeding (BF) Practice	Proportions	
	Boys	Girls
Exclusive BF rate (<4 months)	23.1 per cent	45.5 per cent
Exclusive BF rate (<6 months)	0.0 per cent	9.5 per cent
Predominant BF rate (<4 months)	26.3 per cent	51.2 per cent
Continued breastfeeding rate (12 month)	45.9 per cent	20.4 per cent
Continued breastfeeding rate (24 month)	10.2 per cent	2.1 per cent
Timely complementary feeding rate (6–9 months)	100 per cent	100 per cent

Source: Author's own calculations.

From second day onwards, 33.3 per cent of girls and 18.6 per cent of boys were fed totally on colostrum. For the remaining 66.7 per cent of girls and 81.4 per cent of boys, colostrum was partially discarded. As shown in Table 8.1 exclusive breastfeeding at 4 month was higher for girls (45.5 per cent) than for boys (23.1 per cent). At 6 months, none of the boys was exclusively breastfed in comparison to 9.5 per cent girls. Predominant breastfeeding rates (4 months) were also higher for girls (51.2 per cent) in comparison to boys (26.3 per cent). Median age of breastfeeding was longer for boys (11 months) than for girls (9.5 months).

Top Feeding Practices

Initiation of top milk was delayed for girls (3.4±2.0 months) in comparison to boys (2.5 ± 0.1 months). Most common top milks were diluted cow milk (given to 38.6 per cent of boys and 34.7 per cent of girls), tinned milk (57.3 per cent of boys and 28.0 per cent of girls) and packet milk (12.9 per cent of boys and 10.7 per cent of girls). A small proportion of children also received buffalo milk (6.2 per cent) and a few of them received goat milk (1.4 per cent). Complementary feeding rates at 6 to 9 months of age were similar for boys and girls (Table 8.1). Top feeds were also introduced early to boys in comparison to girls (5.8 ±1.6 months vs 6.8 ± 2.1 months).

Food Consumption Pattern during Weaning Periods

Table 8.2 presents the common food items present in the diet of children aged 6 to 18 months. These were rice (95.5 per cent), *dal* (pulses) (94.1 per cent), potato (94.0 per cent), papaya (83.6 per cent), *muri* (puffed rice) (79.3), *suji* (semolina) (40.5 per cent), fish, eggs, and meat (73.9 per cent), commercially available foods (61.6), biscuits, toast, and bread (82.8 per cent), vegetables (86.6 per cent), chapati (17.0 per cent), and other food items such as sago (24.8 per cent) and barley (9.5 per cent). Difference between the sexes was more marked with respect to consumption of commercially available foods and protein-rich foods like fish, meat, and eggs.

Feeding during Sickness

During the one-year follow-up, feeding practices were observed in 332 diarrhoeal episodes. Of these 162 episodes occurred in boys and 170 in girls.

As depicted in Table 8.3 more girls (78.2 per cent) than boys (55.9 per cent) received breastfeeding during sickness. However, tinned milk was offered more frequently to boys (45.7 per cent) in comparison to

Table 8.2: Food items offered to boys and girls during weaning
(age 6–18 months)

Food item	Proportions	
	Boys	Girls
Rice	96.6	95.5
Dal	96.4 *	94.1*
Chapati	17.0	16.9
Suji (semolina)	54.0 *	40.5*
Muri	78.4	79.3
Barley	10.3 *	8.5 *
Sabudana (sago)	28.5 *	21.1*
Vegetable	87.6	85.9
Potato	94.6	94.0
Papaya	87.4 *	83.6*
Fruits**	49.5 *	34.3 *
Eggs / fish / meat	92.9 *	73.9 *
Cerelac	69.9 *	61.6 *
Biscuit /toast/bread	94.3 *	61.6 *

Notes: * Difference between the sexes is significant at 5 per cent level; ** included
bananas apples, grapes, oranges etc.
Source: Author's own calculations.

girls (30.6 per cent). Amount of top food was restricted in 8.6 per cent
episodes suffered by boys and 11.8 per cent episodes suffered by girls.
Top food was stopped in 8.8 per cent episodes in boys and 4.4 per cent
episodes in girls.

Table 8.3: Feeding practices during sickness (acute diarrhoeal episodes)

Feeding practices	Proportions	
	Boys	Girls
Breastfeeding continued	55.9 *	78.2 *
Top food stopped	8.8	4.4
Top food restricted	8.6	11.8
Quality of food changed	59.9	59.4
Offered tinned milk	45.7 *	30.6 *
Offered ready-made expensive foods**	72.8 *	48.2 *

Notes: * Difference between the sexes was significant at 0.05 level;
** included commercially available tinned foods, biscuits, toasts etc.
Source: Author's own calculations.

Quality of food was changed in 59.6 per cent of episodes. Ready-made foods were offered more often to boys in comparison to girls. Out of 200 (60.2 per cent) episodes where such supplements were given, 118 (59.0 per cent) were among boys in contrast to 82 (41.0 per cent) among the girls. Other common types of food offered during illness included milk (given in 71.3 per cent episodes), rice (66.9 per cent), puffed rice or muri (40.7 per cent), and pressed rice or cheera (35.8 per cent). No gender difference was noted in these foods given to children during sickness.

Customs

A custom of offering first solid food to the child, known as *Annaprashan* or *Mukhebhat*, was performed for 80.0 per cent of boys and 34.7 per cent of girls at 6 months of age. The median age of Annaprashan was 6 months for boys and 7 months for girls. Another very common custom was *Puja*. This was usually done 6 weeks after the birth. In this, a kind of gruel prepared from semolina is offered to God and then it is fed to the child as a good omen. It was done for 80.0 per cent of boys and only 34.6 per cent of girls.

Nutritional Status of Children

Proportion of underweight (WFA) was 49.5 per cent in boys and 56.5 per cent in girls, respectively. Difference in nutritional status (WFA) of boys and girls was noted in each age group but was more marked in the age group of 36–48 months (60.0 per cent of boys vs 87.5 per cent girls).

Grade I and II malnutrition was more common in girls (36.6 per cent and 15.9 per cent) than in boys (9.3 per cent and 10.9 per cent). No difference was noted in grade III malnutrition (5.5 per cent and 5.1 per cent respectively among boys and girls). Proportion of stunting (HFA) was 45.7 per cent in boys and 57.6 per cent in girls. For stunting, the gender gap was maximum in the age group of 36–48 months.

Attitude of Mother

A high proportion mothers (93.1 per cent) considered breast milk as the best for the newborn baby. The rest 6.9 per cent of mothers were undecided. Colostrum was considered as a protective food by 33.1 per cent of mothers, 39.3 per cent of mothers were undecided about the usefulness of colostrum. The rest (27.6 per cent) considered it as a

Table 8.4: Nutritional status by child's gender

Age group (in months)	Sex of child					
	Boys			Girls		
	No. of observations	Proportion under-weight	stunted	No. of observations	Proportion under-weight	stunted
≤12	194	23.7	23.2	206	26.6	24.3
>12–24	203	38.9	41.4	188	53.7	51.1
>24–36	188	57.9	64.4	171	69.5	69.6
>36–48	190	60.0	63.7	160	87.5	86.9
>48	105	52.3	61.9	95	60.0	62.1
Total	880	45.7	49.5	820	57.6	56.5

Source: Author's own calculations.

harmful secretion that should be discarded. A total of 50.3 per cent mothers were of the opinion that the child needs extra milk supplement before four months, 42.8 per cent thought breast milk was sufficient nutrition for infants up to the age of 4 months while 6.9 per cent of mothers remained undecided on this issue.

Tinned milk was considered superior supplement by 69.0 per cent of mothers. Another 17.9 per cent thought cow milk was a better substitute. The remaining 13.1 per cent of mothers were undecided. Tinned food was considered to be a better weaning food by 70.3 per cent of mothers, 7.6 per cent considered home available food as a better supplement while the remaining 22.1 per cent mothers were undecided.

DISCUSSIONS

The study found the existence of gender bias among pre-school children in a rural community of West Bengal. Discrimination in feeding begins with the initiation of breastfeeding. It was delayed by 2.6 hours in girls compared to boys. This could be a reflection of the mother's initial feeling of rejection towards the newborn girl baby. Similar findings were previously reported by Miller (1997). Breast milk is a natural gift to the newborn. In the present study, majority of mothers considered breast milk as the best feed for the neonate. This is corroborated by a study in Ethiopia (Woldegebriel 2002). Breast milk has all the essential nutrients for the infants. Use of prelacteal feeds not only interferes with the natural process of lactation but is also potentially hazardous to newborn, exposing them to risk of infections. In the present study, more girls (93.3 per cent) received prelacteal feeds than boys (70.0 per cent). This could be considered as a substitute for delayed initiation of breastfeeding. However, qualitatively the prelacteal feeds were similar, except that greater proportion of girls received plain water. The study has also found that a high proportion of children (81.4 per cent boys and 66.7 per cent of girls) received breast milk substitutes besides colostrums for the first three days. This is in contrast with the findings of other surveys which reported colostrum consumption at 73 per cent (in Kolkata and adjoining areas of West Bengal) (Kumar 1997). However, in our study none of the mothers fully discarded the colostrum. When the attitude of mothers was tested regarding the usefulness of colostrum, 33.1 per cent mothers considered it to be beneficial for the newborn while 27.6 per cent of mothers believed that it is harmful and hence should be discarded. This is in conformity with the observations made in Nepal (Manandhar 1997). It underlines the need for the education of mothers about the usefulness and protective value of colostrum.

Exclusive breastfeeding is recommended for infants at least up to the age of 4 months and preferably up to 6 months (WHO 1997). Almost all mothers have enough milk for the newborns. However, psychological factors such as mother's worry, her attitude, tiredness, dislikes, rejection of the baby seem to play an important role in the mother's ability to feed her child. In the present study exclusive breastfeeding rates at 4 and 6 months were found higher for girls. The underlying reason could be mother's concern about the insufficiency of breast milk to meet the needs of the infant. More than half (50.3 per cent) of the mothers expressed the view that the child needs extra milk supplement before 4 month. This is in contrast to the observations made in Ethiopia (Woldegebriel 2002), where 80 per cent mothers considered breast milk to be sufficient for the child up to the age of 6 months. In the present study, 69 per cent mothers considered tinned milk as a superior supplement. Boys being considered more precious received it more often. This is similar to the findings of other researchers (Das Gupta 1987; Bhogle 1991). At the age of 4 months, 45.5 per cent of girls were exclusively breast-fed in comparison to 23.1 per cent of boys. Surveys undertaken in different areas of West Bengal reported exclusive breastfeeding rate at 4 months as 11.1–28.6 per cent

(Kumar 1997). At the age of 6 months, 9.5 per cent of girls continued to receive exclusive breastfeeding, while not a single boy was exclusively breast-fed. In a study, exclusive breastfeeding rate of 9.6 per cent was noted at 4–6 months (Nag 1997). However in Nepal and elsewhere higher breastfeeding rates were reported for both the sexes 11 per cent (Manandhar 1997; Kapil et al. 1994). Another notable feature was longer breastfeeding time for boys. Researchers from Bangladesh made similar observations (Hossain and Roger 1988). A few reports from India too indicate the preference for longer breastfeeding for boys (Miller 1997; Bhogle 1991; Rao and Kanade 1992). There is a strong need to undertake more such studies in other areas to assess the actual impact of ongoing breastfeeding promotional activities at community level.

It was encouraging to find cent per cent complementary feeding between the ages of 6 to 9 months. This observation is at variance with the reports from different Indian states (Ghosh 1998). Nevertheless different motives appear to be at work. In the boys it was to meet the demands of growth, whereas in girls the underlying reason was mostly the lack of time on the part of mother to breastfeed them. Girls were offered readily available cheaper supplements in the process of cessation of breastfeeding as continued breastfeeding rates were lower for girls. This becomes obvious on analysing the diet of children aged 6 to 18 months. This is the age when the selection of complementary food plays an important role in the child's nutrition. Good complementary foods should be rich in energy and should also serve as a good source of protein, vitamins, and minerals. The study noted the difference in all food items consumed by the boys and girls. This may be due to delay in Annnaprashan ceremony of girls by one month. Puja ceremony when suji was offered to the child was also more commonly performed for boys. This is in line with the observations made by other researchers (Miller 1997). The contrast was much sharper with regard to protein rich food items like eggs, meat, and fish, which were offered to a higher proportion of boys than girls. There are reports of preferential feeding for boys by several authors (Chen et al. 1981; Das Gupta 1987; Sen and Sengupta 1983; Anyanwu 1995 and others). While others did not find such difference (Backstrand et al. 1997). There is shortage of information on this particular aspect, from West Bengal. Hence there is need to undertake similar studies in different socio-economic strata, for further exploration of the underlying reasons. Principles of healthy feeding practices have yet to percolate at the community level.

Discriminatory feeding practices are reflected in the poorer nutritional status of girls, although nutritional status of both boys and girls was found to be unacceptable. Proportion of underweight and stunting was higher in girls. This is in contrast to the results of the NNMB survey which did not find any difference (Ministry of Human Resource Development 2002). However, in numerous other studies from India, Bangladesh, and other developing countries, girls were found to be more malnourished than boys (Cowan 1990; Srivastava and Nayak 1995; Fauveau et al. 1991; Ghosh et al. 2002; HKI 1994 etc.). In the present study, poorer nutritional status of girls has been noted in all ages but was most marked between 3 to 4 years. After 4 years, the gap narrowed down. This is in line with the observations of Helen Keller International NSP report from Bangladesh (HKI 1994). After the age of 4 years, the child gradually acquires independence and starts sharing with adults which may result in improved nutritional status. The study found no difference in severe malnutrition between boys and girls whereas others reported higher rate of severe malnutrition among girls (Choudhury et al. 2000).

The study has highlighted the prevailing gender differences in the feeding of young children at the crucial juncture of rapid growth and development. Initiation of breastfeeding was delayed for girls. Weaning started early for boys. Boys also received protein-rich items and expensive commercial foods more frequently. Culturally also the girls were discriminated by delaying their Annaprashan ceremony by a month. Discrepancies in feeding practices have resulted in poorer nutritional status of girls. The reason for the observed differences seems to lie in mothers' adopted behaviour rather than lack of resources. This needs to be addressed by a well-planned and directed intervention acceptable at the level of community.

REFERENCES

Anyanwu, S.O. (1995), 'The Girl Child: Problems and Survival in the Nigerian Context', *Scandinavian Journal of Development Alternatives*, March–June, Vol. 14, Nos 1 and 2, pp. 85–105.

Backstrand, J.R., L.H. Allen, G.H. Pelto, and A. Chavez (1997), 'Examining the Gender Gap in Nutrition: An Example From Rural Mexico', *Social Science and Medicine*, June, Vol. 44, No. 11, pp. 1751–9.

Balkrishnan, R. (1994), *Social Context of Sex Selection and the Politics of Abortion in India*, Harvard School of Public Health, Cambridge, pp. 267–86.

Behrman, Richard E. and Victor C. Vaughan (1983), *Nelson Textbook of Pediatrics*, Twelfth Edition, III, MD Publication–W.B. Saunders Company, USA, pp. 26–33.

Bhogle, S. (1991), 'Child Rearing Practices and Behaviour and Development of Girl Child', *Indian Journal of Social Work*, Vol. 52, No. 1, pp. 61–8.

Census of India (2001), *Provisional Population Totals: India*, Office of Registrar General of India, Paper 1 of 2001, New Delhi, (*http://www.Censusindia.net/results/resultsmain.html*)

Chen, L. (1982), 'Where Have the Women Gone? Insights from Bangladesh on the Sex Ratio of India's Population', *Economic and Political Weekly*, March, Vol. 6, pp. 364–72.

Chen, L., E. Huq, and S. D'Souza (1981), 'Sex bias in the Family: Allocation of Food and Health Care in Rural Bangladesh', *Population and Development Review*, Vol. 7, No. 1, pp. 54–70.

Choudhury, K.K., M.A. Hanifi, S. Rasheed, and A. Bhuiya (2000), 'Gender Inequality and Severe Malnutrition Among Children in a Remote Rural Area of Bangladesh', *Journal of Health, Population Nutrition*, and December, Vol. 18, No. 3, pp. 123–30.

Cowan, B. (1990), 'Let Her Die', *Indian Journal Maternal and Child Health*, October–December, Vol. 1, No. 4, pp. 127–8.

Das Gupta, M. (1987), Selective Discrimination Against Female Children in Rural Punjab, India, *Population and Development Review*, Vol. 13, No. 1, pp. 77–100.

Dettwyler, Katherin A. and Claudia Fismman (1992), 'Infant Feeding Practices and Growth', *Annual Review of Anthropology*, Vol. 21, pp. 171–204.

Fauveau, V., M.A. Koenig and B. Wojtyniak (1991), 'Excess Female Deaths Among Rural Bangladeshi Children: An Examination of Cause-Specific Mortality and Morbidity', *International Journal of Epidemiology*, September, Vol. 20, No. 3, pp. 729–35.

Frongillo, E. A. Jr and F. Begin (1993), 'Gender Bias in Food Intake Favors Male Preschool Guatemalan Children', *Journal of Nutrition*, February, Vol. 123, No. 2, pp. 189–96.

Ghosh, S. (1991), 'Girl Child: A Life Time Deprivation and Discrimination', *The Indian Journal of Social Work*, Vol. 52, No. 1, pp. 21–7.

—— (1998), 'Rational Feeding Practices to Prevent Malnutrition', *The Child and Newborn*, Vol. 2, No. 3, pp. 5–6.

Ghosh, S., A. Kilaru, and S. Ganapathy (2002), 'Nutrition, Education, and Infant Growth in Rural Indian Infants: Narrowing the Gender Gap?', *Indian Medical Association*, August, Vol. 100, No. 8, pp. 483–4, 486–8, 490.

Gove, S. (1997), 'Integrated Management of Childhood Illnesses by Outpatient Health Workers: Technical Basis and Overview', *Bulletin of World Health Organization*, Vol. 75 (supplement), pp. 7–24.

Helen Keller International (HKI) (1994), Nutritional Surveillance Project 'Summary Report on the Nutritional Impact of Sex Biased Behavior', HKI, Dhaka, Bangladesh.

Hossain, M. and G.M. Roger (1988), 'Parental Son Preference in Seeking Medical Care for Children Less Than Five Years of Age in Rural Community of Bangladesh', *American Journal of Public Health*, Vol. 78, pp. 1349–50.

Indian Council of Medical Research (ICMR) Bulletin (2000), *Priorities in Child Health*, Vol. 30, No. 9, p. 86.

Kapil, Umesh, D. Verma, S. Narula, D. Nayar, H.P.S. Sachdev, Archana D. Shah, and N. Gnanasekaran (1994), 'Breast-Feeding Practices in Schedule Caste Communities in Haryana State', *Indian Pediatrics*, October, Vol. 31, p. 10.

Kumar, S. (1997), *BFHI Scenario in West Bengal*, World Breastfeeding Week, pp. 7–8.

Manandhar, D.S. (1997), 'Primary Care of Newborn in Nepal', *The Newborn*, National Eonatology Forum, West Bengal, Vol. 3, No. 2, pp. 57–59.

Miller, Barbara D. (1981), *The Endangered Sex, Neglect of Female Children in Rural North India*, Carnell University Press, Ithaca, pp. 83–106.

Ministry of Human Resource Development (2002), 'The Indian Child: A Profile', Department of Women and Child Development, Government of India, p. 61.

Nag, S.K. (1997), 'Changing Scienario in Infant Nutrition', *World Breastfeeding Week*, pp. 19–20.

Park, K. (1997), *Text Book of Preventive and Social Medicine*, 15th edn, M/s Banarsidas Bhanot Publisher, Jabalpur, p. 363.

Rao, S. and A.N. Kanade (1992), 'Prolonged Breast Feeding and Malnutrition Among Rural Indian Children Below Three Years of Age', *European Journal of Clinical Nutrition*, Vol. 46, pp. 187–95.

Satish Kumar (1997), BFHI Scenario in West Bengal, *World Breastfeeding Week*, pp. 7–8.

Sen, A. and S. Sengupta (1983), 'Malnutrition in Rural Children and the Sex Bias', *Economic and Political Weekly*, Vol. 28, pp. 855–64.

Srivastava, S.P. and N.P. Nayak (1995), 'The Disadvantaged Girl Child in Bihar: A Study of Health Care Practices and Selected Nutritional Indices', *Indian Pediatrics*, Vol. 32, No. 8, pp. 911–3.

Woldegebriel, A. (2002), 'Mother's Knowledge and Belief on Breast Feeding', *Ethiopian Medical Journal*, October, Vol. 40, No. 4, pp. 365–74.

WHO/CDD/SER (1991), *Indicators for Assessing Breast-feeding Practices*, WHO, Switzerland, p. 91.

WHO (1997), *Breastfeeding*, WHO, Switzerland.

——— (2000), *Management of Child with Serious Infection and Severe Malnutrition, Guidelines for care at first level in developing countries*, Department of Child and Adolescent Health and Development, WHO, Switzerland.

Appendix A8.1: Operational Definitions

1. Exclusive breastfeeding: The practice of infants receiving only breast milk.
2. Predominant breastfeeding: The practice of infants receiving breast milk as a predominant source of nourishment. The babies also received water and water-based drinks (fruit juices, oral rehydration solution, ritual fluids drops, or syrup). But the children didn't receive non-human milk, food-based fluids, or solids.
3. Continued breastfeeding: The practice of infants receiving breast milk in addition to other foods and liquids.
4. Colostrum: Deep lemon yellow coloured thick secretion of breast for initial 2–4 days after child birth.
5. Prelacteal feed: Feeds given to newborn infants before initiation of breastfeeding. Included plain water, mineral water, glucose, or candy water and honey etc.
6. Top milk: Non-human milk given to infants for nourishment. This includes cow's milk, tinned milk, packet milk, buffalo's milk, and goat's milk.
7. Top food: Solids, semi-solid, and liquids except milk, given to the child for nourishment.
8. Complementary feeding: In addition to breast milk, the infants received solids and semi-solids and other foods and liquids including non-human milk and milk substitutes.
9. Median duration of breastfeeding: Age (in months) when 50 per cent of children are no longer breastfed.
10. Weight for age (WFA): It was computed using NCHS standards. Children with Weight for age Z score <-2 were considered underweight.
11. Grades of Malnutrition: Indian Academy of Pediatrics (IAP) classification was used as follows: Grade I Malnutrition: Median weight for age between 70 per cent and 80 per cent;

    Grade II Malnutrition: Median weight for age between 60 per cent and 70 per cent; and

    Grade III Malnutrition: Median weight for age below 60 per cent.
12. Height/Length for age (HFA): It was computed using NCHS standards. Children with Height/Length for age Z score <-2 were considered stunted.

Health and Nutritional Status of School Age Children
Some Gender and Age Differentials

TARA GOPALDAS* —————————————————— 9

Introduction

About a quarter of the world's population (5–15 years) are school age children. Yet they have received scant attention for nutrition or health services as compared to the pregnant/lactating mother or pre-school child. It was only in 1989 that attention was sharply focused on the poor health and nutritional status of the schooler (UNESCO 1989; Pollitt 1990; Leslie and Jamison 1990; Jamison and Leslie 1990). Gopalan (1975) had cogently argued that the overwhelming emphasis on the pre-school child had unfortunately drawn away attention from health and nutrition programmes for the schoolers who deserve as much attention as they are also severely malnourished. They are the future citizens and parents and if not helped, the quality of human resources would be greatly eroded. This is very true as the schooler (especially the 10+ years category) is virtually treated as an adult. He/she is expected to execute extremely hard physical work in and outside his home: most often has a long walk to school on an empty stomach and is expected to perform well in the classroom. All this without any allowances being made for his/her rapid growth and sexual development which call for enormously increased dietary and nutrient requirements. The social and economic need to invest in the health of this segment has been strongly emphasized (Gopaldas 1989). It is estimated that approximately 87 per cent of the world's school age children will live in the developing countries with the concentration

* I sincerely thank my research colleagues, especially, Sunder Gujaral and all my research scholars for their commitment to the cause of the schooler. I also thank the Ford Foundation and the Partnership of Child Development, Oxford University, UK for their generous financial support in the eighties and nineties, respectively, and for having full confidence in me and in Tara Consultancy Services.

being in Latin America, Africa, and Asia (Leslie and Jamison 1990). Hence, this paper will focus on these three continents. Further, only the most pervasive and dominant nutritional disorders of the schooler and some major factors contributing to this situation in these parts of the world have been referred to.

Dominant Nutritional Disorders (and Contributing Factors) in the Schooler of the Developing World

1. Hunger: Practically all members of the low income group (LIG) families are underfed and are chronically hungry. The schooler of the LIG is no exception. As mentioned earlier, most of them attend school on an empty stomach and suffer short-term hunger which has been shown to affect a child's attention in the classroom (Pollitt et al. 1978; Simeon et al. 1989; Popkin and Lim Ybnez 1982).
2. Endemic Protein–Energy Malnutrition (PEM): It follows that those who are chronically hungry also suffer from PEM of various grades and have a small body size. Small body size in school age children negatively influences physical work (Satyanarayana et al. 1979). Chronic PEM affects behavioural and mental development (Pollitt 1988; Jamison 1986; Mock and Leslie 1986; and Agarwal et al. 1987). Unfortunately, hunger and PEM are manifestations of poverty and a poor environment and cannot be addressed only through snacks/school lunches or mid-day-meal programmes (Sahn et al. 1981).
3. Unsafe Water: Water is the single most important food for man. Unsafe drinking water in most of the rural areas is the cause of several water-borne human parasitic/helminthic diseases of the gastro-intestinal-tract (GIT), that subsequently lead to PEM (Stephenson et al. 1980), nutritional anaemia (Hussein et al. 1981), and vitamin A deficiency (VAD) (Mahalanobis et al. 1979). Providing schools with safe drinking water (tube well) may help somewhat in improving the health and nutritional status of the schooler. In the short term, there appears to be no other way out but to de-infest pre-school and school populations periodically (Pyle 1973). De-infestation measures in the short term are eminently feasible and relatively cost-effective.
4. Iron Deficiency Anemia: This is the most widespread disorder in almost all segments of the population of the developing world; the

schooler is no exception. Among the school age, the pre-adolescent and adolescent groups are most affected (Kashyap and Gopaldas 1987; Srikantia 1989). It has very definite and deleterious effects on physical work capacity (Gopaldas, Kale, and Bhardwaj 1985) and cognition/behaviour (Soewondo, Husaini, and Pollitt 1989; Pollitt et al. 1989; and Seshadri and Gopaldas 1989). Reduction or even eradication of nutritional anaemia is entirely feasible and possibly the most cost-effective input to deliver in an expanded supplementation programme to the schooler. Fortification or direct supplementation have also shown excellent results.

5. IDD: This condition is widely prevalent in the schooler, especially so in the sub-Himalayan belt in India, Bolivia, Peru, and many African countries. IDD even in its milder form affects micro-development, visual perceptual organization, visual motor-coordination, and speed of information processing. Cretinism which affects far less in the population, directly inhibits schooling. Like iron-supplementation/fortification, it is entirely feasible and cost-effective to deliver iodine to the schooler either through iodized salt or through direct supplementation of iodine in oil (Hetzel 1989).

6. VAD: This condition though in its milder form, is far more prevalent in the schooler than in the pre-schooler (Sommer 1982 and International Vitamin A Consultative Group 1979). Vitamin A is not only important for vision but also has important roles to play in morbidity (Sommer 1982), immunity (International Vitamin A Consultative Group), and growth (Graham et al. 1981). Further, hypovitaminosis and nutritional anaemia often co-exist among poor children of these regions (Meija et al. 1977; Mohanram et al. 1977; International Nutritional Anemia Consultative Group 1979). Diets of school age children show the most severe dietary deficits with respect to vitamin A (Kanani 1984). Hence, there is an urgent need to address the twin problems of widespread iron and vitamin A deficiency in this population.

Intestinal Parasitic Infestations and Their Negative Influence on the Nutritional Status of the Schooler

Two broad groups of intestinal parasites of public health nutrition importance are (i) protozoa (for example, Entomoeba Histolytica and Griardia Lamblia) and (ii) helminths (for example, Ascaris

Lumbricoides, Ancylostoma Duodenale, Trichuris Trichuria. These parasites definitely impair nutritional status in the host by several mechanisms such as: affecting enzymatic digestion; mucosal absorption of nutrients; competing for host's nutrients; causing catabolic loss of nutrients; and causing bacterial overgrowth (Solomons and Keusch 1981; Tomkins and Watson 1989). The negative impact of specific helminths/protozoa on nutritional status follows.

Negative Impact of Round Worm or Ascariasis on Nutritional Status: (i) Absorption of fat and protein is impaired. (ii) Absorption of vitamin A is seriously impaired (Sommer 1982). The serum retinol levels are lowered in infested children (Kumar et al. 1976).

Negative Impact of Hookworm (A. duodenale and N. americanus): (i) These helminths are considered to be among the principal etilological factors in the development of anaemia in the tropics and cause anaemia through blood loss (Layrisse et al. 1976).

Negative Impact of Whip Worm (Trichuris Trichuria): (i) Common but unrecognized cause of diarrhoea and dysentery where infection rates are high (Beaver 1961). Hence, cause of malabsorption and loss of nutrients in stools. (ii) Causes blood loss but causation in anaemia is uncertain (Greenberg and Cline 1979).

Negative Impact of the Protozoan Entamoeba Histolytica: (i) Pathogenic to man, causes chronic ill health, recurrent diarrhoea, abdominal pain, and malabsorption of nutrients especially of fat (Chatterjee 1980 and Solomons and Keusch 1981). (ii) Lowers Hb levels. (iii) Lowers serum retinol levels (Beaver 1961; Greenberg and Cline 1979).

Negative Impact of the Protozoan Griardia Lamblia: (i) Aggravates diarrhoea (Madan, Ghosal, and Sengupta 1977). (ii) Lowers Hb levels (Gautam 1980).

Some notable differences: Among helminths, round worm and hookworm were more confined to rural areas, while the protozoal infections were more widespread in slums. The prevalence rate increased with the age of the child and was higher among boys than girls (Kanani 1984).

BRIEF REVIEW OF PREVALENCE LEVELS OF MAJOR NUTRITIONAL DISORDERS IN SCHOOL AGE POPULATIONS, WORLDWIDE

A review of available literature did not yield much information on comprehensive nutritional status surveys on large school age cohorts in the three continents of interest. I have therefore attempted to piece together whatever little information is available and this is in Tables 9.1, 9.2, 9.3, 9.4, 9.5, and 9.6.

I have also included two maps depicting the geographical distribution of IDD and of Xerophthalmia (Maps 9.1 and 9.2).

Table 9.1: Prevalence of parasitic infestations among school children

(per cent)

Region		Prevalence
Latin America		
Peru	Round Worm (*A.Lumbricodes*)	28
Africa		
Southern Tunisia	Round Worm (*A.Lumbricodes*)	17–48
	Amoebiasis (*E. Histolytica*)	2–4
	Giardiasis (*G.Lamblia*)	3–15
Kenya (Nairobi)	Round Worm (*A.Lumbricodes*)	60
	Hook Worm (*A.Duodenale*)	22
	Whip Worm (*T. Trichuris*)	38
Asia		
India	Round Worm (*A.Lumbricodes*)	1
Southern India	Amoebiasis (*E. Histolytica*)	2
	Giardiasis (*G.Lamblia*)	12
Northern India	Round Worm (*A.Lumbricodes*)	10
	Giardiasis (*G.Lamblia*)	27
Eastern India	Round Worm (*A.Lumbricodes*)	25
	Amoebiasis (*E. Histolytica*)	12
	Giardiasis (*G.Lamblia*)	51
	Hook Worm (*A.Duodenale*)	54

Source: Bradfield et al. (1968); Stephenson et al. (1980); Indirabai et al. (1976); Jain et al. (1976); and Kalita (1991).

It is quite evident from Table 9.1 that poverty, poor hygiene, and lack of safe water are the causes of very high levels of parasitic infestations in the school age children of Latin America, Africa, and Asia. In Asia,

**Table 9.2: Prevalence of nutritional anaemia (Hb level < 12 g/dl)
among school children**

(per cent)

Region	Prevalence
Latin America	26
Africa	49
East Asia	22
South Asia	50
World	37
Developed Regions	7
Developing Regions	46

Source: E.M. De Macyer and M.A. Egman (1985).

Table 9.3: Quantitative data on IDA (Hb <129/dl) in schoolers

Age Groups	Baseline Mean ± SEM
6–10 years	
Boys	10.5±0.06 (650)
Girls	10.5±0.05 (644)
11–15 Years	
Boys	10.9±0.06 (581)
Girls	10.5±0.07 (601)
6–15 years	
Boys	10.7±0.04 (1231)
Girls	105±0.04 (1245)

Source: T. Gopaldas (2005).

eastern India has extremely high levels of Giardiasis and of hookworm. In Baroda, the prevalence figures were 44 per cent (boys) vs 35 per cent (girls).

From Tables 9.2 and 9.3 we see that South Asia and Africa lead in having the highest prevalence of nutritional anaemia (Hb level of < 12 g/dl) in school children. This is indeed a shameful state of affairs

Table 9.4: Prevalence of iodine deficiency in school age children

(per cent)

Region	Prevalence
Latin America	
Argentina	50
Bolivia	61
Brazil	15
Ecuador	12
Guatemala	11
Paraguay	16
Peru	22
Venezuela	13
Africa	
Cameroon	62–85
*Ethiopia	10–39
Lesotho	7–22
*Kenya	40–60
*Mali	10
*Nigeria	15
*Olurin	12–50
Senegal	26–40
*Sierra Leonne	25–70
*Zambia	42–59
Asia	
India (Kangra Valley)	47
*Nepal	46
*Bhutan	65

Note: * Separate figures for school age not reported, information abstracted.
Source: Hetzel (1988 and 1989).

Table 9.5: Prevalence of mild VAD in school children

(per cent)

Region	Prevalence
Latin America	
Brazil (North East)	21*
Asia	
Cebu, Philippines	5
Malaysia	16
India	41

Note: * XIB only.
Sources: F.S. Solon et al. (1978); K.W. Tony and Y.H. Cheng (1977); W.R. Simmons (1976); and I. Pant and T. Gopaldas (1986).

Table 9.6: Per cent prevalence of VAD signs and symptoms in Baroda schoolers

Vitamin A Status	Boys			Girls			Total Sample		
	5–9 yrs (204)	10–15 yrs (176)	5–15 yrs (380)	5–9 yrs (159)	10–15 yrs (156)	5–15 yrs (315)	5–9 yrs (363)	10–15 yrs (332)	5–15 yrs (695)
Vitamin A sufficient	62	35	50	62	59	61	62	46	55
Vitamin A deficient	38	65	51	38	41	39	38	54	46
XIA #	14	16	15	20	15	18	17	16	16
XIB @	6	10	8	3	12	7	4	11	8
XIA + XIB	2	6	4	1	3	2	1	5	3
XN *	12	16	14	11	5	8	11	11	11
XN + XIA **	3	8	6	3	4	4	3	6	5
XN + XIB **	2	9	5	0	1	1	1	5	3
XN + XIA + XIB **	0	1	0	0	0	0	0	0	0
Active cases (5+6+7)	5	17	11	3	5	4	4	11	8

Notes: # Conjunctival xerosis by Rose Bengal dye test; @ Bitot spots; * Night-blindness; ** Active cases of Xerophthalmia (Sommer 1982)
Figures in parentheses indicate number of subjects.
Source: T. Gopaldas (2005).

Map 9.1: Distribution of IDD in developing countries

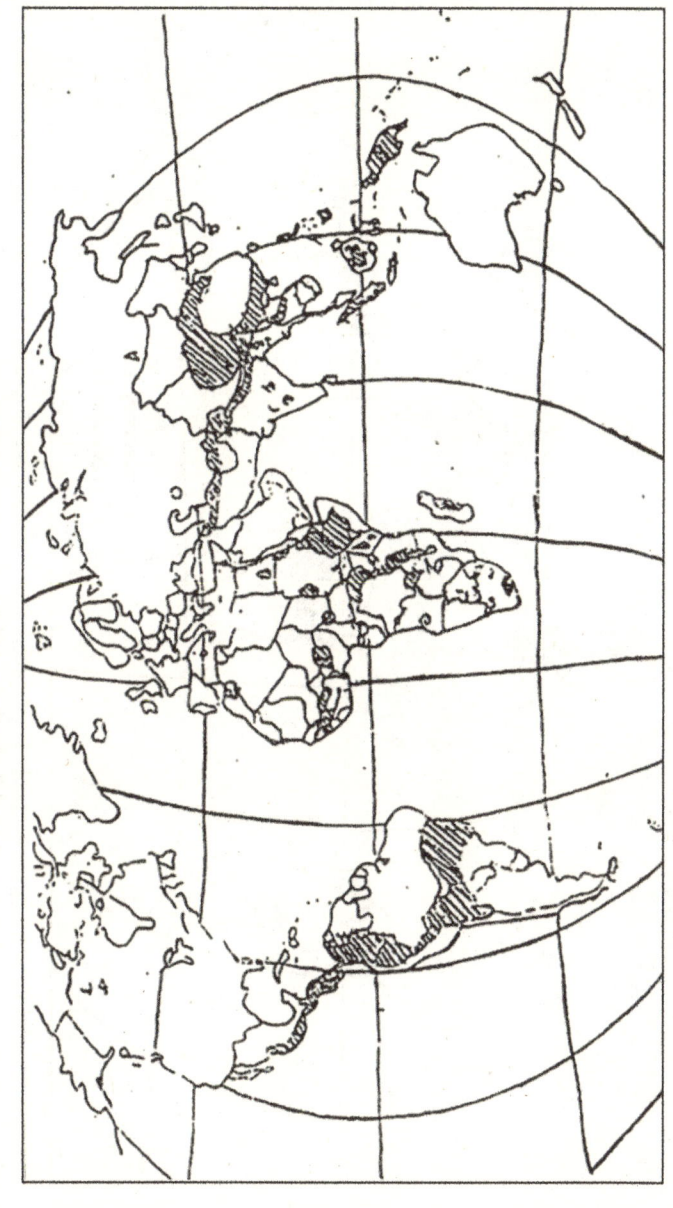

Source: ACC/SCN (1988); Hetzel (1988).

Map 9.2: Geographical distribution of Xerophthalmia, 1986

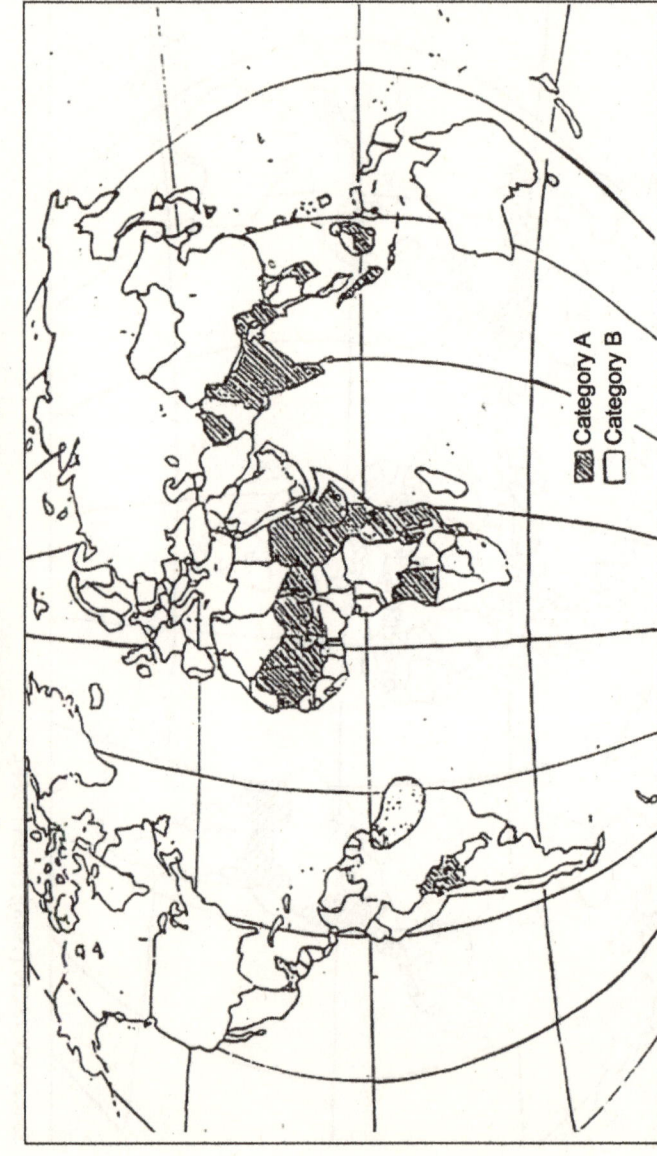

Category A
Category B

Notes: A: Xerophthalmia is a significant public health problem; B: Sporadic cases of xerophthalmia do occur; A: El Salvador, Haiti, Bangladesh, India, Indonesia, Nepal, Sri Lanka, and Philippines.

Source: ACC/SCN (1987); West and Sommer (1987).

as iron-folic acids supplementation is one of the cheapest methods of reducing or wiping out this public nutrition menace.

Table 9.4 shows that iodine deficiency disorder (IDD) has come down substantially worldwide, including in India.

VAD continues to be our biggest public nutrition problem, in *all* population groups. Table 9.5 shows that 50 per cent of the boys depicted pre-clinical or the milder signs of Vitamin A deficiency; The prevalence figure jumped to 65 per cent in the older boys. In the girls it was much less at 39 per cent with only a slightly higher prevalence in the older girls. We can easily combat VAD through supplementation (tablet or capsule form), just two times a year per schooler per year in the classroom.

Table 9.6 shows that in the 5 to 9 years age group there is no difference, with 38 per cent prevalence of VAD among both boys and girls. However, in the older age group (10–15 years) there is a significant difference both by gender and by age. The older boy is most affected (65 per cent) vs the girl (41 per cent) [10–15 years].

BARODA SCHOOL AGE CHILDREN–A CASE STUDY (1980–95)

Since we have worked with school age boys and girls (5-15 years) in about 40 of the free municipal schools out of the existing 200 in Baroda, for over a decade and since we have executed comprehensive intestinal parasitic and nutritional status surveys on large cohorts, I use Baroda as a case study to depict the sad and deplorable parasitic/ nutritional status of these children.

Nutrient Intake

It is evident from Figures 9.1 and 9.2 that the meager home diet failed to meet the RDA of any nutrient. The most noticeable deficit was with regard to Vitamin A.

Growth

We can see from Figure 9.3 that only about half the children (5–15 years) had a normal weight for height index. Older children (10–15 years) had an even poorer growth rate. Among girls (10–15 years), only 31 per cent had a normal growth. As per Waterlow's classification (not shown here), stunting was noted in 40 per cent of all older children, being more prevalent in the older boys versus the older girls.

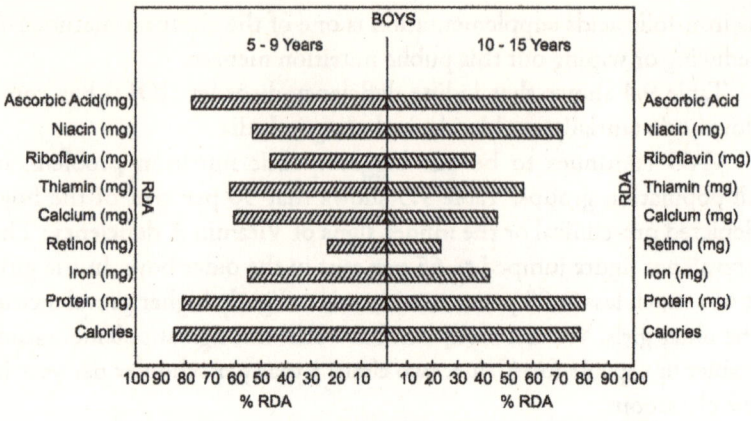

Figure 9.1: Mean nutrient intake of baroda schoolers (boys)

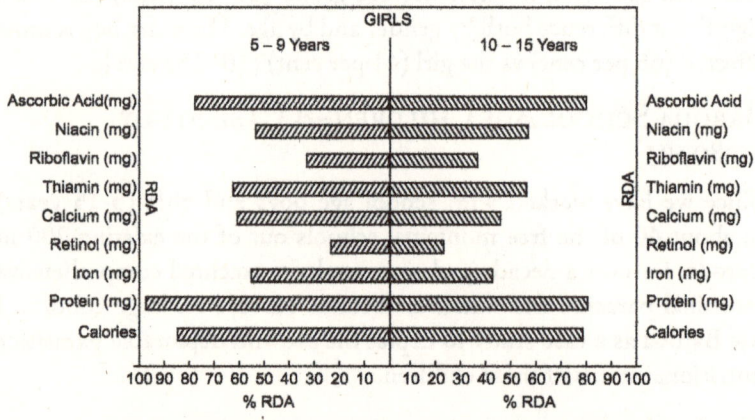

Figure 9.2: Mean nutrient intake of baroda schoolers (girls)

Nutritional Anaemia

Using the WHO cut-offs of 11 g/dl for children (5–9 years) and 12 g/dl for children (10–15 years), we see that as many as 73 per cent of the boys and 67 per cent of the girls were mildly to moderately anaemic (see Figures 9.4 and 9.5).

Intestinal Parasites

Table 9.7 shows that total prevalence was high at 40 per cent with protozoal infection (*E. histolytica* and *G. Lamblia*) being higher (25

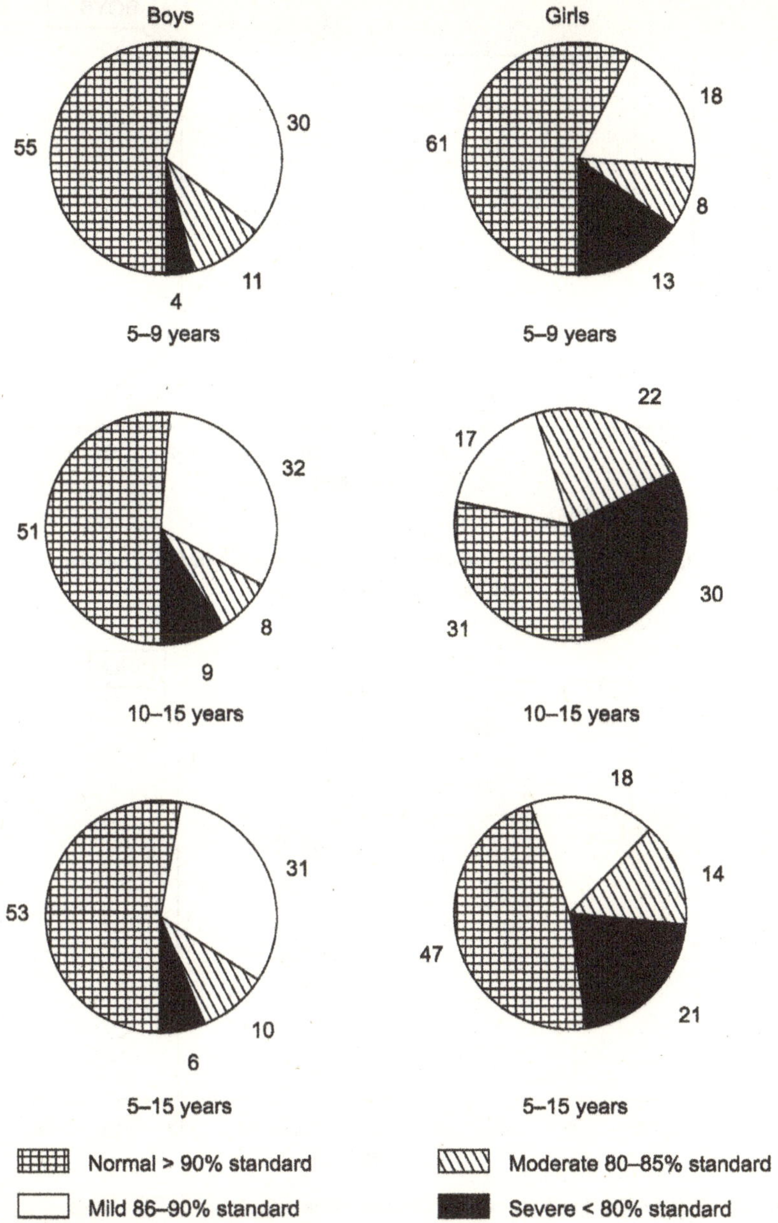

Boys

30
55
11
4

5–9 years

Girls

18
61
8
13

5–9 years

32
51
8
9

10–15 years

22
17
30
31

10–15 years

31
53
10
6

5–15 years

18
14
47
21

5–15 years

▦ Normal > 90% standard   ▨ Moderate 80–85% standard

☐ Mild 86–90% standard   ■ Severe < 80% standard

Source: Gopaldas and Gujral (1996).

Figure 9.3: Distribution of schoolers according to grades of malnutrition by weight for height index

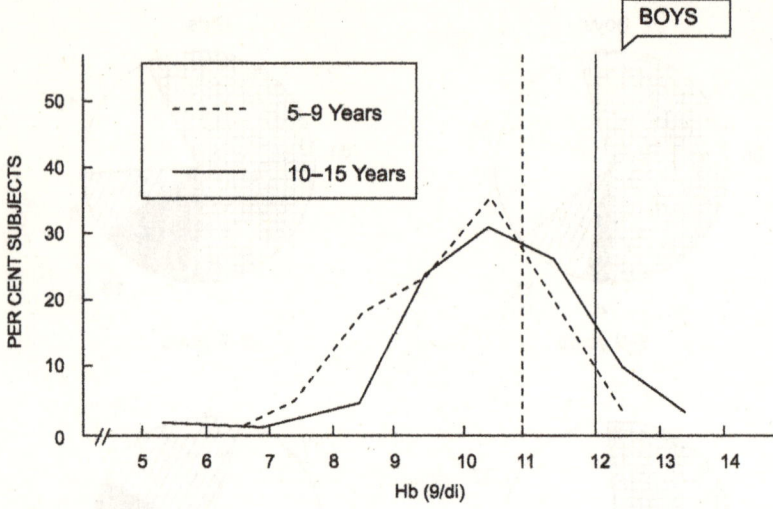

Source: Gopaldas (2005).

Figure 9.4: Frequency distribution of haemoglobin (Hb) values of Baroda subjects (boys)

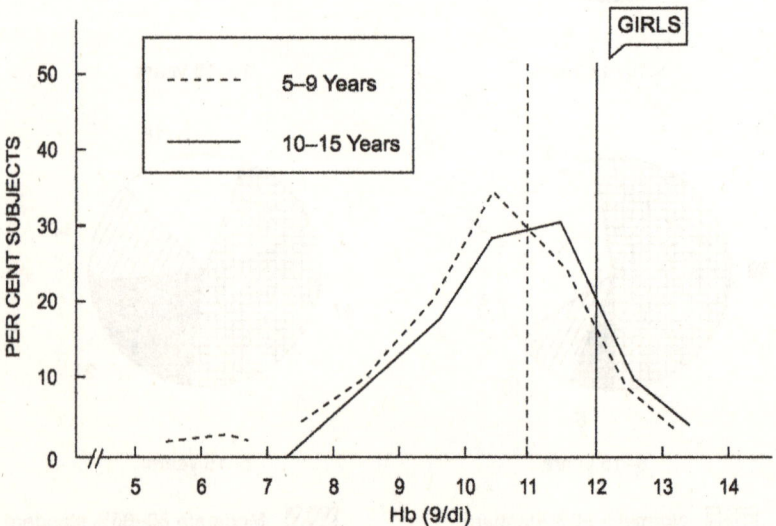

Figure 9.5: Frequency distribution of haemoglobin (Hb) values of Baroda subjects (girls)

Table 9.7: Prevalence of Intestinal Infestation in Baroda Schoolers

Type of Infestation	Boys		Girls		Total Sample	
	No.	per cent	No.	per cent	No.	per cent
E. histolytica	18	17	17	17	35	17
G. lamblia	12	11	6	6	18	9
H. nana	11	10	7	7	18	9
A. lumbricoides	0	0	2	2	2	10
T. trichuria	1	10	1	1	2	10
A. duodenale	1	10	0	0	1	1
Mixed infestation	5	5	3	3	8	4
Nil	61	56	66	65	127	60
Total	109	100	102	100	211	100
Total helminthes	18	17	13	13	31	15
Total protozoa	30	28	23	23	53	25
Total prevalence	48	44	36	35	84	40
Positive history of passing worms	61	34	36	25	97	29

Source: T. Gopaldas (2005).

per cent) than helminthic infection (15 per cent). Boys had higher infection levels than girls.

SOME SUGGESTIONS FOR A QUICK SITUATIONAL ANALYSIS OF THE PARASITIC CUM NUTRITIONAL STATUS OF THE SCHOOL AGE POPULATION

1. There is a paucity of information on parasitic and nutritional status of school age children in the three continents of interest on representative samples using a common and acceptable methodology.
2. It is suggested that all efforts be made to collect the necessary information from secondary data sources to the extent possible.
3. A network of medical and nutritional institutions should be set up in the three continents to compile existing information speedily.
4. We have found it extremely difficult to obtain subject co-operation for stool samples. At least in India there is a social and cultural taboo. Perhaps information could be elicited through focus group interviews or through questioning the child.
5. Older school children can be used to help in anthropometric measurements and in eliciting information on nutritional deficiencies,

ill-health, and physical handicaps. We have found in our child-to-child project that children are quicker to detect ailments and abnormalities in their peer group than the teachers.

6. At the very least, an inter-continental database can be set up wherein the heights and weights of children entering primary school and leaving it can be ascertained. Similarly their Hb levels. This will help in monitoring school health at the most basic level. It will also throw light on the deterioration of health and nutritional status in the older boys and girls (11–15 years).

7. Approximately 30 million underprivileged schoolers (5 to 15+ years) are getting the mid-day meal plus the 'deworming and micronutrient package in the classroom' since 2004 (Gopaldas 2005 and GoI 2007–08).

8. The Government of India is trying its best to extend the mid-day meal and 'the preventive health package' up to high school, on an all-India basis.

REFERENCES

ACC/SCN (1987), First Report on the World Nutrition Situation, ACC/SCN, Geneva.

———— (1988), Supplement on Methods and Statistics to the First Report on the World Nutrition Situation, ACC/SCN, Geneva.

Agarwal, D.K., S.K. Upadhyay, A.M. Tripathi, and K.N. Agarwal (1987), 'Nutritional Status, Physical Work Capacity and Mental Function in School Children', *Nutrition Foundation of India, Scientific Report*, Vol. 6, pp. 67–76.

Beaver, P.C. (1961), 'Control of Soil Transmitted Helminthes', *WHO Public Health Report*, Vol. 10, WHO, Geneva.

Bradfield, R.B., M.V. Jensen, L. Gonzales, and C. Garrayar (1968), 'Effect of Low Level of Iron and Vitamin Supplementation on Tropical Anaemia', *American Journal of Clinical Nutrition*, Vol. 21, No. 1, pp. 57–67.

Chaliha Kalita, M. (1991), 'The Influence of Type of Tea Plantation on the Nutritional Status of Male and Female Plantation Workers of Assam', Ph.D thesis, Department of Foods and Nutrition, M.S. University, Baroda, India.

Chatterjee, K.D. (1980), *Paristology in Relation to Clinical Medicine*, 12th edition, Chatterjee Medical Publishers, Calcutta.

DeMaeyer, E.M., M. Adiels-Tegman (1985), 'The Prevalence of Anaemia in the World', *World Health Statistics*, Quarterly, Vol. 38, pp. 302–16, World Health Organization, Geneva, Switzerland.

Gautam, S. (1980), 'An Exploratory Study to Investigate the Impact of Selected Health Inputs in Mid-Day-Meal Programme Beneficiaries (10–13 years)', M.Sc thesis, Department of Foods and Nutrition, M.S. University, Baroda, India.

Gopalan, C. (1975), 'Nutrition and India's Children', *Assignment Children*, Vol. 29, pp. 51–60.

Gopaldas, T., M. Kale, and P. Bhardwaj (1985), 'Prophylactic Iron Supplementation for Underprivileged School Boys', *Indian Journal Pediatrics*, Vol. 22, pp. 737–43.

Gopaldas, T. and S. Gujral (1996), 'The Pre-Post Impact Evaluation of the Improved Mid-day-Meal Programme', Final Report, Tara Consultancy Services, Gujarat.

Gopaldas, T. (1989), 'Strategies and Approaches to Combat Under Nutrition: India's Eighth Five Year Plan (1990–1995)', Department of Foods and Nutrition, M.S. University, Baroda.

———(2005), 'Improved Effect of School Meals with Micronutrient Supplementation and De-worming', *Food Nutrition Bulletin*, Vol. 26, No. 2, pp. 220–29.

Graham, G.G., M.M. Creed, W.C. McLean, C.H. Kallman, J. Rabold, and E. David Mellets (1981), 'Determinants of Growth among Poor Children: Nutrient Intake – Achieved Growth Relationships', *American Journal of Clinical Nutrition*, Vol. 34, pp. 539–54.

Government of India (2007–08), *Annual Work Plan and Budget of 37 States and Union Territories of India*, Ministry of Human Resource Development, Department of School Education, Literacy and the Midday Meal Division.

Greenberg, E.R. and B.L. Cline (1979), 'Is Trichuriasis Associated with Iron Deficiency Anemia?', *American Journal of Tropical Medicine and Hygiene*, Vol. 28, No. 4, pp. 770–72.

Hetzel, B.S. (1988), 'The Prevention and Control of Iodine Deficiency Disorders', ACC/SCN, Nutrition Policy Discussion Paper 3, pp. 55–61.

——— (1989), *The Story of Iodine Deficiency: An International Challenge in Nutrition*, Oxford University Press, Delhi, pp. 36–52.

Hussein, L., B. Elnaggar, S. Gaafar, and H. Allam (1981), 'Effects of Levels of Iron on Haemoglobin Values of Parasitized School Children', *Nutrition Reports International*, Vol. 23, No. 5, pp. 901–13.

Indirabai, K. and D.P.N.M. Ratna Mallika (1976), 'School Health Service Programme—a Comparative Study of School Children in Tirupathi, Andhra Pradesh', *Indian Pediatrics*, Vol. 13, No. 10, pp. 751–8.

International Nutritional Anemia Consultative Group (1979), 'Iron Deficiency in Infancy and Childhood', A report of INACG.

International Vitamin A Consultative Group (1979), 'Recent Advances in the Metabolism and Function of Vitamin A and their Relationship to Applied Nutrition', A report of the IVACG, Switzerlnd.

Jain, M., U.N. Bhatia, A. Srivastava, D.S. Aggarval, and S. Gupta (1976), 'Amoebiasis in Children in an Urban Community', *Indian Pediatrics*, Vol. 13, No. 2, p. 119.

Jamison, D. (1986), 'Child Nutrition and School Performance in China', *Journal of Development Economics*, Vol. 20, pp. 299–309.

Jamison D.T. and J. Leslie (1990), 'Health and Nutrition Considerations in Education Planning, 2. The Cost and Effectiveness of School Based Interventions', UNU Food and Nutrition Bulletin, Vol. 12, No. 3, pp. 204–14.

Kanani, S. (1984) 'Intervention Studies with Antiparasitics, vitamin A and iron Supplements on Mid Day Meal Programme Beneficiaries', PhD thesis, Deptartment of Foods and Nutrition, M.S. University, Baroda, India.

Kashyap, P. and T. Gopaldas (1987), 'Hematinic Supplementation and Hematological Status of Underprivileged School Girls (8–15 years of age); *Nutrition Research*, Vol. 7, pp. 1127–38.

Kumar, K.A., C.M.S. Siddhu, M.R. Chandra, and K. Kishore (1976), 'Serum Vitamin A Level in Secondary School Children', *Indian Journal of Pediatrics*, Vol. 43, pp. 368–77.

Layrisse, M., M. Roche, and S.J. Baker (1976), 'Nutritional Anemias', in G.H. Beaton, and J.M. Bengoa (eds), *Nutrition in Preventive Medicine*, WHO, Geneva. pp. 55-82.

Leslie, J. and D.T. Jamison (1990), 'Health and Nutrition Considerations in Education Planning, 1. Educational Consequences of Health Problems among School-age Children', UNU Food and Nutrition Bulletin, Vol. 12, No. 3, pp. 191–203.

Lowenstein, F.W. and D.E. O'Connel (1977), 'Health and Nutritional Status of Village Boys 6–11 Years in Southern Tunisia', *Journal of Tropical Pediatrics Environmental Child Health*, Vol. 23, No. 2, pp. 66–72.

Madan, S., S.P. Ghosal, and P.C. Sengupta (1977), 'Intestinal Parasitosis: Its Relation to Diarrhoea in Indian Children', *Indian Pediatrics*, Vol. 14, No. 11, pp. 899–903.

Mahalanobis, D., T.W. Simpson, M.L. Chakraborty, C. Ganguli, A.K. Bhattacharjee, and K.L. Mukherjee (1979), 'Malabsorption of Water Miscible Vitamin A in Children with Giardiasis and Ascariasis', *American Journal of Clinical Nutrition*, Vol. 32, pp. 313–18.

Meija, L.A., R.E. Hodges, G. Arroyave, F. Viteri, and B. Torun (1977), 'Vitamin A Deficiency and Anaemia in Central American Children', *American Journal of Clinical Nutrition*, Vol. 30, pp. 1175–84.

Mock, P.R., and J. Leslie (1986), 'Childhood Malnutrition and Schooling Deficit in the Terai Region of Nepal', *Journal of Development Economic*, Vol. 20, pp. 33–52.

Mohanram, M., K.A. Kulkarni, and V. Reddy (1977), 'Hematological Studies in Vitamin A Deficient Children', *International Journal of Vitamins and Nutrition Research*, Vol. 47, pp. 389–93.

Pant, I. and T. Gopaldas (1986), 'Is vitamin A Deficiency a Public Health Problem in Underprivileged School Boys (5–15 years)', *Nutrition Research*, Vol. 6, pp. 1951–61.

Pollitt, E. (1988), 'A Critical View of Three Decades of Research on the Effects of Chronic Energy Malnutrition on Behavioural Development', in S. Schurch and N.S. Scrimshaw (eds), *Chronic Energy Deficiency: Consequences and Related Issues*, IDECG, Nestle Foundation, Lausanne, Switzerland, pp. 77–93.

———(1990), 'Malnutrition and Infection in the Classroom', UNU *Food and Nutrition Bulletin*, Vol. 12, No. 3, pp. 178–88.

Pollitt, E., P. Hathirat, N.J. Kotchabhakdi, L. Misell, and A. Valyasevi (1989), 'Iron Deficiency and Educational Achievement in Thailand', *American Journal of Clinical Nutrition*, Supplement, Vol. 50, pp. 687–96.

Pollitt, E., R.L. Leibel, and D. Greenfield (1978), 'Brief Fasting, Stress and Cognitive Function', *American Journal of Clinical Nutrition*, Vol. 34, pp. 1526–33.

Popkin, B.M. and M. Lim Ybnez (1982), 'Nutrition and School Achievement', *Social Science of Medicine*, Vol. 16, pp. 53–61.

Pyle, D.F. (1973), 'The Feasibility of Periodic Deworming in Supplementary Feeding Programmes', *Indian Pediatrics*, Vol. 10, No. 8, pp. 507–10.

Sahn DE, B.L. Rogers, and D.P. Nelson (1981), 'Assessing the Uses of Food Aid: PL480 Title II in India', *Ecology of Food and Nutrition*, Vol. 10, pp. 153–61.

Satyanarayana, K., A.N. Naidu, and B.S. Narasinga Rao (1979), 'Nutritional Deprivation in Childhood and the Body Size, Activity and Physical Work Capacity of Young Boys', *American Journal of Clinical Nutrition*, Vol. 32, pp. 1796–1875.

Seshadri, S. and T. Gopalads (1989), 'Impact of Iron Supplementation on Cognitive Functions in Preschool and School Aged Children: The Indian Experience', *American Journal of Clinical Nutrition*, Supplement, Vol. 50, pp. 675–84.

Simeon, D.R., and S. Grantham McGregor (1989), 'Effects of Missing Breakfast on the Cognitive Functions of School Children of Differing Nutritional Status', *American Journal of Clinical Nutrition*, Vol. 49, pp. 646–53.

Simmons, W.R. (1976), 'Xerophthalmia and Blindness in North East Brazil', *American Journal of Clinical Nutrition*, Vol. 29, pp. 116–22.

Soewondo, S., M. Husaini, and E. Pollitt (1989), 'Effects of Iron Deficiency on Attention and Learning Processes in Preschool Children. Bandung, Indonesia', *American Journal of Clinical Nutrition*, Supplement, Vol. 30, pp. 667–73.

Solomons, N.W. and G.T. Keusch (1981), 'Nutritional Implications of Parasitic Infections', *Nutrition Reviews*, Vol. 39, No. 4, pp. 149–61.

Solon, F.S., B.M. Popkin, T.L. Fernandez, and M.C. Latham (1978), 'Vitamin A Deficiency in the Phillipines: A study of Xerophthalmia in Cepu', *American Journal of Clinical Nutrition*, Vol. 31, pp. 360–68.

Sommer, A. (1982), *Nutritional Blindness—Xerophthalmia and Keratomalacia*, Oxford University Press, Oxford, New York.

Srikantia, S.G. (1989), 'Nutritional Deficiency Diseases', in C. Gopalan, and S. Kaur (eds) *Women and Nutrition in India*, Nutrition Foundation of India. Special Publication Series, New Delhi, p. 5.

Stephenson, L.S., B.W.T. Crompton, M.C. Latham, T.W.J. Schulpen, M.C. Nesheim, and A.A.J. Jansen (1980), 'Relationships between Ascaris Infection and Growth of Malnourished Preschool Children in Kenya', *American Journal of Clinical Nutrition*, Vol. 33, pp. 1165–72.

Tomkins, A., and F. Watson (1989), 'Malnutrition and Infection: A Review', Administrative Committee on Coordination/Standing Committee on Nutrition State-of-the-Art Series Nutrition Policy Discussion paper No.5.

Tony, K.W. and Y.H. Cheng (1977), 'Serum Vitamin A levels of Two Rural Communities of Malaysia', *Journal of Tropical Pediatrics and Environmental Child Health*, Vol. 93, pp. 91–93.

UNESCO (1989), *First Technical Report of the News UNESCO Project to Improve Primary School Performance through Improved Nutrition and Health*, UNESCO, Paris.

West, K.P. and A. Sommer (1987), 'Delivery of Oral Doses of Vitamin A to Prevent Vitamin A Deficiency and Nutritional Blindness; a State of the Art Review', Administrative Committee on Coordination/Standing Committee on Nutrition, Nutrition Policy Discussion paper No. 2, p. 5.

Gender Bias and Family Planning Programme in India[†]

AMITABH TEWARI and
SURUCHI TEWARI ————————————— 10

INTRODUCTION

The concept of family planning (FP) is associated with the awareness, conscious thought, and action of a couple regarding their family size and reproductive behaviour. So it is a part of intensely private and personal behaviour of an individual (Tewari 1989). In general, there are hardly any social efforts made regarding an increase in the adoption of family planning practices. But, it is an area where the State is taking initiative and, through policy interventions, trying to popularize the FPP. Although in India the first state-run birth control clinic was established in Mysore in 1930 (GoI 1959), the introduction of the FPP in the five year plan (1951–6) made India the first developing country to do so. In the First FYP, a modest beginning was made when a sum of Rs 65 lakh was allotted to FPP, then in the successive FYPs the amount kept on increasing (Table 10.1). During the last 50 years, various approaches viz. clinic, extension, camp, and cafeteria were adopted at different periods of time. At present the cafeteria approach is the one most practiced. In this approach, health workers/agencies come up with a number of FP devices from which the people can choose the desired one. Moreover, they also get a chance to discuss the pros and cons of each of the devices with the doctors or health workers.

[†] An earlier draft of this paper was presented at a National Seminar organized by J.S. Hindu College, Amroha, on 'Population and Development', 23–24 February 2003. The authors are grateful to Subha Ray, Lecturer, Department of Anthropology, University of Allahabad, for his comments and suggestions.

Table 10.1: Expenditure on FPP in successive FYPs

Plan period	Plan outlays on family welfare programme (Rs crore)	Per cent share to total plan outlays
First Plan (1951–56)	0.6	0.033
Second Plan (1956–61)	5.0	0.109
Third Plan (1961–66)	27.0	0.314
Annual Plan (1966–69)	82.9	1.251
Fourth Plan (1967–74)	285.8	1.800
Fifth Plan (1974–79)	491.8	1.247
Sixth Plan (1980–85)	1309.0	1.342
Seventh Plan (1985–90)	2868.0	1.311
Annual Plan (1990–91)	675.0	1.097
Annual Plan (1992–97)	749.0	1.137
Eighth Plan (1992–97)	6500.0	1.497
Ninth Plan (1997–2002)	15,088.0	2.755
Tenth Plan (2002–07)	27,125.0	3.036

Source: GoI; Various Draft Five Year Plans.

In a patriarchic society like India, men are often the primary decision makers in each and every aspect of life including the decision regarding adoption of FP. The Indian FPP is geared exclusively towards women, thus making it a 'women's business'.

In this chapter an attempt has been made to analyse the gender bias that is inherent in the FPP in India. The analysis in this study is based on secondary data published by the Government of India as well as from various independent researches. The paper is divided into four sections. The first section deals with the existence of gender bias in the FPP. The biological aspects of gender bias have been discussed in the second section while the social aspects of gender bias are dealt with in the third section. Finally, the fourth section presents the conclusions of the study.

GENDER BIAS

The presence of gender bias in the FPP was pointed out as early as 1962 in the report of the Director of Family Planning, it referred to the female bias in the programme, which is focused exclusively on women and neglects the men. Although the FPP was revamped thoroughly after the report, the gender bias prevalent in Indian society clearly manifests itself in the FPP, which still focuses on women to a considerable extent.

The first National Population Policy (1976) sought to encourage state governments to make sterilization 'compulsory for citizens', under certain conditions. It resulted in an unprecedented increase in number of sterilizations. Between April 1976 to March 1977, as many as 8.26 per cent sterilizations were performed. Vasectomies were conducted in places like railway stations and quickly arranged camp-sites. Many men were allegedly forced to undergo sterilization (Maharatna 2002). However, in the new Population Policy Statement (1977) the voluntary nature of the FPP was reaffirmed. As a consequence the number of acceptors of FP, especially male acceptors, declined sharply. This is evident from the fact that the number of vasectomies diminished after 1976–77 (Srinivasan 1998). With this decline in male participation and refusal to come forward for vasectomy, the focus was once again turned towards women. The tubal ligation of women began to rise steadily and became a dominant method of FP especially in this period (Maharatna 2002). During the Seventh FYP (1985–90), there was a slow but steady increase in the number of female sterilizations, women gradually came to the centre of FPP and most of the programmes became women oriented. Both the ICPD held at Cairo in 1994 and the World Conference on Women at Beijing in 1995 highlighted the hitherto neglected area of need of male involvement and the unnecessary and uneven burdening of women with the task of regulating reproduction to meet macro goals (Jayalakshmi et al. 2002). Thus internationally it was accepted that

Table 10.2: Distribution of currently married couples by any modern contraceptive method currently used in India.

(per cent)

Period	Pills	IUD	Condom	Female sterilization	Male sterilization	Periodic abstinence	Total
NFHS-I (1992–3)	1.2	1.9	2.4	27.4	3.5	2.7	36.5
NFHS-II (1998–9)	2.0	2.0	3.0	34.0	2.0	5.0	42.8
NFHS-III (2005–06)	3.1	1.8	5.3	37.3	1.0	7.8	56.3

Source: NFHS-I, NFHS-II and NFHS-III.

FPP policies have imposed overwhelming responsibilities on women for achieving fertility reduction and demographic transition.

Despite this realization, no perceptible change has occurred in the FPP in India. The data from NFHS-I (1992–3), NFHS-II (1998–9) and NFHS-III (2005–06), given in Table 10.2, show marginal male participation in the FPP. The data from NFHS-I reveal that the use of any modern method (pill, IUD, condom etc.) is only 36.5 per cent out of which 27.4 per cent accepted female sterilization while only 3.5 per cent accepted male sterilization. The data from NFHS-II reveal that though the total use of any modern method increased to 42.8 per cent, but male sterilization declined to 2 per cent, while the NFHS-III data show a further decline to only 1 per cent in the male sterilization though female sterilization is marked by a continuous increase (34.1 in NFHS-II and 37.3 in NFHS-III). The present data evidently confirm that in spite of efforts made by the government and the various agencies to popularize male participation in family planning, the situation can still aptly be presented in the words of Ashish Bose (1992), 'Whether we like it or not India's FPP has become primarily a women's programme.'

Even at the policy level there was no change in the approach. This is evident from the views of Karan Singh (1997), one of India's eminent thinkers and former Minister of Health and Family Planning that '...in short (a) revitalization of National Population Policy is needed in which women take an active part. All programmes have to revolve around them.'

The gender bias in the FPP is also manifested in the basket of fertility control methods, which are presently available. Table 10.3 reveals that about 80 per cent of the methods/devices are for women and only 20 per cent are for men. This vast difference in the availability of FP method/devices for men and women irrespective of caste, class, and religion implies that the gigantic share of family planning burden is on the women and the FPP is 'women centred'. In other words, the FPP in India is 'gender centred', 'gender subordinated' and 'gender biased' both in urban and in rural areas (Pattanaik 2002).

In this way male involvement is being undermined in the FPP in India in spite of the fact that men are equally responsible for the increase in family size and also for the rearing of children. Actually the role of men in such matters is of great importance because they are the sole decision makers in the vast majority of Indian families. But the

Table 10.3: Common methods of contraception available

Methods/Devices available for males	Methods/Devices available for females
Reversible method	Reversible methods
Condom	IUD
	Oral pills
	Injectable hormones
	Morning-after pills
	Abortion
Permanent method	Permanent methods
Vasectomy	Tubal ligation
	Hysterectomy

Source: Bal (2002).

paradox is that in spite of encouraging male involvement, most of the efforts and strategies are revolving around the women. It is noteworthy that the gender bias in the FPP has both biological as well as social aspects.

BIOLOGICAL ASPECTS OF GENDER BIAS

So far as the biological aspects are concerned, the process of reproduction and also its control are complex in nature. It is regulated by intricately balanced mechanisms involving the endocrine glands and the accessory sex organs. Without going into the biological details it can be stated that the number of male and female organs and hormones involved in the process of reproduction, which are mentioned in Table 10.4, do not vary much in number. Studies reveal that the approaches envisaged for contraception are the same for both males and females. Broadly speaking, there are as many potential sites or approaches for men as there are for women to achieve contraception (Bal 2002). The physiological basis of various approaches for developing male contraceptives is summarized in Table 10.5. Contraception may be achieved by interrupting the male reproductive process at any of these sites. Despite these biological facts, a very limited number of methods/devices have been developed for men and on the contrary, a very large number have been made available for women.

A survey of research studies on reproductive health published until January 2002 (available at National Library of Medicine, USA), reveals that for every single publication on male reproductive health there are 1.5 for females and for every single clinical trial for male contraception

Table 10.4: Organs and hormones involved in the process of reproduction

Organs		Hormones	
Male	Female	Male	Female
Hypothalamus	Hypothalamus	Follicle	Follicle stimulating
Pituitary	Pituitary	Stimulating	Hormone
Testis	Uterus	Leutinising Hormone	Leutinising
Prostrate	Ovary	One	Hormone
Seminal Vesicle	Cervix	GnRH	GnRH
Penis	Vagina	Testosterone	Oestrogen
	Vulva	Oestrogen	Progesterone
		Inhibin	HCG
			Prolactin

Source: Bal (2002).

Table 10.5: Physiological basis of potential male contraception

Physiological Basis	
Inhibition of hypothalamic pituitary function	Counteraction of GnRH Activity
	Suppression of Gonadotropins
	Inhibition of FSH secretion/sction
Post testicular action	Inhibition of Epididymal sperm maturation
	Anti-sperm-antigen vaccine
	Reversible intra–vasal devices
Direct inhibition of spermatogenic cell in testis.	

Source: Roy et al. (2002).

there are 7.3 for female contraception (Bal 2002). Despite the constraints of this survey of scientific literature, a fact emerges that scientific studies on male reproductive health and contraception are few in comparison to that for females. It indicates gender-based differences even in scientific researches on contraception and population control, even when they are expected to be the most objective.

The gender bias also becomes evident while dealing with health issues. The health concerns of women are being marginalized to achieve the set goals. We cannot overlook the scandal of chemical sterilization of women in India with Quinacrine that was carried out under rhetoric of both choice and reproductive rights till the Supreme Court stepped in to issue a ban (Rao 1998). Health implications for women are proving extremely deleterious, as the focus of reproductive health seems to be seriously misplaced. 'The ICPD converted women health issues to safe abortion and reproductive rights alone; it marginalized issues of comprehensive primary health care and social security, both of which are under attack in [the] new world order' (Qadeer 1995).

The Fourth Report of the Committee on Empowerment of Women pointed to the health disabilities and morbidity that are gender specific. These interventions are conspicuously absent in the currently operating reproductive health services which were put in place as a women centred alternative to the FPP (Rajkrishna 2002). The package of reproductive health appears to 'miss wood for the trees'. In our country, a dominant ideology that seeks to reinforce a dark tradition of Indian womanhood, that of sacrifice, is still being followed and focus is on woman merely as a reproductive being (Rao 2000). There is a need to get rid of diseases and provide equal treatment in all the dimensions. In the present context, it can be stated that 'woman's health should not be subordinated to population goals nor restricted to reproductive matters' (Towards Beijing: Crucial Issues of Concern 1995).

Social Aspects of Gender Bias

The ICPD (1994) recognized the importance of gender based power dynamics for reproductive health within the sexual relationship of men and women. The power in a sexual relationship differs to the relative ability of one partner to act independently, to dominate decision making, partner's wishes, or to control a partner's action (Pulerwitz et al. 2000). Research related to the social aspects of adoption or non-adoption of FP methods/devices and reduction of fertility is focusing more on the factors related to female literacy, women's empowerment, and socio-economic improvement of women as a profound determinant of fertility decisions. But in the haste, a basic fact that fertility change is determined by many interesting social and cultural factors is being ignored. A mere increase in literacy or labour force participation does not indicate increased female autonomy in making decisions on fertility (Rajkrishna 2002). The dominating role played by the males in all the minor and major decisions related to the family and society must also be considered (Heptulla 2000; Schuler et al. 1997). A study based on 13 DHS reveals that an average of 9 per cent of married women with unmet need for FP cite disapproval of their husbands as the main reason for not practicing contraception (Bongaarts and

Bruce 1995). Studies conducted throughout the developing world, have shown that although majority of men 'approve of family planning in the abstract yet they often raise a number of concerns and engender resistance on their own partners for the use of contraceptive' (Green et al. 1995).

Reproductive behaviour, in a country like India, is strongly embedded in broader socially sanctioned constructs (Raju 2001). Gender power relations existing between men and women, place women in a situation where they are often without power and authority in negotiating sexual relations with men. They may also have limited access to contraceptives and the power to use them even when available (Bandewar 2003). Studies indicate that men being the household heads and the primary providers for the family, play a dominant role and many times even become the ultimate determiner. A study conducted in Uttar Pradesh, the most populous state of India, revealed that wives basically agreed with the decision taken by their husbands regarding sexual matters, and most of the time silent consent by the women or lack of protest by them was interpreted as having arrived at a joint decision. Women almost never question the decision of their husband, nor do they enter into any discussion with them (Jayalakshmi et al. 2002). Thus, in Indian patriarchal society, where they enjoy a better position and hold in the society and in policy formulation, males are not ready to take the responsibility for limiting their family size and controlling population growth in a larger perspective.

Moreover, in a number of societies including India, the responsibility for reproductive decisions does not lie only or even primarily with the couple themselves but extends to a wider kin group, particularly the husbands' parents (Caldwell 1982; Knodel et al. 1984; Bandewar 2003; Raju 2001). The data from NFHS on currently married women (CMW), keeping India in focus, reveal that CMW alone cannot decide whether they should have any more children or whether they should wait at least two more years before having another child. In fact, their husbands take decisions related to these matters (NHFS-2, 1998–9). The NFHS-I and NFHS-2 data reveal that 2477 and 2402 CMW respectively cited 'opposition to use of FP methods' as a reason for their inability to adopt them. The categories of the opposition faced by them are shown in Table 10.6.

Table 10.6 reveals that in 1992–3, around 49 per cent of CMW were not using any FP method because of opposition from husbands

Table 10.6: Main reasons for not using any FP methods by CMW

Reasons	CMW not using any method despite willing to do so (NFHS-I)		CMW who never used any method (NFHS-II)	
	Numbers	Percentage	Numbers	Percentage
Opposition by husband	961	38	1235	51.4
Opposition by others	117	4.7	217	9.1
Against religion	1020	41.2	658	27.4
Opposition by self	379	15.3	292	12.1

Source: NFHS-I and NFHS-II (NFHS-III data for these variables is not available till date).

and this percentage shot up to 51 per cent in 1998–9, showing the increasing opposition from husbands. Similarly, the opposition from others (members of the family) is also on the rise. An addition of these two increases the figure to 60 per cent of CMW who are not using FP methods because of opposition from husband and other members of the family. Perhaps the concerns expressed by men regarding the non-adoption of FPP include the fear that they will lose their role as head of the family, that their partners will become promiscuous or adulterous and that they will be ridiculed by other members of the community (Watkins et al.1997; Bawah et al. 1999). Thus, the woman who bears the pain and responsibility of giving birth to a child has very little say in deciding when to have a child, the number of children to have, and whether to use a contraceptive or not. Still women are being made the focus group while decision making by the males is being promoted by attaching the concept of status and power to it. Thus, the differences are not merely sexual but are socially created, promoted, and maintained.

Conclusion

Men are often the primary decision makers in the FP decision yet FP services are geared exclusively towards women, leading men to consider FP as 'woman's business' (AVSC and IPPF/WHR 1998). As a result, the burden of contraceptive use falls on women more heavily (Bruce 1998; Greene and Biddlecom 2000). A Report by United Nations (2000) reveals that worldwide, out of the 58 per cent of married couples who practice any of the available methods for contraception only about 28 per cent practice a method that requires male co-operation (that is, male sterilization, condom, periodic abstinence or withdrawal) while in developing countries this proportion is only about 20 per cent (UN 2000).

Thus, it can be concluded that men are safely walking out of the FPP, as the contraceptive technology is basically female oriented (Bose 2000). As Cohen and Berger (2000) point out, however, fewer contraceptive choices exist for men and, if more male methods/devices were available and social biases were removed the women's burden with regard to contraceptive use could be reduced and the overall level of contraceptive prevalence may rise. So a holistic approach is needed in which men, women, social dynamics, and dimensions should be dealt with as a complex whole and not independently to achieve a major success in programmes like FP, which have deep roots in the cultural constructs of the society. Male participation in the FPP should be promoted so that the burden of women is reduced and an objective approach is adopted.

REFERENCES

AVSC International and IPPF/WHR (1998), *Literature Review for the Symposium on Male Participation in Sexual and Reproductive Health: New Paradigms*, AVSC International and IPPR/WHR, Oaxaca, Mexico.

Bal, V. (2002), 'Gendered Science: Women as Practitioners and Targets of Research', *Economic and Political Weekly*, Vol. 37, No. 62, pp. 5163–7.

Bandewar, S. (2003), 'Abortion Services and Providers Perceptions: Gender Dimensions', *Economic and Political Weekly*, Vol. 24, pp. 2075–81.

Bawah, A.A., P. Akeongo, R. Simons, and J.F. Phillips (1999), 'Women's Fear and Men's Anxieties: The Impact of Family Planning on Gender Relations in Northern Ghana', *Studies in Family Planning*, Vol. 31, No. 1, pp. 54–66.

Bongaarts, and J. Bruce (1995), 'The Causes of Unmet Need of Contraception and the Social Context of Services', *Studies in Family Planning*, Vol. 26, No. 2, pp. 57–75.

Bose, A. (1992), 'India's Family Planning Programme, Getting out of the sterilization Trap', *Indian Journal of Public Administration*, Vol. 38, No. 3, pp. 45–54.

———(2000), 'Population Stabilization in India: Progress and Pitfall', *Yojana*, Vol. 4, No. 8.

Bruce, J. (1998), 'Social Context of Reproductive Health: Acknowledging the Role of Partners and Fostering Partners Support for Reproductive Choice and Health', Unpublished.

Caldwell, J.C. (1982), *Theory of Fertility Decline*, Academic Press, New York.

Cohen, S.I. and M. Berger (2000), 'Partenering: A New Approach to Sexual and Reproductive Health', Technical Paper No. 3, United Nation Population Fund, New York.

Government of India (GoI) (1959), 'Family Planning in India', Director General of Health Services, New Delhi, p. 1.

Green, A. and A.E. Biddlecom (2000), 'Absent and Problematic Men; Demographic Accounts of Male Reproductive Roles', Population and Development Review, Vol. 26, No. 1, pp. 81–115.

Green, C.P., S.I. Cohen, and H.B. Ghouayel (1995), 'Male Involvement in Reproductive Health, including Family Planning and Sexual Health', Technical Report No. 28, United Nations Population Fund, New York

Heptulla, N. (2000), 'Role of Women in Population Stabilisation', Yojana, August.

International Institute for Population Sciences (IIPS) (1995), National Family Health Survey NFHS-2, 1992–93, IIPS, Mumbai.

International Institute of Population Sciences (IIPS) and ORC Macro (2000), National Family Health Survey NFHS-2, 1998–99, Mumbai, India.

www.nfhsindia.com, key indicators of NFHS-III, accessed on 7 June 2007.

Jayalakshmi, M.S., K. Ambani, P.K. Prabhakar, and P. Swain (2002), 'A Study of Male Involvement in Family Planning', Health and Population—Perspectives and Issues, Vol. 25, pp. 113–22.

Knodel, J., N. Havanan, and A. Pramualratana (1984), 'Fertility Transition in Thailand: A Qualitative Analysis', Population and Development Review, Vol. 10, No. 2.

Maharatna, A. (2002), 'India's Family Planning Programme: An Unpleasant Essay', Economic and Political Weekly, March, No. 9.

Pattanaik, B.K. (2002), 'Convergence of Gender Actions and Rural Population Stabilization', Yojana, May.

Pulerwitz, I., S.L. Gortmaker, and W. Dejong (2000), 'Measuring Sexual Relationships Power in HIV/STD Research', Sex Roles, Vol. 42, Nos 7 and 8, pp. 637–60.

Qadeer, N. (1995), quoted in M. Dasgupta, et al. 1998 (ed.) Women's Health in India: Risk and Vulnerability, Oxford University Press, New Delhi.

Rao, M. (1998), 'India's Augean Staldes: The Unfinished Health Agenda in Women's Health', in S. Mukhopadhyay (ed.) Public Policy and Community Action, Manohar, New Delhi.

Rajkrishna (2002), 'Rewinding Population Policy', Economic and Political Weekly, 29 June, pp. 2515–16.

Raju, S. (2001), 'Negotiating with Patriarchy Addressing Men in Reproductive and Child Health', Economic and Political Weekly, December, No. 8, pp. 4589–92.

Reddy, S. Y. (1983), 'Family Planning—Political Will', Yojana, Vol. 44, No. 8.

Roy, S., M.C. Kapilashrami, T.G. Shrivastav, S. Roy, and A. Basu (2002), 'Recent Advances in Hormonal Male Contraception', Health and Population—Perspectives and Issues, Vol. 25, No. 4, pp. 159–76.

Schuller, S.R., S.M. Hashemi, and A.P. Riley (1997), 'The Influence of Women's Changing Roles and Status in Bangladesh's Fertility Transition: Evidence from a Study of Credit Programmes and Contraceptive Use', *World Development*, Vol. 25, No. 4, pp. 563–75.

Singh, K. (1997), 'Population: The More, the Merrier', *Facts For You*, August.

Srinivasan, K. (1998), 'Population Policies and Programmes since Independence', *Demography in India*, Vol. 27, No. 1.

Tewari, A. (1989), 'India's population policy', in S.D. Maurya, (ed.) *Population and Housing Problems in India*, Vol. I, Chugh Publications, Allahabad.

Towards Beijing (1995), A Brief Report on Fourth World Conference on Women, *Yojana*, August.

United Nations (2000), *World Population Monitoring 2000: Population, Gender and Development*, UN Department for Economic and Social Affairs, New York.

Watkins, S.C., N. Rosenberg, and D. Wilkinson (1997), 'Orderly Theories, Disorderly Women' in G.W. Jones, R.M. Douglas, J.C, Caldwell, and R.M. D'Souza (eds), *The Counting Demographic Transition*, Oxford University Press, New York.

Heart Disease among South Asians
Role of Gender

SUMITA DAS SARKAR and
AHANA SARKAR _____ 11

INTRODUCTION

With an increase in life expectancy, the world's population is ageing rapidly. As women live longer than men (Bonita and Howe 1996), an ageing society, which for the most part, is female, is apparent (Mylander 1979), making them more vulnerable to degenerative disease like heart diseases. Within the umbrella of heart diseases, common diseases affecting the heart include CVD, ischaemic heart disease (IHD), coronary heart disease (CHD), and coronary artery disease (CAD).

The CVDs account for a significant proportion of adult deaths globally (Murray and Lopez 1996). Stroke and IHD are the two most common causes of cardiovascular mortality (Murray and Lopez 1996). Therefore, an increase in life expectancy means longer exposure to risk factors for CVD resulting in greater prevalence of CVD. This calls for greater awareness about the importance of CVD as a global health issue. Improvements in survival rates of heart diseases mean more individuals are living with disabilities thus contributing to the burden of society and the economy (Bonita 1998), which points towards the need for primary prevention programmes.

CHD and stroke had been the major cause of death in Western Europe, North America, and Australia/New Zealand for the last few decades (Pearson, Smith, and Poole-Wilson 1998). During the period 1965–90, CVD-related mortality fell by about 50 per cent in Australia, Canada, France, and the United States of America (Lopez 1993). USA has observed a decline in the prevalence rate of CAD (McIntosh 1989; Cooper et al. 2000). However, in developing countries, the prevalence of CVD is increasing (Reddy and Yusuf 1998). It is estimated that by the year 2020, projected disability-adjusted life years (DALYs) for

CVD in India will be substantially high if projections remain constant (Murray and Lopez 1997).

Factors relating to the economic, cultural, and social milieu play a role in explaining the disparities between the developed and developing nations. However, it is of interest to inquire about the interaction of such lifestyle factors and biological factors. CVD must be considered from a life course perspective. As such, the risk of developing CVD is influenced by lifestyle factors such as smoking, drinking, unhealthy diet, lack of exercise, and biological factors such as high blood pressure, high cholesterol, obesity, and diabetes. These factors act at all stages in life, from fetal life to adulthood (Aboderin et al. 2001).

This calls for the examination of heart diseases and their association with biological and lifestyle risk factors, which can be better understood such as South Asians living abroad or in their countries of origin. Within South Asians globally, focus on women is needed in light of gender disparities to understand their specific risk factors.

Heart Disease amongst South Asians and Gender Roles

Amongst South Asians (Indian, Pakistani, Bangladeshi, and Sri Lankan), a very high risk of heart disease (Gupta, Singh, and Verma 2006; Joshi et al. 2007; Jafar, Qadri, and Chauturvedi 2008) and high mortality from CHD has been found (McKeigue and Marmot 1988; Gupta and Gupta 1996). Globally, South Asian populations, regardless of their cultural and religious diversity, have the highest prevalence rate of CAD in comparison with other ethnic groups from Trinidad, Fiji, South Africa, Malayasia, UK, USA, and Canada (Anonymous 1986; Beckles et al. 1986; Miller et al. 1989; Tuomilehto et al. 1984; Sharper and Jones 1959; Danaraj et al. 1959; Lee et al. 2001; Balarajan 1991; Bhopal et al. 1999; Marmot, Adelstein, and Bulusu 1984; Blackledge, Newton and Squire 2003; Enas et al. 1996; Sheth et al. 1999; Anand et al. 2000).

South Asians may be genetically predisposed to heart diseases (Levy and Kannel 2000) and are evolutionarily adapted to survive under conditions of scarcity that may be metabolic and genetic (Neel 1962). The genetic predisposition of South Asians and their exposure to industrialization, urbanization, and westernization may explain their high risk for heart diseases (Pearson 1997; Bhatanagar et al. 1995). As a consequence, levels of cholesterol, blood sugar, or blood pressure that are optimal for people of the West may be sufficient to predispose the South Asians, living in the West, to an increased risk of CAD. In United States of America (US), Europeans have a very high risk of CAD, but the comparative risk for South Asians, living in US, is greater (Enas et al. 1996). Looking in terms of gender differences, the risk for South Asian women compared to European women, was not only greater but higher than the comparative risk between European and South Asian men (Cappuccio 1997). Balarajan (1991) compared mortality rates surveyed in England and Wales in 1970–2 with rates in 1979–83, and found that those who had been born in the Indian subcontinent had the highest death rates from CAD in 1970–2. A decade later in 1979–83, there was an observed rise in mortality due to CAD of 13 per cent in women and 6 per cent in men, among the immigrants from South Asia.

The age of onset for CAD has increased in developed countries, but, in South Asia, it has decreased (Enas, Yusuf, and Mehta 1992; Reddy and Yusuf 1998). Additionally, South Asians are differently susceptible to risk factors for heart disease while living in their own country of origin (that is , India, Bangladesh, Pakistan), pointing towards socio-cultural risk factors such as lifestyle differences. In developed countries such as Canada, the prevalence of CAD is associated with lower socio-economic standards and the rural population, where there are high risk factors such as high dietary fat intake, low physical activity, diabetes, high blood pressure, and obesity (Squires, 1999; Choiniere, Lafontaine, and Edwards 2000). Conversely, urbanized population and higher socio-economic standards in India have been associated with the increasing occurrence of CAD (Reddy 1993). The overall mortality prevalence estimates in India, performed in the last decade, range between 7.6 per cent and 12.6 per cent for urban populations and 3.1 per cent to 7.4 per cent for rural populations (Bahl, Prabhakaran, and Karthikeyan 2001).

Possible causes for this phenomenon may arise from lifestyle differences between urban and rural populations in developed versus developing countries. In India, amongst the rural populations, less fat intake and higher demand of physical labour possibly contribute to the decreased risk of CAD (Begom and Singh 1995). Bonita (1998) suggests that the urban population of India, with higher socio-economic standards, has incorporated the western lifestyle, which may have contributed to the increased prevalence of CAD amongst the population. Conventional CHD risk factors, such as obesity, hypertension, and diabetes, are more prevalent in urban India than rural India (Padmavati 1962). However, the rise in CHD that is seen in rural India has been mostly attributed to smoking and lower educational level (Gupta, Gupta, and Ahluwalia 1994; Rastogi et al. 2004a).

The relevance of such findings about lifestyle risk factors should be noted within the context of gender differences across developing and developed nations. Murray and Lopez (1996) projected deaths from 1990 to 2020, caused by IHD between developed and developing countries and found that while the deaths caused by IHD in women would decrease in 2020 in developed countries, the numbers would increase for women in developing countries.

According to WHO, women in developing countries have lower life expectancy compared to their female counterparts in developed countries (WHO 2000). However, women in developing countries, who have survived beyond middle age, have life expectancy comparable to women in developed countries (WHO 2000). Bonita (1998) also points to the high maternal mortality in developing countries such as Mozambique, Nigeria, and India, leading to a corresponding lower life expectancy for women. Socio-economic differences predict that women in developing countries, surviving beyond middle age, and with decreased susceptibility to maternal mortality and accompanying medical complications, are of higher socio-economic status and are living urbanized, westernized lifestyles within their country of origin, such as India. Access to sufficient health care shows significant disparities between socio-economic status and between genders within different socio-economic levels (International Institute for Population Sciences and ORC Macro 1998–9; Deogaonkar 2004).

Although, the cultural, religious, and geographical variations of the disease in South Asian countries are not yet fully understood (Reddy 1993), studies done in India have shown that differences exist. The prevalence of CAD has been shown to vary when comparing Southern and Northern India (Sarvotham and Berry 1968; Begom and Singh 1995), in rural and urban populations (Reddy 1993), by a population's level of education (Gupta et al. 1994), by diet (Rastogi et al. 2004a) and by levels of physical exercise in urban areas (Rastogi et al. 2004b).Confounding such matters is the obvious role of gender differences.

Literacy rates are higher in South India than in North India (Dutt and Sen, 1992). Females in some northern states (for example, Uttar Pradesh, Bihar, Rajasthan) show the lowest level of literacy, while northern states that are influenced by an urban setting, such as Delhi, show higher rates of female literacy (Dutt and Sen 1992). There is also a male-bias towards rural to urban migration (Dutt and Sen 1992). In India, girls are more likely to be neglected than boys with respect to nutrition (Borooah 2004). Even within educated women in urban settings in India, practice and knowledge of physical activity and its effect on heart diseases is lacking (Vaz and Bhorathi 2003).

Finally, conventional risk factors such as smoking, high blood pressure, high cholesterol, diabetes, and central obesity have been associated with CAD among South Asians (Chadha et al. 1990; McKeigue, Shah and Marmot 1991; Reddy 1993; Pais et al. 1996). Higher coronary mortality rate among South Asians abroad in comparison with other ethnic groups (Beckles et al. 1986; Miller et al. 1989) may be due to diabetes mellitus as an important risk factor for the prevalence of CAD. McKeigue et al. (1991) posit that high IHD rate among South Asians are due to a metabolic syndrome, which is characterized by central obesity, non-insulin dependent diabetes, high triglyceride levels, and a predisposition to impaired glucose tolerance. South Asians living in the UK have a higher rate of heart disease and diabetes (Simmons, Williams, and Powell 1992). When a sample of South Asians living in the UK was asked about their knowledge of heart disease and diabetes, including awareness of risk factors (prevention), their understanding was found to be lacking (Rankin and Bhopal 2001). Other studies looking at South Asians in UK have found that women were less knowledgeable about diabetes, heart disease, their risk factors, and prevention methods, than their male counterparts (Hawthorne and Tomlinson 1999).

CONCLUSION

The decline in CAD mortality during the last few decades in developed countries indicates that CAD is treatable and can be prevented if risk factors are identified and controlled (Cooper et al. 2000). CAD among South Asians across the world is affecting individuals earlier (McKeigue et al. 1993; Enas and Mehta 1995).

The South Asian population, in general, has to be aware of their increased risk for CAD. Most living in their countries of origin are at risk and segregating the high-risk individuals and treating them is an economically unviable option as compared with western countries. Educating the general public as a whole will not only target individuals currently suffering from CAD, but also those who may later develop the disease. Awareness of CAD will help high-risk individuals to seek help early enough so that treatment can be more effective and allow for more timely communication between patients and doctors. Medical professionals in South Asian countries also need to be targeted to tackle the development of the CAD epidemic. Mostly, attention towards South Asians and CAD has been found through comparison with western countries, or, other ethnicities. Future direction for focus is needed on South Asians themselves, as the primary subjects not just within comparative studies. Additionally, the unique role of the women and their risk factors must be addressed. Women have been under-represented in clinical trials; as a result, treatment and outcomes concerning CVD has gender-specific gaps in knowledge (Pilote et al. 2007). Women's gender role as care givers and their social and cultural expectations may make it difficult for them to incorporate healthy lifestyles. Even though heart disease is considered a 'man's disease', it is the most common cause of mortality among women (*World Health Report 1997*; Bonita 1998). It may be that the social stigma of heart disease as a man's disease has hindered South Asian women from seeking medical attention and actively changing their lifestyle such as diet, reducing their risk for diabetes and incorporating physical activities into their daily lives. South Asian women are not encouraged to view CHD as a possibility in their lives.

With continued focus on heart disease amongst South Asians, within their countries of origin and abroad, we may better understand the role of interaction between biological and lifestyle factors, especially when looking at the role of gender. One possible limitation to such inquiry may be grouping South Asians together as a homogeneous population. For example, Nazroo (1997) showed that the prevalence of self-reported CHD was greater amongst Bangladeshis and Pakistanis but lower in Indians, when compared to Europeans. Thus, noting biological, social, and environmental differences by ethnicity, and across gender, are important for a comprehensive understanding of heart disease within South Asians, both as a homogeneous population and as heterogeneous populations with differing risk factors (Bhopal et al. 1999).

REFERENCES

Aboderin, I., A. Kalache, Y. BenShlom, J.W. Lynch, C.S. Yajni, D. Kuch, and D. Yach (2001), 'Life Course Perspectives on Coronary Heart Disease Stroke and Diabetes: Key Issues and Implications for Policy and Research', World Health Organization, Geneva, Retrieved on 10 June 2008, from *http://whqlibdoc.who. int/hq/2001/WHO_NMH_NPH_01.4.pdf.*

Anand, S., S. Yusuf, V. Valdamir, S. Devanesen, K. Teo Koon, P.A. Montague, L. Kelemen, C.Yi, E. Lonn, H. Gerstein, R.A. Hegele, and M. McQueen (2000), 'Differences in Risk Factors, Atherosclerosis, and Cardiovascular Disease Between Ethnic Groups in Canada: the Study of Health Assesment and Risk in Ethnic groups (SHARE)', *Lancet*, Vol. 356, pp. 279–84.

Anonymous (1986), 'Coronary Heart Disease in Indians Overseas', *Lancet*, Vol. 1, pp. 1307–8.

Bahl, V.K., D. Prabhakaran, and G. Karthikeyan (2001), Coronary disease in Indians', *Indian Heart Journal*, Vol. 53, No. 6, pp. 707–13.

Balarajan, R., A.M. Aldelstein, L. Bulusu, and V. Shukla (1984), 'Patterns of Mortality Among Migrants to England and Wales from the Indian Subcontinent', *British Medical Journal*, Vol. 289, pp. 1185–7.

Balarajan, R. (1991), 'Ethnic Differences in Mortality from Ischaemic Heart Disease and Cerebrovascular Disease in England and Wales', *British Medical Journal*, Vol. 302, pp. 560–4.

Barker, D.J.P. (1995), 'Fetal Origins of Coronary Heart Disease', *British Medical Journal*, Vol. 311, pp. 171–4.

Barker, D.J.P., C. Osmond, P.D. Winter, and B. Margetts (1989), 'Weight Gain in Infancy and Death from Ischaemic Heart Disease', *Lancet*, Vol. 2, pp. 577–80.

Beckles, G.L., G.J. Miller, B.R. Kirkwood, S.D. Alexis, D.C. Carson, and N.T. Bryam (1986), 'High Total and Cardiovascular Disease Mortality in Adults of Indian Descent in Trinidad, Unexplained by Major Coronary Risk Factors', *Lancet*, Vol. 1, pp. 1298–301.

Begom, R. and R.B. Singh (1995), 'Prevalence of Coronary Artery Disease and its Risk Factors in the Urban Population of South and North India', *Acta Cardiologia*, Vol. 3, pp. 227–40.

Bhatnagar, D., I.S. Anand, P.N. Durrington, D.J. Patel, G.S. Wander, M.I. Mackness, F. Creed, B. Tomenson, Y. Chandrashekhar, M. Winterbotham, R.P. Britt, J.E. Keil, and G.C. Sutton (1995), 'Coronary Risk Factors in People from the Indian Subcontinent Living in West London and Their Siblings in India'. *Lancet*, Vol. 345, pp. 405–9.

Bhopal, R., N. Unwin, M. White, J. Yallop, L. Walker, K.G.M.M. Alberti, J. Hartland, S. Patel, N. Ahmad, C. Turner, B. Watson, D. Kaur, A. Kulkarni, M. Laker, and A. Tavridou (1999), 'Heterogeneity of Coronary Heart Disease Risk Factors in Indian, Pakistani, Bangladeshi, and European Origin Populations: Cross Sectional Study', *British Medical Journal*, Vol. 319, pp. 215–20.

Blackledge, H.M., J. Newton, and I.B. Squire (2003), 'Prognosis for South Asian and White Patients Newly Admitted to Hospital with Heart Failure in the

United Kingdom: Historical Cohort Study', *British Medical Journal*, Vol. 327, pp. 526–31.

Bonita, R. (1998), *Women, Ageing and Health: Achieving Health Across the Life Span*, 2nd edn, WHO, Geneva.

Bonita, R. and A.L. Howe (1996), 'Older Women in An Ageing World, Achieving Health Across the Life Course', *World Health Statistics Quarterly*, Vol. 49, pp. 134–41.

Borooah, V.K. (2004), 'Gender Bias Among Children in India in Their Diet and Immunisation Against Disease', *Social Science & Medicine*, Vol. 58, pp. 1719–31.

Cappuccio, F.P. (1997), 'Ethnicity and Cardiovascular Risk: Variations in People of African Ancestry and South Asian Origin', *Journal of Human Hypertension*, Vol. 11, pp. 571–6.

Chadha, S.L., S. Radhakrishnan, K. Ramchandran, U. Kaul, and N. Gopinath (1990), 'Epidemiological Study of Coronary Heart Disease in Urban Population of Delhi', *Indian Journal of Medical Research*, Vol. 92, pp. 424–30.

Choiniere, R., P. Lafontaine, and A.C. Edwards (2000), 'Distribution of Cardiovascular Disease Risk Factors by Socioeconomic Status Among Canadian Adults', *Candian Medical Association Journal*, Vol. 2, pp. 162–9.

Cooper, R., J. Cutler, P. Desvigne-Nickens, S.P. Fortmann, L. Friedman, R. Havlik, G. Hogelin, J. Marler, P. McGovern, G. Morosco, L. Mosca, T. Pearson, J. Stamler, D. Stryer, and T. Thom (2000), 'Trends and Disparities in Coronary Heart Disease and Other Cardiovascular Diseases in the United States. Findings of the National Conference on Cardiovascular Disease Prevention', *Circulation*, Vol. 102, pp. 3137–47.

Danaraj, T.J., M.S. Acker, W. Danaraj, W.H. Ong, and T.B. Yam (1959), 'Ethnic Group Differences in Coronary Heart Disease in Singapore: An Analysis of Necropsy Records', *American Heart Journal*, Vol. 58, pp. 516–26.

Deogaonkar, M. (2004), 'Socio-Economic Inequality and Its Effect on Healthcare Delivery in India: Inequality and Healthcare', *Electronic Journal of Sociology*, Vol. 8, retrieved on 10 June 2008 from *http://www.sociology.org/content/vol8.1/deogaonkar.html*

Dutt, A.K. and A. Sen (1992), 'Provisional Census of India 1991', *Geographical Review*, Vol. 82, No. 2, pp. 207–11.

Enas, E.A. and J.L. Mehta (1995), 'Malignant Coronary Artery Disease in Young Asian Indians: Thoughts on Patogenesis, Prevention and Treatment', *Clinical Cardiology*, Vol. 18, pp. 131–5.

Enas, E.A. and A. Senthikumar (2001), 'Coronary Artery Disease in Asian Indians: An Update and Review', *The Internet Journal of Cardiology*, Vol. 1, No. 2, pp. 1–44.

Enas, E.A., S. Yusuf, and J. Mehta (1992), 'Prevalence of Coronary Artery Disease in Asian Indians', *The American Journal of Cardiology*, Vol. 70, pp. 945–9.

Enas, E.A., A. Garg, M. Davidson, V. Nair, B. Huet, and S. Yusuf (1996), 'Coronary Heart Disease and Its Risk Factors in First Generation Immigrant Asian Indians to the United States of America', *Indian Heart Journal*, Vol. 48, pp. 343–53.

Flavell, C.M. (1994), 'Women and Coronary Heart Disease', *Progress in Cardiovascular Nursing*, Vol. 9, pp. 18–27.

Fodor, J.G. and R. Tzerovska (2004), 'Coronary heart disease: is gender important?', *The Journal of Men's Health & Gender*, Vol. 1, No. 1, pp. 32–7.

Gupta, M., N. Singh, and S. Verma (2006), 'South Asians and Cardiovascular Risk: What Clinicians Should Know', *Circulation*, Vol. 113, pp. 924–9.

Gupta, R. and V.P. Gupta (1996), 'Meta-Analysis of Coronary Heart Disease Prevalence in India', *Indian Heart Journal*, Vol. 48, pp. 241–5.

Gupta, R., V.P. Gupta, and N.S. Ahluwalia (1994), 'Educational Status, Coronary Heart Disease, and Coronary Risk Factor Prevalence in a Rural Population of India', *British Medical Journal*, Vol. 309, pp. 1332–6.

Gupta. R., P. Joshi, V. Mohan, K.S. Reddy, and S. Yusuf (2008), 'Epidemiology and Causation of Coronary Heart Disease and Stroke in India', *Heart*, Vol. 94, No. 33, pp. 16–26.

Hart, C.L., D.J. Hole, and S.G. Davey (2000), 'Influence of Early and Later Life on Stroke. Risk Among Men in a Scottish Cohort', *Stroke*, Vol. 31, pp. 2093–7.

Hawthorne, K. and S. Tomlinson (1999), 'Pakistani Moslems with Type 2 Diabetes Mellitus: Effect of Sex, Literacy Skills, Known Diabetic Complications and Place of Care on Diabetic Knowledge, Reported Self-Monitoring Management and Glycaemic Control', *Diabetic Medicine*, Vol. 16, No. 7, pp. 591–7.

International Institute for Population Sciences and ORC Macro (1998–9) *National Family Health Survey (NFHS-II)*, India.

Jafar, T.H., Z. Qadri, and N. Chauturvedi (2008), 'Coronary Artery Disease Epidemic in Pakistan: More Electrocardiographic Evidence of Ischaemia in Women than in Men', *Heart*, Vol. 94, pp. 408–13.

Jensen, L. and K.M. King (1997), 'Women and Heart Disease'. *Critical Care Nurse*, Vol. 17, pp. 45–53.

Joshi, P., S. Islam, P. Pais, S. Reddy, P. Dorairaj, K. Kazmi, M.R. Pandey, S. Haque, S. Mendis, S. Rangarajan, and S. Yusuf (2007), 'Risk Factors for Early Myocardial Infraction in South Asians Compared with Individuals in Other Countries', *Journal of the American Medical Association*, Vol. 297, pp. 286–94.

Lee, J., D. Heng, K.S. Chia, S.K. Chew, B.Y. Tan, and K. Hughes (2001), 'Risk Factors and Incident Coronary Heart Disease in Chinese, Malay and Asian Indian Males: The Singapore Cardiovascular Cohort Study', *International Journal of Epidemiology*, Vol. 30, pp. 983–8.

Levy, D. and W.B. Kannel (2000), 'Searching for Answers to Ethnic Disparities in Cardiovascular Risk' *Lancet*, Vol. 356, pp. 266–7.

Lopez. A.D. (1993), 'Assessing the Burden of Mortality from Cardiovascular Disease', *World Health Statistics Questionnaire*, Vol. 46, pp. 91–6.

Marmot, M.G., A.M. Adelstein, and L. Bulusu (1984), 'Immigrant Mortality in England and Wales 1970–78: Causes of Death by Country of Birth', *Office of Population Censuses and Surveys [OPCS]*, xii (Studies on Medical and Population Subjects no. 47), p. 145.

McIntosh, H.D. (1989), 'Risk Factors for Cardiovascular Disease and Death: A Clinical Perspective', *Journal of American College of Cardiology*, Vol. 14, pp. 24–30.

McKeigue, P.M. and M.G. Marmot (1988), 'Mortality from Coronary Heart Disease in Asian Communities in London', *British Medical Journal*, Vol. 297, pp. 903.

McKeigue, P.M., G. Shah, and M.G. Marmot (1991), 'Relation of Central Obesity and Insulin Resistance with High Diabetes Prevalence and Cardiovascular Risk in South Asians', *Lancet*, Vol. 337, pp. 382–6.

McKeigue, P.M., J.E. Ferrie, T. Pierpont, and M.G. Marmot (1993), 'Association of Early-Onset Coronary Heart Disease in South Asian Men with Glucose Intolerance and Hyperinsulinemia', *Circulation*, Vol. 878, pp. 152–61.

Miller, G.J., G.I. Beckles, G.H. Maude, D.C. Carson, S.D. Alexis, S.G.L. Price, and N.T. Byam (1989), 'Ethnicity and Other Characteristics Predictive of Coronary Heart Disease in a Developing Community: Principal Results of the St. James Survey, Trinidad', *International Journal of Epidemiology*, Vol. 18, pp. 808–17.

Mosca, L., J.E. Manson, S.E. Sutherland, R.D. Langer, T. Manolio, and E. Barrett-Connor (1997), 'Cardiovascular Disease in Women: A Statement for Healthcare Professionals from the American Heart Association: Writing Group', *Circulation*, Vol. 96, pp. 2468–82.

Murray, C.J.L. and A.D. Lopez (eds) (1996), *Global Health Statistics: A Compendium of Incidence, Prevalence and Mortality Estimates for Over 200 Conditions*, Harvard University Press, Cambridge.

——— (1997), 'Alternative Projection of Mortality and Disability by Cause 1990–2020, Global Burden of Disease Study', *Lancet*, Vol. 349, pp. 1498–1504.

Mylander, M. (1979), 'Continuities and discontinuities', *Women and Health*, Vol. 4, p. 322.

Nazroo, J. (1997), *The Health of Britain's Ethnic Minorities*, Policy Studies Institute, London.

Neel, J.V. (1962), 'Diabetes Mellitus: A "Thrifty" Genotype Rendered Detrimental By "Progress"?', *American Journal of Human Genetics*, Vol. 14, pp. 353–62.

Padmavati, S. (1962), 'Epidemiology of Cardiovascular Disease in India, Ischemic Heart Disease', *Circulation*, Vol. 25, pp. 711–17.

Pais, P., J. Pogue, H. Gerstein, E. Zachariah, D. Savitha, S. Jayprakash, P.R. Nayak, and Yusuf Salim (1996), 'Risk Factors for Acute Myocardial Infraction in Indians: A Case Control Study', *Lancet*, Vol. 348, pp. 358–63.

Pearson, T.A. (1997), 'Global Perspective on Cardiovascular Disease', *Evidence-based Cardiovascular Medicine*, Vol. 1, pp. 4–6.

Pearson, T.A., S.C Smith, and P. Poole-Wilson (1998), 'Cardiovascular Speciality Societies and the Emerging Global Burden of Cardiovascular Disease, A Call to Action', *Circulation*, Vol. 97, pp. 602–04.

Pilote, L., K. Dasgupta, V. Guru, K.H. Humphries, J. McGrath, C. Norris, D. Rabi, J. Tremblay, A. Alamian, T. Barnett, J. Cox, W.A. Ghali, S. Grace, P. Hamet, T. Ho, S. Kirkland, M. Lambert, D. Libersan, J. O'Loughlin, G. Paradis, M. Petrovich, and V. Tagalakis (2007), 'A Comprehensive View of Sex-Specific Issues Related to Cardiovascular Disease', *Canadian Medical Association Journal*, Vol. 176, No. 6, pp. S1–44.

Rankin, J. and R. Bhopal (2001), 'Understanding of Heart Disease and Diabetes in a South Asian Community: Cross-Sectional Study Testing the 'Snowball' Sample Method', *Public Health*, Vol. 115, pp. 253–60.

Rastogi, T., K.S. Reddy, M. Vaz, K. Spiegelman, D. Prabhakaran, W.C. Willet, M.J. Stampfer, and A. Ascherio (2004a), 'Diet and Risk of Ischemic Heart Disease in India', *American Journal of Clinical Nutrition*, Vol. 79, pp. 582–92.

Rastogi, T., M. Vaz, K. Spiegelman, K.S. Reddy, A.V. Bharathi, M.J. Stampfer, W.C. Willet, and A. Ascherio (2004b), 'Physical Activity and Risk of Coronary Heart Disease in India', *International Journal of Epidemiology*, Vol. 33, pp. 759–67.

Reddy, K.S. (1993), 'Cardiovascular Diseases in India', *World Health Statistics Quarterly*, Vol. 46, pp. 101–7.

——— (2004), 'Cardiovascular Diseases in Non-Western Countries', *New England Journal of Medicine*, Vol. 350, pp. 2438–40.

Reddy, K.S. and S. Yusuf (1998), 'Emerging Epidemic of Cardiovascular Disease in Developing Countries', *Circulation*, Vol. 97, pp. 596–601.

Sapru, R.P. (1983), 'Cardiovascular and Non-Tuberculous Chest Diseases. An Estimate of the Size of the Problem in India', *Annals of the National Academy of Medical Sciences (India)*, Vol. 19, pp. 179–93.

Sarvotham, S.G. and J.N. Berry (1968), 'Prevalence of Coronary Heart Disease in an Urban Population in Northern India', *Circulation*, Vol. 37, pp. 939–53.

Sharper, A.G. and K.W. Jones (1959), 'Serum-Cholesterol, Diet and Coronary Heart Disease in Africans and Asians in Uganda', *Lancet*, Vol. 2, pp. 534–7.

Sheth, T., N. Cyril, M. Nargundkar, S. Anand, and S. Yusuf (1999), 'Cardiovascular and Cancer Mortality Among Canadians of European, South Asian and Chinese Origin from 1979 to 1993: An Analysis of 1.2 Million Deaths', *Journal of Canadian Medical Association*, Vol. 161, pp. 132–8.

Simmons, W.R., and M.J. Powell (1992), 'Prevalence of Diabetes in Different Regional and Religious South Asian Communities in Coventry', *Diabetic Medicine*, Vol. 9, No. 5, pp. 428–31.

Squires, B.P. (1999), 'Cardiovascular Disease and Socioeconomic Status', *Canadian Medical Association Journal*, Vol. 162, No. 9, supplement.

Tuomilehto, J., P. Ram, R. Eseroma, R. Taylor, and P. Zimmet (1984), 'Cardiovascular Diseases in Fiji: Analysis of Mortality, Morbidity and Risk Factors', *Bulletin of World Health Organization*, Vol. 62, pp. 133–43.

Vaz, M. and A.V. Bhorathi (2003), 'An Exploratory Study of Perceptions and Practices Related to Physical Activity in Women College Teachers and Students in Bangalore, South India', *Health Education Journal*, Vol. 62, No. 4, pp. 316–25.

Wingate, S. (1991), 'Women and Coronary Heart Disease: Implications for the Critical Care Setting', *Focus on Critical Care*, Vol. 18, pp. 212–20.

WHO (1997), *World Health Report 1997—Conquering Suffering, Enriching Humanity*, World Health Organization, Geneva, p. 42.

——— (2000), 'Women, Ageing and Health', retrieved 10 June 2008, from *http://www.who.int/mediacentre/factsheets/fs252/en/*

On Some Measures of Gender Discrimination

MANORANJAN PAL and
PREMANANDA BHARATI _____ 12

Amartya Sen (2001)[1] illustrated with examples the different kinds of inequality between men and women that exist in most parts of the world. These are: (i) mortality inequality, (ii) natality inequality, (iii) basic facility inequality, (iv) special opportunity inequality, (v) professional inequality, (vi) ownership inequality, and (vii) household inequality. Mortality inequality may be ascribed to differential treatments by the society to females starting from childhood. By natality inequality, Sen wanted to mean sex-selective abortion that is illegally practised in some countries. In many countries, females get less opportunities than males, for example, opportunity of schooling or participating in social functions etc. Females also miss special opportunities like those for higher education, professional training etc. Job prospects for women in many countries are less bright than those for men. The number of women employed gradually decreases if one goes to more and more senior positions. Besides, there exists severe inequality of ownership of properties. Inequality between male and female members within the household has also been observed. It is even taken for granted in many countries that women would do household work regardless of whether they do outside work or not. Sen's capability approach can also be used to see gender inequality (Robeyns 2003; 2005). Nussbaum (1995; 2000) has also produced a very careful and elaborate list. Since capabilities are nothing but 'functionings', Robeyns describes how to measure 'functionings' based on individual-level data.

Achievement of gender equality requires the full participation of all segments of society in the decision-making processes and in the

---

[1] A shortened version of this chapter was published in *The New Republic* on 17 September 2001.

allocation of resources. The process of achieving gender equality is not at all satisfactory in India. Forced marriage, marriage of under-aged girls and bride burning are still prevalent in India. Substantial differences between women and men have also been noted in the context of health and well-being. Aspects of health and nutrition come to the forefront for children, especially for under-5 year olds.

Many measures of gender inequality and gender segregation have been proposed and are being proposed in the literature. Most of these are ad hoc measures. Bharati et al. (2008) showed that there are gender differences and spatial variations in the nutritional status of children in India. Gender difference is not very pronounced and almost disappears when the effects of age and socio-demographic variables are removed. Mehrotra (2007) reviewed the human development status of women in Asian countries and examined the demographic dimensions, and the social and human consequences of discrimination between male and female members in the society.

The aspects of gender discrimination in child care practices in India were discussed by Nangia and Roy (2007). They use NFHS data for rounds 1 and 2. A gender disparity index was prepared by them for each of the indicators of child care considered in this study namely, immunization of children, duration of breastfeeding, health care of sick children, nutritional status, mortality of children in different ages, and their educational attainment. The study showed that gender disparity has declined in some spheres of child care. Arokiasamy and Pradhan (2007) also adopted a multiple indicator approach to study patterns of gender bias in India on the basis of a series of female by male ratios with respect to school attendance, use of preventive and curative health care services, and child nutrition status. Significant gender differences have been revealed with respect to each of these indicators. Except for South Indian states, the odds of female children being underweight, and discriminated against in preventive and curative care and in school attendance have been found to be significant.

Mohanty (2007) used two separate econometric models—a sample selection model and a household fixed effects model—to examine gender disparities in child schooling in India. The chapter found very strong evidence of gender bias in the overall schooling outcomes, yet it uncovered no significant gender discrimination in intra-household allocation of schooling resources favouring the male child, once the child is enrolled in a school. Kundu (2007) analysed gender disparity by the method of Benefit Incidence Analysis (BIA) in the incidence of government expenditure on education across expenditure classes.

Mukhopadhyay and Majumder (2007) analysed the data from Censuses and the Sample Registration System of India for different years and tried to see the extent of dissimilarity between males and females over time on different aspects of health, education, and employment. The study showed that significant differences exist in almost all the aspects and also discussed some implications of these findings. Chakraborty and Sinha (2007) examined the intertemporal and spatial trends of juvenile sex ratio and socio-economic determinants of the spatial variations in the relative neglect of the girl child in India.

Non-availability of gender disaggregated data sometimes put a constraint on the analysis of gender bias among children. Studies have indicated that the girls often receive less attention from parents than the boys. Intra-household differences on food consumption were seen to be prominent in some regions. Pal (2008) proposed a model for the estimation of gender inequality in the average consumption of calories in households from National Sample Survey Organization (NSSO) data and found no significant difference in calorie intake between male and female members within the household. Also, those who work on gender issues, should be aware of relevant data to be collected in order to see gender inequality. One can refer to the World Bank data on sex-disaggregated indicators on population, labour, education, enrolment ratios, life expectancy, and maternal mortality which are published on an annual basis. For baseline data on the gender issues, one can also see CIDA (1996 a; b; c)[2] and UN (1995). Beck (1999) stressed the need for developing a national level data base of gender sensitive indicators which can support national level planning towards gender equality (also see Commonwealth Secretariat 1999). Mathematical and statistical modeling and hence analysis of sex-disaggregated data should thus come to the forefront of research on gender issues as pioneered by Atkinson (1970), Anand and Sen (1997) and as carried out by Bardhan and Klasen (1999), Nussbaum (1995; 2000), Pressman (1988; 1998; 2000), Robeyns (2003; 2005), and others.

The 73rd Amendment of the Indian Constitution is an important event in the history of gender empowerment in India. Women have

[2] Canadian International Development Agency.

moved one step forward in participating in *Gram Panchayats* and other political activities. It is hoped that the initiatives of the GoI would narrow down the gender inequality in the country. It is also necessary for women to become more politically aware and conscious about the programmes and schemes that are available for their development.

UNDP introduced the GDI and GEM in 1995 to augment the HDI. The need for sex-disaggregated data was thus stressed by UNDP and Commonwealth in international conventions and declaration.[3]

Besides GDI and GEM, other measures of gender equality/inequality have also been proposed in the literature. The sex ratio (FMR or MFR), the Index of Relative Equity proposed by Anand and Sen (1997), GPG etc. are worth mentioning. The measures of gender segregation, strictly speaking, cannot be viewed as measures of gender inequality, but some modifications of these segregation measures may well be regarded as measures of gender inequality. The authors propose some measures that can be derived from the existing measures of inequality by decomposing these to within and between population groups—the groups being male and female populations.

Sex ratio is perhaps the oldest measure of gender inequality proposed in the literature. It is defined as the ratio of male population to female population, the MFR or the ratio of female population to male population, the FMR. Since women have lower age specific mortality rates than men do, the ideal FMR is some value which is greater than 1 (Sen 2001).[4] It is argued that more enlightened regions have higher FMR values than those in less developed regions. Thus FMR value is regarded as an indicator of development.

The FMR of child female-male ratio (CFMR) and adult female-male ratio (AFMR) persons for the 43rd, 50th, and 55th rounds of NSSO, separately for rural and urban sectors (Tables 12.1 and 12.2) have been calculated from the data given in Siddhanta et al. (2003). These figures confirm our popular idea that less developed states have lower values of FMR. AFMR was greater than 1 for all the periods in both rural and urban sectors of Kerala. CFMR was also close to 1 or

---

[3] For example, Platform for Action of the Fourth UN World Conference on Women in Beijing in 1995 and Commonwealth Plan of Action on Gender and Development in 1995.

[4] The FMR in North America and Europe is around 1.05. However, the FMR in the world is around 0.97, which is not only less than 1.05 but also less than 1.

Table 12.1: Sex ratios in different states in India for the 43rd, 50th, and 55th rounds of NSS, rural sector

States	43rd round		50th round		55th round		50th minus 43rd		55th minus 50th	
	CFMR	AFMR	CFMR	AFMR	CFMR	AFMR	CFMR	AFMR	CFMR	AFMR
Andhra Pradesh	0.966	1.005	1.019	1.023	0.973	1.007	0.053	0.018	-0.046	-0.016
Assam	0.839	0.883	0.787	0.897	0.877	0.913	-0.052	0.014	0.090	0.016
Bihar	0.861	0.941	0.841	0.924	0.875	0.946	-0.020	-0.017	0.034	0.022
Gujarat	1.086	0.976	0.959	0.968	0.877	0.935	-0.127	-0.008	-0.082	-0.033
Haryana	0.806	0.942	0.959	0.968	0.789	0.912	0.153	0.026	-0.170	-0.056
Karnataka	0.944	1.070	0.965	1.006	0.844	0.981	0.021	-0.064	-0.121	-0.025
Kerala	0.976	1.191	0.969	1.214	0.974	1.198	-0.007	0.023	0.005	-0.016
Maharashtra	0.869	0.988	0.917	1.000	0.976	0.995	0.048	0.012	0.059	-0.005
Madhya Pradesh	0.911	0.959	0.893	0.939	0.959	0.905	-0.018	-0.020	0.066	-0.034
Orissa	0.923	0.962	0.983	0.995	0.908	0.995	0.060	0.033	-0.075	0.000
Punjab	0.732	0.926	0.787	1.002	1.102	0.986	0.055	0.076	0.315	-0.016
Rajasthan	0.853	1.006	0.930	0.968	0.935	0.973	0.077	-0.038	0.005	0.005
Tamil Nadu	0.949	1.020	0.975	1.046	0.927	1.034	0.026	0.026	-0.048	-0.012
Uttar Pradesh	0.829	0.937	0.851	0.947	0.872	0.960	0.022	0.010	0.021	0.013
West Bengal	0.940	0.963	0.964	0.980	0.938	0.943	0.024	0.017	-0.021	-0.037

Source: Data from 43rd, 50th, and 55th rounds of NSS.

Table 12.2: Sex ratios of different states in India for the 43rd, 50th, and 55th rounds of NSS, urban sector

State	43rd round		50th round		55th round		50th minus 43rd		55th minus 50th	
	CFMR	AFMR	CFMR	AFMR	CFMR	AFMR	CFMR	AFMR	CFMR	AFMR
Andhra Pradesh	0.925	1.007	0.951	0.980	0.948	0.976	0.026	-0.027	-0.003	-0.004
Assam	0.850	0.888	0.912	0.922	0.915	0.846	0.062	0.034	0.003	-0.076
Bihar	0.982	0.957	0.856	0.805	0.837	0.824	-0.126	-0.152	-0.019	0.019
Gujarat	0.978	0.917	0.958	0.969	0.944	0.946	-0.020	0.052	-0.014	-0.023
Haryana	0.840	0.908	0.929	0.865	0.982	0.952	0.089	-0.043	0.053	0.087
Karnataka	0.950	0.968	0.963	0.957	0.958	0.964	0.013	-0.011	-0.005	0.007
Kerala	0.955	1.102	0.948	1.107	0.986	1.124	-0.007	0.005	0.038	0.017
Maharashtra	1.030	0.907	0.921	0.933	0.955	0.902	-0.109	0.026	0.034	-0.031
Madhya Pradesh	0.949	0.877	0.922	0.887	0.957	0.882	-0.027	0.010	0.035	-0.005
Orissa	0.866	0.836	0.942	0.855	0.888	0.900	0.076	0.019	-0.054	0.045
Punjab	1.007	0.894	0.899	0.945	0.880	0.915	-0.108	0.051	-0.019	-0.030
Rajasthan	0.942	0.900	0.882	0.915	0.949	0.922	-0.060	0.015	0.067	0.007
Tamil Nadu	0.915	1.006	1.008	0.988	0.920	1.019	0.093	-0.018	-0.088	0.031
Uttar Pradesh	0.864	0.816	0.915	0.874	0.848	0.848	0.051	0.058	-0.067	-0.026
West Bengal	1.037	0.852	0.882	0.898	0.883	0.910	-0.155	0.046	0.001	0.012

Source: Data from 43rd, 50th, and 55th rounds of NSS.

more than 1 in both the sectors. Note that Kerala is known for its high literacy rates.

According to Sen, women's gainful employment and literacy play a significant role in improving FMR. Kerala is one example which stands for literacy. Female life expectancy in Kerala is also very high. Kerala also has other features which may influence FMR values. The Nairs of Kerala have the custom of female ownership of property. Moreover, about 20 per cent population in Kerala is Christian.

The HDI was introduced in the very first issue of HDR in 1990. It is a composite index comprising three components: (i) life expectancy at birth (LEI), (ii) weighted average of educational attainment and enrolment ratio (EAI), and (iii) standard of living index (SLI). The HDI is just the simple average of these three indices. Symbolically, the HDI can be defined as HDI = (LEI+EAI+SLI)/3.

As can be seen from the formula, the composite index HDI uses only the simple arithmetic mean of the concerned variables and ignores the distributional features especially the male–female differences. We can not say that two countries with the same overall means have the same development index even if one country has a large differences between men and women than the other country? Development of all groups in a uniform manner should be the aim of every nation.

The GDI is one way of looking at uniform development as far as male and female populations are concerned. The GDI uses same variables as the HDI (that is, LEI, EAI, and SLI), but gives due consideration to male and female populations. It first finds the LEI, EAI, and SLI values separately for male and female populations and then suitably combines them to get LEI_{ede}, EAI_{ede}, and SLI_{ede}. Finally, the GDI is found from the following simple average:

$$GDI = (LEI_{ede} + EAI_{ede} + SLI_{ede})/3.$$

Thus, the GDI uses the same formula for combining the different components as in HDI except that here the EDE value of each component is found by taking gender into consideration.

The GEM measures the relative empowerment of women and men in political and economic spheres of activity. It is a composite index with three components. The first component represents political participation and decision-making power, the second component represents economic participation and decision-making power and the last component reflects power over economic resources. It is again the simple arithmetic mean of the three components, but here the components are different from those of the HDI and GDI.

Choice of the different components of GDI and GEM, their corresponding weighting system, and even the aversion to inequality parameter are somewhat arbitrary and are not rigorously based on objective criteria. Thus, there is some scope for refining these measures.

The GPG is defined as the difference between the poverty rates[5] of female-headed households $(PovR_f)$ and other households $(PovR_o)$, respectively (Christopher et al. 1999). The possible reasons for GPG are: (i) the difference between education levels of women who head households and those of the heads of other households, the education level being positively correlated with the income; (ii) gender difference in income even for the same work; and (iii) gender segregation which puts women into jobs with low pay.

Gender segregation means the tendency of men and women to be employed in different occupations/work places though it is not exactly what we mean by gender inequality. It need not be due to gender inequality or gender discrimination. The segregation measures consider the deviation of male/female employment from that of the overall population. A perfect segregation occurs when there is only female employment or only male employment in each occupation/work place. A large number of gender segregation measures have been proposed in the literature (Harrison 2002).

Though the gender segregation measures cannot be interpreted as measures of gender inequality, we can introduce vertical and horizontal measures of segregation. If the occupations are arranged in an hierarchical manner, that is, from lowest to highest occupation or in the reverse order then the resulting index is known as vertical segregation index. We can also find the horizontal segregation index by considering different organizations for a given or similar occupations. Horizontal segregation index can be regarded as gender inequality.

The measures of gender discrimination have been derived from the general measures of inequality (of size distributions, say, income) such as coefficient of variation, Lorenz ratio etc. Giving the same weight to male and female population, it was seen that most of the derived

---

[5] The poverty rate is calculated as the percentage of families whose income falls BPL (for their family size and type) in a given year.

measures have the same form—the absolute difference between the two group means divided by the sum of the two group means, the normalizing term. It is very simple, intuitively appealing, and satisfies the most desirable properties of a measure of gender inequality.

MEASURES DERIVED FROM MEASURES OF INCOME INEQUALITY

Suppose $I(x_1, x_2, ..., x_n)$ is a measure of income inequality and the population is divided into K mutually exclusive and exhaustive groups with $n_1, n_2, ..., n_K$ observations. Let us replace the x_i values by their respective group means. We thus get the between group index as:

$$I_b = I((m_1, m_1, ... m_1), (m_2, m_2, ... m_2), ..., (m_K, m_K, ... m_K)),$$

where $m_1, m_2, ..., m_K$ are repeated $n_1, n_2, ..., n_K$ times respectively. The difference between the inequality measure and the between-group inequality measure may be regarded as a measure of within-group inequality.[6] I_b can be regarded as a measure of gender inequality if the population is divided into two groups—males and females. Thus from each measure of income inequality we shall get a measure of gender inequality of income. Moreover, the variable need not be restricted to the income variable only. We can take any quantitative characteristic or even a dummy variable signifying whether a person is getting a particular facility or not. In case of dummy variable with values 0 and 1, 1 denoting existence, the mean will give the proportion of persons getting the facility within the group.

Let us now consider the existing measures and get the corresponding gender inequality measures using this formula.

+ Coefficient of Variation (CV)

$$I_{GCV} = \sqrt{(n_1 n_2)} \, |m_1\text{-}m_2|/(n_1 m_1 + n_2 m_2) = \sqrt{(n_1 n_2)} \, |m_1\text{-}m_2|/(nm),[7]$$

[6] More generally any inequality measure can be decomposed into three parts as $I = I_b + I_w + I_r$, where I_b = between-group inequality, I_w = within-group inequality and I_r = the remainder term. Thus, strictly speaking if there is a remainder term then $I_w \neq I - I_b$.

[7] The formula for coefficient of variation, assuming that the observations are x_1, $x_2, ..., x_n$, is CV = SD/AM, where SD = standard deviation $= \sqrt{\frac{1}{n}\sum_{i=1}^{n}(x_i - \bar{x})^2}$, and AM = arithmetic mean $= \bar{x}$. Putting $x_i = m_1$ for male or m_2 for female, we get the required formula for gender inequality corresponding to CV. Other measures of gender inequality can be derived in a similar manner.

where $n = n_1 + n_2$, the total number of observations and $m = (n_1 m_1 + n_2 m_2)/n$, the overall mean.

- Relative Mean Deviation (RMD)[8]

$$I_{GRMD} = 2(n_1 n_2) |m_1 - m_2| / (n(n_1 m_1 + n_2 m_2))$$
$$= 2(n_1 n_2) |m_1 - m_2| / (n^2 m).$$

- Lorenz Ratio (LR)[9]

$$I_{GLR} = (n_1 n_2) |m_1 - m_2| / (n(n_1 m_1 + n_2 m_2)) = (n_1 n_2) |m_1 - m_2| / (n^2 m).$$

- Standard Deviation of Logarithms (SDL)[10]

$$I_{GSDL} = \sqrt{(n_1 n_2)} |\ln(m_1) - \ln(m_2)| / n.$$

- Elteto-Fryges Measures(EF)[11]

Here we assume that $m_1 < m_2$.

$$I_{GEF1} = (n_1 m_1 + n_2 m_2) / (n m_1) = m / m_1,$$
$$I_{GEF2} = m_2 / m_1 \text{ and}$$
$$I_{GEF3} = (n m_2) / (n_1 m_1 + n_2 m_2) = m_2 / m.$$

- Theil's Entropy Measure(T)[12]

$$I_{GTE} = (n_1 m_1 / (nm)) \ln(m_1 / m) + (n_2 m_2 / (nm)) \ln(m_2 / m).$$

- Atkinson's (1970) Measure(A)[13]

$$I_{GA} = 1 - \{(1/n)(n_1 m_1^{1-\varepsilon} + n_2 m_2^{1-\varepsilon})\}^{1/(1-\varepsilon)} / m.$$

Most of these measures have simple forms. Not all these measures lie within the desired range of an index number, that is, in between 0

---

[8] RMD is $\frac{1}{n} \sum_{i=1}^{n} |x_i - \bar{x}| / \bar{x}$.

[9] LR is defined as $LR = 1 - \frac{1}{n^2 \mu} \sum_{i=1}^{n} (2(n-i)+1)\hat{x}_i = \frac{1}{2n^2 \mu} \sum_{i=1}^{n} \sum_{j=1}^{n} |x_i - x_j|$, where $\mu = \bar{x}$ and $\hat{x}_i$ s are x_i values arranged in increasing order.

[10] SDL is defined as $\sqrt{\frac{1}{n} \sum_{i=1}^{n} (\ln x_i - \overline{\ln x})^2}$, where $\overline{\ln x} = \sum_{i=1}^{n} \ln x_i / n$.

[11] EF measures are defined as m/m_1, m_2/m_1, and m_2/m, where m is the overall mean, m_1 is the mean of incomes $< m$, and m_2 is the mean of incomes $> m$.

[12] Theil's Entropy measure is defined as $T = \sum_{i=1}^{n} \frac{x_i}{\bar{x}} \log\left(\frac{x_i}{\bar{x}}\right)$.

[13] Atkinson's measure of inequality is $A_\varepsilon = 1 - \left[\frac{1}{n} \sum_i \left(\frac{x_i}{\bar{x}}\right)^{1-\varepsilon}\right]^{\frac{1}{1-\varepsilon}}$, where $\varepsilon > 0$, and represents the degree of inequality aversion.

and 1, because of the fact that the original measures of inequality do not lie in the desired range.

Inequality between two groups should not depend on the number of observations in each group, because the existing nature of treatment or exploitation, if any, to any of the persons does not change if one person from any of the groups is inducted in or removed from the population. Thus equal weight should be given to each group. The idea of giving equal weight forces us to deviate from the usual concept of original measures of inequality from which these measures have been derived. These measures may be named as gender discrimination indices. A gender discrimination index thus gives the degree of discrimination observed between two groups by comparing two representative persons taken one from each group. We thus have three concepts of differences between men and women: gender inequality, gender segregation, and gender discrimination.

The respective measures take the following simpler forms if we take $n_1 = n_2 = n/2$.

- $I_{GCV} = |m_1 - m_2| / (m_1 + m_2)$.
- $I_{GRMD} = |m_1 - m_2| / (m_1 + m_2)$.
- $I_{GLR} = (1/2)|m_1 - m_2| / (m_1 + m_2)$.
- $I_{GSDL} = |\ln(m_1) - \ln(m_2)| / 2$.
- $I_{GEF1} = (m_1 + m_2) / (2m_1)$,
- $I_{GEF2} = m_2 / m_1$ and
- $I_{GEF3} = (2m_2) / (m_1 + m_2)$.
- $I_{GTE} = (m_1 / (m_1 + m_2))\ln(2m_1 / (m_1 + m_2)) + (m_2 / (m_1 + m_2))$
  $\ln(2m_2 / (m_1 + m_2))$.
- $I_{GA} = 1 - 2((m_1^{1-\varepsilon} + m_2^{1-\varepsilon})/2)^{1/(1-\varepsilon)} / (m_1 + m_2)$.

As we can see the formula for I_{GCV} now coincides with the formula for I_{GRMD}. Also, many of these measures still do not lie between 0 and 1. However the gender discrimination measures can be made to lie in the [0,1] interval just by taking the following simple transformations.

- $I_{CVG} = I_{GCV} = |m_1 - m_2| / (m_1 + m_2)$.
- $I_{RMDG} = I_{GRMD} = |m_1 - m_2| / (m_1 + m_2)$.
- $I_{LRG} = 2\,I_{GLR} = |m_1 - m_2| / (m_1 + m_2)$.
- $I_{SDLG} = 1 - \exp(-I_{GSDL}) = |\sqrt{m_1} - \sqrt{m_2}| / \sqrt{m_2}$.

- $I_{EF1G} = 1 - 1/I_{GEF1} = |m_1-m_2|/(m_1+m_2)$,
- $I_{EF2G} = 1 - 1/I_{GEF2} = |m_1-m_2|/\max(m_1,m_2)$, and
- $I_{EF3G} = 2(1 - 1/I_{GEF3}) = |m_1-m_2|/\max(m_1,m_2)$,

where $\max(m_1,m_2)$ is the maximum of m_1 and m_2.

- $I_{TEG} = I_{GTE}/\ln(2)$.
- $I_{AG} = I_{GA}/(1-2^{-\varepsilon/(1-\varepsilon)})$ for $0 < \varepsilon < 1$, and

    $= I_{GA}$ for $\varepsilon = 0$ or > 1.

Now we have four indices I_{CVG}, I_{RMDG}, I_{LRG}, and I_{EF1G} equal to $|m_1-m_2|/(m_1+m_2)$. The three special cases of I_{AG} are worth mentioning. These are when ε tends to 1, 2, and ∞.

$I_{AG}|_{\varepsilon\to1} = 1 - \sqrt{(m_1m_2)}/((m_1+m_2)/2) = (\sqrt{m_1}-\sqrt{m_2})^2/(m_1+m_2)$.

$I_{AG}|_{\varepsilon=2} = 1 - ((1/m_1+1/m_2)/2)^{-1}/((m_1+m_2)/2)$

    $= ((m_1-m_2)/(m_1+m_2))^2$.

$I_{AG}|_{\varepsilon\to\infty} = |m_1-m_2|/(m_1+m_2)$.

$|m_1-m_2|/(m_1+m_2)$ thus signifies the situation with extreme discrimination aversion. The above discussion leads to a natural and very simple index of gender discrimination which is $|m_1-m_2|/(m_1+m_2)$.

CONCLUSION

The major limitation of all the indices of gender inequality, gender segregation, and gender discrimination, is that they do not provide information on the wider social pattern—how the women are oppressed, if at all. It does not say anything about social relations between men and women. The indices should be complemented by gender analysis. The cause as well as the effect of low and high values of the indices from the agreed norm should be thoroughly investigated so that some policy prescription towards gender equality can be given.

REFERENCE

Anand, Sudhir and Amartya Sen (1997), 'Gender Inequality in Human Development: Theories and Measurement', Human Development Report Office Occasional Paper no. 19, New York, United Nations Development Programme (UNDP), http://hdr.undp.org/docs/ publications/ ocational_papers/oc19a.htm.

Arokiasamy, P. and J. Pradhan (2007), 'Gender Bias Against Female Children In India', Paper presented at the seminar on Gender Issues and Empowerment of Women, organized by the Social Sciences Division, Indian Statistical Institute, February, Kolkata.

Atkinson, Anthony B. (1970), 'On the Measurement of Inequality', *Journal of Economic Theory*, Vol. 2, No. 3, September, pp. 200–63.

Bardhan, Kalpana and Stephan Klasen, (1999), 'UNDP's Gender Related Indices: A Critical Review', *World Development*, Vol. 27, pp. 985–1010.

Bharati, S., M. Pal, and P. Bharati (2008), 'Determinants of Nutritional Status of Pre-School Children in India', *Journal of Biosocial Science*, Vol. 40, pp. 801–14.

Beck, Tony (1999), *A Quick Guide to Using Gender Sensitive Indicators*, Commonwealth Secretariat, Marlborough House, London, UK.

Chakraborty, Lekha S. and D. Sinha (2007), 'Declining Juvenile Sex Ratio in India: Trends and Determinants', Paper presented at the seminar on Gender Issues and Empowerment of Women, organized by the Social Sciences Division, Indian Statistical Institute, February, Kolkata.

Christopher, K., P. England, K. Ross, T. Smeeding, and S. McLanahan (1999), 'The Sex Gap in Modern Nations: Single Motherhood, the Market and the State', LIS Working Paper, Luxemberg.

CIDA (1996a), *Developing Baseline Gender Indicators and Analysis for Country Programme Planning: A Resource Guide*, CIDA, Asia Branch Hull, (author: T. Beck).

——— (1996b), *Guide to Gender-Sensitive Indicators*, CIDA, Asia Branch Hull (authors: T. Beck, and M. Stelcner).

——— (1996c), *The Why and How of Gender-Sensitive Indicators: A Project Level Handbook*, CIDA, Asia Branch Hull, (authors: T. Beck, and M. Stelcner).

Commonwealth Secretariat (1999), *Using Gender Sensitive Indicators: A Reference Manual for Governments and other Stakeholders*, Gender Management System Series, London (author: T. Beck).

Harrison, Jane (2002), 'Gender Segregation in Employment in Australia: A Workplace Perspective', Working Paper No. 186, *Economics*, Murdoch University, Austrlia.

Kundu, P. (2007), 'Incidence of Public Expenditure on Education: Viewing through a Gender Lens', Paper presented at the seminar on Gender Issues and Empowerment of Women, organized by the Social Sciences Division, Indian Statistical Institute, February, Kolkata.

Mehrotra, S. (2007) 'Capability Deprivation of Women: Are Women Holding Up Half the Sky in Asia?', Paper presented at the seminar on Gender Issues and Empowerment of Women, organized by the Social Sciences Division, Indian Statistical Institute, February, Kolkata.

Mohanty, I. (2007), 'Gender Discrimination in Child Schooling: Why do we observe it?', Paper presented at the seminar on Gender Issues and Empowerment of Women, organized by the Social Sciences Division, Indian Statistical Institute, February, Kolkata.

Mukhopadhyay, B.K. and P.K. Majumder (2007), 'Status of Gender-Differentials and Trends in India: Population, Health, Education and Employment', Paper presented at the seminar on Gender Issues and Empowerment of Women, organized by the Social Sciences Division, Indian Statistical Institute, February, Kolkata.

Nangia, P. and T.K. Roy (2007), 'Gender Disparity in Child Care in India: Findings from Two National Family Health Surveys', Paper presented at the seminar on Gender Issues and Empowerment of Women, organized by the Social Sciences Division, Indian Statistical Institute, February, Kolkata.

Nussbaum, Martha (1995), 'Gender Issues and Empowerment of Women, Human Capabilities, Female Human Beings', in Martha Nussbaum, and Jonathan Glover, (eds), *Women, Culture and Development*, pp. 61–104, Oxford University Press, Oxford UK.

———(2000), *Women and Human Development: The Capabilities Approach*, Cambridge, University Press, Cambridge.

Pal, M. (2008), 'Estimation of Gender Inequality in the Average Consumption of Calories in the Households from NSSO Data', Paper presented at the ISI/ Academia Sinica/ISM joint conference held during 19–20 June 2008 in Taipei.

Pressman, Stephen (1988), 'The Feminization of Poverty: Causes and Remedies', *Challenge*, Vol. 31, pp. 57–61.

———(1998), 'The Gender Poverty Gap in Developed Countries: Causes and Cures', *Social Science Journal*, Vol. 35, pp. 275–86.

——— (2000), 'Explaining the Gender Poverty Gap in Developed and Transitional Economics', Working Paper No. 243, Luxemberg Income Study, CEPS, Luxemberg.

Robeyns, Ingrid (2003), 'Sen's capability Approach and Gender Inequality: Selecting Relevant Capabilities', *Feminist Economics*, Vol. 9, Nos 2 and 3, pp. 62–92.

——— (2004), 'Measuring Gender Inequality in Functionings and Capabilities: Findings from the British Household Panel Survey', in Bharati, Pal, Ghosh and Vasulu (eds) *Gender Disparity: Its Manifestations and Implications*, Oxford University Press, India.

——— (2005), 'Measuring Gender Inequality in Functioning and Capabilities: Findings from the British Household Panel Survey', in Bharati and Pal (eds), *Gender Disparity: Its Manifestations and Implications*, Anmol Publishers, India.

Sen, Amartya (2001), 'Many Faces of Gender Inequality', *The Frontline*, India, 9 November.

Siddhanta, S., D. Nandy, and S.B. Agnihotri (2003), 'Sex Ratios and "Prosperity Effect": What Do NSSO Data Reveal?', *Economic and Political Weekly*, 11 October, pp. 4381–04.

UN (1995), *The World's Women, 1970–1990: Trends and Statistics*, Social Statistics and Indicators, Series K, No. 12, United Nations, New York.

Gender Dimorphism
Discrimination in Rural India, 1930–1975

ARAVINDA MEERA GUNTUPALLI
and ALEXANDER MORADI ————————— 13

INTRODUCTION

Mean body stature of a population is used by many researchers as a measure of net nutrition and living standards (Fogel et al. 1983; Komlos 1985; Steckel 1995; and Strauss and Duncan 1998). Measures of height are employed as the principal index of nutritional status for males and females as both laboratory experiments on animal populations and observational studies of human populations have led physiologists and nutritionists to conclude that anthropometric measurements are reliable indices of the extent of malnutrition. Stature is also recommended by the (World Health Organization Working Group 1986) and other international agencies to assess the nutritional status of populations. In this context, our study attempts to understand gender discrimination in India by using dimorphism in stature from the period of Great Depression (1930) to the 1970s.

The chapter is organized as follows: First, we clarify the meaning of 'gender dimorphism in stature' and its applicability for measuring gender discrimination by arguing that stature measure has particular advantages compared to other commonly used indicators. After a detailed discussion about the data sources and construction, we present the secular trend in height dimorphism in seven Indian states from 1930 to 1975. Thereafter, we explore the impact of several economic variables such as agricultural output, poverty, real wages, development expenditures, and the impact of monsoon rainfall on gender dimorphism in stature through a regression analysis. Finally, we present the conclusion.

Dimorphism in Stature: A New Indicator of Gender Discrimination

The use of stature for measuring health and nutrition rests on a well-defined pattern of human growth between childhood and maturity. The average annual increase in height is the greatest during infancy, falls sharply up to age 3, and then falls more slowly during the remaining pre-adolescent years. This growth pattern reflects the interaction of genetic, environmental, and socio-economic factors during the period of growth. According to Eveleth and Tanner (1976), 'Two genotypes which produce the same adult height under optimal environmental circumstances may produce different heights under circumstances of deprivation. Thus children who would be the taller in a well-off community would be smaller under poor economic conditions. If a particular environmental stimulus is lacking at a time period when it is essential for the child, then the child's development may be stunted'. In this context, we rely on Baten (2000) who found the effect of environmental conditions during the first three years to be so overwhelmingly strong that later influences on growth had only a very small impact on final adult height.

Studies, mostly of prehistoric populations, found a decrease in male/female height differences under conditions of nutritional stress and an increase in dimorphism with improved diet (Brauer 1982; Gray and Wolfe 1980; Stini 1985). According to these studies, males are generally more susceptible to fluctuations in nutritional quality and show greater impairment in long bone growth compared to females, who are more stable under similar food deficits. Moreover, in times of chronic dietary deficiencies, selection would operate to reduce body size with respect to energetic efficiency putting males at an additional disadvantage.[1] Therefore, body size is positively correlated with the degree of sexual dimorphism in height (Clutton-Brock and Harvey 1984) and a development for smaller/larger body size should result in reduced/increased height dimorphism. Since nutritional conditions improve in our study period, an increasing dimorphism in stature could just be a natural biological response if the above argument holds.[2]

---

[1] We wonder whether a higher mortality of tall people or a larger fertility of small people is a likely cause for selection in contemporary times.

[2] The improvement of nutritional conditions is clearly evident from the positive

Does the view of a 'biological' response hold in a contemporary and global perspective? In using Food and Agriculture Organization (FAO) data on calorie supply available for human consumption we are able to approximate the overall nutritional situation in a region.[3] A low calorie supply indicates poor nutritional conditions and a high one means abundance, in which nutritional needs can be sufficiently met. In the global sample from Jürgens (1990), male and female mean heights are astonishingly well explained by calorie supply (Figure 13.1). For both genders, the regression coefficients are positive and highly significant with R-squares well above 50 per cent pointing to a very good fit. Moreover, the regression lines run nearly parallel. Therefore, mean stature of both females and males are increasing with food supply generally at the same rate and height of both genders reacts on improvements in nutritional conditions in a very similar manner. Taking the difference between the mean heights of the gender expressed as a percentage of male height confirms this assessment (Figure 13.2).[4] We find that dimorphism in stature is not increasing with total food supply and the relation between dimorphism and nutrition is insignificant. Moreover, only 0.03 per cent of the observed variance in gender dimorphism can be explained by the overall nutritional situation suggesting that other factors play a more important role. Additionally, South Asia is located clearly above the regression line, which means that India has much larger dimorphism in stature than other countries on average. Similarly, during the Orissa food crisis (1930s) and Kerala grain crisis (1965–6) period our data indicate not only a clear decline in the height of both men and women but also increasing dimorphism (which means greater decline in the stature of women compared to men).

Summing up, we cannot find any support that gender dimorphism in stature is affected by overall nutritional conditions in a biological

---

secular trend in stature of both males and females from our study sample. The secular trend in mean height is also evident from the more representative NFHS survey (Guntupalli 2003), for example, females from rural India born in 1975 are 0.6 cm taller than their counterparts born 25 years before.

[3] Derived from the Food Balance Sheets available at *http://apps.fao.org/*. We have weighted the country-wise data on calories according to the share of its population in the region. The figures correspond to the mean food supply available for the time period 1961–2000.

[4] We thank Jörg Baten for the suggestion regarding the use of percentage.

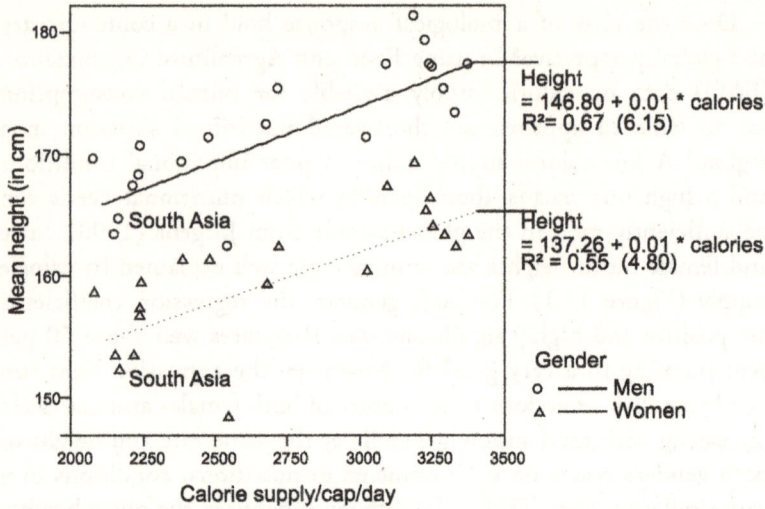

Notes: Regions included are North America, Northern Latin America, Southern Latin America, North Europe, Central Europe, Eastern Europe, South-Eastern Europe, France, Iberian Peninsula, North Africa, West Africa, South-East Africa, Near East, South Asia, China, South-East Asia, Australia, Japan/Korea (see Jürgens 1990 for details). We have additionally included figures provided by the World Bank LSMS surveys for Ghana 1960-70 and the Ivory Coast 1960–70 as well as the height of the NCHS (US) reference population at age 18; t-values in parentheses below the regression equation.

Sources: Jürgens 1990, World Bank LSMS Surveys for Ghana and the Ivory Coast 1960–70, and the NCHS (US).

Figure 13.1: Relationship between mean height and food supply in a global sample

manner. Therefore, one should not consider increasing dimorphism as biologically induced from the nutritional improvements in contemporary India.

In what way does 'gender dimorphism' differ from 'sexual dimorphism'? Human beings exhibit sexual dimorphism in size, shape, and behaviour. It is common knowledge that males have a larger stature than females, more robust cranial and facial features, along with greater muscularity and strength (Frayer and Wolpoff 1985). To be more specific, the terms 'gender discrimination' and 'gender dimorphism' that are used frequently in this study are not measuring sexual dimorphism ascribed by biology, anatomy, hormones, and physiology but gender dimorphism in stature, which is constructed through psychological, cultural, and social means and when the intra-household allocation

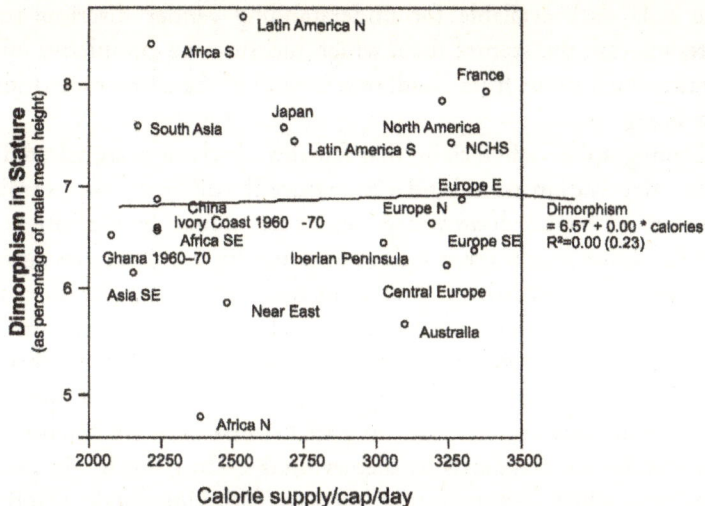

Sources: Jürgens 1990, World Bank LSMS Surveys for Ghana and the Ivory Coast 1960–70, the NCHS (US), and the FAO Food Balance Sheets (1961–2000).

Figure 13.2: Relationship between dimorphism in stature and food supply

of resources favours one gender disproportionately. This can be attributed to differential access to food, health facilities, and education due to 'son preference.' We take support from a very recent study by Borooah (2004). Based on a sample of over 4000 children between the ages of 1 and 2 years in India, he found it less likely that girls would be immunized against disease and would receive a nutritious diet. A study by Brennan et al. (1997), based on immigrant and local Indians demonstrates that the male to female mean height ratio was higher in northern than in southern India and greatest for higher social classes. They suggest that differences in the ratio of male to female height can be used together with sex differences in death rates as indicators of differential treatment of female children.

What are the advantages of gender dimorphism when compared to other commonly used indicators? Some scholars have used mortality as an indicator to measure gender discrimination. First of all, there is a paucity of systematic evidence and research work to show long-term changes in the health of Indian women based on state-wise mortality data. Additionally, life expectancy, mortality, and nutrition data are available for the pre-1975 periods for the population of India as a whole and not for specific states to understand regional changes.

The only data available for understanding gender discrimination state-wise are the stature data, which measure the cumulative effect of nutritional status from childhood instead of the current nutritional well-being.

Demographers often claim that females' life chances are affected by greater deprivation in food and it is measured by differences in mortality. A review of female disadvantage on access to food by DeRose et al. (2000), shows that there is lack of evidence for a general bias against females in calories. However, we argue that data on access to food and calorie consumption do not show the real gender discrimination due to some methodological problems, especially systematic bias (Strauss and Duncan 1998). We also argue that this is due to the fact that female requirements are lower in part because they are smaller and this was determined partly by dietary intake. Thus, low intake causes small size, which in turn can be used to justify low intake (DeRose et al. 2000).

The problem with the use of malnutrition and mortality data is the fact, that there is no clear argument that shows the relation between these two indicators. A country level study by Hill and Upchurch (1995) shows no link between female malnutrition and excess female mortality. Basu (1989) found that even though boys in Delhi have higher malnutrition rates than girls, they have lower death rates. The recently declining Indian sex ratio received a lot of attention and this indicator was used by many researchers for measuring gender discrimination in India. It was argued by Mayer (1999) that education, employment, and mortality data are better indicators compared to sex ratio for measuring gender discrimination. In this context where there is growing research and criticism regarding the use of calorie consumption, life expectancy, mortality and sex ratio data, we are using height data as an indicator to measure gender discrimination in nutrition and health. Apart from this, our study is completely exploratory as there is no information available on measuring gender discrimination based on stature dimorphism, especially for India.

Data on Stature in Rural India

The National Nutrition Monitoring Board (NNMB) carried out a nutrition survey in 1975–9, which was repeated in 1988–90 and 1996–7 covering rural areas in the Indian states of Andhra Pradesh, Gujarat, Karnataka, Kerala, Maharashtra, Orissa, and Tamil Nadu

(National Institute of Nutrition 1999). In each state, about 125 villages from eight geographically distant districts were selected in the first survey. The second and third survey, covered a total of 120 and 100 villages per state. Particularly, in each and every survey about 30 villages were totally replaced by new ones. Mean heights for both sexes who were older than 20 years were reported in five-year age groups that reduced bias from age heaping. We exclude the age groups above 50 years since individuals start to lose stature rapidly from this point of time (Baten and Murray 2000). This study is based on 21,914 men and 29,248 women aged 20–50 (or between 100 and 750 per age group, sex, and survey).

We converted the age groups into birth cohorts by assuming the measurement to be carried out in the middle of the survey period. For each survey and state, a time series of our gender dimorphism measure was constructed by taking the difference between male and female mean height, which is expressed as a percentage of male height. Accordingly, the youngest four birth cohorts of each survey are approximately overlapping with the subsequent one. This allows us to test whether the change in the sampled villages has an impact on the level or trend of gender differences in height.

A necessary condition for consistency between the surveys is that gender dimorphism based on the same birth cohorts should be relatively similar, so that the deviations represent just fluctuations from random sampling. However, for Karnataka, Kerala, and Orissa the first and second surveys do not produce identical results and show considerable deviations (Table 13.1). The reasons for these inconsistencies can be attributed to changes in sampling design and coverage over the time period of these three surveys. In fact, the figures on mean income per capita reported by NNMB suggest that poorer households were presumably selected in the second survey compared with the first one.[5] Thus, anyone who compares the development of the various measures between the surveys (also in a cross-sectional sense) without

[5] Based on a comparison with figures of the NSS on mean per capita expenditures in the rural economy of those states, which shows an increase of about 10 per cent while the NNMB households reported a decrease of about 7 per cent in per capita income. The scarce information given by the National Institute of Nutrition 1999 does not allow a more precise assessment.

Table 13.1: Mean differences of dimorphism between the surveys (based on the same birth cohort)*

(mean differences in per cent)

State	(Survey I–Survey II)	Number of runs crossing 0	(Survey II–Survey III)	Number of runs crossing 0
Andhra Pradhesh	0.083	3	0.218	1
Gujarat	−0.087	1	0.430	0
Karnataka	0.618	2	0.321	2
Kerala	−1.280	0	−0.262	1
Maharashtra	−0.317	3	0.103	3
Orissa	1.166	0	−0.019	3
Tamil Nadu	−0.238	1	0.688	2
Total	0.002	–	0.333	–

Note: *Based on four observations per state.
Source: NNNB Consecutive Surveys.

taking into account the differential composition of the population is mistakenly interpreting sampling effects as real changes.[6]

We suspect that migration and mortality might also be responsible for the inconsistencies. However, a regression indicates no structural influence of time on the differences in gender dimorphism among the surveys, which means no significant bias due to higher mortality of smaller individuals. Since the growth period of severely stunted individuals continues until their early twenties (Brennan et al. 1994) another source of inconsistency could be still growing individuals in the age group 20–25. This would result in a higher mean stature in the age group 30–35 of the same birth cohort when measured ten years later. Indeed, we find a significant downward bias in the age group 20–25 for both males and females. Nevertheless, the bias disappears when we take height differences between males and females (apparently both males and females face the same prolonged growth problem and height difference nullifies this effect).

Without doubt, NNMB nutrition surveys still represent the unique and most representative source available for male and female heights despite these irregularities. Moreover, the divergent series (Karnataka,

---

[6] We could not find any analyses of these surveys (for example, National Institute of Nutrition Monitoring Bureau (1999) or Venkaiah et al. (2002), which control for sampling effects in some manner.

Kerala, and Orissa) follow nearly a parallel trend. Therefore, pooling the three surveys to obtain a single index, that represents a large number of individuals with a broad spectrum, is definitely advantageous. However, before averaging we first standardize the levels to avoid spurious leaps due to a switch from one survey to another. This means, that the series are shifted on the vertical axis until the differences becomes 0 on average. For deciding which of the NNMB surveys is most representative, we chose the survey, in which the levels of female mean heights match mean height of NFHS-2 rural women (International Institute for Population Sciences (IIPS) and ORC Macro 2000). Furthermore, we weight the data points according to the number of individuals in the birth cohorts. Consequently, we obtain consistent information on the secular trend of gender dimorphism in rural India. Nevertheless, one should be cautious about the interpretation of levels, especially where shifts are large (Karnataka, Kerala, and Orissa). For this reason we do not intend to observe the level but the trend of gender discrimination.

We illustrate the procedure by taking the example of Karnataka (Figure 13.3). The first survey indicates a larger gender dimorphism. Nevertheless, there is an agreement with both subsequent surveys in the increase in dimorphism between 1940 and 1955. In contrast, a

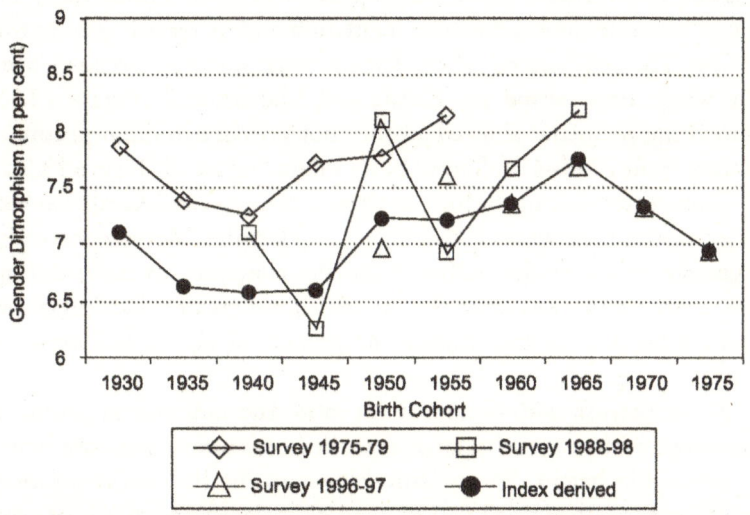

Source: NNMB Consecutive Surveys in Karnataka.

Figure 13.3: Gender dimorphism in stature according the NNMB surveys in Karnataka

naive averaging with the lower height differences of the second survey would result in a levelling of height dimorphism for this period. Although we cannot definitely decide which of the surveys represents the true level, the comparison with female mean heights based on the representative NFHS would point to the third one.

THE SECULAR TREND IN GENDER DIMORPHISM IN STATURE, RURAL SOUTH INDIA 1930–70

In all the seven Indian states we observe a secular trend of increasing mean heights for both males and females, although the trend slows down somewhat in the 1960s. In total, the nutritional and health status improved in the long run. However, our measure suggests that in some Indian states the males benefit more from the development than the females (Figures 13.3, 13.4, and 13.5). In Orissa, for instance, gender dimorphism increased considerably, pointing to the female disadvantage, except for the 1950s, when there was a short improvement. A similar development could be observed in Andhra Pradesh till 1950 where decrease in gender inequality starting in the 1950s continued until the end of the study period. Contrastingly, in Karnataka, dimorphism stagnated before the Second World War and showed an inverted U trend with a peak in 1965. In Tamil Nadu, the initial decrease slowed down to stagnation and increased again in the 1970s. The only states, where female discrimination declined over the whole time period are Kerala and Maharashtra (Figure 13.5). Surprisingly, Gujarat showed a continuous decline in dimorphism in stature from 1945–65 followed by an increasing trend (Figure 13.5).

As expected, during the food crisis period, Orissa and Kerala showed a decrease in the stature of both males and females. More importantly, a greater decline in the stature of females compared to males during this crisis period was observed, which shows greater discrimination and female disadvantage during the periods of nutritional stress or crises.

A comparison with decennial sex ratio data indicates in general a negative correlation, so that an increase in the sex ratio is associated with a decrease in height dimorphism. However, the Pearson correlation coefficient is rather small (−0.31) and only significant to 10 per cent confidence level. Thus, the relationship is not very close and there are remarkable deviations for some states. This is not an unexpected result given that both indicators have strong complementary characteristics

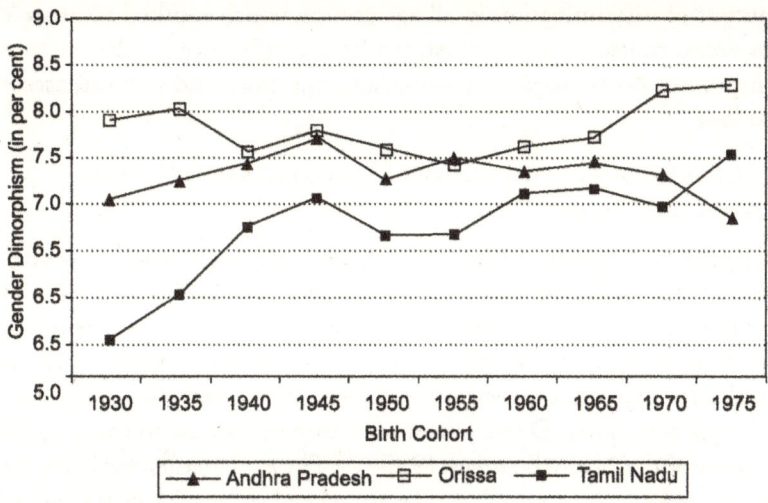

Source: NNMB Consecuting Surveys.

Figure 13.4: Gender dimorphism in stature in Andhra Pradesh, Orissa, and Tamil Nadu

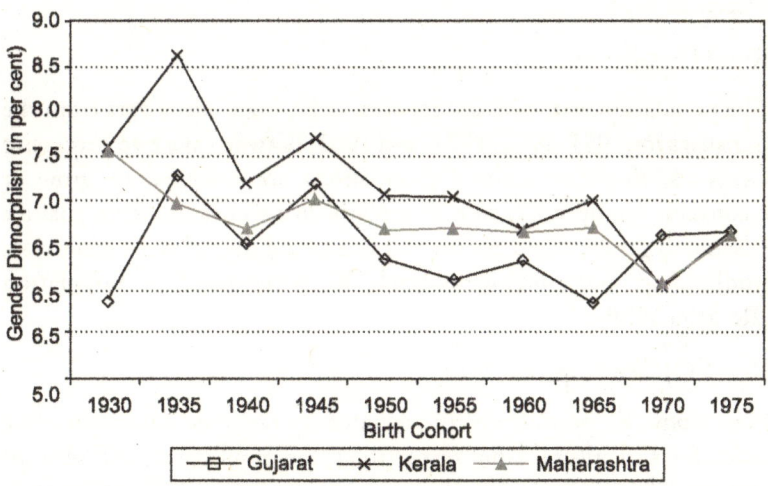

Source: NNMB Consecuting Surveys.

Figure 13.5: Gender dimorphism in stature in Gujarat, Kerala, and Maharashtra

in measuring gender discrimination. The sex ratio measures the output of discrimination in all age groups, which resulted ultimately in excess mortality. In contrast, the height difference is affected by a disproportionate burden of workload, morbidity, and reduced access to food.

DETERMINANTS OF GENDER DIMORPHISM IN RURAL INDIA, 1955–75

The general hypothesis that we want to test here is whether gender discrimination is increasing in poor times, during which care and investment in girls is reduced disproportionately. The regression analysis is restricted to the time period 1955–75 due to lack of available data on explanatory variables at the state level for pre-independent India. Dimorphism in stature refers now to the original figures of the NNMB survey 1996–7.[7] The explanatory variables are organized in such a way that they are related to conditions the adults faced during early childhood. Data for all our explanatory variables are drawn from the database of Özler et al. (1996) except for information on rice output, which is from Sanghi et al. (1998). The definition of the indicators from the above data sets and expected relationships are presented here.

Rural Population

The population estimates are constructed using Census data from the Censuses for 1951, 1961, 1971, and 1981. Between any two successive Censuses, the state-sectoral populations are assumed to grow at a constant (compound) rate of growth. We would expect a positive relation to gender dimorphism as it was found that income, education, landholding, and nutritional levels are determined by population (Rodgers 1989).

Real SDP Per Capita

State domestic product (SDP) deflated by the state consumer price index for agricultural labourers is the value of all goods and services produced by the agricultural sector. We consider SDP as a general indicator of economic development in rural areas.

---

[7] Using the proposed index for assessing the secular trend would not alter the results, because changes in both series are very similar.

Poverty Gap Index

The poverty gap index measures the mean distance below the poverty line as a proportion of the poverty line where the mean is taken over the whole population, counting the non-poor as having zero poverty gap. This indicator will help us to understand gender dimorphism in the context where poverty is argued to increase gender discrimination (World Bank 1981).

Rural Real Wages

It consists of annual state-level data on agricultural wage for male labourers. Since there is no univariate relationship between changes in the poverty gap index and rural real wages, we obtain additional information on the development of income in rural India. If care for girls has a higher income elasticity, we should find a negative relationship with dimorphism. However, female discrimination is also present in the Indian labour market and increases in men's wages could result in a rising wage differential between the genders.[8] Then, future economic returns on investment in boys might increase, reducing incentives for expenditures on girls. If this effect outweighs, rural real wage would have a positive impact on dimorphism.

Development Expenditures

State development data include State expenditure on economic (rural development, irrigation, and flood control) and social services (education, medical and public health, family welfare, water supply, and sanitation). We argue that with the increase in development programmes women should benefit in the absence of gender differentiated programmes.

Rain Data

The monthly average rainfall by state is the simple average of actual rainfall and refers to the four months in the monsoon season. The total amount and the time of monsoon rainfall is a very important input factor in the production of crops, for example, we find a significantly positive correlation between rainfall and per capita output growth in

[8] Based on cross-sectional data on an urban agglomeration in Uttar Pradesh in 1995, Kingdon (1998), for example, found a 45 per cent gender earnings gap after controlling for human capital differences.

rice and wheat.[9] This suggests that rainfall is a good approximation of overall food supply. By affecting supply, rain also becomes a significant determinant of inflation in rural prices. Net consumers have to pay less for food, which should result in an increase in total food consumption. Therefore, growth in rainfall indicates good years with a relative abundance. A negative impact of rainfall on gender dimorphism would point to a general pattern, which we have already found for Orissa and Kerala, that care for girls is reduced disproportionately in the presence of food shortages and crises.

The standard deviation of rainfall refers to the yearly growth rates observed in a five-year period. We include this control variable as rainfall changes from year to year and the beneficial effects outlined above might be highly volatile.

Rice Output

We have used rice output data to construct a rice per capita index. We took the total quantity of yearly rice output in each state and divided it by the yearly rural population. We include this measure as a direct proxy for the availability of food as rice is not only the major staple crop in most of these states but was also the dominant food crop until the 1970s in several states. With the choice of rice we do not neglect the states of Gujarat and Maharashtra, since rice is still among the major food crops during the time period of our study.

As can be observed from the secular trends in dimorphism an up is often followed by a down in the series (significant during the whole period only for Gujarat, Kerala, and Maharashtra). We attribute this to age heaping problems still present in five-year age groups and mostly for individuals born before Indian Independence. Therefore, we include the lagged dependent variable to control for this pattern, which, however, becomes insignificant.

The regression results reveal very interesting insights (Table 13.2). State fixed effects are insignificant in regression (1). Therefore, we exclude them in regression, (2) followed by other insignificant variables in regression, and (3) to reduce problems of overspecification. The growth in the state net domestic product of the agricultural sector has no impact on dimorphism. The reason might be, that SDP is a very

---

[9] The Pearson correlation coefficient between rice and rain is 0.743 based on all states, and 0.630 for wheat and rain in Gujarat and Maharashtra.

Table 13.2: OLS-determinants of the development of
dimorphism in height, 1955–75

Model	(1)	(2)	(3)
Constant	−2.320 (−0.66)	0.416 (0.27)	−0.019 (−0.04)
Dimorphism $_{t-1}$	−0.096 (−0.26)	−0.116 (−0.42)	
Rural Population (in per cent)	0.594 (0.43)	−0.478 (−1.15)	−0.413 (−1.55)
Real SDP per capita of agricultural sector (in per cent)	0.027 (0.63)	0.003 (0.08)	
Rural Real Wage (in per cent)	−0.006 (−0.27)	−0.021 (−1.33)	−0.022* (−1.82)
Poverty Gap Index (in per cent)	0.044 (0.56)	0.089 (1.56)	0.095* (1.84)
State Development expenditures (in per cent)	−0.021 (−1.15)	−0.023 (−1.58)	−0.026** (−2.47)
Rice output/capita (in per cent)	0.030 (1.21)	0.042** (2.53)	0.046*** (4.06)
Rainfall during monsoon months (in per cent)	−0.087** (−2.56)	−0.084** (−2.65)	−0.091*** (−5.88)
STDEV(growth in yearly rainfall)	0.038** (3.08)	0.037*** (3.43)	0.038*** (5.36)
Time indicator	0.048 (0.30)	−0.036 (−0.30)	
State Fixed Effects (p–value)	0.744		
N	24	24	24
R^2–adj.	0.171	0.278	0.396

Notes: Kerala is not included in the regression due to unavailability of data. Except for the time indicator and the standard deviation in the growth of yearly rainfall all variables are expressed in averaged growth rates based on the period the birth cohort is born; t-values based on the Huber/White/Sandwich estimator of variance. In the case of fixed effects, the reference category represents Andhra Pradesh; */**/** denote significance at the 10 per cent/5 per cent/1 per cent confidence levels.
Sources: NNNB Surveys, database of Özler et al. (1996), and Sanghi et al. (1998)

general indicator of economic development, that neglects important aspects of well-being like nutrition and health, which should primarily influence dimorphism. In contrast, income growth measured by rural real wages and the poverty gap index has a significantly negative influence on gender dimorphism in stature, which confirms that discrimination against girls is increasing with poverty in a temporal and cross-sectional dimension.

In general, State development expenditures decrease gender discrimination measured by height. Unfortunately, we cannot identify which of the State services is responsible for the total beneficial effect. However, we would expect a negative influence especially from investment in education. Water supply could considerably reduce the workload of mothers of carrying water and in combination with sanitation might additionally reduce children's morbidity, independent of the gender. Special area programmes, investment in general infrastructure, and nutritional programmes targeting poor districts might also have a discrimination decreasing effect. In contrast, we would expect investment in health facilities to increase gender dimorphism because of a bias against girls in the utilization of health facilities, which, however, still offers both genders a better health status than no access at all. Moreover, as the example of Kerala demonstrates, policies could improve non-discriminatory access to health. In sum, the beneficial effect of State expenditures is an important result as it indicates that the State could actively reduce gender bias against girls, thus improving their nutritional and health status.

At first glance, the regression coefficient of rice output per capita suggests a discrimination increasing effect. However, for a proper interpretation the high collinearity between rain and rice output must be taken into account, which makes a ceteris paribus assumption extremely unreasonable. Rainfall during monsoon is an important input in the production of rice. The relationship is highly significant at the 1 per cent level, and 53 per cent of the variation in growth of rice output can be explained by the rainfall variable. In five-year periods, in which rainfall increased by one per cent, rice output per capita usually rises by 0.56 per cent. This means that the net effect on dimorphism is negative as a one per cent increase in rainfall first decreases dimorphism by 0.09 per cent while the predicted increase in rice output (0.56 x 0.046) does adjust the extent by reducing the figure to 0.07 per cent. It follows that dimorphism will only rise if rice output is disproportionately increased by other means. In India in the 1950s and 1960s, output of crops increased because of an expansion in the cultivated area (Kabra 1990). Labour input is a complementary production factor to land. Since women contribute an important share of the labour force in rice cultivation (Dyson and Moore 1983), an increasing workload could reasonably reduce the care for girls in the short term.

There are additional causal chains through which the adjustment could work. Rice is also sold for cash to urban centres, so that in times of good harvests, food consumption might be less than the figures for rain suggest. While the generated income should generally be considered as a possibility to spend more on the care of children, it is unclear, whether girls get their share from these windfall gains. Moreover, by increasing supply, rainfall also affects rural prices in a significantly negative way. Therefore, during times of relative food abundance, income grows with output less than linearly.

The positive effect of the standard deviation in the yearly rainfall should be interpreted in a similar manner. A large standard deviation means that rainfall as well as harvests, income, and food supply are highly volatile in the five-year period. Obviously, this volatility has more detrimental consequences for girls than for boys.

The fit of our model turns out to be astonishingly well with about 40 per cent of the variance in dimorphism explained by the independent variables. The findings also support our view that height dimorphism is a valid indicator of gender discrimination. All the determinants point to the fact that gender dimorphism in stature becomes smaller if the overall nutritional situation improves.

SUMMARY

In this study we have used a new measure 'Gender Dimorphism in Stature' and have argued that this can be used as an indicator for gender discrimination by comparing global data on stature and calorie availability. By using stature differences, we have explored inter-state differences and the trend of gender discrimination. Kerala, as expected, showed decreasing gender discrimination whereas Orissa showed an increasing trend from 1930–75. During the food crisis period in both Kerala and Orissa, an increase in gender dimorphism was observed, pointing to a rise in gender discrimination.

Our findings suggest that poverty makes a direct contribution to an increase in female discrimination and based on this we recommend that nutrition and health programmes should take special consideration of poor women. Another important finding was the relation of stature differences to various aspects of agriculture. Surprisingly, we see an increasing discrimination with an increase in rice output (at a given input of monsoon rain). We argue that this is due to higher participation of women in rice cultivation, which would provide them with less time for child care, especially for the female child. We have also found decreasing discrimination with a rise in rural wages, which might be due to a subsequent investment on the female child's food and health. Interestingly, monsoon rainfall plays a very important role in reducing discrimination by increasing output and decreasing food prices. At the same time, we find that fluctuations in rainfall (higher standard deviation in rain) favour boys and not girls.

The major recommendation that emerges from our argument is that increase in expenditure for development programmes decreases gender discrimination. However, we do not know the contribution of individual programmes such as health, transport, labour welfare, and nutrition in reducing discrimination. Nevertheless, the logic of the argument that we have developed here has an attribute that makes gender dimorphism in stature unique among various arguments on gender discrimination in India. Stature, being an outcome of nutrition and health, definitely serves as a complementary indicator for measuring gender discrimination compared to conventional ones. Finally, we recommend 'gender dimorphism in stature' for measuring gender discrimination in future research.

REFERENCES

Basu, AM. (1989) 'Is Discrimination in Food Really Necessary for Explaining Sex Differential in Childhood Mortality?', *Population Studies*, Vol. 43, No. 2, pp. 193–210.

Baten, J. (2000), 'Height and Real Wages: An International Comparison', *Jahrbuch fuer Wirtschaftsgeschichte*, Vol. 11, pp. 17–32.

Baten, J. and J. Murray (2000), 'Heights of Men and Women in 19th Century Bavaria: Economic, Nutritional, and Disease Influences', *Explorations in Economic History*, Vol. 37, pp. 351–69.

Borooah, V.K. (2004), 'Gender Bias among Children in India in their Diet and Immunisation against Disease', *Social Science and Medicine*, Vol. 58, pp. 1719–31.

Brauer, G.W. (1982), 'Size Sexual Dimorphism and Secular Trend: 'Indicators of Subclinical Malnutrition', in R.L. Hall, (ed.) *Sexual Dimorphism in Homo Sapiens: A Question of Size*, Prager, New York, pp. 245–59.

Brennan, L., J. McDonald, and R. Shlomocuitz (1997), 'Sex Differences in Indian Height at Home and Abroad', *Man in India*, Vol. 77, pp. 105–18.

——— (1994), 'The Heights and Economic Well-Being of North Indians under British Rule', *Social Science History*, Vol. 18, pp. 272–307.

Clutton-Brock, T.H. and P.H. Harvey (1984), 'Comparative Approaches to Investigating Adaptation', in J.R. Krebs and N.B. Davies, *Behavioral Ecology, An Evolutionary Approach*, pp. 7–29

DeRose, L.F., M. Das, and S.R. Millman (2000), 'Does Female Disadvantage Mean Lower Access to Food ?', *Population and Development Review*, Vol. 26, No. 3, pp. 517–47.

Dyson, T. and M. Moore (1983), 'On Kinship Structure, Female Autonomy, and Demographic Behavior in India', *Population and Development Review*, Vol. 9, No. 1, pp. 35–60.

Eveleth, P.B. and Tanner (1976), *Worldwide Variations in Human Growth*, University Press, Cambridge.

Fogel, R.W., S.L. Engerman, R. Flood, F. Friedman, R. Margo, K. Sakoloff, R. Steckel, J. Trussell, G. Villaflor, and K. Wachter (1983), 'Secular Changes in American and British Stature and Nutrition', *Journal of Interdisciplinary History*, Vol. 14, No. 2, pp. 445–81.

Frayer, D.W. and M.H. Wolpoff (1985), 'Sexual Dimorphism', *Annual Review of Anthropology*, Vol. 14, pp. 429–73.

Guntupalli, M.A. (2003), 'The Health Status of Indian Women: A Study Based on Height, BMI and Anemia', Working Paper presented at International Convention of Asia Scholars, Singapore, 19–22 August.

Gray, J.P. and L.D. Wolfe (1980), 'Height and Sexual Dimorphism of Stature among Societies', *American Journal of Physical Anthropology*, Vol. 53, pp. 441–56.

Hill, K. and D.M. Upchurch (1995), 'Gender Differences in Child Health: Evidence from the Demographic and Health Surveys', *Population and Development Review*, Vol. 21, No. 1, pp. 127–51.

International Institute for Population Sciences (IIPS) and ORC Macro (2000), *National Family Health Survey (NFHS-2), 1998–99*: IIPS, Mumbai.

Jürgens, H.W. (1990), *International Data of Anthropometry*, International Labour Office, Geneva.

Kabra, K.N. (1990), *Political Economy of Public Distribution of Food in India*, Ajanta Publications, New Delhi.

Kingdon, G.G. (1998), 'Does the Labour Market Explain Lower Female Schooling in India', *Journal of Development Studies*, Vol. 35, No. 1, pp. 39–65.

Komlos, J. (1985), 'Stature and Nutrition in the Habsburg Monarchy: The Standard of Living and Economic Development', *American Historical Review*, Vol. 90, pp. 1149–61.

Mayer, P. (1999), 'India's Falling Sex Ratios', *Population and Development Review*, Vol. 25, No. 2, pp. 323–43.

National Nutrition Monitoring Bureau (1999), 'Report of Second Repeat Survey, Rural', NNMB Technical Report series, No. 18, ICHR, National Institute of Nutrition, Hyderabad.

Özler, B., M. Ravallion, and G. Datta (1996), *A Database on Poverty and Growth in India*, Policy Research Department, World Bank: Washingtion, DC.

Rodgers, G. (1989), *Population Growth and Poverty in Rural South Asia*, Sage Publications, New Delhi.

Sanghi, A., K.S.K. Kumar, and Jr. J.W. Mckinsey (1998), *India Agriculture and Climate Data Set*, World Bank, *http://www-esd.worldbank.org/indian/database.html*

Strauss, J. and T. Duncan (1998), 'Health, Nutrition, and Economic Development', *Journal of Economic Literature*, Vol. 36, pp. 766–817.

Steckel, R.H. (1995), 'Stature and the Standard of Living', *Journal of Economic Literature*, Vol. 33, No. 4, pp. 1903–40.

Stini, W.A. (1985), 'Growth Rates and Sexual Dimorphism in Evolutionary Perspectives', in R.I. Gilbert and J.H. Mielke (eds.), *The Analysis of Prehistoric Diets*, Academic Press, Orlando, pp. 191–226.

Venkaiah, K., K. Damayanti, M.U. Nayak, and K. Vijayaghavan (2002), 'Diet and Nutritional Status of Rural Adolescents in India', *European Journal of Clinical Nutrition*, Vol. 56, pp. 1119–25.

WHO Working Group (1986), 'Use and Interpretation of Anthropometric Indicators of Nutritional Status', *Bulletin of the World Health Organization*, Vol. 64, No. 6, pp. 929–41.

World Bank (1981), *World Development Report*, World Bank, Washington D.C.

A New Measure of Gender Bias[†]

DIGANTA MUKHERJEE[*] ——————— 14

Introduction

It has been well documented in the economics and sociological literature that parents exhibit preference for sons across geographical, economic, and social boundaries. Adult sons are expected to provide economic support and hence having more sons is always desirable (Das 1987; Lahiri 1984; Miller 1981; ORG 1983). On the other hand, daughters are supposed to create an economic burden for the parents in terms of dowry etc. As a consequence, parents desire a high proportion of sons. This chapter attempts to quantify this feeling of bias of the parents as revealed by a few simple characteristics of the offspring. In this paper, we look at the parents' decision problem at the procreation stage rather than at the stage of household budget allocation where the daughters are discriminated against in terms of expenditure on health and education. A large literature has developed that deals with this latter issue. See Rose (1999), Dutta and Panda (2000), Chakrabarty (2000), Schultz (2001) and the references cited therein for some recent investigations along this line.

While this preference is generic, as it is not possible for the parents to pre-determine the sex of their unborn children, realizing an ideal

[†] An older version of the chapter, under a slightly different name, was accepted for presentation at the 13th World Congress of the International Economic Association, held in Lisbon, September 2002.

[*] I am grateful to Peter J. Lambert of University of York, Kunal Sengupta of CESP, Jawaharlal Nehru University, Rajlakshmi Mallik of Loreto College, Amita Majumder and Debrup Chakraborty of Indian Statistical Institute, Stephen Jenkins and Elena Bardasi of University of Essex, and Dave Mare of Motu Research Trust, New Zealand for their invaluable help. I would also like to thank the seminar participants at the Department of Economics, Jadavpur University and Economic Research Unit, Indian Statistical Institute, Kolkata and Arunachal University, Itanagar for their active participation and insightful comments. The usual disclaimer applies.

outcome is not possible directly. But there are indirect methods by which the parents can improve the proportion of sons among their children. The most common ones that have been documented in the literature are the following.

Better health care for sons affects the sex composition of the surviving children (Bardhan 1974, 1982). Surprisingly, this does not effect the sex ratio at the national level. The sex ratio at birth (boy per girl, surviving children) varies between 1.02 and 1.14 across regions and over a long time period for India. This is also true for most western countries (Waldron 1983, 1987). Recent research on genetics shows that, at the family level, there is no bias towards either sex (Rodgers and Doughty 2001). Thus, for demographic purposes, the sex of any given child may be considered a random event with the probability of having a boy being 0.513 (sex ratio = 1.05). In this paper, for simplicity, we take this probability to be ½. This does not bias our measure significantly.

The second and more drastic method of doing this is the use of sex selective abortion (Park and Cho 1995; Yi, Liao, and Cho 1997). This involves the use of simple chemical tests to determine the sex of an unborn child. Sex selective abortion has not yet become such a significant factor in determining the sex ratio in India (Arnold 1997; Dasgupta and Bhat 1995; Nair 1996). Although the data on stillbirths is very difficult to get for Indian families (usual surveys record only surviving children), we may safely assume that this will not affect our analysis in any significant manner.

The third and, in a way, the most benevolent method for achieving a higher proportion of sons is to practise DSB. This means that the parents stop having children when they think that they have enough (in absolute or relative terms) sons. Amin and Mariam (1987), Arnold (1997), Arnold and Zhaoxiang (1986), De Silva (1993), Rahman et al. (1992), Sarma and Jain (1974) provide evidence of such behaviour.

As a consequence of the above, we have the following broad observations that are supported by data: (i) families with a large number of children will have a large proportion of daughters (Park and Cho 1995) and (ii) for a given family size, socio-economic characteristics of couples who want a higher proportion of sons will be the same as those who have a higher proportion.

In this paper, we focus on modelling the third method of achieving a better proportion of sons by the parents, namely DSB. Our aim here is to measure the extent of DSB that the parents practice at the family level. This is arguably a difficult task. The exact stopping rule followed by a couple depends on both magnitude (desired proportion) and intensity (how determined they are to have their desired number of sons) of their feeling of bias. There have been very few earlier attempts at developing a theory towards the measurement of son preference (Ben-Porath and Welch 1976; Davies and Zhang 1997).

There have been some empirical attempts at this measurement problem. Coombs (1979), Coombs, Coombs, and McClelland (1975), Coombs and Sun (1978), Kwon and Lee (1976), Widmer, McClelland, and Nickerson (1981) are a few of the recent papers in this area. Recently, Clark (2000) attempted a very extensive analysis using survey data for India asking each couple about their actual and ideal proportion or number of sons. She shows that ideal figures are related to the age of mother, education, caste, residence (rural/urban), religion, and geographic region. Her analysis relies on sex ratios (proportions) of the stated preferences and actual figures.

This paper hypothesizes a simple measure of (male) gender bias based on an idea akin to DSB. This measure uses data on only the actual distribution of children (and not stated ideal numbers, which is suspect in any context). In particular, it uses the actual (age, sex) composition of children in a family. In the second section we formulate the procreation decision by parents as a dynamic utility maximization problem and hence show that changes in the sex ratio are more important in gauging the extent of bias of the parents than the actual proportions. That is, a couple's decision to procreate further is affected more by a favourable or adverse change in the sex ratio than the actual value of the ratio. We discuss this in greater detail in Remark 14.1.

In this context, it is important to know whether the observed (revealed) bias is actually a good proxy for the inherent (subjective) bias of the parents. This will be ensured if the parents have control over their number of children. For a country like India, FP facilities are widely and cheaply available in the form of contraceptives etc. Also, in recent years, awareness in this context has improved considerably through the ministrations of health workers. Thus, at least for our empirical exercise (see below), we can be reasonably certain of being able to observe data that closely resembles the inherent bias in the population.

We go on to suggest a simple measure that captures these changes. The simplification we have achieved for our measure relies on certain assumptions. But the justification for these assumptions lies in the fact that otherwise the problem would be too complex to capture using a simple functional form. Very few empirical studies exist, focussing on the distribution of children, due to the lack of such simplified measures. We believe that there exists a strong need for economic insights and inferences in this area. Here, we have purpose-built a measure that facilitate this. Another implicit justification would be if our measure throws up plausible inferences.

In the third section, we have worked out the shape of the theoretical distribution of our bias measure and carried out an illustrative empirical exercise estimating family level gender bias using NSSO 50th round data from Tamil Nadu, a state of India. The last section offers some concluding remarks.

MOTIVATION AND METHODOLOGY

We first sketch our model of male bias for parents. In the ensuing discussion, we will always assume that any future child is a male with probability ½. To develop notation, we consider our data or primitive to be the vector of children in a family with k children: $(c_1, c_2 \ldots c_k)$, where $c_i = 1$ (0) if child is male (female). The vector is ordered according to age. That is, the sex of the eldest child is recorded in c_1 and so on.

We assume that the parents face a dynamic problem of optimal stopping time in terms of utility maximization. Let $p_k = \sum_{i=1}^{k} c_i / k$ be the proportion of male children in the family when the family has k children. Let the utility of the parents be a function of the number of children, n, along with the proportion of male, p_n. Thus, the parents' utility function is given by $u = u(n, p_n)$.

After the kth procreation, the utility of the parents is given by $u(k, p_k)$. If they attempt again, the expected utility will be given by

$$Eu_{k+1} = \frac{1}{2}u(k+1, \frac{k}{k+1}p_k + \frac{1}{k+1}) + \frac{1}{2}u(k+1, \frac{k}{k+1}p_k) , \qquad (14.1)$$

where the first (second) term in the expected utility expression in (14.1) depicts the possibility where a male (female) child is born in the $(k+1)^{st}$ attempt. So the parents will try again, after the kth procreation, if $Eu_{k+1} > u(k, p_k)$. We take the following assumption regarding the shape of the utility function:

A 14.1: $\Delta u / \Delta k < 0$ for $k \geq k_0$, that is, utility is decreasing in k, the number of children, after some critical number k_0.

In other words, the parents may, at first, like having more children, when they have only a few. However, after some stage, additional children are undesirable per se, the only motivation for further procreation is having additional sons. This assumption is very reasonable in terms of affordability (in terms of both resource and time) and the urge for continuation of lineage. The critical number, k_0, may depend on many socio-economic factors like biological supply children (fecundity), social location, income, size of the family, etc.

A 14.2: (a) For parents who are male biased, $u(k, p_k) > u(k, p'_k)$ for a given k and $p_k > p'_k$.

(b) For parents who are female biased, the reverse inequality holds.

The above assumptions imply the following.

Remark 14.1: A one-time increase in p_k would discourage parents with high male bias to try again (if they are beyond k_0).

Proof: The requirement of $k > k_0$ is due to the fact that for $k \leq k_0$, simply adding to the number of children is utility augmenting. In this situation, expected utility may be unambiguously increasing and hence, in that range, our proposition may not hold.

By high male bias we imply that the rate of increase of $u(k, p_k)$ with respect to p_k is large and positive. Now, given p_k, the gain potential from another procreation, through improvement of p_k (if a male is born), is

$$(1 - p_k)/(k+1)(= p_k \frac{k}{k+1} + \frac{1}{k+1} - p_k)$$ and the loss potential (when there

is a female birth) is $(p_k)/(k+1)(= p_k - \frac{k}{k+1} p_k)$. That is, overall benefit potential decreases if there is a favourable change in p_k. Given that expected utility is now decreasing in k, for a couple with high male bias after experiencing an increase in p_k, it becomes more likely that they will value the status quo $u(k, p_k)$ more than the expected utility, Eu_{k+1}, given by equation (14.1).

Remark 14.2: The stopping time or the maximum number of attempts by the parents will be finite.

Proof: As $k \to \infty, \dfrac{1}{k+1} \to 0,$, so $Eu_{k+1} \approx u(k+1, p_k) < u(k, p_k)$ for $k \geq k_0$.

We now postulate a reasonable quantification of male bias. In general, the measure of bias is:

$B = B(c_1, c_2 \ldots c_k$). We now take recourse to the following simplifications.

We can reasonably assume that the measure B will depend on the total number of children and the stopping state or the sex of the last child (c_k). Also the total number of children, k, helps to get the measure in a ratio form (dimension free number). c_k captures the stopping state which is important in the sense that it reflects what you want at the end (may be waiting for this to happen).

Remark 14.1 shows that a male (female) biased couple would be encouraged to continue procreation if there is a favourable change in the direction of movement of the quantity p_k. That is, an increase (decrease) after a sequence of decreases (increases). Again, this is equivalent to the occurrence of a male or 1 (female or 0) after a series of 0s (1s). These occurrences can be tracked if we count the occurrence of the pairs (0, 1) or (1, 0) in the vector $(c_1, c_2 \ldots c_k$). For this, we use the notation k_{01} = number of (0,1) pairs and k_{10} = number of (1,0) pairs in $(c_1, \ldots, c_k)$. Thus, we postulate the following.

k_{10} (k_{01}) captures attitude to risk exposure revealed through another attempt of procreation even after a detoriation (improvement) in the ratio. Once achieving (0, 1), if one attempts again, we assume that it indicates less male bias. Similarly, we take it that after the occurrence of the pair (1, 0), similar behaviour implies more male bias.

These behavioural assumptions, in turn, implicitly suggest that the underlying utility function might exhibit convexity in the p_k term. This is at variance with the usual concavity assumption on utility functions but given the nature of the variable, this is not implausible.

Note that we are ignoring the effect of infant mortality on our utility maximization problem. An additional child may be demanded to replace a dead child. Given that female births are systematically underreported in many developing countries like India (Rose, 1999 and many others) and female infanticide is not rare; the implication of this simplification for our measure is that, in expected terms, we are underestimating the value of k_{10} and hence gender bias. A solution to this problem increases our data requirement. For our present discussion, we are ignoring this component.

We now state our next assumption. We assume that our measure of bias depends on only the factors that we have discussed so far. That is, we simplify the measure to the following form.[1]

A 14.3: $B = B(k, c_k, k_{10}, k_{01})$.
Now, as we have said that the presence of the number of children, k, as an argument of the bias function is solely to make it a dimension free pure number. Hence, given that the maximum value of k_{01} and k_{10} can be $[k/2]$, we simplify the measure of bias to the following.

A 14.4: $B = B\left(c_k, \dfrac{k_{01}}{[k/2]}, \dfrac{k_{10}}{[k/2]} \right)$, where B is decreasing (increasing) in

the second (third) argument.

We now go for a further simplification to two directional components, one in terms of {0,1} switches (female direction) and one with {1,0} (male direction). This will help us in our empirical exercise later. We assume that the marginal effect of k_{01} on the measure of bias B is independent of the value of k_{10} and vice versa. More precisely, we are assuming

A 14.5: $\dfrac{\Delta^2 B(.)}{\Delta k_{10} \Delta k_{01}} = 0$

This is analogous to the assumption that $\dfrac{\partial^2 B(.)}{\partial k_{10} \partial k_{01}} = 0$ in the continuum

situation. This kind of assumption imposes a separability restriction on the measure under consideration.

Some algebra demonstrates that the implication of (A 14.5) is that the measure B becomes additively separable in these two components. That is, we have

$$B = B_M\left(c_k, \dfrac{k_{10}}{[k/2]} \right) + B_F\left(c_k, \dfrac{k_{01}}{[k/2]} \right)$$

The impact of c_k is assumed to be in assigning relative weight to the factors $\dfrac{k_{10}}{[k/2]}$ and $\dfrac{k_{01}}{[k/2]}$. As c_k can only take two possible values (0 or 1) we can, without loss of generality, assume that:

[1] Ideally, one should also take account of k_0 here. But, as we do not have an estimate for it, for the time being this lacuna is ignored.

$$B_M\left(c_k, \frac{k_{10}}{[k/2]}\right) = G_M\left(\frac{k_{10}}{[k/2]}\right) w_M(c_k) \text{ and}$$

$$B_F\left(c_k, \frac{k_{01}}{[k/2]}\right) = G_F\left(\frac{k_{01}}{[k/2]}\right) w(c_k)$$

where $w_M(c_k) + w_F(c_k) = 1$ (as these are meaningful in the relative sense). From the above discussion, obviously, $G_M(G_F)$ is increasing (decreasing) in k_{10} (k_{01}) as k_{10} (k_{01}) is directly (inversely) related to male bias.

More simply, we can now finally rewrite our measure of bias B as

$$B = G_M\left(\frac{k_{10}}{[k/2]}\right) w(c_k) + G_F\left(\frac{k_{01}}{[k/2]}\right)(1 w_F(c_k)) \qquad (14.2)$$

$w(c_k)$ is the importance attached to B_M with $w(1) + w(0) = 1$, $w(1) \geq w(0)$. G_M captures the male direction. So, if last child is a male, this gets higher weight.

Note: This measure works for $k \geq 2$ only (not defined for k=0 and 1). This is not a serious shortcoming as with realized k=0 or 1, a manifestation of bias is not possible.

Finally, to illustrate our concept through a simple functional form, we postulate:

A 14.6: $B_F = \left\{1 - \frac{k_{01}}{[k/2]}\right\}[1 - w(c_k)]$ and $B_M = \frac{k_{10}}{[k/2]} w(c_k)$

This is a simple special case of the general form (14.2). For the empirical part of our paper, in the next section, we will consider this special case only. This is one simple measure that illustrates our idea. As k_{01} is inversely related to male bias, so we take $1 - k_{01}/[k/2]$ as an indicator of male bias. Similarly, k_{10} is directly related to male bias, so male bias is assumed to be linearly increasing in k_{10}. In our empirical illustration, we have tried $w(1) = 0.9$ (BIAS90) and 0.70 (BIAS70). As B is assumed to be linear in G_M and G_F, considering any two distinct values of $w(c_k)$ is sufficient. Using the value of B for these two choices, one can generate a complete family of distributions of B for all permissible values of $w(c_k)$.

One may note the difference of the measure suggested in (14.2) with conventional measures like the sex ratio. Our measure does not look at the ratio $\Sigma c_i/k$ or the simple proportion of males in the distribution of children, because this ratio has probabilistic components to it. Given our assumption of equal probability of a male or female child, $\sum c_i$ is binomially distributed, given k. Also, the intention of the parents is better captured by looking at the sequence of offspring rather than the final proportion. So we look at shifts in the ratio and corresponding stopping rules.

The number of shifts from male to female (1 to 0) that is allowed by the parents indicates their intensity of bias towards a male child or intensity of desire for more boys. Conversely, if the parents allow for more children even after favourable shifts from female to male (0 to 1), a lack of such bias is exhibited.

Example 14.1: Consider the vector of offspring (0, 0, 0, 0, 0, 0, 0, 1). This reveals a couple who has a high degree of bias and waited till the 8th child to get a son. For this, the computed value of bias, using our measure given by equation (14.2), under the assumption (A 14.6), is 0.225 [with $w(1)=0.70$]. This value turns out to be higher than the conventional measure (say, sex ratio = 0.125) which would suggest a lower male bias.

Note that $(1,1)$ (or $(0,0)$) also imply improvement (or deterioration) in ratio, but we want to focus on shifts, so we only look at $(1,0)$ or $(0,1)$ pair. One might look at longer strings and study changes of a higher order, but that will complicate the intuition and also lower the number of admissible data points (if we look at strings of length 3, we can only look at data for which $k \geq 3$, etc.).

Finally, we discuss another class of examples about which our measure cannot say anything. These are the sequences (0, 0, ..., 0, 0) and (1, 1, ..., 1, 1), which, according to subjective judgement, show a large degree of bias. However, for these two sequences, as both k_{01} and k_{10} are equal to 0; the value of the measure will be $w(0)$ or $w(1)$. This causes some indeterminacy in the pattern of bias which we will discuss later. However, it is to be noted that in our set-up the generic probability of any future child being male is equal to ½. With this assumption, both the strings are equally likely (for any given size). Hence the values $w(0)$ or $w(1)$ will also occur with equal probability and, in expected terms, the resulting distribution will remain unbiased.

Distributional Considerations

Theoretical Distribution

To facilitate empirical application, one needs to look at the shape of the theoretical distribution that our proposed measure of gender bias should have, when the underlying population exhibits no bias in either direction. That is, when the sequence of offspring, for any family size, is completely random. To generate such a distribution, we assume that for the population under consideration the number of children in a family, n, follows a Poisson distribution with parameter 2.5 (this is approximately the average number of children per mother for the selected households in our sample). The Poisson process assumption is an intuitively reasonable one and is commonly used to model birth processes. Thus, for each possible value n of the Poisson random variable ($n = 0, 1, 2...$) we consider all possible vectors of children $\underline{c}$ of length n. Each offspring is assumed to be a male with probability ½ (as already mentioned in the first section). For each n, there are 2^n possibilities. The bias measure is computed for each of these possibilities and hence the theoretical distribution of the measure for each n is constructed by giving equal weightage to each possibility (given n, all possibilities are equally likely). A sample of our method of calculation is presented here.

Example 14.2: Consider a family with the ordered sequence of offspring given by (boy, girl, girl, boy, boy). This translates into the vector of offspring $\underline{c} = (1, 0, 0, 1, 1)$ and $k = 5$. For this, one can compute $k_{10} = 1$, $k_{01} = 1$ and $c_k = 1$. Hence, the measure of bias for this family, as given by (14.2), is BIAS70 = 0.5 and BIAS90 = 0.5. Again consider another vector $\underline{c} = (0, 1, 0, 1, 0, 0)$. One can similarly calculate $k = 6$, $k_{10} = 2$, $k_{01} = 2$, and $c_k = 0$. Hence BIAS70 = 0.433333 and BIAS90 = 0.36667.

To get the overall theoretical distribution, we then combine each of these distributions (one for each value of n) with weight equal to the probability of realization of that particular value of n, given by the Poisson model [for example, $P(n = 3) = e^{-2.5} \dfrac{2.5^3}{3!}$ etc.].

See Figure 14.1 for the theoretical distribution of our gender bias measure for the 'no' bias case for $w(1) = 0.70$ (BIAS70) and $w(1) = 0.90$ (BIAS90). The x-axis in both the diagrams depicts the range of

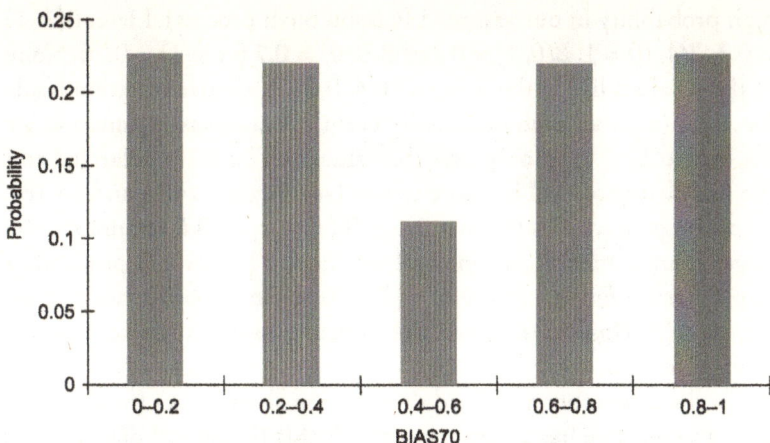

Figure 14.1a: Theoretical distribution of BIAS70

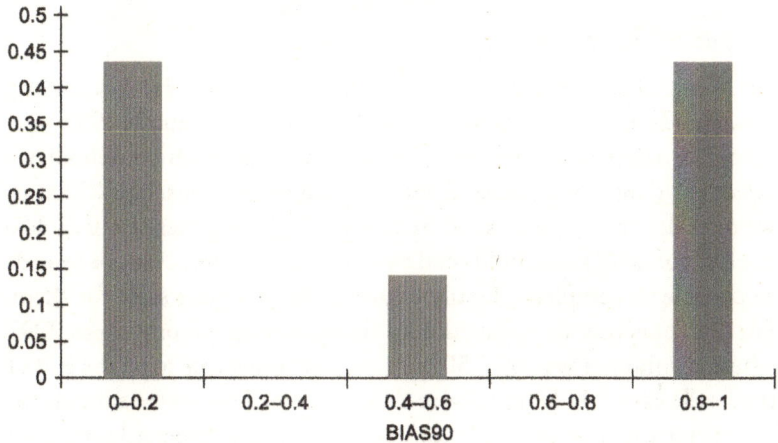

Source: Author's calculations.

Figure 14.1b: Theoretical distribution of BIAS90

values of the bias measure (BIAS70 and BIAS90, respectively) divided into five equal intervals 0 to 0.2, 0.2 to 0.4 etc. The y-axis shows the probability of the bias measure taking a value in each interval. The distribution is symmetric around 0.5 in general and U-shaped. The peaks are more pronounced for higher values of $w(1)$.

The U-shape of the theoretical distribution is actually a consequence of the choice of values for $w(1)$ and the intervals of values that we have chosen for the figure. Consider all possible cases for $n = 2$ (which has a high probability in our assumed Poisson birth process). Here, $B(1, 1)$ = 0.3, $B(1, 0)$ = 1, $B(0, 1)$ = 0 and $B(0, 0)$ = 0.7 for $w(1)$ = 0.70. None of these values lies in the interval $[0.4, 0.6]$. A similar situation holds for $n = 3$ (another high probability event). Analogous explanation for the case $w(1)$ = 0.90, only now the values will be more polarized and the middle region will be more sparse (see Figures 14.1a and 14.1b). The strings $(c_1,..., c_n)$ such that $0.4 \leq B(c_1,..., c_n) \leq 0.6$ require n to be larger than 3. Hence, this interval will have a low overall probability of occurrence for any choice of $w(1) > 0.6$. On the other hand, if we choose $w(1)$ close to 0.5, then the measure becomes less sensitive to changes in $(c_1,..., c_n)$.

To check whether a realized distribution shows more (or less) bias than average, one has to compare it with this theoretical distribution. For this, standard non-parametric tests like the goodness-of-fit or the Kolmogorov–Smirnov test may be used.

Empirical Illustration

We now illustrate the pattern of male bias distribution among households in rural Tamil Nadu, using NSSO 50th round (1993–94) data. The sample included 3901 households. From each household, we select the family originating from the head of the household. That is, we consider the children sired by the head. Among these households, the head of 2092 households had two or more children. Also, one needs to consider a completed family to get to the stopping state for them. For this purpose, we selected only those families among these 2092 where the mother was aged 50 or more (assuming this to be the end of the fertile age). 241 families were thus selected. These were suitable for our exercise and constituted our final sample. As mentioned earlier, we ignored the effect of lack of information on dead children.

For each of the families, the ordered sequence $\underline{c}$ is constructed by looking at the age and sex of each child. Then, this vector is used for computing the value of the bias measures. The Histograms for the distribution of BIAS70 and BIAS90 are shown in Figures 14.2a and 14.2b. The x-axis is same as in Figures 14.1a and 14.1b. The y-axis now shows the observed proportional frequency in each interval of values, computed from our data. From these, one can see that both the distributions have approximately the U-shape as predicted by the discussion above. But, in both diagrams, the left peak is shifted to the right indicating a slightly higher bias than expected. On the other

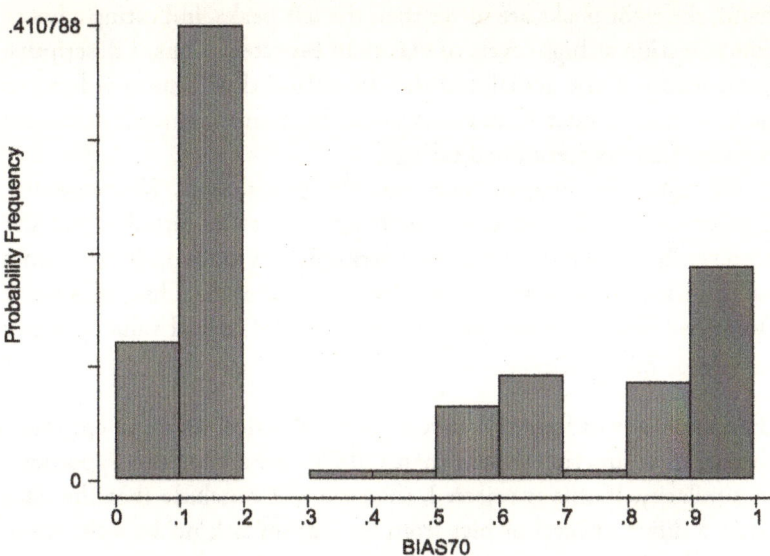

Figure 14.2a: Histogram showing the proportional frequency distribution of BIAS70

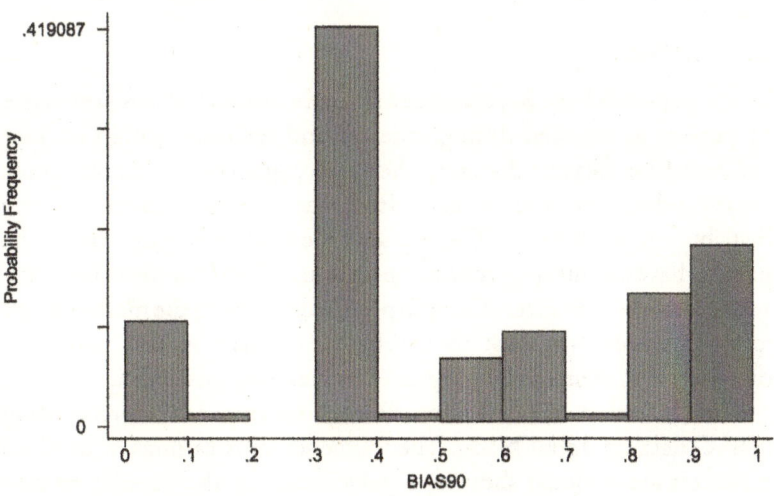

Source: Author's calculations.

Figure 14.2b: Histogram showing the proportional frequency distribution of BIAS90

hand, the right peaks are lower than the left peaks, indicating a lower concentration at high levels of bias than expected. Thus, a descriptive comparison of the actual and the theoretical distribution is hard to make in this context. One needs to employ non-parametric statistical tests for that (as mentioned earlier).

For example, suppose one uses the one-sample, Kolmogorov–Smirnov test in this context. The hypothesis to be tested is that the empirically observed frequency distribution is statistically the same as the theoretical distribution already computed. This calls for a two-sided Kolmogorov–Smirnov test and the critical value at 5 per cent level of significance is $\frac{1.36}{\sqrt{n}}$ = 0.0876 here (n = 241). So, if the maximum difference between the theoretical and the empirical distribution function is less than 0.0876, we accept the hypothesis of similarity. If this is rejected, then we will conclude that the data show a different level of bias from the benchmark 'no' bias situation. One-sided alternatives like 'more' or 'less' biased can be similarly tested against, using appropriate critical value ($\frac{1.22}{\sqrt{n}}$). For the illustration at hand, the hypothesis of similarity is rejected using either BIAS70 or BIAS90. In fact, the alternative of 'more biased' is supported.

CONCLUSION

In this paper we have hypothesized a simple measure of son preference by parents as revealed through the age and sex composition of their children. Our measure does not take into account the stated preferences or any other information apart from the realized situation of the distribution of children. The measure looks at how many times the parents have attempted procreation after an increase or decrease in the sex ratio of their children. Our purpose in developing the methodology is to emphasize the lack of theoretical research in this particular direction that seems to be pregnant with exciting possibilities.

We illustrated our definition through an empirical exercise using NSSO data on Tamil Nadu. The frequency distributions of our bias measures are bimodal showing a polarization of the population into low and high bias segments with a sparse middle region as predicted by the theoretical discussion. But, the actual and theoretical distributions also show certain differences which have to be tested statistically for significance to conclude whether the realized distribution is more (or less) biased than average. Our illustration shows a higher level of bias in terms of such a test.

REFERENCES

Amin, R. and A.G. Mariam (1987), 'Son Preference in Bangladesh: an Emerging Barrier to Fertility Regulation', *Journal of Bio-Social Science*, Vol. 19, pp. 221–28.

Arnold, F. (1997), 'Gender Preferences for Children'. Demographic and Health Surveys', *Comparative Studies*, Vol. 23.

Arnold, F. and L. Zhaoxiang (1986), 'Sex Preference, Fertility, and Family Planning in China', *Population and Development Review*, Vol. 12, No. 2, pp. 221–46.

Bardhan, P. (1974), 'On Life and Death Questions', *Economic and Political Weekly*, Vol. 9, Special Number, pp. 1293–1304.

———(1982), 'Little Girls and Death in India', *Economic and Political Weekly*, Vol 17, No. 36, pp. 1448–50.

Ben-Porath, Y. and F. Welch (1976), 'Do Sex Preferences Really Matter?', *Quarterly Journal of Economics*, Vol. 90, No. 2, pp. 285–307.

Chakrabarty, M. (2000), 'Gender Bias in Children in Rural Maharashtra—An Equivalence Scale Approach', *Journal of Quantitative Economics*, Vol. 16, No. 1, pp. 51–65.

Clark, S. (2000), 'Son Preference and Sex Composition of Children: Evidence from India', *Demography*, Vol. 37, No. 1, pp. 95–108.

Coombs, L. (1979), 'Prospective Fertility and Underlying Performances: A Longitudinal Study in Taiwan', *Population Studies*, Vol. 33, pp. 447–55.

Coombs, L, and T.H. Sun (1978), 'Family Composition Preference in a Developing Culture: The Case of Taiwan, 1973', *Population Studies*, Vol. 32, No. 1, pp. 43–64.

Coombs, C., L. Coombs, and G. McClelland (1975), 'Preference Scales for Number and Sex of Children', *Population Studies*, Vol. 29, No. 2, pp. 273–98.

Das, N. (1987), 'Sex Preference and Fertility Behaviour: A Study of Recent Indian Data', *Demography*, Vol. 24, pp. 517–30.

Dasgupta, M. and P.N.M. Bhat (1995), 'Intensified Gender Bias in India: A Consequence of Fertility Decline', Centre for Population and Development Studies, Harvard University, Working Paper No. 95-03.

Davies, J.B. and J. Zhang (1997), 'Effects of Gender Control on Fertility and Children's Consumption', *Journal of Population Economics*, Vol. 10, pp. 67–85.

De Silva, W.I. (1993), 'Influence of Son Preference on the Contraceptive Use and Fertility of Sri Lankan Women', *Journal of Bio-Social Science*, Vol. 25, pp. 319–31.

Dutta, B. and M. Panda (2000), 'Gender Bias in India', *Journal of Quantitative Economics*, Vol. 16, No. 1, pp. 81–103.

Kwon, T.H. and H.Y. Lee (1976), 'Preferences for Number and Sex of Children in a Korean Town', *Bulletin of the Population and Development Studies Centre* (Seoul), Vol. V, pp. 1–11.

Lahiri, B. (1984), 'Demand for Sons Among Indian Couples by Rural-Urban Settlement Size', *Demography India*, Vol. 13, Nos 1 and 2, pp. 120–32.

Miller, B. (1981), *The Endangered Sex: Neglect of Female Children in Rural North India*, Cornell University Press, Ithaca, N.Y.

Nair, P.M. (1996), 'Imbalance of Sex Ratio of Children in India', *Demography India*, Vol. 25, No. 2, pp. 177–87.

(Operations Research Group) ORG (1983), *Family Planning Practices in India: Second all India Survey*, Operations Research Group, Baroda.

Park, C.B. and N.H. Cho (1995), 'Consequences of Son Preference in a Low-Fertility Society: Imbalance of the Sex Ratio at Birth in Korea', *Population and Development Review*, Vol. 21, No. 1, pp. 59-84.

Rahman, M.J., J. Akbar, F. Phillips, and S. Becker (1992), 'Contraceptive Use in Matlab, Bangladesh: The Role of Gender Preference', *Studies in Family Planning*, Vol. 23, No. 4, pp. 229–42.

Rodgers, J.L. and D. Doughty (2001), 'Does Having Boys (or Girls) Run in the Family?', Paper presented at the Annual Meeting of the Population Association of America, *Chance*, Vol. 14, No. 4, pp. 8–13.

Rose, E. (1999), 'Consumption Smoothing and Excess Female Mortality in Rural India', *Review of Economics and Statistics*, Vol. 81, No. 1, pp. 41–9.

Sarma, D.V.N. and A.K. Jain (1974), 'Preference for Sex of Children and Use of Contraception among Women Wanting No more Children in India', *Demography India*, Vol. 3, No. 1, pp. 81–104.

Schultz, T.P. (2001), 'Women's Roles in the Agricultural Household: Bargaining and Human Capital Investments', in B.L. Gardner and G.C. Rausser (eds), *Handbook of Agricultural Economics 1A*, Elsevier, Netherlands.

Waldron, I. (1983), 'Sex Differences in Human Mortality: The Role of Genetic Factors', *Social Science and Medicine*, Vol. 17, No. 6, pp. 321-33.

——— (1987), 'Patterns and Causes of Excess Female Mortality among Children in Developing Countries', *World Health Statistical Quarterly*, Vol. 40, pp. 194–210.

Widmer, K., G. McClelland, and C. Nickerson (1981), 'Determining the Impact of Sex Preference of Fertility: A Demonstration Study', *Demography*, Vol. 18, No. 1, pp. 27–37.

Yi,Y., T.F. Liao, and N.H. Cho (1997), 'Male-Child Preferences and Sex-Selective Abortions in Korea', Paper presented at the Annual Meeting of the Population Association of America.

Gender Bias in Mortality?
'An Update on Missing Women'[†]

STEPHAN KLASEN
and CLAUDIA WINK[*] ———————— 15

INTRODUCTION

Nearly 20 years ago, Amartya Sen estimated that some 100 million women are 'missing' as a result of excess female mortality in parts of the developing world, most notably South Asia, China, West Asia, and parts of North Africa (Sen 1989, 1990b). Coale (1991) and Klasen (1994) used more precise demographic techniques and arrived at figures that varied between 60 million (Coale) and 90 million (Klasen). All three estimates confirmed the enormous toll excess female mortality was exacting on women in these parts of the world.[1]

All these estimates of 'missing women' were based on demographic information of the 1980s and early 1990s. Since then, there has been considerable speculation about current trends of gender bias in mortality with some observers suggesting a falling intensity while others predicting the opposite (for example, Klasen 1994; Das Gupta and Mari Baht 1997; Drèze and Sen 1995; Mayer 1999; Croll 2000). Figure 15.1 shows recent projections by the United Nations

[†] We would like to thank Amartya Sen for having inspired us to work on this issue over the past several years and thank three anonymous referees and participants at a workshop at the University of Munich for helpful comments and suggestions. We also want to thank Katarina Smutna and Andreas Beivers for excellent research assistance.

[*] This paper is a slightly revised and abridged version of a paper that appeared in 2002 in the *Population Development Review*, Vol. 28, pp. 285–312, (reprinted with permission).

[1] For a more thorough discussion of Sen's contribution to this field of research and the ensuing debate about estimating the number of missing females, see Klasen and Wink (2003).

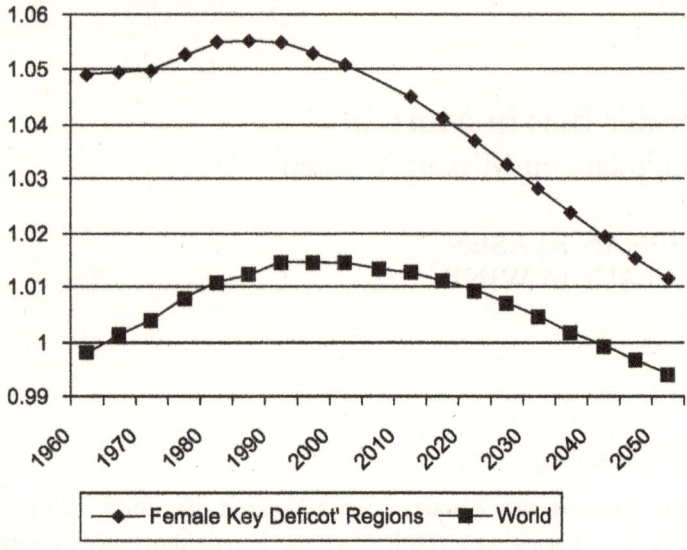

Note: Female deficit regions include East Asia, West Asia, Southern Asia, and North Africa.
Source: United Nations (1999).

Figure 15.1: Sex ratio (global and in female deficit regions)

Population Division of the sex ratio (number of males divided by number of females) in the world and in the regions where males outnumber females. These estimates suggest that the sex ratio in the female-deficit regions, after rising steadily since 1960, is estimated to have peaked around 1985 and then believed to have decline a quite sharply. Given the high share these regions have in the world's total population, a turning point in the global sex ratio, after a similar rise since 1960, is estimated for 1995.[2]

---

[2] Using a decomposition based on three groups (Europe, female-deficit regions, and remaining countries), one can show that some 30 per cent of the global rise between 1960 and 1995 is due to increases in the sex ratio in Europe, about 15 per cent due to the increase in the sex ratio in female-deficit countries and the remaining 55 per cent are due to the increase in the share of female-deficit countries, among the world's population and the converse decline of European populations, where females outnumber males. The increase in the sex ratio in Europe is largely related to the falling demographic importance of the male cohorts that were heavily decimated during World War II.

Around 2000, nearly all countries with considerable excessive female mortality have conducted new censuses which allows us to see whether there has indeed been a worsening or an improvement. By examining the latest Census returns and updating the number of 'missing women', we show that the number of missing women has continued to rise in absolute terms to some 65–107 million, depending on the assumptions used. In relative terms (as a share of women alive), it has, however, improved in most countries, regardless of the assumptions used. After significant improvements in Bangladesh and Pakistan, India now has the highest share of missing females. While improved female education and employment opportunities have generally reduced excess female mortality, the increased use of sex-selective abortions has had the opposite effect of raising the number of missing women, particularly in China, but increasingly also in India.

THE CONCEPT AND MEASUREMENT OF MISSING WOMEN

While one way to assess the survival-disadvantage of females is to examine age-specific mortality patterns by sex, such data are often not available or reliable in many poor countries. Also, it may be of interest to examine the cumulative impact of past and present gender bias in mortality on the populations alive today.

Thus, a second method to assess the impact of gender bias in mortality is to compare the actual population sex ratio (the number of males divided by the number of females at the most recent census) with an 'expected' population sex ratio that would obtain given equal survival opportunities of the sexes. If the actual ratio exceeds the expected, the additional number of women that would have to be alive to equate the actual with the expected sex ratio is the number of 'missing women' at that point in time.[3]

It is based only on the population sex ratio which is likely to be the most reliable demographic figure in developing countries, as it 'only' requires an accurate Census count but no accurate monitoring of vital statistics. Also, as a stock measure, it allows an estimate of

[3] By holding the number of men constant in that hypothetical calculation, the implicit assumption (as also in the other method) is that the number of women could be increased without correspondingly reducing the number of males. Since the distribution of survival chances is, at least in part, a zero-sum game, this assumption, it is not clear whether one could indeed increase the number of females without at least somewhat reducing the number of males.

the cumulative impact of gender bias in mortality on the population alive today.

The critical question in the calculation of the number of missing women is the expected sex ratio that would obtain in the absence of discrimination. Since no society in the world, past or present, has been entirely gender-neutral in the allocation of resources, opportunities, and behavioural patterns, it is quite difficult to speculate on the sex ratio in the absence of gender discrimination. For example, the high female survival advantage in European countries is not a sign of discrimination against males in the allocation of resources, but is, in part, related to male behavioural patterns, mainly smoking, drinking, dangerous driving, and a higher incidence of violence against oneself and others, that reduce their life expectancy considerably vis-à-vis females (Waldron 1993).

In his illustrative calculations to get a sense of the enormity of the problem, Sen simply used the population sex ratio prevailing in SSA as a benchmark (Sen 1989, 1990, 1992). This generated a total of over 100 million missing women in the regions most affected by gender bias in mortality, which are South Asia, China, the Middle East, and North Africa (see Sen 1989, 1990; Klasen 1994).

In a more precise demographic assessment of the phenomenon, Coale argued that the 'expected sex ratio' of a population is not a constant but instead depends on four factors (Coale 1991; see also Klasen 1994): first, the sex ratio at birth which differs from parity but indicates a slight male excess in all populations. Viewed in isolation, this would suggest an expected population sex ratio favouring males. Although Coale (1991) suggested that the excess of males at birth is constant, evidence from the biomedical literature, long-time series from developed countries as well as cross-section and panel analyses from today's world all suggest that the sex ratio at birth rises with overall health conditions.[4] Table 15.1 shows regressions predicting the sex ratio at birth in a cross-section of countries, based on overall

---

[4] There is a large literature documenting that the sex ratio in utero is considerably higher than at birth, and that the sex ratio of miscarriages, spontaneous abortions, and stillbirths is much larger than the sex ratio at birth. As a result, improving health conditions that reduce the incidence of miscarriages and stillbirths will then increase the sex ratio at birth which is consistent with the secular trends in the sex ratio at birth. For a detailed discussion see Klasen (1994) and Chahnazarian (1986). Whenever better health and nutrition lowers the rates of such spontaneous abortions

Table 15.1: Life expectancy and the sex ratio at birth

Sample	(1) Non-African	(2) African	(3) Only African-Americans	(4) All Combined
Constant	0.991 (64.61)***	0.888 (21.51)***	0.982 (69.14)***	0.957 (64.61)***
Life Expectancy	0.00087 (4.14)***	0.00216 (3.35)**	0.00070 (3.07)*	0.00134 (6.35)***
African Population (dummy)				−0.0157 (4.17)***
Adj. R-Squared	0.071	0.254	0.458	0.326
N	212	31	11	243

Notes: *** refers to 99.9 per cent significance, ** to 99 per cent, and * to 95 per cent significance levels.
Sources: United Nations (1984, 1987, 1993, 1999), US Department of Health and Human Services (1991).

health conditions, which is proxied by life expectancy at birth.[5] The regressions in columns 2 and 3 are then done for countries where Africans form the vast majority as well as for African-Americans in the USA at different points in time as it has been shown that African populations (and populations of African descent in the Caribbean and the US) have a significantly lower sex ratio at birth.[6] Regression 4 then combines all the data and just uses a dummy variable for African populations.

---

and miscarriages and reduces the incidence of stillbirths, the sex ratio at birth will consequently increase.

[5] The data are based on sex ratios at birth reported in the Demographic Yearbooks of the last 20 years and typically include several observations per country at different time periods. Countries included in the sample must have complete birth registration, at least 5000 births per year, no evidence of sex-selective abortions, and, in the first regression, must not contain a significant portion of African populations,

[6] This is not only apparent from data on sex ratios at birth in Africa, but also from Africans in the US and the Caribbean and has been well-documented (for example, Teitelbaum 1970; Teitelbaum and Mantel 1971; Chahnazarian 1986; James 1984; Khoury et al. 1983). For a more detailed discussion, see Klasen (1994). While it is likely that sex ratios at birth in other regions of the world are not uniform but also differ slightly and that, due to the high genetic diversity of Africa, the sex ratio at birth is likely to differ within Africa, these differences have not been found to be large enough that they can be detected with some certainty in available demographic data.

Column 1 indeed shows a significant positive relationship between the two variables and suggests that 10 years of greater longevity are associated with a 0.9 percentage point higher sex ratio at birth.[7]

Column 2 shows the regressions for countries with African populations (from Africa, the Caribbean, and African-Americans in the US). As expected, we see an overall lower sex ratio at birth (in the constant), but also a much stronger influence of life expectancy on the sex ratio at birth. If we restrict the sample to African-Americans in the US at 11 points in time (from the 1940 to 1988), the impact of longevity is smaller and more similar to the other regions, but the difference in the level of the sex ratio at birth prevails.

The fourth regression pools the data from the non-African and African populations and includes a dummy for African populations. Life expectancy continues to exert a significant influence on the sex ratio at birth with the coefficient being about half-way between the non-African and the African regressions. Also, the dummy for African populations again shows the lower sex ratio at birth of some 1.6 percentage points prevailing among them, even if one controls for the influence of life expectancy.

Clearly, the sex ratio at birth has to be considered in calculating the expected population sex ratio and its relationship to overall health conditions has to be taken into account. In the estimates here, we use column 1 one to predict sex ratios for all countries except those with African populations, and column 3 for African populations.[8]

Second, the sex ratio depends on the expected sex specific mortality rates that would exist in a society without gender bias in mortality. Coale (1991) suggested using the Princeton Model Life Tables as the benchmark for non-discriminating societies. The Model Life Tables are made up of some 240 life tables from all parts of the world (but with a heavy predominance from Europe) dating largely from the mid-19th century up until the mid-20th century (Coale, Demeny, and Vaughan 1983). They are aggregated into four regional groupings ('West', 'East', 'North', and 'South') based on observed differences in the patterns of mortality, especially the relationship between childhood and adult

---

[7] Klasen (1994) produced a regressions based on only 62 observations (all of which are contained in the augmented analysis here) with nearly identical results. See Klasen and Wink (2003) for more details.

[8] We use regression 3 due to possible concerns about data quality in the African observations. To check results, we also use regression 2 and report the results.

mortality rates, and then calculated for different mortality levels assuming stable populations (see Coale, Demeny, and Vaughan, 1983 for details).[9] Although the populations that make up these model life tables were also not gender neutral in all respects, from a demographic point of view they are likely to approximate sex-specific mortality rates in non-discriminating societies more closely than most other possible assumptions. In particular, the behavioural patterns leading to high excess male deaths in today's societies (relating to traffic accidents and smoking) were not widespread, the incidence of reported gender bias in mortality is generally low (especially when compared to today's episodes, Klasen 1999), and maternal mortality rates, which could also distort expected mortality patterns, were quite comparable to some of today's developing regions. At the same time, the epidemiological transition from high to low mortality populations, including sex-specific differences in that transition, are well-represented in the model life tables and can serve as a good basis for comparison.

All four sets of the model life tables show a considerable female survival advantage in infancy and in older age groups (particularly above age 50). In between, women only enjoy a survival advantage in moderate to low mortality environments; in high mortality environments (with female life expectancy below 40), girls suffer from higher mortality than boys, particularly in the Tables 'West' and 'South', while adult women in high mortality environments additionally suffer from slightly higher mortality than men of the same age in the 'East' and 'South' Tables.[10] In the 'North' Tables, based on the mortality experience of Scandinavian countries, this female disadvantage is generally the smallest. While Coale (1991) relied on the model life tables 'West' in his assessment, Klasen (1994) suggested that these tables were underestimating gender bias in mortality, particularly in high mortality environments, as the countries that formed the basis for those model life tables had themselves experienced episodes of

[9] Stable populations are populations that exhibit constant fertility and mortality rates and thus a constant age structure of the population. The Model Life Tables can also be used for 'quasi-stable' populations that exhibit constant fertility but uniformly declining mortality levels as such populations also generate a stable age structure. See Coale, Demeny, and Vaughan (1983); Coale (1991), and the discussion below.

[10] On the other hand, women's survival advantage in infancy and older ages is larger in the 'East' tables which consequently generates the highest number of implied 'missing women' below.

moderate to excess female mortality, particularly in the 19th century. This was shown by finding that the model life tables 'West' assumed that girls between 1–20 have higher mortality rates than boys in high mortality environments which is contrary to the biological evidence and likely to be related to actual episodes of gender bias in mortality in the 19th century (for example, Klasen 1998, 1999; Humphries, 1991; McNay, Humphries, and Klasen 1998). Instead, Klasen argued that the model life tables 'East' give the least biased estimate.

Using any of the model life tables would imply that over the life cycle, men will suffer from higher mortality rates than females, particularly in infancy and old age which accords well with the biological literature on the subject (see Waldron 1983, 1993, 1998). As a result, we would expect that the male excess at birth is progressively eroded as people age. In high mortality environments, parity between males and females of a cohort is expected to be achieved by the age 10–20; in low mortality environments, it is only achieved after age 50.

This combination of a male excess among the young and a female excess among the old (and the middle-aged, depending on the overall mortality environment), clearly implies that the age structure of the population, which is largely driven by fertility patterns, will have an impact on the expected sex ratio. The population growth rate and the resulting age structure is, therefore, the third factor that influences the expected sex ratio of a population. Countries experiencing high population growth and thus a large share of young people have a higher expected sex ratio than populations with low fertility and thus a larger share of the elderly.

Last, the expected sex ratio might be influenced by international migration if such migration is unbalanced in its gender make-up. While there is significant migration taking place involving the countries that experience 'missing women' problems, this does not have a large effect on the 'missing women' calculation and was, in view of the paucity of reliable data to factor in this effect, not considered by Sen (1989), Coale (1991), or Klasen (1994).

Based on the model life tables 'East' for the mortality level and population growth prevailing in the early 1970s,[11] and a sex ratio

---

[11] As the statistics are calculated for stable or 'quasi-stable' populations, it is necessary to adjust for the fact that most not only have falling mortality but also falling fertility levels. To accomplish this, Coale (1991) did not take the fertility levels of

Table 15.2: Number of missing women, latest estimates (based on model life tables 'East' and adjusted sex ratio at birth)

	Estimate for 1980s and early 1990s						New Estimate based on Most Recent Censuses and Demographic Estimates							
	Year	Actual Number of Women	Actual Sex Ratio	Expected Sex Ratio	Missing (Number)	Women (per cent)	Year	Actual Number of Women	Actual Sex Ratio	Expected Sex Ratio at Birth	Expected Sex Ratio	Expected Number of Women	Missing (Number)	Women (per cent)
China	1990	548.7	1.060	0.997	34.6	6.3	2000	612.3	1.067	1.050	1.001	653.2	40.9	6.7
Taiwan	1990	9.8	1.071	0.998	0.7	7.3	1999	10.8	1.049	1.052	1.002	11.3	0.5	4.7
South Korea	1985	20.2	1.002	1.003	−0.0	−0.1	1995	22.2	1.008	1.047	1.000	22.4	0.2	0.7
India	1991	407.1	1.079	0.986	38.4	9.4	2001	495.7	1.072	1.037	0.992	535.7	40.0	8.1
Pakistan	1981	40.0	1.105	0.998	4.3	10.8	1998	62.7	1.081	1.042	1.003	67.6	4.9	7.8
Bangladesh	1981	42.2	1.064	0.977	4.6	8.9	1991	54.1	1.059	1.038	0.991	57.9	3.7	6.9
Nepal	1981	7.3	1.050	0.975	0.6	7.7	1991	9.3	0.995	1.035	0.994	9.3	0.0	0.1
Sri Lanka	1981	7.3	1.040	1.005	0.3	3.4	1991	8.6	1.005	1.052	1.006	8.6	0.0	0.0
West Asia	1985	55.0	1.073	1.002	3.9	7.1	2000	92.0	1.043	1.042	1.002	95.8	3.8	4.2
of which:Turkey	1985	25.0	1.027	0.996	0.8	3.2	1990	27.9	1.027	1.047	1.003	28.5	0.7	2.4
Syria	1981	7.3	1.050	1.000	0.4	5.0	1994	6.7	1.047	1.048	1.016	6.9	0.2	3.1
Afghanistan	1979	6.3	1.059	0.965	0.6	9.7	2000	11.1	1.054	1.024	0.976	12.0	0.9	8.0
Iran	1986	24.2	1.046	1.001	1.1	4.5	1996	29.5	1.033	1.039	1.996	30.6	1.1	3.7
Egypt	1986	23.5	1.049	0.998	1.2	5.1	1996	29.0	1.048	1.044	1.003	30.3	1.3	4.5
Algeria	1987	11.3	1.024	0.997	0.3	2.7	1998	14.5	1.018	1.043	1.005	14.7	0.2	1.2
Tunisia	1984	3.4	1.038	0.993	0.2	4.5	1994	4.3	1.021	1.043	1.000	4.4	0.1	2.1
SSA	1990	253.0	0.980	0.962	4.9	1.9	2000	307.0	0.987	1.017	0.982	308.6	1.6	0.5
Total (Comparable)		1123.9			86.8	7.7		1355.1					94.7	7.0
Total (World)		1491.7			95.9	6.4		1763.1					99.4	5.6

Notes: Total Comparable includes China, India, Pakistan, Bangladesh, Nepal, West Asia, and Egypt. Total world additionally includes Taiwan, South Korea, Iran, Algeria, Tunisia, and Afghanistan. Turkey and Syria are subsumed in West Asia and thus not added separately. The expected sex ratio at birth is based on regression 1 in Table 15.1 (regression 3 for SSA). Figures for West Asia, SSA, Afghanistan, and Sri Lanka are based on estimates prepared by the United Nations Population Division based on national Census and other demographic information; all others are based on new Census data. Countries considered by Sen, Coale, and Klasen are shown in bold and a total for these regions is reported as Total (comparable),

Sources: Registrar General (2001); United Nations (1999, 2000); State Statistical Bureau (2001); and Statistical Bureau of Taiwan (2001).

at birth predicted by regression 1 in Table 15.1, the left-hand panel of Table 15.2 shows the number of missing women in the 1980s and early 1990s in the countries most affected by gender bias in mortality. These figures differ slightly from Klasen (1994) due to final adjustments made to preliminary Census returns in China, India, and Egypt that had been used in Coale (1991) and Klasen (1994),[12] and slight differences due to the expanded regression predicting the sex ratio at birth.[13] The set of countries considered has also been expanded to include other regions and countries where gender bias in mortality might be a problem. In particular, we now also include Afghanistan, Taiwan, South Korea, Sri Lanka, Iran, Algeria, Tunisia, and SSA.[14] The countries considered by Sen, Coale, and Klasen in the earlier publications are shown in bold and a total is reported for just those regions (called 'total comparable').

When considering the countries included by Sen, Coale, and Klasen, the total number of missing women for the 1980s and early 1990s, using our preferred estimation methodology, stands at 86.8 million. When using Sen's assumption of the expected sex ratio prevailing in SSA, the number increases to 102 million; using Coale's assumption of the model life tables 'West' and a fixed sex ratio at birth, the number drops to some 58 million. India had the highest absolute number of missing women in the early 1990s. Among the countries considered in earlier studies, the largest relative problem, indicated by the share

---

the time of the Census but those prevailing some 20 years earlier to generate roughly average fertility levels for the cohorts alive at the Census time. We also adopt this approach (see also below).

[12] Most notable was the downward revision of the sex ratio in China from 1.066 to 1.060 which thereby reduced the number of missing women by some 3.3 million (regardless of the assumption used to generate the expected sex ratio). In contrast, revisions to the figure from India and Egypt increased the number of missing women by 0.9 million and 0.1 million, respectively.

[13] Moreover, the mortality assumption for Bangladesh in the early 1970s was changed as was the actual sex ratio in West Asia which was erroneously reported to be 1.060 in Coale (1991) and, by implication, Klasen (1994). The sex ratio reported in the source given is 1.073 (United Nations 1991).

[14] The choice of countries was driven either by evidence of sex ratios above one or findings in the literature about gender bias in mortality. Malaysia and the Philippines also have a slight excess of males but it is unclear to what extent this is due to sex-selective migration. These are, therefore, not included. We also show the data for Turkey and Syria, two countries that are subsumed under the West Asia region. They are not counted in the totals.

of missing females, appears to be in Pakistan, followed closely by Bangladesh, and India, while more moderate problems exist in West Asia, Nepal, China, and Egypt.

The additional countries considered also show a substantial number of missing women, bringing the total number of missing women to some 96 million. Particularly noteworthy are the considerable problems of missing women in Afghanistan and Taiwan, while more moderate problems appear in Sri Lanka, Iran, Tunisia, and Algeria. In SSA there also appears to have been a slight problem of missing women, which is not as readily apparent due to the lower sex ratio at birth prevailing there, but which is consistent with mortality statistics from the region (see Klasen 1996a, b).

AN UPDATE ON THE NUMBER OF MISSING WOMEN

Based on the same assumptions of our preferred methodology, but more recent demographic information, the right-hand panel of Table 15.2 shows updated estimates of the number of missing females in the world.

Beginning with the global figure, the comparable figure shows an increase in the number of missing women from 87 million to 95 million. Thus the cumulative impact of gender bias in mortality is exacting an increasing absolute toll on women worldwide. While this points to an absolute worsening, it suggests a slight relative improvement. The population in the countries suffering from excess female mortality increased by some 18 per cent while the number of missing women increased by 'only' about 8 per cent. As a result, the share of missing women (as a share of women alive) has fallen from 7.7 per cent to 7 per cent.

The largest drop, in percentage terms, occurred in Nepal, where results from the 1991 Census suggest that the problem of missing women has all but disappeared. This sudden drop of the sex ratio is, as will be shown below, is not very plausible so that this result should be treated with some caution. The drop, in percentage terms, is also considerable in Bangladesh, Pakistan, and West Asia, where the share of missing women dropped by 2–3 percentage points. The fall is more modest in India and Egypt where it dropped by some 0–2 percentage points. In China, the share of missing women actually rose by 0.4 percentage points, adding another 6.3 million 'missing women'. As a result of the considerable improvements in Pakistan and Bangladesh, India now has the dubious distinction of having the largest share of missing women in the world. Similar trends also exist in the expanded set of countries considered. While there has been an increase in the total number of missing women from just below 96 million to over 99 million, the share of missing women fell from 6.4 per cent to 5.6 per cent. The absolute number of missing women fell in most countries and in virtually all countries there has been a significant reduction in the share of missing women. Particularly noteworthy is the virtual disappearance of the phenomenon in Sri Lanka, and great improvements in Taiwan and in Iran, although there may be confounding factors in the latter country.[15] In SSA the share of missing women is estimated to have fallen. This conclusion should be treated with caution due to the poor quality of demographic data and due to the sensitivity to the assumption about the sex ratio at birth. Using regression 2 in Table 15.1 to predict the sex ratio at birth, the share of missing women stands at a much higher 2.7 per cent and there are over 8 million missing women. Also, the change in the share of missing women is sensitive to the assumption of the correct sex ratio at birth (see below).[16]

When examining the factors underlying this relative improvement, one can distinguish between changes in the expected sex ratio and changes in the actual sex ratio. With the exception of South Korea, the expected sex ratio has increased in all other countries included. The main reason for this is the increase in the expected sex ratio at birth due to improved longevity in these countries. In other words, due to this effect, we would have expected sex ratios to increase in

---

[15] The heavy and predominantly male losses during the Iran–Iraq War might partly contribute to the fall in the sex ratio. Some of these losses should already have been apparent in 1986 which suggests that the number of 'missing females' is underestimated in both Census counts.

[16] In Afghanistan, the problem persists at a high level but non-existing demographic information which is substituted by estimates from the United Nations makes any guesses on the actual trends hazardous. It is likely that the anti-female policies adopted by the recently deposed Taliban government, which included a prohibition on female education and employment as well as much worse health access for women, has worsened the situation considerably. On the other hand, continual warfare over the past 20 years will have exacted a heavy and likely male-dominated toll which will further distort the calculation of missing women.

most parts of the world. The higher longevity has a second effect on the expected sex ratio. In populations that are growing and thus have a large share of young people, expanded longevity actually increases the expected sex ratio at birth as males benefit relatively more from an equiproportionate mortality decline as the male excess at birth now survives to higher ages and males have higher mortality rates to begin with. Conversely, falling population growth rates in some (though not all) regions would have also reduced the expected sex ratio at birth as the populations would age and thus females would predominate more. Since the expected sex ratios increased everywhere except in South Korea, the first two effects are dominating the third.

What, however, happened to actual sex ratios? With the exceptions of China, South Korea, and SSA where it increased slightly, it has fallen in all other regions. The decreases vary considerably. The largest decrease (which appears implausible) was in Nepal, but there were also substantial decreases in Pakistan, Bangladesh, and West Asia. In Egypt and India the decreases were slight. In countries that were not included in Coale (1991) and Klasen (1994), most have experienced decreases in their sex ratio. In Iran, Turkey, Syria, Tunisia, Taiwan, and Algeria there were reductions in the sex ratio of varying degrees. The largest drop was experienced in Sri Lanka where the sex ratio dropped from 1.040 in 1981 to an estimated 1.005 in 1991 (Klasen 2001).

Had gender bias in mortality remained constant in relative terms, we would have expected rising sex ratios in all regions except South Korea. Combined with population growth, this would have led to drastically rising numbers of missing women. In reality, the actual sex ratios dropped in most regions and countries and the actual decline, despite an expected increase, is responsibly for the slight decline in the share of missing women in most countries, although existing population growth ensured that the absolute number of missing women increased in quite a few countries.

In a sensitivity analysis (discussed in detail in Klasen and Wink 2002), we show that the reported trends in gender bias in mortality are not sensitive to the choice of a different reference standard such as the one used by Sen or Coale, although they do affect the estimated total number of missing females (as we would expect from the above discussion). Thus, we can be quite confident that these results are rather robust.

Explaining Trends in Gender Bias in Mortality

From Table 15.2 we can generate the following stylized facts regarding trends in gender bias in mortality. While in absolute terms, the number of missing women has increased, in relative terms it is falling in most places. Particularly sharp reductions, in relative terms, occurred in North Africa, and parts of South Asia, most notably Nepal, Bangladesh, and Pakistan (from very high levels). In Sri Lanka, it entirely disappeared and in India it has been slightly reduced. China, South Korea, and Sub-Saharan Africa experienced a deterioration. What factors are driving this trend towards such an uneven relative improvement?

Before discussing this it is important to briefly review the most important findings on both the mechanisms and the socio-economic causal factors associated with excess female mortality.[17] Most studies have shown that the most important process driving excess female mortality is unequal access to health care which is leading to higher mortality of young girls (for example, Chen et al. 1981; Hazarika 2000; Alderman and Gertler 1997; Croll 2000; Basu 1992; Klasen 1999; Timaeus, Harris, and Fairbairn 1998), while differences in access to nutrition appear to be smaller if present at all (Chen et al. 1981; Somerfelt and Arnold 1999, Basu 1992; Hazarika 2000; Sen and Sengupta 1983; Hill and Upchurch1995).

This comparative neglect of female children, which is generally worse in rural areas, appears to be particularly severe for later-born girls and among them even worse for girls with elder sisters (Das Gupta 1987; Muhuri and Preston 1991, Klasen 1999, Drèze and Sen 1995).

In addition, sex-selective abortions seem to have played an increasing role in some countries experiencing missing women, most notably China, South Korea, and possibly India (Croll 2000; Banister and

[17] We will not discuss possible epidemiological factors that could generate changes in sex-specific mortality rates. To the extent that they are related to the epidemiological transition that is similar to the one experienced in the countries included in the model life tables, these factors are controlled for in the calculation of missing women. To the extent that they differ, it is very difficult to assess these issue with any certainty as cause of death data are largely lacking in most developing countries.

Coale 1994; Registrar General 2001). The most important evidence of this is the rising observed sex ratios at birth which appears to be indeed due largely to sex-selective abortions rather than the under-registration of female infants (Croll 2000; Banister and Coale 1994).

While these appear to be the most important processes generating gender bias in mortality, there is now an increasing literature on the most important underlying socio-economic causes of this neglect of female children. Cross-sectional evidence suggests that high sex ratios and high relative female mortality are associated with low female employment opportunities (for example, Rosenzweig and Schultz 1982; Murthi, Guio, and Drèze 1995; Klasen 2001; Sen 1990a). In addition, higher female education appears to lower excess female mortality, although the effects of this appear to be non-linear (World Bank 2001;Murthi, Guio, and Drèze 1995; Das Gupta 1987; Drèze and Sen 1995).

Apart from these factors associated with female empowerment and their economic independence, there are a number of customs and cultural practices that appear to hurt females in some regions. Among them are virilocal marriage patterns, great importance attached to ancestry worship undertaken by sons, high dowry payments for brides, and processes of emulating the upper strata of society (for example, Dyson and Moore 1983; Drèze and Sen 1995; Croll 2000).

Also, it appears that scarcity of economic resources is a necessary, but not sufficient condition for gender bias in mortality. While it is usually the case that households must be forced to ration scarce health care and nutrition resources for the differential treatment of girls to emerge, in many countries the poorest sections of the population experience less gender bias in mortality than slightly richer groups (see, for example, Murthi, Guio, and Drèze 1995; Klasen 1999, 2001; Drèze and Sen 1995), which is presumably related to greater female economic independence and fewer cultural strictures observed by the poorest sections of the population.

Lastly, state policy can critically influence gender bias in mortality. To the extent that the state provides free access to nutrition and health care, the need to ration scarce household resources is lessened, which can particularly help disadvantaged girls. Similarly, state activism in the field of female education and employment can improve the situation of girl children. Conversely, strict family planning policies such as the one-child policy in China can heighten discriminatory practices as couples will try to ensure that their registered and surviving child is a boy.[18]

In Table 15.3, we present some regression results to illustrate some of the findings. The first regression tries to explain the percentage of missing women in an international panel with 47 observations. The observations include all countries and periods listed in Table 15.2,[19] augmented by another 16 observations (two per country) from the most populous countries in Latin America and South East Asia. As these regions do not have significant problems of gender bias in mortality, their inclusion should add variation to be explained and thus allow a more precise estimate of the effects of the various exogenous factors on the incidence of missing women.[20] The regression shows a strong negative influence of female literacy on the share of missing women. Higher female literacy thus has a sizeable influence in reducing gender bias in mortality. Female labour force participation also reduces gender bias in mortality although the effect is not significant. This particular result should be treated with some caution as the database for female labour force participation (ILO 2000) is very weak and data quality and comparability across countries is likely to be a serious problem. Moreover, not all types of female labour force participation appear to help women to the same extent (see also Berik and Bilginsoy 2000) In particular, the relatively high observed female labour force participation in East Asia does not appear to help women there as shown by the interaction term. Apart from measurement issues, one interpretation is that other factors that lead to significant gender bias in mortality dominate the effect of female labour force participation (Croll 2000). The large and significant regional dummy variables show that female labour force participation and female literacy are unable to explain all of the variation in gender bias in mortality; these influences are largely related to State policy as well as some customs and cultural practices that have been described earlier. The time trend variable suggests a

[18] See Klasen (1999) for a more detailed development of these arguments.
[19] The 1991 observation for Nepal is deleted as it appears not to be reliable. See discussion below.
[20] The results are, however, robust to the exclusion of these Latin American (Brazil, Mexico, Colombia, and Argentina) and South East Asian (Indonesia, Thailand, Malaysia, and the Philippines) countries.

Table 15.3: Determinants of missing women in the world and within India

	(1) Worldwide Panel Regression		(2) Panel Regression of India's States 1971–91	(3) Sex Ratios in 1961–2001
Constant	3.96 (2.35)**	Constant	114.38 (18.06)***	114.42 (52.01)***
Female Labour Force Participation	−0.025 (0.75)	Female Labour Force Participation (Main Workers only)	−0.21 (3.54)***	
East Asia*FLFP	2.57*** (3.02)	Female Literacy	−0.20 (1.80)*	−0.15 (3.70)***
Female Literacy	−0.077***(5.18)	Male Literacy	−0.06 (0.62)	
East Asia	−3.99 (1.06)	Total Fertility Rate	0.20 (0.21)	
South Asia	6.44*** (6.17)	Infant Mortality Rate	−0.03 (1.87)*	
Middle East + North Africa	3.22*** (3.69)	Urbanization Rate	0.26 (3.80)***	
SSA	0.027* (1.95)	Population Density	0.007 (2.10)**	0.011 (4.17)***
South East Asia	2.99*** (3.57)	South Dummy	−6.81 (5.23)***	−8.24 (7.39)***
Second Observation	−0.045 (0.97)	East Dummy	−5.16 (3.63)***	−7.04 (5.70)***
		West Dummy	−2.67 (1.66)	−1.18 (0.88)
		1961 dummy		−4.23 (2.06)**
		1971 dummy	−3.15 (2.00)*	−3.13 (1.68)*
		1981 dummy	−3.16 (2.79)***	−3.34 (1.99)**
		1991 dummy		−1.105 (0.81)
Adj. R–Squared	0.871		0.872	0.577
N	47		43	75

Notes: *** refers to 99 per cent, ** to 95 per cent, and * to 90 per cent significance levels. Absolute value of t-statistics in brackets. In regression 1, the omitted category is Latin America. In regressions 2 and 3, the omitted region is North and the omitted time dummy is 1991 in regression 2 and 2001 in regression 3. The states included are grouped into four regions: North consisting of Haryana, Himachal Pradesh, Punjab, Madhya Pradesh, Rajasthan, and Uttar Pradesh, East consisting of Bihar, Orissa, and West Bengal, South consisting of Andhra Pradesh, Karnataka, Kerala, and Tamil Nadu; and West consisting of Gujarat and Maharashtra. In regression 2, the observations for West Bengal and Bihar in 1971 are dropped as there are missing values. The literacy rates refer to the population 6 and older who are literate, and the female labour force participation rate is simply the number of female main workers divided by the total female population.

Sources: ILO (2000); Wink (2000); and Registrar General (2001).

slight, but insignificant improvement between the first and second observation from each country.

Regressions 2 and 3 analyse the large inter-state variation in sex ratios in India.[21] We present two panel regressions here. The first estimates a more complete model predicting the sex ratio of India's largest states.[22] For this model we only have data for 1971 to 1991. Independent variables are those used in related studies on India (for example, Murthi et al. 1995; Drèze and Murthi 2001) and include the total fertility rate, urbanization, female labour force participation, male and female literacy, population density, and infant mortality.[23] The second model is more restricted but allows us to include 1961 and 2001 in the panel data analysis.[24] A number of interesting results emerge. First, the results confirm the importance of female labour force participation and female literacy in reducing gender bias in mortality, while male literacy has no significant impact (see also Murthi et al. 1995). Second, population density is associated with increasing sex ratios while urbanization has the opposite effect, a subject that deserves closer scrutiny. Third, reduced fertility does not appear to influence the sex ratio as was feared by some authors (Das Gupta and Mari Baht, 1997).[25] Fourth, there remain sizeable

[21] Note that these are actual sex ratios and not the share of missing women which would be the difference between actual and expected sex ratios. The latter is very difficult to calculate for India's states over such a long time period.

[22] The states included are grouped into four regions: North consisting of Haryana, Himachal Pradesh, Punjab, Madhya Pradesh, Rajasthan, and Uttar Pradesh, East consisting of Bihar, Orissa, and West Bengal, South consisting of Andhra Pradesh, Karnataka, Kerala, and Tamil Nadu, and West consisting of Gujarat and Maharashtra. In regression 2, the observations for West Bengal and Bihar in 1971 are dropped as there are missing values.

[23] As in related studies, female labour force participation refers to the share of all women who report to be main workers in the Census, and literacy to the share of males and females above age 6 who are literate. Other data from India report different labour force participation rates but generally similar regional differentials. For more details, see Bardhan and Klasen (1999). We also estimated regressions that weight observations according to population size of India's states but the results are very similar.

[24] To ensure that the differences in results between the two regressions are not driven largely by omitted variable bias, we also estimate the reduced model for the period 1971 to 1991. The results were very similar to the 1961–2001 regression shown in column 3.

[25] See also Drèze and Murthi (2001) for a similar finding.

regional variations captured by the dummy variables. They are likely to be related to cultural practices as well as state policies that differ dramatically across regions in India (Drèze and Sen 1995; Dyson and Moore 1983). Lastly and in contrast to the global regression, there appears to be a time trend suggesting a worsening of sex ratios. This may partly capture the effects of a rising expected sex ratio due to improved longevity (and its impact on the sex ratio at birth and mortality patterns) and differential population growth within India that has recently been much higher in states with high sex ratios,[26] but it may also point to the intensification of gender bias, particularly with regard to sex-selective abortions, which is also consistent with the increasing imbalance in the sex ratio at birth and the sex ratio of 0–4 year olds in India (Registrar General 2001).[27] An interpretation of the aggregate evidence would thus be to suggest that improving female education and labour force participation in recent years has helped to reduce the gender bias in mortality while more effective methods of discrimination (especially sex-selective abortions) have worsened matters which is captured by the worsening time trend.

The reduced regressions for 1961–2001 largely support this picture. Improved female literacy has helped to reduce sex ratios[28] while the worsening time trend has partly offset this, and may indeed be due to the greater incidence of sex-selective abortions.

[26] While between 1961 and 1981, population growth did not differ greatly between states with high and low sex ratios, between 1981 and 1991, and 1991 and 2001, the decadal population growth rate in states with high sex ratios was 5.3 and 10.6 percentage points larger, respectively, than in states with a low sex ratio. In 1991–2001, where this difference was largest, this effect would have led to an increase in the sex ratio of about 0.15 percentage points so that the overall drop in the sex ratio of some 0.7 percentage points is quite remarkable.

[27] The time trend may also give some indication of possible under-enumeration of females. In particular, the fact that there is little difference in the dummy variable for 1971 and 1981, and between 1991 and 2001 may support the contention that the 1971 and 1991 Censuses were underestimating the number of females and thus the worsening time trend was mitigated by better enumeration in the subsequent Census (see Dyson 2001).

[28] In these reduced regressions, male or female literacy have a similar impact suggesting that it is overall literacy rather than female literacy in particular that is driving the results. But this result is likely to be driven by the omission of female labour force participation as can be seen in the expanded regression in column 1.

Based on these findings about the factors influencing the survival patterns of girls, a tentative interpretation of current trends can be attempted. While Klasen and Wink (2002) discuss all regions where gender bias in mortality is a problem, in this abridged version we will concentrate only on South and East Asia.

East Asia

In East Asia, we experience a falling trend of gender bias in mortality in Taiwan, and rising gender bias in China. In South Korea, we see a slight worsening, albeit from a very low level. In Taiwan and South Korea, rapidly rising prosperity has reduced the need to ration scarce resources and has sharply improved female education and employment opportunities (World Bank 2001). At the same time, there continues to be considerable discrimination against female infants which by now appears to have shifted largely to sex-selective abortions. In South Korea, the sex ratio at birth has increased to above 1.1 in the early 1990s which points to a considerable incidence of sex-selective abortions. However, due to very low overall fertility rates, the demographic impact of this worrying phenomenon is smaller than elsewhere (Croll 2000), while the survival advantage of females in older age groups now has a considerably larger demographic impact. Similarly, Taiwan has unusually high sex ratios at birth which appear to be linked to sex-selective abortions (Croll 2000).

China is the country that has experienced a rising overall sex ratio and a rising share of missing women. This is despite considerable improvements in the first few decades of Communist rule where the expansion of free public health services and public provision of nutrition greatly reduced the previously existing great discrimination against female children (see Drèze and Sen 1989, 1995; Klasen 1993, 1999). The most important reasons for the deterioration in recent years appear to be two-fold. First, the significant changes in the organization of public services in connection with the economic reforms that began in the late 1970s. This involved the dissolution of the communes which had previously provided free health care and food. Now the provision of these goods is largely back into the hands of households which allows discriminatory practices to re-emerge (Drèze and Sen 1995; Banister 1987; Klasen 1993, 1999). Second, the one-child policy has sharply increased the incentive of parents to discriminate against female children as they want to ensure that the officially registered child is a boy. This policy has led parents to adopt several strategies to achieve this goal including the abandonment of girl children, illegal adoptions, hiding of girls, the refusal to get the one-child certificate in the case of a first-born girl, and an increasing incidence of sex-selective abortions (for example, Banister 1987; Banister and Coale 1994; Johannson and Nygren 1991; Junhong 2001; Klasen 1999). The rising sex ratio at birth is testimony to these strategies although it is unclear to what extent the different strategies mentioned are responsible for this rise in the sex ratio to above 1.15 in the 1980s and 1990s (Croll 2000; Junhong 2001). Clearly the one-child policy is among the most important underlying causes for intensified gender bias in mortality in China, while improving overall health conditions, incomes, female education, and employment opportunities have extended female life spans.

South Asia

In South Asia, we saw dramatic progress in Nepal and Sri Lanka, large progress in Bangladesh and Pakistan, and moderate progress in India. Beginning with Nepal, recent Censuses showed dramatic variations in the sex ratio. In 1961 it was alleged to be 0.91, rising to 1.05 in 1981, and falling again to 0.99 in 1991. While some of these oscillations are due to male migration and return to India, there are serious questions about the validity of these findings. In particular, the drop of the sex ratio in 1991 appears highly implausible. One way to see this is to examine the ratio of 20–24 year old women in 1991 to 10–14 year old girls in 1981. In the impossible case of no mortality in the intervening years one would expect as many 10–14 year olds in 1991 as 0–4 year olds in 1981, that is, the ratio would be 1. In fact, it is 1.09; and the ratio of 25–29 year old women in 1991 to 15–19 year old women in 1981 is an even more implausible 1.15 (Central Bureau of Statistics 1995). This points either to improved enumeration of females in 1991, or under-enumeration of males. Existing analyses of mortality trends continue to point to higher mortality of girls between 1 and 4 years, although the extent of excess female mortality is smaller than elsewhere in South Asia (Pradhan 1997). Given the paucity of data, it is difficult to specify at present the extent of improvement.

In Pakistan, there has been a considerable reduction in the sex ratio in 1998 which followed an earlier reduction in the 1981 Census. But these improvements came from extremely high levels. In 1972, the population sex ratio stood at 1.14, and dropped to a very high 1.10 in 1981 (Government of Pakistan 1995). A part of the improvement is likely to be related to improved enumeration of females, as can be seen when one compares the age structure of the two Censuses. At the same time, there appears to have been a real improvement as well, mostly related to improved female education, employment opportunities, and rising urbanization. But clearly, female disadvantage prevails as can also be seen in considerably higher post-neonatal and child mortality rates of female children (Wink 2000).

In Bangladesh, there have been steady reductions in the sex ratio since 1974. While some of this might also be related to improved enumeration of females in later Censuses, there also appear to have been real improvements which can also be seen from mortality statistics (Wink 2000). Rapidly rising female education (from a very low level) and improving employment opportunities (aided by the greater availability of micro-credit to women) [29] are likely causes for these improvements from a low base.

Sri Lanka is a country that has experienced a dramatic turnaround in gender bias in mortality. The sex ratio declined from 1.15 in 1951 more or less continuously to an estimated 1.00 in 1991. Data on mortality differentials bear out these changes (Nadarajah 1983; Langford and Storey 1993). Critical to the success in Sri Lanka were the free provision of food and health care which obviated the need for households to ration these vital resources differentially and ensured adequate access for girls. Investments in female education and employment added to this positive trend (see Drèze and Sen 1995; Klasen 1999).

Lastly, we turn to India. Here we see a slight reduction in the sex ratio in the 2001 Census after a deterioration in 1991. In fact, the 2001 results are similar to the 1981 results and there are reasons to believe that some of the oscillations are also due to better female enumeration (Dyson 2001). While some authors had predicted an improvement in the sex ratio (Drèze and Sen 1995; Wink 2000), others predicted a worsening of the situation (Das Gupta and Mari Bhat 1997; Mayer 1999). In fact, several opposing trends seem to operate here. On the one hand, there is evidence of clear improvements in female survival,

---

[29] See Pitt and Khandker (1998) and the literature cited therein for evidence that would support this suggestion.

particularly in older ages. The relative mortality of females above age 15 has steadily improved over the past decades and is now below the mortality of males in all age groups above 25, while there has been little progress in younger age groups (Wink 2000; Drèze and Sen 1995). Conversely, the sex ratio among 0–4 year olds has steadily increased, pointing to increasing disadvantage of young girls or to increasing sex-selective abortions. The latest Census results point particularly to the rise of the latter phenomenon which is consistent with the rise in the sex ratio at birth (Registrar General 2001; Drèze and Murthi 2001).

The regression results of Table 15.3 support these opposing trends. On the one hand, rising female employment opportunities and rising female literacy have helped reduce gender bias in mortality. Particularly, the rising female literacy is predicted to have contributed to a considerable drop in the sex ratio.[30] Unfortunately, this is offset by the impact of rising population density on the sex ratio as well as the time trend predicting ever-rising sex ratios. This time trend is consistent with greater access to means of discrimination, particularly through the increased recourse to sex-selective abortions. Thus, in India there appears to be a precarious balance between improving underlying conditions for women and simultaneously 'improved' methods of sex-selection which appear to largely offset each other and ensure that India is now the country with the highest share of missing women.

Conclusion

While the number of missing women has risen in absolute numbers over the past 10 years, there appears to be a relative improvement in the share of missing women, suggesting that the phenomenon has stabilized at a high level. Thus the projections made by the UN Population Division shown in Figure 15.1 have been highly prescient when they predicted a peak in the sex ratio in female-deficit countries around 1990, although the predicted decline has been smaller than was anticipated. Regional analyses point to definite improvement in North Africa and West Asia, some improvements in South Asia which, however, appear overstated and are partly related to better enumeration

[30] Changes in female labour force participation between 1971 and 1991 would have led to a drop in the sex ratio by 0.8 percentage points. Changes in female literacy would have led to a drop in the sex ratio of 6.8 percentage points. This massive improvement, which on its own would have led to near parity in the sex ratio, is nearly fully offset by the impact of rising population density and the time trend of increasing sex ratios.

of females, and deterioration in China related largely to its strict FP policies. Improvements in Bangladesh and Pakistan ensure that India now has the largest share of missing females in the world, and only a slightly lower absolute number of missing women than China.

Improving female education and employment continue to be important avenues for lowering the sex ratio. These are important areas of state intervention. In addition, state policies can intervene by directly delivering adequate nutrition and health care for girls which has shown remarkable success in Sri Lanka, Kerala, and pre-transition China. Lastly, the increasing ability to discriminate against girls, particularly in the advent of sex-selective abortions, necessitates increasing intervention to reduce the underlying causes of gender bias in mortality. Despite slight improvements in recent years, it does not appear that the problem will disappear rapidly on its own, as suggested by the estimates from the UN in Figure 15.1. Instead, greater efforts are needed to combat this most egregious form of gender discrimination in the coming years.

References

Alderman, H. and P. Gertler (1997), 'Family Resources and Gender Differences in Human Capital Investments: The Demand for Children's Medical Care in Pakistan', in L. Haddad, J. Hoddinott, and H. Alderman (eds) *Intrahousehold Resource Allocation in Developing Countries: Models, Methods, and Policy*, Johns Hopkins Press, Baltimore.

Bardhan, P. (1974), 'On Life and Death Questions', *Economic and Political Weekly*, Vol. 9, pp. 1283–1304.

Bardhan, K. and S. Klasen (1999), 'UNDP's Gender-Related Indices: A Critical Review', *World Development*, Vol. 27, pp. 985–1010.

Banister, J. (1987), *China's Changing Population*, Oxford University Press, New York.

Banister, J. and A. Coale (1994), 'Five Decades of Missing Females in China', *Demography*, Vol. 31, pp. 459–79.

Basu, A. (1992), *Culture, the Status of Women, and Demographic Behaviour*, Oxford University Press, Oxford.

Berik, G. and C. Bilginsoy (2000), 'Type of Work Matters', *World Development*, Vol. 28, pp. 861–78.

Central Bureau of Statistics (1995), *Statistical Year book of Nepal: 1995*, National Planning Commission, Nepal.

Chahnazarian, A. (1986), 'Determinants of the Sex Ratio at Birth', PhD Dissertation, Princeton University, Princeton.

Chen, L., E. Huq., and S. D'Souza (1981), 'Sex Bias in the Family Allocation of Food and Health Care in Rural Bangladesh', *Population and Development Review*, Vol. 7, pp. 55–70.

Coale, A. (1991), 'Excess Female Mortality and the Balance of the Sexes', *Population and Development Review*, Vol. 17, pp. 517–23.

Coale, A., P. Demeny, and B. Vaughan (1983), *Regional Model Life Tables and Stable Populations*, Princeton University Press, Princeton.

Croll, E. (2000), *Endangered Daughters*, Routledge, London.

Das Gupta, M. (1987), 'Selective Discrimination against Females in Rural Punjab, India', *Population and Development Review*, Vol. 13, pp. 77–100.

Das Gupta, M. and P.N. Mari Baht (1997), 'Fertility Decline and Increased Manifestation of Sex Bias in India', *Population Studies*, Vol. 51, pp. 307–15.

Drèze, J. and A. Sen (1989), *Hunger and Public Action*, Clarendon Press, Oxford.

—— (1995), *India Economic Development and Social Opportunity*, Clarendon Press, Oxford.

Drèze, J. and M. Murthi (2001), 'Fertility, Education, and Development: Evidence from India', *Population and Development Review*, Vol. 27, pp. 33–63.

D'Souza, S. and L. Chen (1980), 'Sex Differences in Mortality in Rural Bangladesh', *Population and Development Review*, Vol. 6, pp. 257–70.

Dyson, T. (2001), 'The Preliminary Demography of the 2001 Census in India', *Population and Development Review*, Vol. 27, pp. 341–56.

Dyson, T. and M. Moore (1983), 'On Kinship Structure, Female Autonomy, and Demographic Behaviour in India', *Population and Development Review*, Vol. 9, pp. 35–57.

Government of Pakistan (1995), *Pakistan Statistical Yearbook 1995*, Federal Bureau of Statistics, Karachi.

Hazaraki, G. (2000), 'Gender Differences in Children's Nutrition and Access to Health Care in Pakistan', *Journal of Development Studies*, Vol. 37, pp. 73–92.

Hill, K. and D. Upchurch (1995), 'Gender Differences in Child Health: Evidence from the Demographic and Health Surveys', *Population and Development Review*, Vol. 21, pp. 127–51.

Humphries, J. (1991), 'Bread and a Pennyworth of Treacle', *Cambridge Journal of Economics*, Vol. 15, pp. 451–73.

ILO. (2000), *Estimates and Projections of the Economically Active Population, 1950–2010*, ILO, Geneva.

James, W. H. (1984), 'The Sex Ratio of Black Births', *Annals of Human Biology*, Vol. 11, pp. 39–44.

Johansson, S. and O. Nygren (1991), 'The Missing Girls of China: A New Demographic Assount', *Population and Development Review*, Vol. 17, pp. 35–51.

Junhong, C. (2001), 'Prenatal Sex Determination and Sex-Selective Abortion in Rural Central China', *Population and Development Review*, Vol. 27, pp. 259–82.

Khoury, M., J. Erickson, and L. James (1983), 'Paternal Effects on the Human Sex Ratio at Birth: Evidence from Interracial Cases', *American Journal of Human Genetics*, Vol. 36, pp. 1103–8.

Klasen, S. (1993), 'Human Development and Women's Lives in a Restructured Eastern Bloc', in A. Schipke, and A. Taylor (eds) *The Economics of Transformation: Theory and Practise in the New Market Economies*, Springer, New York.

—— (1994), 'Missing Women Reconsidered', *World Development*, Vol. 22, pp. 1061–71.

Klasen, S. (1996a), 'Nutrition, Health, and Mortality in Sub Saharan Africa: Is there a Gender Bias?', *Journal of Development Studies*, Vol. 32, pp. 913–33.

—— (1996b), 'Rejoinder', *Journal of Development Studies*, Vol. 32, pp. 944–8.

—— (1998), 'Marriage, Bargaining, and Intrahousehold Resource Allocation', *Journal of Economic History*, Vol. 58, pp. 432–67.

—— (1999), 'Gender Inequality in Mortality in Comparative Perspective', (mimeo), University of Munich.

—— (2001), 'Warum fehlen 100 Millionen Frauen auf der Welt? Eine ökonomische Analyse', in O. Fabel and R. Nischik (eds) *Femina Oeconomia: Frauen in der Ökonomie*, Rainer Hampp München (forthcoming).

Klasen, S. and C. Wink (2003), 'Missing Women: Revisiting the Debate', *Feminist Economics*, Vol. 9, pp. 263–99.

—— (2002), 'A Turning-Point in Gender Bias in Mortality? An Update on the Number of Missing Women', *Population and Development Review*, Vol. 28, pp. 285–312.

Kynch, J. and A. Sen (1983), 'Indian Women: Well-Being and Survival', *Cambridge Journal of Economics*, Vol. 7, pp. 363–80.

Langford, C. and P. Storey (1993), 'Sex Differentials in Mortality Early in the 20th Century: Sri Lanka and India Compared', *Population and Development Review*, Vol. 19, pp. 263–82.

Mayer, P. (1999), 'India's Falling Sex Ratio', *Population and Development Review*, Vol. 25, pp. 323–43.

McNay, K., J. Humphries, and S. Klasen (1998), 'Death and Gender in Victorian England and Wales: Comparisons with Contemporary Developing Countries', DAE Working Paper No. 9801, Department of Applied Economics, Cambridge.

Muhuri, P. and S. Preston (1991), 'Mortality Differential by Sex in Bangladesh', *Population and Development Review*, Vol. 17, pp. 415–34.

Murthi, M., A. Guio, and J. Drèze (1995), 'Mortality, Fertility, and Gender Bias in India: A District-Level Analysis', *Population and Development Review*, Vol. 21, pp. 745–82.

Nadarajah, T. (1983), 'The Transition from Higher Female to Higher Male Mortality in Sri Lanka', *Population and Development Review*, Vol. 9, pp. 317–25.

Pitt, M and S. Khandker (1998), 'The Impact of Group-Based Credit Programs on Poor Households in Bangladesh: Does the Gender of Participants Matter?', *Journal of Political Economy*, Vol. 106, pp. 958–96.

Pradhan, A. (1997), *Nepal Family Health Survey 1996*, Ministry of Health, Kathmandu.

Registrar General (2001), *Provisional Population Totals*, Ministry of Home Affairs, New Delhi.

Rosenzweig, M. and T.P. Schultz (1982), 'Market Opportunities, Genetic Endowments, and Intra-Family Resource Distribution', *American Economic Review*, Vol. 72, pp. 803–15.

Sen, A. (1982), 'Food Battles: Conflicts in the Access to Food', 12th Coromandel Lecture delivered on 13 December 1982 in New Delhi, Coromadel Fertilisers Limited, New Delhi.

Sen, A. (1984), *Poverty and Famines*, Oxford University Press, Oxford.

—— (1989), 'Women's Survival as a Development Problem', *Bulletin of the American Academy of Arts and Sciences*, Vol. 43, pp. 14–29.

—— (1990a), 'Gender and Cooperative Conflict', in I. Tinker, (ed.) *Persistent Inequalities*, Oxford University Press, New York.

—— (1990b), 'More than 100 Million Women are Missing', *The New York Review of Books*, 20 December 1990.

—— (1992), 'Missing Women', *British Medical Journal*, Vol. 304, pp. 586–7.

Sen, A. and S. Sengupta (1983), 'Malnutrition of Rural Children and the Sex Bias', *Economic and Political Weekly*, Vol. 18, pp. 855–64.

Somerfelt, E. and F. Arnold (1998), 'Sex Differentials in the Nutritional Status of Young Children', in United Nations (ed.) *Too Young to Die*, United Nations, New York.

State Statistical Bureau (2001), *Communique on Major Figures of the 2000 Population Census*, National Bureau of Statistics, Beijing.

Statistical Bureau of Taiwan, (2001), *Population Estimates of Taiwan*, Taipei.

Tabutin, D. (1991), 'La Surmortalité Feminine en Afrique du Nord de 1965 à Nos Jours', *Population*, Vol. 4, pp. 833–54.

Teitelbaum, M. (1970), 'Factors Affecting the Sex Ratio in Large Populations', *Journal of Biosocial Sciences*, Supplement 2, pp. 61-71.

Teitelbaum, M. and N. Mantel (1971), 'Socio-economic Factors and the Sex Ratio at Birth', *Journal of Biosocial Sciences*, Vol. 3, pp. 23–41.

Timaeus, I., K. Harris, and F. Fairbairn (1998), 'Can Use of Health Care Explain Sex Differentials in Mortality in the Developing World?', in United Nations (ed.) *Too Young to Die*, United Nations, New York.

United Nations (1991), (Various Years), *Demographic Yearbook*, United Nations, New York.

—— (1999), *World Population Projections: Sex and Age*, United Nations, New York.

—— (2000), (Various Years), *Demographic Yearbook*, United Nations, New York.

US Department of Health and Human Services (1991), *Vital Statistics of the United States*, Government Printing Office, Washington DC.

Visaria, P. (1961), 'The Sex Ratio of the Population of India', Monograph 10, Census of India 1961, Office of the Registrar General, New Delhi.

Waldron, I. (1983), 'The Role of Genetic and Biological Factors in Sex Differences in Mortality', in A. Lopez and L. Ruzicka (eds) *Sex Differentials in Mortality*, Australian National University Press, Canberra.

—— (1993), 'Recent Trends in Sex Mortality Ratios for Adults in Developed Countries', *Social Science Medicine*, Vol. 36, pp. 451–62.

—— (1998), 'Sex Differences in Infant and Early Childhood Mortality', in United Nations (ed.) *Too Young to Die*, United Nations, New York.

Wink, C. (2000), 'Weibliche Übersterblichkeit in Entwicklungsländern. Diplomarbeit', University of Munich, Department of Economics, Munich.

World Bank (2001), *Engendering Development*, The World Bank, Washington DC.

Contributors

PREMANANDA BHARATI, Biological Anthropology Unit, Indian Statistical Institute, Kolkata, India, bharati@isical.ac.in

VANI K. BOROOAH, Applied Economics, University of Ulster, Newtownabbey, Northern Ireland, United Kingdom, vk.borooah@ulster.ac.uk

ELIZABETH M. BYRON, Harris Interactive, Washington, D.C., USA, beth.byron@yahoo.com

BINA FERNANDEZ, School of Politics and International Studies, University of Leeds, UK, b.fernandez@leeds.ac.uk

TARA GOPALDAS, Tara Consultancy Services, Bangalore, India, meghakeroo@dataone.in

ARAVINDA MEERA GUNTUPALLI, MRC Epidemiology Resource Centre and Associate member, Centre for Research on Ageing, University of Southampton, Southampton General Hospital, Southampton, UK, aravindaguntupalli@gmail.com

SRIYA IYER, Faculty of Economics and Fellow of St. Catharine's College, University of Cambridge, Cambridge, UK, Sriya.Iyer@econ.cam.ac.uk

STEPHAN KLASEN, Department of Economics, University of Göttingen, Germany, sklasen@uni-goettingen.de

AMAL MANDAL, Department of Political Science, Tufanganj College, West Bengal, India

KOUMARI MITRA, Department of Anthropology and Coordinator of International Development Studies, Faculty of Arts, University of New Brunswick, Canada, kmitra@unb.ca

ALEXANDER MORADI, University of Sussex, UK, A.Moradi@sussex. ac.uk

DIGANTA MUKHERJEE, Usha Martin Academy, Salt Lake, Kolkata, India, digantam@hotmail.com

MANORANJAN PAL, Economic Research Unit, Indian Statistical Institute, Kolkata, India, manoranjan.pal@gmail.com

APARNA PANDEY, Regional Directorate of Ministry of Health and Family Welfare and Regional Leprosy Training and Research Institute, Chhattisgarh, India, draparna07@gmail.com

SUMITA DAS SARKAR, Canadian Blood Services, Toronto, Canada, ksarka001n@rogers.com

AHANA SARKAR, Department of Community Health and Epidemio- logy, Queen's University, Kingston, Canada, 6as34@queensu.ca

LISA C. SMITH, Technical Assistance to NGOs (TANGO), Tucson, lsmith@chuparosa.us

MADHURA SWAMINATHAN, Sociological Research Unit, Indian Statistical Institute, Kolkata, India, madhura@isical.ac.in

AMITABH TEWARI, Department of Economics, Allahabad Degree College (An Associate College of University of Allahabad), Allahabad, India, amitabhtewari@gmail.com

SURUCHI TEWARI, Department of Anthropology, University of Allahabad, Allahabad, India, suruchitewari@gmail.com

CLAUDIA WINK, KfW- German Development Bank, Germany, Claudia.Wink@kfw.de